ALSO BY DAVID O. STEWART

The Summer of 1787

The Trial of

PRESIDENT ANDREW JOHNSON

and the

FIGHT FOR LINCOLN'S LEGACY

IMPEACHED

David O. Stewart

SIMON & SCHUSTER
New York   London   Toronto   Sydney

SIMON & SCHUSTER
1230 Avenue of the Americas
New York, NY 10020

First Simon & Schuster hardcover edition June 2009

SIMON & SCHUSTER and colophon are registered trademarks of Simon & Schuster, Inc.

For information about special discounts for bulk purchases, please contact Simon & Schuster Special Sales at 1-866-506-1949 or business@simonandschuster.com

The Simon & Schuster Speakers Bureau can bring authors to your live event. For more information or to book an event, contact the Simon & Schuster Speakers Bureau at 1-866-248-3049 or visit our website at www.simonspeakers.com.

Designed by Dana Sloan

Manufactured in the United States of America

1   3   5   7   9   10   8   6   4   2

Library of Congress Cataloging-in-Publication Data
Stewart, David O.
Impeached : the trial of President Andrew Johnson and the fight for Lincoln's legacy / by David O. Stewart.—First Simon & Schuster hardcover ed.
p.   cm.
"Simon & Schuster nonfiction original hardcover"—T.p. verso.
Includes bibliographical references.
1. Johnson, Andrew, 1808–1875—Impeachment.   2. United States—Politics and government—1865–1869.   3. Lincoln, Abraham, 1809–1865—Influence.   I. Title.
E666.S84   2009
973.8'1092—dc22   2009003346
ISBN: 978-1-4165-4749-5

To My Mother

CONTENTS

Contents

IMPEACHED

IMPEACHED

PREFACE

[T]his was no ordinary political crisis. It was not a struggle for office, or a contest about a tariff . . . , but a dispute that followed hard on a terrible civil war. It was the reconstruction of the Union that was at issue.

GENERAL ADAM BADEAU, 1887

AFTER FINISHING *The Summer of 1787* about the writing of the Constitution, I wanted to pick up the Constitution's story at its next critical moment. To form a union from thirteen quarreling states, the Philadelphia Convention patched together a number of rough compromises, prominent among them agreements about slavery and the allocation of power between the federal and state governments. Those political bargains held up for seventy years. During those decades, a web of accommodation and mutual forbearance bound the nation together. Three times, painful compromises over slavery kept the states united. Arguments over the powers of the sovereign states flared and subsided and flared anew. By 1861, contention over slavery and state powers overwhelmed the constitutional structure. Eleven Southern states seceded and fought a savage four-year war to be no part of the United States.

That war exposed fundamental flaws in the founding document. Slavery could no longer be papered over. It had to be abolished. The national government's power over the states had to be reinforced. A commitment to equality and the right to vote had to be embraced. From 1865 to 1870, the Thirteenth, Fourteenth, and Fifteenth Amendments remade the Constitution in those ways.

Yet the central constitutional drama of this critical era was not the prolonged battle over the new amendments. Rather, the nation came

1

closest to tearing itself apart, again, during the impeachment struggle between Congress and President Andrew Johnson in the spring of 1868. Accused by the House of Representatives of eleven offenses ("Articles of Impeachment"), Johnson endured a lengthy Senate impeachment trial, escaping conviction and removal from office by a single vote.

I first studied Johnson's impeachment trial twenty years ago, when I defended Walter L. Nixon, Jr., a federal judge from Mississippi, in an impeachment case before the Senate. I needed then to understand what offenses constitute "high crimes and misdemeanors" under the Constitution, and thus support impeachment. Naturally, I turned to the Johnson case, the only presidential impeachment trial to that point. My study yielded mostly confusion.

The principal players in the case were unfamiliar: Congressmen Thaddeus Stevens and Benjamin Butler led the prosecution; in opposition were former Supreme Court Justice Benjamin Curtis and attorney William Evarts. The eleven impeachment articles, which were the indictment of the president, were impenetrable, even for a lawyer. The Senate's rulings on legal issues—what was a "high crime" or "high misdemeanor," and what evidence could be heard—were inconsistent, even incoherent. Those seeking to drive Johnson from the White House were passionate, but the charges against him seemed technical and legalistic. The conflict focused on Johnson's attempt to fire his secretary of war. How, I wondered, could the president not have the power to do that? And yet Johnson almost was convicted on those baffling impeachment articles.

This time around, with greater time and study, I appreciated better how this confrontation grew from irreconcilable disagreements over how to reconstruct the nation after secession and civil war. Johnson was a Southern Democrat, elected on the Republican ticket in 1864, who became president because of the tragic assassination of Abraham Lincoln. Johnson took a narrow view of federal powers under the Constitution. Untroubled by gruesome racial violence in the South, or by the replacement of slavery with a brutal form of agricultural peonage, he wanted Union troops to withdraw quickly from the region. Sovereign Southern states, he believed, should be left to manage their own affairs.

Congress, overwhelmingly Republican and including no representatives from ten Southern states, disagreed. Congressional Republicans were enraged that former Confederates would be rewarded for their treason by swiftly regaining control over their states. Most Republicans wanted power in those "reconstructed" states to be reserved to men who had been loyal to the Union. They insisted that the freed slaves must be protected from white violence. Many wanted the freedmen to have the vote so they could elect state governments that would treat them fairly.

As the dispute between Johnson and congressional Republicans grew more rancorous, constitutional questions became central. Johnson insisted that he was defending the Constitution "as it is," preserving the original vision of the Founding Fathers. Congressional Republicans insisted that the Constitution, and the Union, had to change. When Congress resorted to its ultimate constitutional weapon against the president—impeachment and removal from office—calls to arms rang through the North and South. The nation's future hinged on whether impeachment would work well enough to prevent a plunge back into civil war. Could the Constitution mediate this fierce battle within the government itself? When the nation slid into civil war in 1861, the Constitution was no help. Would it perform any better seven years later?

This was a great testing for the Constitution and the nation. For many years, the conventional telling of the impeachment story portrayed it as a hairsbreadth escape from congressional despotism. By this traditional account, the presidency survived because a few heroic Republicans in the Senate refused to join the vengeful Northern harpies who hated Andrew Johnson for attempting to heal the nation's wounds. That conventional view is a cartoon version of the actual struggle, and ignores much of the historical record. As president, Johnson inflicted many more wounds on the nation than he healed, while votes for his acquittal were purchased with political deals, patronage promises, and even cash.

Andrew Johnson was an unfortunate president, an angry and obstinate hater at a time when the nation needed a healer. Those who opposed him were equally intemperate in word and deed. It was an intemperate time. The tempests of the Civil War still triggered high emotions. Yet Johnson's opponents, often described as demonic impeachers, defended the principles of fairness and equality that represent the finest parts of the American tradition, which they also were fighting to incorporate in the Constitution. The impeachment process proved cumbersome and exasperating, but ultimately achieved exactly the goal for which the Framers of the Constitution designed it: the peaceful resolution of a grave national crisis.

An unexpected part of the story is one that was difficult to see at the time and has been mostly ignored ever since: the corruption and bribery that surrounded the Senate trial. Though the passage of 140 years has covered many tracks, there remains substantial evidence that rogues and blackguards brandished fat wads of greenbacks and portfolios bulging with government appointments in order to keep Andrew Johnson in office, or to drive him out. The rascals included corrupt tax collectors, bent Indian agents, greedy financial manipulators, and political bosses. Assembling the facts surrounding these extraordinary events required historical detective work that was both fascinating and frustrating. The effort drew on my experiences as a criminal defense lawyer in cases involving private and public corruption. Though hard conclusions are elusive with this part of the story, the evidence paints an unsettling portrait of boodle and payoffs that might well have determined one of the critical moments in America's history.

As long as the Constitution holds the nation together, the story of the Johnson trial will be an important one. Twice in my lifetime, impeachment has stopped the nation in its mad rush to the great American future. Richard Nixon resigned in August 1974 rather than face the impeachment articles approved by the House Judiciary Committee. Bill Clinton was the second president in history to be impeached by the House of Representatives; after a brief proceeding in the Senate, he was acquitted on all charges. Yet those episodes pale when compared to the fervor that rocked the nation in 1868, when Andrew Johnson stood accused before the Senate sitting as a court of impeachment. At that moment, only the impeachment clauses of the Constitution stood between the nation and a second Civil War.

1

BAD BEGINNINGS

SPRING 1865

> This Johnson is a queer man.
>
> ABRAHAM LINCOLN, EARLY 1865, AFTER
> JOHNSON PROPOSED TO SKIP HIS OWN
> INAUGURATION AS VICE PRESIDENT

ANDREW JOHNSON OF Tennessee felt shaky on the morning of March 4, 1865. Despite the cold rain that was drenching Washington City, it should have been the most gratifying day of his fifty-six years. At noon, he would be sworn in as vice president of the United States. A man who never attended a day of school would become the nation's second-highest official. Still, despite the excitement of his own Inauguration Day, Johnson did not feel right. It might have been the lingering effects of a fever that had struck him over the winter. Or it might have been nerves—a month before, he had proposed not to attend the inauguration at all, only to be overruled by the president, Abraham Lincoln. Or it might have been the residue of a hard-drinking celebration the night before.

Johnson had a good deal to celebrate. With determination and talent, he had built a tailoring business in his home town of Greeneville in the hill country of East Tennessee. He prospered in real estate deals and rose steadily through every level of government, serving as alderman, mayor, state senator, congressman, governor, and senator. Now he would become vice president, one step from the pinnacle of American politics.

5

Banner for the Lincoln-Johnson ticket in the 1864 election.

He was proud of his plain origins and his high achievements. He had a right to be.

It was a daunting time to come to the highest level of the American government. After almost four years of slaughter that took 600,000 lives on both sides, the Civil War was coming to its ghastly close. Somehow the nation would have to be reunited—"reconstructed" was the favored term. President Lincoln worked to temper the military victory with compassion for the defeated, to quench both the rebellion and the fiery politics that kindled it, knitting together the bitter enemies of a long war. To restore a shared sense of being Americans, he preached national unity. Lincoln's Republican Party had changed its name to the "Union Party" for the 1864 election. Picking Johnson—a Southerner and a Democrat—to run for vice president had been part of that message of national unity.

Until the Republicans nominated him for vice president, Johnson was best known for a single courageous act. In 1861, the senators and congressmen from eleven Southern states had to decide whether to follow their states into rebellion. Only one, Senator Andrew Johnson of Tennessee, stood with the Union. Since 1862, Johnson had been Tennessee's military governor, struggling to manage a state crisscrossed by contending armies. By adding Johnson to their ticket, Republicans hoped to appeal to Democrats and show that they were not just a Northern party. Though Lincoln's modern reputation now towers over the era, he feared the judgment of his countrymen in the 1864 election. On August 23, just a few weeks before the voting began, he confessed in a private memorandum that he expected the voters, weary of the long and bloody war, to reject him and return the Democratic Party to power.

In the election, Lincoln and Johnson won 55 percent of the vote, carrying all but three states, while the Republican Party won dominating majorities in Congress. Republicans had a 149-to-42 margin in the House of Representatives and controlled the Senate, 42 to 10. Having Johnson on the ticket probably helped, though far more important was a rush of Union military successes—the fall of Atlanta, the conquest of Mobile Bay, and victories in Virginia's Shenandoah Valley.

The procession for the Lincoln and Johnson inauguration stepped off from the White House at 11 A.M. Thousands of marchers, dripping wet, plunged into streets thick with mud. The military escort included units of white soldiers and some of Negro troops, followed by brass bands, fire companies drawing their engines, and the lodges of Odd Fellows and Masons. Lincoln and Johnson did not march. They were already in the Capitol Building, sixteen blocks away, out of the nasty weather.

The vice president's ceremony was to be in the Senate chamber, familiar ground for Johnson. Standing in that chamber in the winter of 1861, he had pledged never to abandon his country. "I am unwilling," he declared then, "to walk outside of the Union which has been the result of the Constitution made by the patriots of the Revolution." Now, four years later, the Senate was vertically segregated for his inauguration. The galleries above, except for the press and diplomatic seats, were reserved for ladies. The Senate floor held members of Congress, executive officials, and the diplomatic corps. Lincoln's seven-man Cabinet was at the very front, to the right of the main aisle.

Before the ceremony began, Johnson waited in the office of Vice President Hannibal Hamlin, the man the Republicans dumped from their ticket to make room for Johnson. Hamlin, an antislavery man from Maine, had offered too few political advantages for the critical election. Sitting with Hamlin and Hamlin's son, a Union Army general, Johnson was out of sorts. "Mr. Hamlin," he said, "I am not well, and need a stimulant. Have you any whiskey?"

Vice President Hamlin, a teetotaler, had banned the sale of liquor in the Senate restaurant. To accommodate his guest, he sent out of the building for a bottle. When the whiskey arrived, Johnson tossed down a tumbler of it, straight. Feeling reinforced, he announced that his speech at noon would be the effort of his life. Then he polished off a second glass of whiskey. Word came that it was time to start. Hamlin offered Johnson his arm. The two men passed a few steps down the corridor when Johnson turned back to the vice president's office. He quickly poured out a third glass of whiskey and drank it down. Hamlin looked on in amazement, according to his son: "[K]nowing that Johnson was a hard drinker, [Hamlin] supposed that he could stand the liquor he had taken." Unfortunately, on his own Inauguration Day, he could not.

Arm in arm, the outgoing and incoming vice presidents entered the Senate Chamber. They took their places on the dais. Hamlin began with brief and gracious remarks, thanking the Senate for its courtesies toward him as its presiding officer for the last four years. It was Johnson's turn. He faced the gathering. A solidly built man of medium height, Johnson was an experienced and confident speaker. His oratorical style was forceful and direct, with an adversarial edge that could inflict injury on his opponents. Johnson spoke that day without notes, as he usually did, but could not be heard well at first. Quickly, the audience could tell that something was wrong. Johnson's face glowed a luminous red. His sentences were incomplete, not connected to each other. At the biggest moment of his life, on the most prominent stage he had ever occupied, the man was drunk.

"Your president is a plebeian," Johnson announced. "I am a plebeian—glory in it—Tennessee has never gone out of the Union—

I am going to talk two and a half minutes on that point, and want you to hear me—Tennessee has always been loyal."

Hamlin tugged on Johnson's coat from behind. "Johnson," he hissed, "stop!"

Johnson looked down at the Cabinet members arrayed before him. Calling to each by name, he advised them to remember that their power came from the people. When he got to the secretary of the navy, Gideon Welles, memory failed. Leaning over to a Senate official, Johnson asked in a stage whisper, "What is the name of the secretary of the navy?" Johnson continued, reminding the chief justice that his power, too, derived from the people. Hamlin tugged Johnson's coat again, imploring him to desist. Johnson, elated by the moment or simply oblivious, rambled on.

Sitting closest to the dais, the Cabinet Secretaries began to mutter among themselves. "All this is in wretched bad taste," complained At-

President Andrew Johnson.

torney General James Speed, adding, "The man is certainly deranged." Speed closed his eyes as Johnson kept on speaking. "Johnson is either drunk or crazy," whispered Navy Secretary Welles, whose name had eluded the new vice president. War Secretary Edwin Stanton, his features petrified, replied, "There is something wrong." The postmaster general's face flushed with embarrassment. A few of the senators and congressmen smirked. Most fidgeted anxiously, shifting in their seats, "as if in long-drawn agony." One senator placed his head on the desk before him. A Supreme Court justice showed an expression of "blank horror." Johnson spoke for more than fifteen minutes.

After a period, President Lincoln entered the Senate with several others. Hamlin took direct action. He stood to administer the oath of office to his successor. After mumbling the oath, Johnson grabbed the Bible on which his hand rested. Brandishing it before the crowd, he cried out, "I kiss this Book in the face of my nation of the United States." The mortifying spectacle was over.

Luckily, the rain relented, allowing the president to take his oath outdoors, on a platform on the east side of the Capitol. The dignitaries, shaking their heads in dismay, filed out of the Senate. They joined thousands who waited to hear Lincoln's Second Inaugural Address. The gloom and anxiety of Johnson's ceremony dissipated in the fresh air, scrubbed clean by the rain. As the tall president stepped forward to speak, an observer wrote, "the sun burst forth in its unclouded meridian splendor and flooded the spectacle with glory and light." With biblical cadences and a triumphant sadness, Lincoln's prepared speech gave Americans the reasons for their terrible sacrifices during the war. He also spoke, stirringly, of peace.

Fondly do we hope, fervently do we pray, that this mighty scourge of war may speedily pass away. Yet, if God wills that it continue until all the wealth piled by the bondsman's two hundred and fifty years of unrequited toil shall be sunk, and until every drop of blood drawn with the lash shall be paid by another drawn with the sword, as was said three thousand years ago, so still it must be said "the judgments of the Lord are true and righteous altogether."

With malice toward none, with charity for all, with firmness in the right as God gives us to see the right, let us strive on to finish the work we are in, to bind up the nation's wounds, to care for him who shall have borne the battle and for his widow and his orphan, to do all which may achieve and cherish a just and lasting peace. . . .

Lincoln's eloquence could not wash out the stain of Johnson's rant. Many in the audience knew Johnson from his long public career. They knew he appreciated liquor. A Tennessee rival once recalled uncharitably that Johnson always "enjoyed the meanest whiskey hot from the still, . . . stuff which would vomit a gentleman." A visitor to Johnson's office in Tennessee had concluded that he "took more whisky than most gentlemen would have done, and I concluded that he took it pretty often."

But Johnson had never been drunk on a public occasion, and certainly not on such an important one. A few days later, Lincoln offered the best defense he could to Hugh McCulloch, secretary of the treasury. "I have known Andy Johnson for many years," the president said. "He made a bad slip the other day, but you need not be scared; Andy ain't a drunkard." More candid was the letter of a Michigan senator to his wife: "The Vice President Elect was too drunk to perform his duties & disgraced himself & the Senate by making a drunken foolish speech."

The verdict was universal. Johnson's speech, which he wanted to be the effort of his life, had been a disaster. Treasury Secretary McCulloch thought the new vice president humiliated his friends. A future member of Johnson's Cabinet wrote that the vice president "disgusted all decent people who heard him." The appalling quality of his performance was captured by the correspondent from the *Times* of London, whose reporting was not inhibited by any feelings of national pride:

All eyes were turned to Mr. Johnson as he started, rather than rose, from his chair, and, with wild gesticulations and shrieks, strangely and weirdly intermingled with audible stage whispers, began [his] address. . . . [Johnson's] behavior was that of an illiterate, vulgar, and drunken rowdy, and, could it have been displayed before any other legislative assembly in the world, would have led him to his arrest by the serjeant-at-arms. . . . Mr. Johnson was so proud of the dignity into which fate had thrust him that he boasted of it in the language of a clown and with the manners of a costermonger.

11

The vice president retired from the Washington scene for several days, recuperating at a nearby estate. He was back in Washington later in March, but rarely presided over the Senate, choosing to stay out of sight. The injury to Johnson's stature could not be calculated. From that day on, whenever he made a controversial statement, many assumed he had been drunk.

Six weeks after the inauguration, on the morning of April 15, Abraham Lincoln lay dead, struck down by an assassin's bullet. John Wilkes Booth, an acclaimed actor and Confederate sympathizer, had organized a desperate conspiracy to kill the North's leaders. Booth himself shot Lincoln at Ford's Theater, inflicting the head wound that took the president's life. At the same time, a second man attacked Secretary of State William Seward in his home, where Seward was recuperating from a broken jaw and dislocated shoulder suffered in a recent carriage accident. The assailant almost crushed the skull of Seward's son, stabbed two other men, then slashed open Seward's face and arm. A third conspirator was assigned to kill Andrew Johnson at his room at Kirkwood House. That man, after having a drink to steady his nerves, thought better of the enterprise and hightailed it out of town.

In life, Lincoln had been a controversial figure. He won the presidency in 1860 with only a plurality of the popular vote. His reelection in 1864 was no landslide; he commanded 55 percent of the vote in an election that did not include the Southern states still in rebellion, where he would have been lucky to get one vote in ten. The tragedy of his death began to chip away at any clay feet. The historical Lincoln would eclipse the real Lincoln, rising as a figure of almost mythic resonance for Americans. The president who succeeded Lincoln was bound to be judged by high standards.

Andrew Johnson took the oath of office as the nation's seventeenth president between ten and eleven on the morning of April 15, in his room at Kirkwood House. The days were turbulent. The war was ending. Six days before, Robert E. Lee and the Army of Northern Virginia had surrendered at Appomattox Court House. Joseph Johnston's army in North Carolina would yield in a week. The states would be reunited. To Johnson would fall great challenges. He would need to relieve the enmity born of four years of vicious bloodletting. He would need to bring North and South together, recreating a shared national identity. He would need to help integrate four million freed slaves into American society. As a Southerner and a Democrat who stood by the Union, he could serve as the bridge between the nation's warring regions, fostering peace and reconciliation. Or, as a Southerner and a Democrat, he could perpetuate the sectional hatred that brought war in the first place.

2

PRESIDENT JOHNSON

APRIL 1865

I am for a white man's government in America.

ANDREW JOHNSON, WINTER 1865

THE NEW PRESIDENT respected Mary Lincoln's grief, assuring the widow that she could remain in the White House as long as necessary. Johnson set up his temporary office in the Treasury Building, where he remained for the next six weeks. He hired secretaries for the heavy work ahead. Notable among them was Colonel William G. Moore, a thirty-seven-year-old army officer whose diary would provide an invaluable window into Johnson's presidency.

The nation began to learn about its new president, beginning with his appearance. Johnson was fastidious, always neat in dress and person, and usually struck a serious, thoughtful manner. After meeting the president, British novelist Charles Dickens was impressed, finding his face "very powerful in its firmness . . . , strength of will, and steadiness of purpose."

Johnson's sharp sense of his own dignity had to make the memory of his inauguration all the more painful. By emphasizing his "plebeian" origins, Johnson had granted an unguarded glimpse of his inner heart. Johnson's father drowned when the future president was a small boy. Apprenticed to a tailor in Raleigh, North Carolina, at age ten, the future president labored for five years at the whim of his master, an experience

14

not all that distant from slavery. At fifteen, the rebellious apprentice ran away with his brother, fleeing into South Carolina for almost two years before returning and resolving matters with his former master. With his mother and stepfather, Johnson led a cart into the Appalachian Mountains, finally settling in Greeneville, Tennessee, to start a new life. Through Johnson's impressive rise, the rebellious apprentice would continue to dwell within the man, making him angry and resentful at times when it would have been far better not to be.

In an era when politics was never far from violence, Johnson demonstrated ample personal courage. Once, told that an assassin awaited him at a public meeting, Johnson started his speech by placing a pistol before him. After describing the threat, Johnson roared out, "I do not say to him, 'Let him speak,' but 'let him shoot!' " After long seconds of silence, Johnson remarked with satisfaction, "It appears I have been misinformed."

When Mrs. Lincoln finally left Washington, Johnson's family filled the White House—Eliza, his wife of almost forty years, two daughters (one married, one widowed), one of his two surviving sons, and five grandchildren. When little ones interrupted presidential meetings, their grandfather indulged them; visitors were expected to do the same. One of the president's few recreations was to skip stones with the grandchildren in nearby Rock Creek.

An indeterminate illness often kept Eliza Johnson in bed. During the White House years, the president worked across the hall from her sickroom, looking in on her during the day. She, in turn, tried to moderate his searing temper. A White House worker remembered her staving off eruptions by gently touching the president's arm and saying, "Now, Andrew." The Johnsons had endured the deaths of a son and a son-in-law. Their older surviving son was a notorious alcoholic.

Though Johnson maintained a warm family circle, he kept the world at bay. In a letter, he advised a daughter "to be friendly with all and too friendly with none." In times of stress, the self-educated Johnson sought solace in historical and political books. One close aide wrote that the president was "lonely in the center of forty millions of people, and unhappy even to miserable, on that pinnacle of power." Johnson's bodyguard remembered his employer as "the best hater I ever knew."

The new president had little humor. An aide referred to Johnson's "grim presence," adding, "in almost daily contact with him for over two years, I never saw him smile but once." There are no funny Andrew Johnson stories, no recorded flashes of wit or self-deprecation. He once claimed to like circuses and minstrel shows, then added that he rarely attended them because he "never had much time for frivolity."

When it came to slavery and blacks, Johnson held the conventional views of Southern whites. Some of Johnson's early statements were virulently racist. In a congressional speech in 1844, he explained that blacks were "inferior to the white man in point of intellect—better calculated in physical structure to undergo drudgery and hardship," and also stood "many degrees lower in the scale of gradation . . . between God and all that he had created than the white man." Johnson opposed one bill that year because it "would place every splay-footed, bandy-shanked, hump-backed, thick-lipped, flat-nosed, woolly headed ebon-colored negro in the country upon an equality with the poor white man." Those who met with Johnson, including former slave Frederick Douglass, concluded that his racist views were strongly held. Johnson did not support emancipation of the slaves until the third year of the Civil War.

His views on race did not change when he became president. He confided to a friend in late 1865 that "everyone would, and must admit that the white race was superior to the black." In his annual message to Congress in December 1867, Johnson proclaimed that "negroes have shown less capacity for government than any other race of people," adding, "no independent government of any form has ever been successful in their hands," but rather ended with "relapse into barbarism." Stressing "[t]he great difference between the two races in physical, mental, and moral characteristics," the president warned his countrymen: "Of all the dangers which our nation has yet encountered, none are equal to those which must result from the success of the effort now [being made] to Africanize the half of our country." For Johnson, black political power in the South would be a greater evil than the Civil War, or even slavery.

In the first days after the assassination, Senator Benjamin Wade of Ohio acclaimed the new president. A leading Radical Republican, Wade decided that he preferred Andrew Johnson to Lincoln. "Lincoln had too much of the milk of human kindness," he explained, "to deal with these damned rebels." The new president showed little evidence, at first, of that handicap. Johnson sounded like a man bent on vengeance, repeatedly insisting that "[t]reason must be made infamous and traitors punished." When Wade suggested hanging a baker's dozen of Confederate leaders, Johnson objected that the number must be higher.

The president's enthusiasm for revenge pitted him against General-in-Chief Ulysses S. Grant. At the surrender at Appomattox Court House, Grant had paroled General Lee and his soldiers in return for their pledge not to take up arms again. The new president bridled at Grant's leniency. "I frequently had to intercede for Gen'l Lee and other paroled officers," Grant testified later. "The President at that time occupied exactly the reverse ground . . . that they should be tried and punished." The dispute with Johnson placed Grant's honor at stake. He had given his word to soldiers who would not have surrendered if they thought they could be executed for treason. Ultimately, the president abandoned his effort to prosecute former Confederate officers.

In his first weeks as president, Johnson searched for footing in the difficult political situation. He asked Lincoln's entire Cabinet to stay on, a course that implied a continuation of Lincoln's policy of reconciliation with the South. With Secretary of State Seward incapacitated by his accumulated injuries, Johnson relied heavily on Edwin Stanton, the able secretary of war.

The greatest challenge facing Johnson was reconstruction: reconstruction of the Southern states, and reconstruction of the Union with the South in it. For months, Northern leaders had argued over this question. Lincoln was inclined to set easy terms for Southerners to create new state governments, and then to return to the Union. During the war, when Union troops occupied large parts of Arkansas, Louisiana, and Tennessee, Lincoln allowed the formation of state governments with the participation of only 10 percent of each state's voters from the 1860 election.

Radical Republicans, a term used to describe the most adamant opponents of slavery, criticized Lincoln's approach. They insisted that the leaders of the rebellion should be disqualified from the new governments. They argued that the nation must reconstruct the South as something new, not merely restore Confederate state governments. According to Thaddeus Stevens of Pennsylvania, the Radical chairman of the House Ways and Means Committee, what was needed was "a radical reorganization of southern institutions, habits, and manners." The prospect, he admitted, "may startle feeble minds and shake weak nerves," but "[s]o do all great improvements in the political and moral world. It requires a heavy impetus to drive forward a sluggish people. When it was first proposed to free the slaves, and arm the blacks, did not half the nation tremble? The prim conservatives, the snobs, and the male waiting-maids in Congress, were in hysterics."

The argument over reconstruction included a central legal disagreement. Radicals contended that the Southern states were conquered territories, or had committed suicide, and thus could be governed by the victorious United States in any way it saw fit. The Constitution gives Congress the power to ensure that each state has a "republican form of government," the Radicals pointed out, and Congress had to do so for the "new" Southern states. Stevens, the most determined advocate of radical change, demanded that large Southern plantations be confiscated and distributed to the freedmen. The Constitution, he added, must be amended to match the new reality of the United States, vindicating the promise of equality in the Declaration of Independence. He thought the nation was "like a giant that had outgrown its garments, and if its new constitutional garment would not fit, it must be enlarged."

Johnson, in contrast, embraced the principle that the states were sovereign entities joined in an indissoluble union. He held the metaphysical view that despite the acts of secession and four years of war, the Southern states never left the Union. "There is no such thing as reconstruction," he said six weeks after taking office. "These States have not gone out of the Union, therefore reconstruction is not necessary." He denied the national government's power to intrude on state prerogatives, certainly not to vindicate such a foggy notion as a "republican form of government." It made no sense to him that the Congress could tell the states what to do. As he explained to a British interviewer:

> The States had brought Congress into existence, and now Congress proposed to destroy the States. It proposed to abolish the original and elementary principle of its being. It was as if the creature turned round on the creator and attempted to destroy him.

After the war, in Johnson's view, the federal government had only to help Southerners form their governments. Once formed, those sovereign state governments had the untrammeled right to do what they thought best. He might nudge Southern leaders to adopt certain policies—he suggested they extend the vote to black men who could read or owned $250 of real estate—but he denied the power of the federal government to dictate those policies. Most of all, he wanted the Southern states quickly to reconstitute their governments, elect representatives to Congress, and resume their role in the nation.

Johnson thus became the leading advocate of states' rights, of preserving "the Constitution as it is," without changes beyond the prohibition of slavery in the Thirteenth Amendment. He had an almost mystical confidence in the Constitution drafted in 1787, never mind that it had not prevented a calamitous civil war. An aide remarked that Johnson stood apart from established religions but "[i]f he had a bible at all, as far as I could learn, it was the Constitution of the United States."

Shortly after Johnson became president, War Secretary Stanton presented a plan for the reconstruction of North Carolina that he had developed for Lincoln. Under the plan, the president would appoint a governor for the state. That governor would call a convention to write a new state constitution that, at a minimum, would bar slavery and rescind secession.

Johnson issued the North Carolina plan on May 29, 1865, six weeks after taking office, largely as Stanton had prepared it. Johnson's action included two controversial elements. First, it signaled that he would exclude Congress from the process of reconstructing the state's government. Lincoln had proceeded the same way during the war, but he had been exercising emergency war powers as commander-in-chief of the armed forces. This was now peacetime. Those powers had evaporated. Though Johnson could not invoke emergency war powers, as a practical matter he could act on his own because Congress was in recess, not scheduled to meet again until December, more than six months away. Johnson could have called Congress back into session but chose not to do so. He preferred to take advantage of the opportunity to shape the restored Southern states on his own. By cutting Congress out of his reconstruction effort, Johnson courted conflict with that body.

In addition, Johnson rejected Stanton's recommendation that the freed slaves of North Carolina be guaranteed the right to vote. For Johnson, the Southern states, not the federal government, should decide the rights of the freedmen and freedwomen. Secretary of State Seward explained this policy in simple terms: "According to the constitution those citizens acting politically in their respective states must reorganize their state governments. We cannot reorganize for them." In a separate proclamation, the president began to recede from his demand for vengeance against the "traitors." His proclamation granted amnesty for all but the wealthiest and most powerful former Confederates, including restoration of their voting rights. Only six weeks after the end of the war, the former rebels were to regain control of their own governments, without any role for the freed slaves.

An early challenge to Johnson's policy came from Thad Stevens of Pennsylvania, who would swiftly become the new president's leading opponent. Then seventy-two years old and in his sixth term in Congress, the Radical leader was a bold, polarizing figure. Stevens shared with Johnson both humble birth and a largely fatherless childhood. Stevens's father, a farmer and surveyor in northern Vermont, slid into drink, finally drifting away from the family. Stevens's determined mother put her clever second son through Dartmouth College. Stevens made the most of that advantage when he moved to Pennsylvania, becoming a feared lawyer and an iron manufacturer of middling success.

Perhaps the greatest influence on this future political powerhouse was one Stevens never escaped—a club foot that marked him in an era when many were intolerant of physical handicaps. A neighbor recalled that other boys would "laugh at him, boy-like, and mimic his limping walk," which "rankled" young Thad. Though he ultimately stood six feet tall and developed a strong, athletic constitution, Stevens always confronted the popular superstition that his deformity was the work of the devil. Those painful early experiences helped form the future politician. Stevens's lameness—not to mention that of his older brother, who had *two* club feet—contributed to a dark, sardonic outlook that could intimidate both friends and foes. It also led him to sympathize with underdogs, the poor, those with afflictions of any kind. A congressional colleague recalled that Stevens "seemed to feel that every wrong inflicted upon the human race was a blow struck at himself."

Nineteenth-century America had no greater underdogs than the slaves in the South, and Stevens became both a fervent opponent of slavery and one of the least prejudiced white men in public office. As a lawyer before the war, he represented escaped slaves and opposed the slave catchers who searched for supposed fugitives. Neighbors told stories of Stevens purchasing freedom for slaves. His Lancaster home served as a stop on the Underground Railroad for blacks fleeing bondage. For his last nineteen years, Stevens's home was maintained by Lydia Smith, a "mulatto, who in her youth had great beauty of person." Stevens always treated her with respect, addressing her as "Mrs. Smith" and including her in social exchanges as an equal. Whispers insisted that the two were lovers. He never answered the whispers.

In the House of Representatives, Stevens's stern will and slashing rhetoric commanded respect and won him the leadership of the Republican majority. Another Republican remembered that most legislators chose not to tangle with the Radical from Lancaster: "[M]any a new member was extinguished by his sarcastic thrusts." An adversary recounted Stevens using a single sentence to "lay a daring antagonist sprawling on the ground . . . the luckless victim feeling as if he had heedlessly touched a heavily charged electric wire." One enchanted observer granted Stevens "the very front of Jove himself. Nothing can terrify him, and nothing can turn him from his purpose."

Stevens's greatest weapon was a dry sense of humor, which struck "like lurid freaks of lightning," launched "with a perfectly serious mien,

Rep. Thaddeus Stevens of Pennsylvania, Radical Republican leader.

or . . . a grim smile." Walking a narrow path one day, he encountered a rival who refused to let him pass, growling, "I never stand aside for a skunk." Giving way, Stevens replied equably, "I always do." Advised that President Johnson was "a self-made man," Stevens answered that he was "glad to hear it, for it relieves God Almighty of a heavy responsibility." For one thrust, Stevens used President Lincoln as his foil. When Lincoln asked if a proposed Cabinet appointee would steal, the congressman answered, "I don't think he would steal a red-hot stove." Hearing of the remark, the appointee demanded a retraction. Old Thad obliged. He reminded Lincoln of his statement that the appointee would not steal a red-hot stove, then added, "I now take that back."

Stevens could mock his own pretensions. After typhoid fever caused his hair to fall out, he wore a lush wig to conceal his baldness. One observer thought Stevens wore the hairpiece so haphazardly that it was "at the first glance recognized as such." A female admirer evidently missed the telltale signs and requested a lock of the congressman's hair. Ever gallant, Stevens yanked off the wig and offered her all of it.

By mid-May of 1865, Stevens was troubled that Johnson had recognized the "restored" government of Virginia, which was created during the war but existed mostly as an idea, not a reality. The Pennsylvanian insisted that only Congress could reconstruct the Southern states. In response to the president's proclamation on Virginia, Stevens delivered a letter that made no pretense to courtesy. Johnson's action was "beyond my comprehension," he wrote, "and may provoke a *smile*, but can hardly satisfy the judg[men]t of thinking people." Stevens advised Johnson to call Congress into session to address the question. Otherwise, many would "think that the executive was approaching usurpation." Icily, Johnson made no reply to the leading figure in the House of Representatives.

Seven weeks later, Stevens sent another letter to the president. Following the model set in his North Carolina proclamation, Johnson was appointing governors for each Southern state, instructing them to call conventions to write new state constitutions. Then, Johnson intended, the Southern states could resume their places in the national government. Admitting to "a candor to which men in high places are seldom accustomed," Stevens came straight to the point: "Among all the leading Union men of the North with whom I have had intercourse, I do not find one who approves of your policy . . . [which] will greatly injure the country." Like Stevens's earlier letter, this one asked Johnson to wait for congressional action. Once more, Johnson did not deign to reply.

For the other Southern states, the president issued proclamations like the one for North Carolina. Nurtured by Johnson, the seceded states wrote new constitutions, formed new governments, and chose congressmen and senators to send to Washington. Behind the scenes, Johnson advised Southerners to follow a moderate course and not restore former Confederates to power, but these were mere suggestions. For Johnson, the states must choose their own way. According to the newly appointed governor of South Carolina, the president asked only "that I write him occasionally and let him know how I was getting on in reconstructing the state." Johnson's designee as governor of Virginia complained that on critical issues he could get neither instruction nor advice from the president.

Instead of reconstructed Southern states led by men committed to the Union, Johnson spawned resurrected Confederate governments that bristled with former rebels in high office. The new Southern governments embarrassed the president who so recently demanded the punishment of traitors, yet Johnson made no public objection. The sovereign states, for him, could do as they wished.

Two features of the new Southern state governments threatened immediate trouble for Johnson. The first was the nature of the men chosen to serve as congressmen and senators from the seceded states. Most, according to a congressional report in 1866, were "notorious and unpardoned rebels, men who could not take the prescribed oath of office, and who made no secret of their hostility to the government and the people of the United States." They included ten former Confederate generals and five more army officers of lower rank, seven former members of the Confederate Congress, and three men who were members of conventions that voted to secede in 1861. That many of the new state officials had initially opposed secession in 1861 and reluctantly followed their states into rebellion—traits that may have made them moderates in the eyes of other Southerners—made no difference to Northerners who were outraged by the specter of "unrepentant secessionists" in the halls of Congress. Having started and fought a war that cost hundreds of thousands of Northern lives, these former Confederates proposed to take the reins of power in the national government they had attacked with vast armies. The presence of such men in Washington City, one congressional leader recalled, "inflamed" Northern congressmen, driving many "to act from anger."

Johnson knew that the Southern states were following a reckless and arrogant course, but he would defend to the death their right to do so. He wrote anxiously to the provisional governor of Georgia after learning that all of that state's new congressmen had been so involved in the Confederate cause that none could take the oath of office required for Congress. One of Georgia's new senators was Alexander H. Stephens, who had been vice president of the Confederacy and was then under indictment for treason. Stephens's selection, Johnson wrote privately, was "exceedingly impolitic." Yet the president made no public objection to the Southerners' choices.

Equally incendiary, the restored Confederate governments began to adopt "black codes" that "practically deprived the negro of every trace of liberty." One Republican called them "a striking embodiment of the idea that although the former owner has lost his individual right of property in the former slave, 'the blacks at large belong to the whites at large.' " Though specific terms varied from state to state, the pattern was for "[t]hat which was no offense in a white man [to be] a heinous crime, if committed by a negro." Vagrancy laws allowed the arrest of idle blacks, who would be put to work by local governments or loaned out to private employers—in short, a straightforward restoration of slavery. Blacks were denied the right to serve on juries, to testify in court, to own property. These "Johnson governments" certainly would never allow the freedmen to vote. Johnson raised no objection to the black codes, either.

The president's silence on these Southern actions told Southern whites that he was on their side. In a Mississippi hotel, one confided that Johnson "don't believe much in the niggers, neither, and when we're admitted into Congress we're all right." Beginning in late May of 1865, when Johnson announced the terms for North Carolina's new government, white Southerners came to expect the president would help them restore much of their former lives. According to one traveler, men in the South "quoted the North Carolina proclamation, and thanked God that there had suddenly been found some sort of breakwater against Northern fanaticism." By the end of 1865, a Northerner traveling in the South found that whites assumed "that the President had gone over to the so-called Democratic party, and would use the whole power of his office to break down the so-called Black Republicans." Northerners began to fret, in the words of Radical Ben Wade of Ohio, that Johnson was dissipating "the whole moral effect of our victories over the rebellion," while "the golden opportunity for humiliating and destroying the influence of the Southern aristocracy has gone forever."

This fear grew as the president implemented his program for granting amnesty to Southerners who took up arms. Johnson's amnesty program did not include several categories of rebels, notably those owning taxable property worth more than $20,000. Those rich Southerners would have to beg the president for their pardons. The grandees who had snubbed the former tailor's apprentice for decades would have to seek mercy from President Andrew Johnson. They did so in droves. For months during the second half of 1865, the White House was clogged with wealthy Southerners, hat in hand, asking for their pardons.

Initially the pardon program seemed to express Johnson's resentment of the Southern aristocracy, forcing the rich to crawl to him for dispensation. His lifelong class hostility was captured in the jibe that "[i]f Andy Johnson were a snake, he would hide in the grass and bite the heels of rich men's children." But Northerners came to detest the pardon process, fearing that Johnson was being seduced by those who solicited his favor. Not only were the former rebels getting their pardons, but they also were tying the president ever more closely to the traditional Southern power structure. "They kept the Southern President surrounded by an atmosphere of Southern geniality," complained one New England reporter, "Southern prejudices, Southern aspirations." With a heavy daily diet of Southern visitors, Johnson "heard little else, was given time to think little else." By 1866, Johnson had granted individual pardons to more than 7,000 Southerners.

As the days of 1865 grew shorter, Johnson's honeymoon period as president was drawing to a close. With no Congress to inhibit him, he had swiftly reconstituted Southern state governments, ignoring the views of Republicans like Stevens. But the Republicans were coming. Soon they would arrive in Washington City with the overwhelming majorities they won in the 1864 election: 42 to 10 in the Senate, and 149 to 42 in the House. To avoid a challenge from these powerful Republicans, Johnson would have to demonstrate that his policy had succeeded, that his efforts—often called "presidential reconstruction"—were restoring justice and prosperity. Though no policy could have achieved those goals so quickly, the violence and poverty that oppressed the South would galvanize the opposition to Johnson.

3

LAND OF REVOLUTION

NOVEMBER 1865

Nothing renders society more restless than . . . a revolution
but half accomplished.

CARL SCHURZ, 1865

THE SCARS OF civil war ran fresh and deep across the land. In the
North, the sacrifice of men and treasure had been appalling. An
estimated 360,000 Union troops died of all causes. The towns and roads
seemed littered with amputees, soldiers who survived the brutal medical
practices of the age, constant reminders of the war's murderous price.
But the North had won, and few battles had been waged on its soil.
Through the northern and western states, 23 million people gathered
themselves for a burst of economic expansion that would transform
the continent. The industrial energy devoted to wartime production
would be directed to building railroads to connect the Atlantic with the
Pacific.

In the South, the human losses—260,000 soldiers dead—were a
greater proportion of the population, while the physical wreckage was
far worse. Nine million Southern whites and four million freed slaves
faced fearsome challenges. Travelers were staggered by the destruction
and poverty.

In Virginia's Shenandoah Valley, a visitor saw neither fences nor
crops. Northern Virginia showed few signs of human industry, only an

occasional wan, half-cultivated field. In Richmond and in Columbia, South Carolina, chimneys stood forlornly, surrounded by ash, blackened walls, and piles of bricks. Some shops had goods, but no one had money to buy them. Atlanta had burned also, leaving both races homeless. Blacks and whites lived in makeshift shelters on the edge of town, in clusters that looked like "fantastic encampment[s] of gypsies or Indians." Young men were scarce in Charleston, birthplace of secession, which had become

> A city of ruins, of desolation, of vacant houses, of widowed women, of rotting wharves, of deserted warehouses, of weed-wild gardens, of miles of grass-grown streets, of acres of pitiful and voiceful barrenness.

The Southern economy stood still. For slave owners, emancipation represented a massive loss of capital. According to a calculation prepared for Johnson, the South lost roughly 30 percent of its wealth when the slaves walked away from its plantations. As economic activity dwindled, whites and blacks faced idleness. In one town, "People on Main Street sat out on the sidewalks gossiping and smoking, some with tables playing chess, backgammon and cards. As the sun moved they moved from one side of the street to the other to get the shade."

For all the travail of daily life, a single sea change became the focus of political and social energy in the South. Four million blacks—almost one-third of the people in the region—were now free. Whites and blacks would have to work out what that freedom was, a process that was bound to be painful. By far the greater share of pain would be felt by the impoverished, unschooled, and weaponless freedmen. Most owned only the clothes on their backs. Somehow they had to provide for themselves in a hostile land. But for whites, too, emancipation brought upheaval.

Most Southern whites rejected any suggestion that the freed people could be equal to them. A visiting writer concluded that Southerners viewed the former slave as "an animal; a higher sort of animal, to be sure, than the dog or the horse, but, after all, an animal." Political rights for the former slaves, such as voting, seemed "the most revolting of all possibilities . . . [a] degradation upon a gallant people."

The changes brought by emancipation reached into every human interaction. How should a free black person address a white person? How could he or she walk on the street? Should a black step aside for whites? What if a white person acted improperly? Could a freedman object? The freed slaves wanted to act as equals. Whites were shocked. As one visitor observed, they "perceive[d] insolence in a tone, a glance, a gesture, a failure to yield enough by two or three inches in meeting on the sidewalk."

First came the simple act of traveling through the countryside. Blacks, in theory at least, now could come and go as they pleased, could walk the roads at any time of the day or night. In the early postwar months, and to the dismay of Southern whites, many freed slaves did just that. A Northern traveler reported that "the highroads and by-ways were alive with footloose colored people." Some searched for family members who had been sold or carried into other states. Some fled angry masters or sought better work. Some longed to see what was on the other side of the hill. A black waiter explained the phenomenon: "You know how a bird that has been long in a cage will act when the door is opened; he make a curious fluttering for a little while. It was just so with the colored people. They didn't know at first what to do with themselves. But they got sobered pretty soon."

The overthrow of slavery forced a shift to new labor arrangements. Often the results were harsh. Some freedmen were "turned off" farms where they had lived and worked for years. The owners did not care to pay them, or had no money to do so, so they sent them away. Some masters did not tell their slaves of emancipation, keeping them in bondage for months beyond the war's end. The transition to paying for labor was tortuous. The former slaves had little bargaining power. Most knew only farm work yet had no land of their own. Without experience in making contracts for wages, many entered into yearlong contracts at rock-bottom wages, or for a share of the crop. Mississippi required proof every January that each freedman had a labor contract for the coming year. Some worked an entire year only then to be driven off the land, unpaid. Blacks who violated their contracts faced imprisonment and involuntary, unpaid labor. As one Northern correspondent summarized it, the "black codes" adopted by Johnson's state governments allowed the states to "call them freedmen, but indirectly make them slaves again."

Conflicts flared when the former masters used physical force against their workers, as they were accustomed to do. Most whites thought it impossible that blacks would work without coercion. A Virginian acknowledged that "[a] good many of the masters forget pretty often that their niggers are free, and take a stick to them, or give them a cuff with the fist."

Southern whites responded to emancipation in complicated, sometimes contradictory ways. Many, believing that the freed people could never provide for themselves, predicted that they would simply die out. One South Carolinian insisted that "being left to stand or fall alone in a competitive struggle for life with a superior race, [the freedmen] would be sure to perish." Abolitionists, he gloated, "would find they had exterminated the species." But the freed slaves did not disappear. Indeed, many government records show that more whites than blacks took advantage of postwar food handouts.

Some whites embraced the fanciful notion of sending the blacks someplace else—Africa, Texas, Peru, the Sandwich Islands, any place but where they were. Then, the whites argued, Southern fields could be worked by industrious German immigrants. Problems quickly emerged with this solution: there was neither transportation for four million freed slaves, nor a place to send them, nor any significant interest among the freedmen in leaving.

The whites' refrain turned to the need to "keep the nigger in his place." A North Carolinian explained in the fall of 1865 that he would vote for political candidates who promised to do just that: "If we let a nigger git equal with us, the next thing we know he'll be ahead of us."

Racial violence spread. White assaults on blacks erupted during the commonplaces of daily life. If freed slaves did not touch their hats to their former masters, they were saucy, unendurable. Whites railed when Negroes resisted beatings, seeing resistance as insubordination. One Southerner swore that "nothing would make me cut a nigger's throat from ear to ear so quick as having him set up his impudent face to tell that a thing wasn't so when I said it was so." A New York correspondent wrote that "half-a-dozen times, in the course of a single day, I observed quarrels going on between negroes and white men."

The violence overwhelmed the peacemaking efforts of officials of the Freedmen's Bureau, established by Congress in March 1865 to aid both whites displaced by the war and former slaves making the transition to freedom. Thinly sprinkled through the region, Bureau agents were supposed to secure fair treatment for the freedmen and prevent the reintroduction of slavery under another name. Many Bureau agents were startled by racial attacks they could not restrain. In his first ten days in Greensboro, North Carolina, a Bureau agent received two cases of whites shooting blacks. "The fact is," he explained, "it's the first notion with a great many of these people, if a Negro says anything or does anything that they don't like, to take a gun and put a bullet into him." In the interior of South Carolina, a monthly Bureau report recorded the whipping of a freedman and his children while tied to stakes, the whipping of another who also received a knife wound to the face, and the beating and unexplained disappearance of a freedwoman. A group of North Carolina whites went on a "spree," whipping pro-Union whites, castrating and murdering a black man, then shooting other blacks, including two young boys. In Columbia, South Carolina, a correspondent reported the shooting of a Negro "as if he had been only a dog,—shot at from the door of a store, and at midday!" When a black mistakenly cut down a tree on a white man's farm in Virginia, the white man "deliberately shot him as he would shoot a bird."

In the summer of 1865, President Johnson sent Carl Schurz, an ambitious German-American politician, to examine conditions in the South. Schurz's report was chilling:

> I saw in various hospitals negroes, women as well as men, whose ears had been cut off or whose bodies were slashed with knives or bruised with whips, or bludgeons, or punctured with shot wounds. Dead negroes were found in considerable number in the country roads or on the fields, shot to death, or strung on the limbs of trees. In many districts the colored people were in a panic of fright, and the whites in an almost insane state of irritation against them.

Another presidential agent placed the blame on the Southern state governments nurtured by Johnson. In South Carolina, he reported, Johnson's appointed governor had "put on their legs a set of men who . . . like the Bourbons have learned nothing and forgotten nothing."

By 1866, the violence would become organized. Southern whites formed terrorist groups with chivalric names—the Knights of the Golden

Circle, the Knights of the White Camellia, the Teutonic Knights, the Sons of Washington, the Knights of the Rising Sun, and the Ku Klux Klan. As many as a hundred masked and hooded riders could descend on a homestead or town, killing and maiming at will.

The Southern violence turned Northern observers into cynics. "[T]o knock [a Negro] down with a club," wrote a New Englander, "or tie one of them up and horsewhip him, seems to be regarded as only a pleasant pastime." A stableman in South Carolina, he added, "cut off a negro boy's ear last week with one blow of a whip, and tells of the act as though it were a good joke."

The assailants rarely faced punishment from state or local authorities. In South Carolina, a white killed a black man who was stealing corn. He was tried and exonerated. An ex-Confederate official told of a white man in Texas who whipped his former slave woman for insolence; when the woman's husband protested, the former master shot him. The wounded husband was jailed for assault; the former master went free. A Freedmen's Bureau report for South Carolina explained that "it is difficult to reach the murderers of colored people, as they hide themselves and are screened by their neighbors." A Bureau agent in North Carolina told Congress that he knew of many murders of blacks by whites; in none were charges brought. A Union general posted to Mississippi in 1865 and 1866 testified, "Murder was quite a frequent affair against freedmen everywhere in that community, and the commission of crimes of a lesser grade was still more frequent." He knew of no occasion when a white was punished for an offense against a freedman.

At the end of 1865, General Grant asked army commanders in the South to report on the violence. Commanders in only five states responded (the Carolinas, Mississippi, Georgia, and Tennessee). They described more than 200 assaults on blacks and 44 murders. Much of the violence, however, went unreported. No estimate of the murders and violence in the South after the war is entirely reliable, but the numbers were consistently dreadful.

The carnage was worst in Texas, with its huge distances and wild frontiers. By 1868, an army commander reported that "the murder of negroes is so common as to render it impossible to keep accurate count of them." The records of the Freedmen's Bureau yield a dispiriting catalog of reasons for the murders of black Texans in the postwar years:

[The] freedman did not remove his hat when he passed [a white man], negro would not allow himself to be whipped; freedman would not allow his wife to be whipped by a white man; he [the victim] was carrying a letter to a Freedmen's Bureau official; kill negroes to see them kick; wanted to thin out niggers a little; didn't hand over his money quick enough; wouldn't give up his whiskey flask.

In 1865 and 1866, more than 500 whites were indicted in Texas for murdering blacks; none was convicted. During the 1868 election campaign, an estimated 2,000 Negroes were murdered in Texas.

A bureau agent in Mississippi captured the lawlessness of that time and place:

Men, who are honorable in their dealings with their white neighbors, will cheat a negro without feeling a single twinge of their honor; to kill a negro they do not deem murder; to debauch a negro woman they do not think fornication; to take property away from a negro they do not deem robbery. . . .

While the president worked to return Southern state governments to the former rebels, the army drew the impossible assignment of keeping a lid on the region's cauldron of race hatred. At the end of the war, no institution enjoyed as much stature in the North as the army. After Lincoln's death, no individual could rival the prestige of General-in-Chief Ulysses Grant. Still, both the army and Grant were ill suited to the task of governing more than one-third of the country. The army shrank quickly after the Confederate surrender in April 1865, from 1 million men to fewer than 50,000. Thousands of federal troops remained in the South to keep the peace—enough soldiers to enrage white Southerners, yet not enough to protect the freedmen. Even more galling to Southern whites, many of those soldiers were blacks, former slaves. Without homes or employment to return to, colored troops were willing to remain in uniform. In September 1865, the army commander in Mississippi had thirteen infantry regiments; twelve were black.

Southern whites blanched at "the degradation of being guarded by these runaway slaves of theirs. To be conquered by the Yankees was humiliating, but to have their own negroes armed and set over them they felt to be cruel and wanton insult." Forty years later, a Southerner remembered with horror the experience of having "an alien race, an ignorant race, half-human, half-savage, above them." Freedom for the slaves, she concluded, "was inversion, revolution."

The man in the White House shared those feelings. In September 1865, President Johnson sent a telegram to the army commander in East Tennessee, his home region. The president insisted that Negro troops be withdrawn from the area, which the Negro soldiers had "converted into a sink of pollution." His own house in Greeneville, Johnson protested, was being used as a "rendezvous for male and female negroes who have been congregated there, in fact making it a common negro brothel." The commander replied that he had no alternative to Negro troops. He added, without elaboration, that the president's son-in-law had lodged a white family in the president's home.

The duties of occupation were far different from those of combat. As one general wrote, "you have not only to be a soldier, but must play the politician," a part which many soldiers found "not only difficult but disagreeable." General William Tecumseh Sherman complained that the Army was "left in the breach to catch all the kicks and cuffs of a war of races, without the privilege of advising or being consulted beforehand." A third general, detailed to the Freedmen's Bureau, stressed how difficult it was to keep peace with white Southerners who say "they are overpowered, not conquered," and who "regard their treason as a virtue, and loyalty as dishonorable."

The assignment was a minefield, the conflicts unceasing. Black soldiers felt resentment toward the region that had practiced slavery so long, while many Southerners nursed hatreds from the war. As Chief Justice Salmon P. Chase wrote during a Southern tour in May 1865, "As yet the rebels are disarmed only, not reconciled, hardly acquiescent." Southern whites brought lawsuits against army officers for false arrest, damage to property, murder, and assault. Local officials arrested federal soldiers for small infractions of local ordinances. Far more alarming were the outright murders of soldiers. In South Carolina in 1865, three soldiers from Maine were "shot from behind, . . . killed because they were Yankees." Five more were killed in the western part of the state. Two Freedmen's Bureau agents were murdered in Mississippi, another in

Texas. Texas grand juries refused to indict those accused of shooting down Union soldiers. State militias and "home guards" posed an armed threat to federal troops and complicated many situations.

The Army's task would grow more difficult after political warfare broke out between Congress and the president over how reconstruction should proceed. From month to month, the Army's mandate, and precise instructions, would change dramatically as Congress enacted a new statute, or Johnson's attorney general issued a new interpretation of the last one, or the president replaced a regional military commander to soften the occupation, which he did repeatedly.

In the coming conflict between Johnson and the Congress, control of the Army would become the great prize. Countervailing pressures drew its senior officers—particularly Grant and his second, William T. Sherman—into highly political situations. During a critical point in the contest for control of the Army, Sherman wrote to Grant, "We ought not to be involved in politics, but for the sake of the army we are justified in trying at least to cut this Gordian knot, which they do not appear to have any practicable plan to do."

There would never be enough troops and Bureau agents to pacify the angry South. At its peak, the Freedmen's Bureau had only 900 agents, some of whom sympathized with Southern whites, not with the freedmen. To patrol the Rio Grande border with Mexico and to occupy all of Texas, the Army had only 5,000 men.

The situation between 1865 and 1867 satisfied no one. The president had returned the state governments to the control of former Confederates, which infuriated Stevens and many Northerners. Southern black codes stoked their rage higher, as did the president's amnesty program, while the freed slaves remained at the mercy of their former masters, enjoying only fitful protection from the Army and the Freedmen's Bureau. In November of 1865, as the new Southern senators and congressmen began to arrive in Washington City, the fear spread among Republicans that Johnson was allowing the South to control the national government it had spurned only four years before. Effective reconstruction required a political strategy, not a military one, and that would require agreement between Congress and the president. Instead, the two branches of the government were spoiling for a showdown.

4

THE OPPOSITION GATHERS

DECEMBER 1865

> Contemning all applause, defying all censure, incapable of meekness, . . . this man [Thaddeus Stevens] has no ambition. . . . [N]o position in the gift of his State or of the United States could give him the power which he now holds in the House of Representatives. . . . [He is the] greatest . . . of the politicians.
>
> *GALAXY MAGAZINE*, JULY 1866

IN LATE NOVEMBER, a few days before Congress was to begin its new session, Thaddeus Stevens invited a group of Republican chieftains to his modest home near the Capitol. From his post as chairman of the House Ways and Means Committee, Stevens aimed to mobilize the new Congress. His message was urgent: Congress must save the nation from the policies of Andrew Johnson. Stevens had a plan to do that.

The Republicans at the meeting enjoyed large majorities in Congress, but were a fractious lot. Across the spectrum, from the Radicals through the moderates to the conservatives, strong personalities kindled sharp clashes. Indeed, uniting Republicans was often beyond the powers of even Old Thad. For the next two years, Republican unity would be produced largely by the infuriating actions of the man in the White House.

After Stevens, the best-known Radical was Senator Charles Sumner of Massachusetts, a strapping dandy at six feet four who started in life as an academic lawyer lecturing at Harvard. Never adept in extemporaneous exchanges, Sumner disdained Senate debate. He preferred to rise up to his full height and deliver powerful written addresses that sparkled with classical allusions. When the Massachusetts senator prepared a major speech, his landlord could hear his "magnificent voice rehearsing . . . [before a mirror] studying the effect of his gestures by the light of lamps placed at each side of the mirror." Sumner costumed himself for his orations, favoring bright colors, particularly "a brown coat and light waistcoat, lavender-colored or checked trousers, and shoes with English gaiters."

After delivering a harsh anti-South speech in 1856, Sumner was at his Senate desk when a South Carolina congressman began beating him with a cane. With his legs trapped under the desk and no one coming to his aid, Sumner absorbed the blows until he fell unconscious. He did not recover for more than two years. Though Sumner's credentials as an abolitionist were impeccable, a contemporary insisted that his "love for the negroes [is] in the abstract," and that the New Englander was "unwilling to fellowship with them."

Much about Sumner was in the abstract. For all his oratorical prowess, he was not an effective legislator. A Radical colleague observed that in twenty-three years as a senator, Sumner sponsored a single bill that became law; it barred the naturalization of Mongolians as U.S. citizens.

The obstacle was the vast Sumner ego. When an old friend expressed unhappiness that the senator had not called on her, Sumner explained that because of his involvement in great public questions, he had "quite lost interest in individuals." Even the taciturn Ulysses Grant could score off the New Englander's gigantic self-regard. Told that Sumner did not believe in the Bible, Grant replied, "No, he didn't write it."

Where Sumner was a product of Boston drawing rooms, Bluff Ben Wade of Ohio was a man of the frontier. Thin and wiry, dressed unfailingly in a black suit with a black stovepipe hat, his voice was shrill, his words plain and often profane. Days after Sumner's brutal beating in 1856, Wade proclaimed on the Senate floor that if anyone else wished to throttle free discussion, "let us come armed for the combat; and although you are four to one, I am here to meet you." As he waited for Southerners to challenge him, Wade boasted to friends that his choice of dueling weapons would be squirrel rifles at thirty paces. He also conspicuously placed two pistols on his Senate desk when he took his seat. No Southerner challenged him or tried to beat him to a bloody pulp. One Northerner exulted in the Ohioan's "manliness, courage, vehemence, and a certain bulldog obduracy truly masterful."

The best tale of Wade's pugnacity came from a congressman who rode with him to view the First Battle of Bull Run in the summer of 1861. When Union troops stampeded from the battlefield in a frenzy, desperate to get to safety, some encountered an unexpected barrier. Brandishing his squirrel rifle, the sixty-year-old Wade had upended two carriages to block the road. He manned the barricade with two other legislators and the Senate's sergeant-at-arms. With "hat well back, his gun in position, his party in line," the senator called out, " 'Boys, we'll stop this damned runaway.' " Facing "the onflowing torrent," the legislators held back the tide for "a fourth of an hour," then yielded the position to a senior army officer.

Because Wade would be elected president pro tem of the Senate in 1867, and thus become next in line for the presidency under the laws of the day, his penchant for controversy would be a major influence on whether Congress would expel Andrew Johnson from office. Wade's

Senator Ben Wade of Ohio, Radical Republican and
President Pro Tem of the Senate in 1867–68.

strong views and frontier idiom, with liberal Anglo-Saxonisms, alienated less radical Republicans. According to future President James A. Garfield, conservatives found Wade to be "a man of violent passions, extreme opinions, and narrow views."

A westerner by the geography of the 1860s, Wade believed in cheap money and high tariffs, positions that alarmed the sound-money men of the Republican Party. An advocate for human rights, he supported the eight-hour workday and the ability of women to own property. Wade explained his support for female suffrage in homely terms: "If I had not thought my wife to be as intelligent as I, or as capable of voting understandingly, I would not have married her." In 1864, Wade's frustration with President Lincoln's lenient ways with Southerners led the Ohioan to join a fiery manifesto that denounced Lincoln (his fellow Republican) in the midst of the presidential campaign. In short, Wade terrified Republican conservatives and moderates (the terms were sometimes used interchangeably).

The leading moderate Republican in the Senate, William Pitt Fessenden of Maine, could not abide either Wade or Sumner. Some regarded the lean, reserved Fessenden to be the Senate's finest legislator, though one observer thought he might easily be overlooked in a crowd. The man from Maine could employ an acid sarcasm. Confronting the claim that Nevada needed only "a little more water, and a little better society" to become a state, Fessenden snapped, "That's all that hell wants."

Fessenden's talents won for him important assignments in the Senate, and he served for key months in 1864 as Lincoln's treasury secretary. Yet Fessenden, "a martyr to dyspepsia," could be ill tempered. He once referred to Charles Sumner as the "meanest and most cowardly dog in the parish." Sumner fired back in a newspaper interview, claiming that Fessenden entered Senate debate "as the Missouri enters the Mississippi and discolors it with temper, filled and surcharged with sediment."

With his "cold, dry, severe manner," Fessenden never got along with Ben Wade. In 1867, he would oppose Wade in the contest to be president pro tem of the Senate. Wade's handy victory would cement Fessenden's resentment toward Wade and the Radicals who voted for Wade. The resentment was reciprocal. Radicals knew that the senator from Maine tried to maintain friendly relations with President Johnson, even as he despaired of the president's policies. After almost a year of pitched battle between Congress and Johnson, Fessenden could still write to a friend, "Say what they will, Andy is a good hearted fellow." Fessenden's estrangement from the Radicals—and his contempt for Ben Wade—would figure significantly in the impeachment struggle.

John Bingham of Ohio led the moderate and conservative Republicans in the House of Representatives. With long fair hair and sharp blue eyes, the slender Bingham had a nervous, intense quality and was memorably described as "the best-natured and crossest-looking man in the House."

Sporting credentials as a superior lawyer, Bingham had been the lead "House manager" (prosecutor) in the 1862 impeachment trial of a Tennessee judge who accepted an office in the Confederate government. Bingham also prosecuted the Booth conspirators, convicting all of them before a military commission. One of Johnson's Cabinet members considered Bingham "a shrewd, sinuous, tricky lawyer." His lasting legacy is the first section of the Fourteenth Amendment, which requires that the states provide "due process of law" and "equal protection of the laws" because Bingham insisted that they must. Yet Bingham quarreled frequently with the Radicals, even with the ferocious Stevens. One observer thought the Ohioan achieved eloquence only in the face of "provocation, contradiction, and interruption," as the "more frequently he was interfered with and baited in the discussion, the more vigorous was his logic."

For this cantankerous group of Republicans to pull together, they would have to face a common foe of distressing proportions. In only seven months, Andrew Johnson had transformed himself into just such a figure. The Republicans also would need the leadership of someone with the political skills to pry Johnson's hands from the rudder of the government and then steer the nation in an entirely different direction. Only Thaddeus Stevens could perform that role.

Historical depictions of Stevens usually emphasize his iron will, portraying him as a single-minded zealot never deterred from his path. The Pennsylvanian surely was fierce in pursuit of the goals he cared deeply about, but this traditional portrait neglects the vision, tactical sense, and charm that a legislative leader must have in order to command the loyalty of self-interested politicians. Even though he was a harsh adversary on the floor of the House, Stevens maintained cordial relations with many foes. As one put it, "politically we differed, . . . personally we were the best of friends." Another remembered him as "above the vulgar habit of allowing differences of political opinion to disturb social relations." One colleague fondly recalled that Stevens "made more fun for me to laugh at than any other man in Congress." Despite the passion of his convictions, Stevens was practiced in the art of compromise. Even Andrew Johnson agreed that Stevens would accept the best deal he could get under the circumstances. "I always liked him for it," the president said in late 1866. "A practical man."

To defeat the policies of the president and substitute his own, Stevens would need all of the weapons in his possession.

Stevens's guests traveled to his house through a largely unimpressive city. From the very first, when John Adams moved into the White House in 1800, Washington City tended to disappoint Americans. The capital seemed small and muddy, not a proper setting for titanic national dramas. When the Civil War came in 1861, only Pennsylvania Avenue was paved, yet even there the mud could stop an entire mule team. Other streets alternated between mud and dust, depending on the weather. Plain homes were widely spaced. Without sewers, a longtime resident wrote, "The Capital of the Republic had more mal-odors than the poet Coleridge ascribed to ancient Cologne."

The war transformed Washington from a sleepy Southern town of 60,000 to a military camp of 250,000, crowned by the mighty Capitol dome, which was completed in time for the inauguration in March 1865. For four years, the city was overrun by armies of soldiers, by the men and women who supported them and collected wartime taxes, and by former slaves in flight from their owners.

When the armies left, the city shrank to 100,000 souls. Government buildings still dominated, but more ambitious private residences began to rise. The federal bureaucracy retracted a bit, but not to its prewar dimensions. To accommodate those clerks and other workers—and the congressmen and lobbyists who descended on a seasonal basis—the city spawned a forest of boardinghouses. Due to the limited hygienic resources at most boardinghouses, the Capitol basement included a row of hot-water baths so congressmen could clean up before striding out onto the national stage.

In those days before congressional office buildings, public business often was conducted in hotel lobbies, barrooms, and private homes. A restaurant notice poked fun at the uprooted congressmen who frequented it: "Members of Congress will go to the table first, and then the gentlemen. Rowdies and blackguards must not mix with the Congressmen, as it is hard to tell one from the other."

For those with the resources, Washington City could offer better than the basic boardinghouse. Willard's Hotel, the National Hotel, and the Metropolitan lined Pennsylvania Avenue between the White House and the Capitol. Finer homes clustered toward the White House end of the nation's main street. Near the Capitol, most dwellings were simple, the streets unpaved and mostly unlighted.

Having prospered as a lawyer and iron manufacturer, Stevens could afford better than a boardinghouse. In an area just west of the Capitol, which is now part of the National Mall, he set up housekeeping with Mrs. Smith at 213 South B St., a two-story structure. The neighborhood was quiet, its streets mostly empty. A newspaper correspondent described the dwelling as "a small dilapidated brick house." The location was convenient to several faro houses where the congressman liked to gamble in the evenings, particularly Pemberton's on Pennsylvania Avenue. Some of these establishments aped the luxuries of a London men's club, but Stevens concentrated on gambling, not amenities. He also bet heavily on elections, risking $100,000 on one governor's race in Pennsylvania. There is no record that he ever lost more than he could afford.

In late November of 1865, the powerful politicians in Stevens's parlor shared a dire view of the nation's dangers. They deplored the new state governments in the South and the black codes they had adopted. They were incensed that former Confederates were arriving to take seats as senators and congressmen. The outcome of the Civil War, they feared, was being reversed, with ex-rebels regaining power and the freedmen delivered into a different form of bondage. All that blood, all that sacrifice, all would have been spent for naught.

For Stevens and his guests, the Union victory could be preserved only by excluding from power the men who led the secession, and by protecting the freed slaves. Stevens urged an ambitious program for challenging President Johnson's minimal reconstruction of the South. As one recalled, the determined man from Pennsylvania "at once assumed dominating control in opposition to the President's plan." To that end, he proposed to streamline Congress. He wanted to slice through the pontificating speeches and backroom deal-making, the corrosive disagreements between the House and the Senate, all of which paralyzed legislative action. Stevens wanted a fighting Congress, one that could take on the president and defeat him. Never before or since has anyone succeeded with such a plan. The Republican leaders unanimously approved Stevens's strategy.

The first step was to bar from Congress the new Southern representatives and senators who would support Johnson's policies. The Constitution provided a simple tool for this job. Each house of Congress has the exclusive power to decide whether a member has been elected properly and is entitled to take his seat. If the Republicans used that power to exclude the Southerners, their majorities would be unassailable.

On December 4, Edward McPherson, clerk of the House of Representatives, opened the new session by calling the roll of congressmen. McPherson had a special relationship with Stevens. As a young man, he read law with Stevens, then parlayed the older man's support into a congressional seat from the Gettysburg area. Now McPherson executed his mentor's plan. As he read the roll, he left out every congressman from the eleven seceded states. When a Tennessee representative asked to be recognized, McPherson refused to brook any interruption. When the roll call was done, the Tennessean tried again. McPherson protested that he could not recognize the man since his name had not been called. After Stevens pressed to move on to other business, the Southerner begged to speak. "I cannot yield [the floor]," Stevens replied calmly, "to any gentleman who does not belong to this body."

The Southerners had no recourse. The House had the power to exclude them, and did so; the Senate soon exercised its own power to exclude the senators from the South. Under the Constitution, President Johnson could do nothing to prevent those exclusions. To ensure that the Southern representatives would leave town, Congress refused to pay their living expenses. The Thad Stevens Express was rolling down the track.

The second step in Stevens's plan involved creating a combined

"Awkward Collision on the Grand Trunk Columbia R.R."
Between "A.J." and "Thaddeus."

House-Senate committee to address Reconstruction. The Joint Committee on Reconstruction—sometimes called the Joint Committee of Fifteen—would "inquire into the condition of the states which formed the so-called Confederate States of America, and report whether they, or any of them, are entitled to be represented" in Congress. This joint committee would compile a single factual record that would underlie congressional proposals for dealing with the South. Through the Joint Committee, Republican leaders in the House and Senate would be able to work out their differences in private, not in acrimonious contests over competing legislative proposals. In fact, the Joint Committee would become a powerful tool for shaping Reconstruction. Without debate, the House approved the Joint Committee on a straight party vote; the Senate concurred eight days later.

Stevens and his Radical allies, who comprised only a third of Congress, could not dominate the Joint Committee. Though Stevens was on that committee, he conceded the chairmanship to the "moderate" Fessenden of Maine and left off more polarizing Radicals like Charles Sumner and Ben Wade. The Committee of Fifteen included two other Republican moderates who would play central roles in the impeachment trial, John Bingham of Ohio and Senator James Grimes of Iowa. Even though Stevens and the Radicals were a minority on the committee, they would use it to direct the public agenda for Congress, and the nation. Johnson's navy secretary warned the president that the Joint Committee was "revolutionary"; he described it as "an incipient conspiracy." If Stevens had heard those accusations, he might well have answered, "Exactly."

5

A GOVERNMENT DIVIDED AGAINST ITSELF

JANUARY–JUNE 1866

The war between the President and Congress goes on. . . . At each session [the Radicals] add a shackle to his bonds, tighten the bit in different places, file a claw or draw a tooth, and then when he will be bound up, fastened, and caught in an inextricable net of laws and decrees, more or less contradicting each other, they tie him to the stake of the Constitution and take a good look at him, feeling quite sure he cannot move this time. But then Seward, the Dalila of the piece, rises up and shouts: "Johnson, here comes the radicals with old Stevens at their head; they are proud of having subjected you and are coming to enjoy the sight of you in chains." And Samson summons all his strength, and bursts his cords and bonds with a mighty effort, and the Philistines (I mean the Radicals) flee in disorder to the Capitol to set to work making new laws stronger than the old, which will break in their turn at the first test. . . .

GEORGES CLEMENCEAU, SEPTEMBER 1867

AT THE START of 1866, Congress set off on two paths to reconstruct the South. Charged with developing long-term solutions, the Joint

Committee of Fifteen asked the president to take no further steps on Reconstruction until it could act. He replied, carefully, that he planned no further action at the moment. With that hedged assurance, the Joint Committee formed five subcommittees of three members each to inquire into conditions in specific Southern states. Over the next several months, the subcommittees heard 145 witnesses, including 35 Union Army officers and 71 Southerners (six of them black). The hearings assembled, as Stevens intended, a damning litany of Southern persecution of freedmen and whites who had supported the Union. That litany would provide the essential factual context for the political struggles of the next two years.

Simultaneously, the full committee confronted a startling consequence of the Thirteenth Amendment, which banned slavery forever when it was ratified in December 1865. A new political reality became urgent. The constitutional prohibition against slavery had the perverse effect of increasing the political power of the Southern states. Based on a painful compromise struck when the Constitution was written in the summer of 1787, each slave had been counted for political purposes as three-fifths of a human being. Thus, when allocating congressmen among the states, and when assigning electoral votes in presidential elections, every one hundred slaves counted as sixty "persons."

The abolition of slavery made the three-fifths ratio obsolete. Because of what a New York congressman called a "moral earthquake [that] has turned fractions into ciphers," each black person now would be counted in full, not as three-fifths. This "moral earthquake" had a precise mathematical impact. With four million freedmen counted as full persons, the rebel states would be able to claim twenty-eight *more* congressmen— and twenty-eight *more* electoral votes—than they had in 1860. The penalty for provoking and losing the brutal civil war would be a substantial increase in the political power of the South. For many Northern politicians, this outcome seemed completely outrageous.

In only two weeks, the Joint Committee produced a draft constitutional amendment—it would be the fourteenth—to correct this arithmetical outrage. The proposal stated that if a state denied the right to vote on the basis of "race or color," then citizens of those excluded races would be omitted from the calculations allocating congressmen and electoral votes among the states. Instead of counting as three-fifths of a person for political purposes, or as a full person, blacks would not count at all unless the state gave black men the vote. Though most Northern states also denied voting rights to blacks, their Negro populations were small enough that the amendment would have little impact on their share of congressional seats. But blacks were in a majority in Mississippi and South Carolina, and were close to it in Louisiana, Alabama, and Georgia. The draft Fourteenth Amendment would dramatically slash the political power of those Southern states unless they extended the vote to the freedmen. This proposal reflected practical politics as well as a commitment to equal rights. Because the freedmen were expected to vote overwhelmingly for Republican candidates, Stevens and his allies wished to support their right to vote.

The issue of suffrage, though, proved to be even more complex. In a day-long stemwinder on the Senate floor, Sumner of Massachusetts insisted that the proposal did not go far enough. The freedmen's right to vote must be guaranteed directly, he demanded, as it was in his home state, not merely encouraged in this roundabout fashion. Harkening to the 200,000 blacks who served in the Union Army, Sumner insisted, "If he was willing to die for the Republic surely he is good enough to vote."

The Democratic leader of the House, James Brooks of New York, attacked the amendment from another quarter, warning of the risks of equality. Western states would lose seats in Congress because of the amendment's impact on "coolies" there. Then he pointed to the most obvious limitation on the suffrage: that women did not vote. Brandishing letters from suffragists Susan B. Anthony and Elizabeth Cady Stanton, Brooks promised an amendment to grant women the vote, proclaiming to great applause, "I am in favor of my color in preference to any other color, and I prefer the white women of the country to the negro." Female suffrage would empower New England states, which had seen many males leave for opportunity in the West and South. Brooks also questioned whether states would lose the right to impose literacy tests or property qualifications, all of which could prevent Negroes from voting (and would be employed for that purpose for another hundred years). With the proposed amendment mired in such questions, President Johnson made it clear that he opposed any constitutional change at all.

While the Joint Committee wrestled with the constitutional amendment, the full Congress addressed conditions in the South, particularly the black codes adopted by Johnson-sponsored state governments. Senator Lyman Trumbull of Illinois, who defied characterization as a Radical or a moderate, met with Johnson at the White House to gather the president's views about two bills he was pressing to aid the freedmen. Trumbull went away convinced that Johnson would accept both bills. Passed in late January, Trumbull's Freedmen's Bureau bill extended the life of that agency, which was the nation's most important effort to protect the former slaves. The legislation authorized the bureau to help freedmen enforce contracts, own property, testify in court, and own arms. Trumbull's second bill, the proposed Civil Rights Act, would reverse the black codes. It specifically conferred citizenship upon all persons born in the United States, guaranteeing to them the same civil rights "enjoyed by white citizens."

The Freedmen's Bureau bill was first to reach the president for his signature, and it presented a critical decision for Johnson. Until this point, his party identity had been clouded. Though a Southern Democrat for his whole life, he was elected on the Republican ticket and retained Lincoln's Republican Cabinet. The legislation came from a Congress in which Republicans enjoyed two-thirds majorities in both houses. This could be an opportunity for Johnson to work with Congress and also to demonstrate his compassion for the freedmen. He would be joining the effort to do justice for those who labored in bondage for so long.

The president saw the occasion differently. For him, the bill presented an opportunity to stop the Radicals in their tracks and to protect the states from federal power. He confided to a Cabinet member his concerns about "the extraordinary intrigue which he understood

*Johnson vetoes the Freedmen's
Bureau Bill.*

was going on in Congress," which aimed at "nothing short of a subversion or change in the structure of the government." Thad Stevens and his allies, the president believed, intended "to take the government into their own hands, . . . and to get rid of him." Andrew Johnson would never back down from a challenge to his authority.

Johnson vetoed the Freedmen's Bureau bill with a message calculated to infuriate Republicans. Turning a blind eye to racial violence in the South and the abject condition of the freed slaves, Johnson could not "discern in the condition of the country anything to justify" the powers proposed for the Bureau. The freedman, he assured the nation, is "not so exposed as may at first be imagined"; and if he thinks he is, he "possesses a perfect right to change his place of abode." Nothing could justify the expense of the Freedmen's Bureau, he concluded, or the expansion of federal powers at the expense of the states, or the bill's substitution of military trials for the right of Southern whites to trial by jury in their own courts. The president's concern for Southern whites, and his indifference to the former slaves, led a Radical newspaper to describe his approach as one that "ties up the children so that they shall not bite the rabid dog, and turns loose the rabid dog so that he can protect the children."

The veto message ended with a crescendo of defiance, a passage written by Johnson himself. He chastised Congress for enacting legislation for the South after refusing to seat the Southern representatives. He claimed the right to press this critique because, as president, he was "chosen by the people of all the States." Yet Johnson ignored the impact of the war on his own election in 1864. The citizens of the Confederacy had not voted for him any more than they voted for the congressmen and senators then seated in the Capitol. By his own logic, he could claim no greater legitimacy than could Congress. Indeed, Johnson's challenge to Congress only emphasized his own shaky political foundation. Selected for the Republican ticket as a symbol of unity between North and South, and then elected with Republican votes, he now chose to obstruct the policies of that party. Most Republicans insisted that voters chose Abraham Lincoln, *not* Johnson, and that he violated his obligation to those voters by opposing the party's legislation.

Johnson's veto met with groans and anger across the North. An Iowa newspaper declared him "the most deliberately bad man out of prison in the republic." The *Pittsburgh Commercial* urged the president's friends "to tell him plainly that persistence in the path he has taken must lead to fatal estrangements," a view echoed by the Radical *Chicago Tribune*, which declared that Johnson "has severed himself from the loyal [Republican] party and united with its enemies, North and South." Southern newspapers, in contrast, applauded the president's courage and determination. One pronounced him "all right on the negro question."

Republicans in Congress reacted swiftly. Senator Trumbull felt betrayed. He had sought the president's views on the legislation, and Johnson had raised no objection. Now the president vetoed the bill outright. Without the legislation, Trumbull insisted, the freedmen "will be tyrannized over, abused, and virtually reenslaved." Nevertheless, the Senate failed on February 20 to muster the two-thirds majority required to pass the bill over Johnson's veto.

Without any attempt at compromise or negotiation, Johnson had won the first round with Congress. For a bull-headed politician like him, the successful veto and the angry cries of his opponents meant only one thing—that he should step up his attack against Stevens and the Radicals. Attack had been his style for almost forty years in public life, and he was not about to change.

Johnson did not wait long. On the night of Washington's Birthday, February 22, political supporters congregated outside the White House and called for remarks honoring the first president. They got a full dose of Andrew Johnson of Tennessee.

At times enraged, at times self-pitying, for an hour and ten minutes the president complained that "an irresponsible central directory"—that is, the Joint Committee of Fifteen—was assuming "nearly all the powers of Congress," thereby "concentrat[ing] the powers of the government in the hands of the few." To the penitent South, he extended "the right hand of fellowship." No such hand reached out to those "men—I care not by what name you call them—still opposed to the Union." When the crowd called upon him to name those "other" men who were enemies of the nation, Johnson was ready:

> Suppose I should name to you those whom I look upon as being opposed to the fundamental principles of this Government, and as now laboring to destroy them. I say Thaddeus Stevens, of Pennsylvania.

President Johnson addressing Washington's Birthday crowd at the White House, 1866.

I say Charles Sumner, of Massachusetts. I say Wendell Phillips [the abolitionist], of Massachusetts.

The president thus embraced the former rebels as patriots and denounced the Radicals as traitors. But he was not done. Johnson went on to imply that those named Radicals not only were enemies of the government, but actually were plotting his murder: "I have no doubt [their] intention was to incite assassination." He offered himself as a willing sacrifice, asking only that "when I am beheaded I want the American people to be the witness." Stirred by his looming martyrdom, Johnson asked to be laid on an altar to the Union so "the blood that now warms and animates my existence shall be poured out as a fit libation to the Union of these States." A grisly libation, to be sure.

Johnson had misplayed his hand. Rather than acting the statesman who wished to unify the nation, he behaved like a political brawler with a grandiose self-image. Many deplored the speech, particularly what a moderate Republican recalled as its "low tone, its vulgar abuse." Others suspected that it was the product of hard drinking. His own secretary of the treasury, Hugh McCulloch, called it a "very imprudent speech" that "turned not only the Republican party but the general public sentiment of the Northern States against him." A Johnson ally estimated that the speech cost the Democrats 200,000 votes in the fall elections.

Johnson's divisiveness—his unrelenting us-versus-them attitude—drove away those who might have supported him. Fessenden, chair of the Joint Committee of Fifteen and Johnson's best hope for an ally among leading Republicans, found "relief" in the president's "folly and wickedness." The Maine senator wrote in a private letter that "[t]he long agony is over. He has broken the faith, betrayed his trust, and must sink from detestation into contempt."

The criticism caused Johnson to dig in even deeper. In late March, Trumbull's Civil Rights bill cleared Congress. Once more the president vetoed, offering a pastiche of objections that pandered to many prejudices. The bill would guarantee civil rights not only for blacks, he warned, but also for "the Chinese of the Pacific States, Indians subject to taxation, [and] the people called Gipsies." He criticized the statute's supposed discrimination against immigrants, was saddened that blacks were not yet worthy of citizenship, and feared that the law would incite racial intermarriage. His real dismay, however, was that the law "would operate in favor of the colored and against the white race," which would "resuscitate the spirit of rebellion."

This time the veto did not stand. Johnson's inflammatory language and unwillingness to compromise was stiffening his opponents in Congress. The law's author, Trumbull of Illinois, meticulously dissected Johnson's veto message, adding his own feelings that the president had deceived him. Having invited the president to comment on the draft legislation, Trumbull reported, he never received "the least objection to any of the provisions of the bill." By a single vote in the Senate, the bill was enacted over Johnson's objection. Over a glass of claret with an aide, the president was unrepentant. "Sir, I am right," he declared. "I know I am right and I am damned if I do not adhere."

For many, Johnson's veto of the Civil Rights bill of 1866 would stand as his defining political blunder, setting a tone of perpetual confrontation with Congress that prevailed for the balance of his presidency. That veto, along with his veto of the Freedmen's Bureau legislation and Washington's Birthday speech, fundamentally eroded his support among congressional Republicans. For Andrew Johnson, there would be no compromises and no negotiations with his congressional adversaries. The political life of the nation would be reduced to a simple contest of will and power.

Congress responded in kind. When a vacancy arose on the Supreme Court in the spring of 1866, Johnson nominated Henry Stanberry of Ohio, the lawyer who drafted much of the veto message on the Civil Rights Act. Rather than allow the president to place his man on the high court, Congress eliminated the seat. To ensure that Johnson would never appoint a judge to the Supreme Court, the legislation provided that the Court would shrink to seven justices when the next vacancy occurred. A pattern for ineffective government was forming. Dismayed by Johnson's exercise of presidential powers, Congress would eliminate or hedge those powers, thereby infuriating the man in the White House even more.

Over the next three months, two bloody incidents undermined the president's sunny vision of conditions in the South and reinforced the Radicals' insistence that only federal action could protect the freedmen and Southern supporters of the Union (often called Unionists). First, in early May 1866, came a three-day riot in Memphis, in Johnson's home state. After a dispute over a carriage collision, white police and firemen stormed through black neighborhoods of South Memphis while nearby federal troops did nothing. Forty-six blacks and two whites were killed. Hundreds of buildings burned. When it was over, a local newspaper wrote, "Thank Heaven the white race are once more rulers in Memphis." General Ulysses Grant had a different reaction. Southern whites were becoming more defiant, he warned the *New York Times*: "A year ago they were willing to do anything; now they regard themselves as masters of the situation."

Equally bloody was an episode in New Orleans in late July, when white police attacked a black political meeting. At least 47 blacks were killed and over 100 wounded; 1 policeman died of sunstroke. Arriving a day after the mayhem, General Philip Sheridan reported that the attack was "so unnecessary and atrocious as to compel me to say that it was murder." A day later, Sheridan's feelings were stronger: "It was not a riot; it was an absolute massacre."

A few Johnson loyalists tried to blame the Radicals for the violence, but most Northerners laid the responsibility at the president's feet. One Republican reported that after Memphis and New Orleans, Americans began to ask, " 'Does this mean that the rebellion is to begin again?' " A Radical congressman wrote in a magazine article that the president "has thrown himself into the arms of the South." By some measures, some former slaves were beginning to make progress. In May 1866, the Freedmen's Bureau reported more than seventy schools in Texas were teaching the children of freedmen and were wholly self-sustaining. Many Northerners came to the South to teach those children. Yet the same report found that when federal troops withdrew from an area, violence against blacks increased.

Through the early months of 1866, as Johnson's missteps and Southern violence shifted public opinion to favor Congress, the Joint Committee turned again to the nascent Fourteenth Amendment. After Charles Sumner's insistence on Negro suffrage torpedoed Stevens's simple proposal to fix the three-fifths rule, the panel confronted at least seventy proposed versions. Pressure built for the amendment to address many issues in addition to congressional representation.

Once more, the scene shifted to Thad Stevens's parlor on South B Street, behind the Capitol Building. Early one morning, Mrs. Smith opened the door for Robert Dale Owen, the idealistic son of Robert Owen, the Scottish visionary who had founded the utopian community of New Harmony, Indiana. As chair of a wartime commission on the freed slaves, Robert Dale Owen authored a report that inspired the founding of the Freedmen's Bureau. Now, in late March 1866, he had an idea for breaking the impasse over the Fourteenth Amendment.

Seated in Stevens's parlor, with bearskins on the floor and panther skins on the walls, Owen outlined a draft amendment that blended several elements and took a gradual approach. After ten years, racial discrimination in voting or civil rights would be banned; until then, persons who were barred from voting in a state because of their race could not be counted in the allocation of congressional representatives among the states. The Owen draft also proposed to bar repayment of debts incurred by the Confederate states. "Read that to me again," Stevens said. After chewing the matter over, he was sold.

"We've had nothing as good as this, or as complete," he pronounced. "It would be likely to pass, too; that's the best of it. We haven't a majority, either in our committee or in Congress, for immediate [Negro] suffrage." He promised to put Owen's draft before the Joint Committee. Owen had less luck with Fessenden of Maine, the Joint Committee chairman, who heard him out silently. John Bingham's reaction was more positive.

During the first half of April, the Joint Committee worked over Owen's proposal, finally approving a version of it and adding Bingham's pet language that the states must provide to their citizens "due process of law" and "equal protection of the laws." By imposing those requirements directly on the states, Bingham's provision could work a fundamental shift in power between the federal and state governments. Both Congress and federal courts could enforce those guarantees against the states. The traditional principle of state sovereignty, which had encouraged secession and which still inspired Andrew Johnson's policies, would be reduced, limited by federal protection for individual rights.

The Joint Committee did not release the proposed amendment for several weeks because Fessenden fell ill. In the interim, political resistance mounted to Negro suffrage—even Negro suffrage that would be delayed for ten years—and the Joint Committee dropped that provision. The members concluded that three-fourths of the states would not ratify voting rights for blacks "in any degree or under any restriction." When the revised version of the amendment emerged at the end of the month, with the suffrage provision stripped out, the president still denounced it to his Cabinet, then leaked minutes of his remarks to the newspapers.

Few now remember the provisions of the Fourteenth Amendment that caused the greatest debate in 1866. Bingham's airy guarantees of due process and equal protection—which would remake America in the twentieth century—drew relatively little comment. Focusing on practical matters, Johnson and other opponents trained their fire on the provision that stripped federal voting rights from those who had "voluntarily adhered to the late insurrection, giving it aid and comfort." In the coming debates, that provision would be weakened steadily. The final version merely barred from federal office those who had taken an oath to support the United States Constitution but then "engaged in insurrection or rebellion." Of course, Negro suffrage was long gone, replaced by a version of Stevens's original idea, which would reduce congressional representation for any state where the right to vote was "in any way abridged." That provision would survive to the final version of the Fourteenth Amendment, but it would never be enforced through long decades when many states systematically denied voting rights to blacks.

With Congress poised to approve the Fourteenth Amendment on June 13, Stevens did not rejoice. "Don't imagine," he told a friend, "that I sanction the shilly-shally, bungling thing that I shall have to report to the House." When he closed the House debate on the amendment, one observer thought he "looked so feeble, the great old man, it makes me sorry." Nevertheless, the packed chamber hung on his words.

As a younger man, he said, he dreamt of freeing American institutions "from every vestige of human oppression, of inequality of rights, of the recognized degradation of the poor, and the superior caste of the rich." His "bright dream" had vanished, he said, so Congress had merely "patched up the worst portions of the ancient edifice, . . . leaving it, in many of its parts, to be swept through by the tempests, the frosts, and the storms of despotism." In closing, Stevens revealed a willingness to compromise that he often concealed.

> Do you inquire why, holding these views and possessing some will of my own, I accept so imperfect a proposition? I answer, because I live among men and not among angels; among men as intelligent, as determined, and as independent as myself, who, not agreeing with me, do not choose to yield their opinions to mine. Mutual concession, therefore, is our only resort, or mutual hostilities.

Despite his disappointment, Stevens voted for the amendment, which received the two-thirds vote needed to submit it to the states for their approval. If three-fourths of them ratified it, the amendment would become part of the Constitution.

With the amendment on its way to the states, President Johnson mobilized for battle. In an official statement, he expressed "grave doubts" about the provision's wisdom. He also questioned its validity, since the

Southern states were not then represented in Congress. Meeting with one Cabinet member, "he expressed himself in the most decided terms of hostility" to the amendment. Johnson urged state legislators in the South to reject it or delay voting on it.

Two Republican congressmen learned firsthand of the president's bellicose mood. Calling at the White House when the row between the president and Congress was "at its height," they hoped to "smooth over the differences." They had misjudged their president. "He received us politely enough," one remembered, "and without mincing any words he gave us to understand that we were on a fool's errand and he would not yield." Thereafter, the two congressmen joined the extreme Radicals in the House and always voted with them. Johnson could have that effect on people.

6

---◆◆◆---

POLITICAL WAR

JULY—NOVEMBER 1866

We have got to fight Johnson because he will fight us.

SENATOR LYMAN TRUMBULL, JULY 2, 1866

WITH ONE EYE on the congressional elections that loomed in the fall of 1866, Johnson resolved to carry the fight to his foes. The president, according to his own treasury secretary, "was a combatant by temperament. If he did not court controversy, he enjoyed it." Elected on the Republican ticket, Johnson longed to cut himself free from that party. He did not share its principles, its goals, or its brief history. Yet many of his old colleagues in the Democratic Party mistrusted his pro-Union stance during the war. The time was ripe, Johnson decided, to launch a new party, conservative yet pro-Union, that would support his political agenda and his personal ambitions.

The president's closest adviser, Secretary of State Seward, described Johnson's strategy as a subtle one. He intended to prod the Radicals into taking extreme positions. Once Stevens and his ilk were flushed into the open, Johnson aimed to appeal to Republicans who could not stomach the Radicals, and to Democrats who were uncomfortable with that party's ambivalence toward the Civil War. In mid-June, just after congressional approval of the Fourteenth Amendment, he resolved to call a convention of a new "Union" party, borrowing the name used by the Republicans in 1864.

It was a bold step, but not without potential. Political parties were more fluid in those days. The Republican Party, which ruled Congress and had won the last two presidential elections, was barely a decade old.

Launching the new party gave the president a chance to address nagging personnel issues in his Cabinet, still made up of Lincoln holdovers. There would be no change at the State Department. In the year since the assassination, the president had come to trust William Henry Seward, calling him "faithful, firm and reliable . . . a truly great man." Small and slender, with a prominent nose and an addiction to fine cigars, the polished, playful Seward had largely recovered from the carriage accident and assassination attempt of the year before, though knife wounds had robbed one side of his face of most expression. He also had suffered the loss of his wife, who died only weeks after the assassination attempt. Still, Seward regained his vigor and his usually sunny disposition. One contemporary called Seward both a charming talker and a good listener, "a characteristic rare among men who have been long accustomed to lead."

A devoted supporter of President Lincoln, Seward transferred that loyalty to Johnson. Contemporaries saw the secretary of state's influence in many of the new president's policies. One Republican thought it was Seward who persuaded Johnson to abandon the vindictive rhetoric of his first days in office and then brought the Tennessean around to the laissez-faire policy followed in allowing Southern whites to establish their own governments. Some thought the adviser's influence at the White House had its roots in the pivotal role of Seward's allies in pushing the Republican Convention of 1864 to nominate the man from Tennessee for vice president. Whatever their political history from 1864, Seward and Johnson developed a particularly close relationship as president and secretary of state.

Though many Southerners viewed Seward as a rabid abolitionist before the Civil War, the reality was different. In the supercharged days of early 1861, with Southern states seceding and no one sure if the nation would survive, Seward was a voice of conciliation, insisting that slavery should be preserved in those states where it already existed but prevented from expanding. Radicals like Thaddeus Stevens were enraged. Through the war, Seward adhered to his conciliatory, gradualist views while many Republicans became Radicals. When Lincoln proposed the Emancipation Proclamation in 1862, Seward urged him to wait for a better moment. By war's end, the secretary of state was largely out of step with his own party. He strongly approved Johnson's controversial speech on Washington's Birthday 1866 and showed relatively little interest in the plight of the freedmen. The secretary of state, insisting that Johnson was implementing Lincoln's policies, urged the immediate seating of Southern congressmen and senators. He was content to return Southern state governments to the control of former Confederates. In a public letter, Seward endorsed the president's call for the Union Party convention.

Other members of the Cabinet, however, were entirely too Republican for Johnson's taste. By asking all Cabinet members to join the call for the new Union Party convention, he intended to force some from office. Three responded by resigning, as Johnson had hoped. Out went the postmaster general, the secretary of the interior, and the attorney general, replaced by Johnson loyalists. Now the president could redirect the thousands of patronage jobs in those agencies. In that era before civil service reform, every federal job could be filled for solely political reasons, making patronage appointments a key to political power. According to his new secretary of the interior, the president now pledged to use that patronage for "the true friends of the Country."

For months, Republicans had been complaining that Johnson was replacing that party's loyalists in favor of Democrats. From Maryland to Illinois to Missouri, Johnson's appointments dismayed the Republican faithful. By summertime, many postmasters, tax collectors, and Indian agents would face demands that they support the new Union Party or lose their jobs. In the seven months before June of 1866, Johnson removed 52 postmasters; over the next four months, more than 1,600 would be sacked for political reasons. He also turned to the tax collection machinery, which one Maine Republican described as "all-pervasive in its character," with thousands of officials serving at the president's pleasure. In a single building, the New York Custom House, 1,200 political appointees levied duties on goods imported through the nation's busiest port. Those highly coveted jobs featured indoor work, no heavy lifting, and plenty of opportunity for graft, both petty and grand.

Republicans watched helplessly as the president turned political custom on its head, delivering to the losing Democrats the spoils of the Republican victory in 1864. Johnson's use of patronage reminded Republicans of the political reversal they suffered at the hands of John Wilkes Booth. To a party man, it was unnatural.

Senator Fessenden complained that the president was filling federal offices in Maine with "copperheads and flunkies." ("Copperhead" was a derogatory term used during the Civil War to describe Northern Democrats who supported a negotiated peace with the Confederacy.) In Ohio, Senator John Sherman groused that Johnson was "turning out good men—sometimes wounded soldiers—merely because they adhered to their party convictions, and putting in men who opposed the war."

Fortified by the president's greater control over federal patronage, Johnson and his allies focused their energies on the founding of the Union Party. Its convention would meet in Philadelphia in the second week of August.

Johnson's Cabinet purge was fatally incomplete, failing to reach the prickly secretary of war, Edwin Stanton of Ohio and western Pennsylvania. It was no secret in Washington that Stanton's loyalty to Johnson was uncertain. Though he answered to the president, the war secretary sympathized strongly with the Radicals. For six months, Johnson had been mulling over candidates to succeed Stanton. Stanton himself, recognizing his compromised position, toyed with the thought of resigning. Yet, month after month, the war secretary remained awkwardly in office. For nineteen months more, Stanton would be a painful stone in Andrew Johnson's shoe.

Compact and bristling with energy, Edwin Stanton was one of the most difficult people ever to head a federal agency. At a personal level, he could be both insufferable and baffling. Ulysses Grant wrote in his memoirs that Stanton "cared nothing for the feelings of others. In fact it seemed to be pleasanter to him to disappoint than to gratify." Stanton's shifting moods kept others off balance. "[O]ften petulant, irritating, and senselessly unjust," according to a contemporary, he also could be "one of the most amiable, genial, and delightful conversationalists I have ever met." The war secretary seemed "proud of the fact that he had more personal and political enemies than any prominent officers of the government."

Stanton's bad temper had its roots in personal tragedies. The death of his first wife and a daughter, followed by his brother's suicide, haunted him as a younger man. After his second marriage, an infant son died in 1862. Stanton's own health was erratic, worsened by long workdays and fits of asthma. When stress laid him low, he lived on mush and milk, but kept working.

Stanton had been a formidable trial lawyer, developing a national renown. An Ohioan described Stanton, when young, as always in a hurry; with age, he became abrupt. While defending an 1855 patent infringement case brought by Cyrus McCormick, inventor of a reaping machine, Stanton was contemptuous of a tall Illinois lawyer who was added to the trial team. Referring to Abraham Lincoln, Stanton asked, "Where did that long-armed creature come from and what can he expect to do in this case?" Stanton blocked Lincoln from any active role in the trial. Luckily for Stanton, the future president had a gift for overlooking personal slights.

Secretary of War Edwin Stanton.

Stanton's first service in Washington City came in late 1860, while Democratic President James Buchanan feebly watched the country slide toward secession and civil war. Acting as attorney general for the last four months of Buchanan's term, Stanton was suspected of slipping Cabinet secrets to the incoming Republicans. When Lincoln's first war secretary proved unequal to the job, Stanton took over with an efficiency that earned Lincoln's gratitude and trust. Behind glistening spectacles and the beard of an Old Testament prophet, Stanton was curt, incisive, and forceful. "Folks come up here and tell me there are a great many men who have all Stanton's excellent qualities without his defects," Lincoln said. "All I can say is, I haven't met 'em; I don't know 'em." A Republican congressman paid tribute to Stanton's work ethic: "He lived in the War Office, literally; his bed was there; his food was there; his presence in his own household was a rare event."

Yet as Stanton fed his gargantuan appetite for work, his modest store of people skills atrophied. According to one contemporary, a Stanton subordinate "had to be a mere cipher, so dictatorial and despotic was he."

The relationship between Stanton and Andrew Johnson began pleasantly, even respectfully. When Johnson left his post as military governor of Tennessee in early 1865, Stanton wrote with admiration of Johnson's service "in a position of personal toil and danger, perhaps more hazardous than was encountered by any other citizen or military officer in the United States." In the days immediately after Lincoln's assassination, Johnson leaned heavily on the war secretary. Tensions arose quickly, though, when Johnson rejected Stanton's proposal to include Negro suffrage as part of the new state government for North Carolina.

While Johnson steadily moved away from the Republican Party that had placed him in office, Stanton edged toward its Radical wing. By February 1866, Navy Secretary Gideon Welles was sure that Stanton had thrown in with the Radicals, but was not sure whether "the President is fully aware of that fact." In truth, Johnson referred privately to his war secretary's duplicity, declaring that he knew no man who could be more obsequious than Stanton. However deferential Stanton might be in person, his opposition to Johnson's policies drove many official actions. Sitting atop the War Department, Stanton was perfectly placed to thwart Johnson's efforts to empower Southern state governments. In

April, Johnson proclaimed that the Southern rebellion was over, an act that left army commanders unsure whether they could still enforce martial law in the South. With Stanton's connivance, General Grant circulated a confidential instruction that commanders should continue to use martial law as needed, and that the president could not direct the Freedmen's Bureau's actions.

Those actions frustrated Johnson, and more like them followed. In July, Grant authorized commanders to arrest lawbreakers when civil authorities failed to do so, exactly contrary to the president's wish that state governments resume control over law enforcement. The war within the Johnson Administration emerges in the explanation offered by one of Grant's senior aides: "A Cabinet Minister [Stanton] and the General of the Army [Grant] were doing their utmost to thwart the President," the aide wrote, because "the President himself, and all but one of his legal advisers, were engaged in the effort to subvert or pervert the declared will of the people." According to Grant's aide, Stanton and the general-in-chief "concerted constantly how best to execute the intent of Congress in spite of [Johnson,] whom Stanton at least deemed a guilty conspirator." In his escalating war with Congress, Johnson did not command the loyalty of his own senior officials.

In May, a Radical congressman reported Stanton's assurance that the secretary of war was "heart & soul with us." Though Stanton claimed to "loathe Johnson's politics," he confided that "good men demand him to stay in the Cabinet." Oddly, despite his mistrust of Stanton, Johnson still listened to the war secretary's advice. By summertime, Navy Secretary Welles concluded that even though Stanton was "treacherous," the secretary of war yet could influence the president's decisions.

The president continued to vacillate on whether to keep Stanton at the War Department. Musing with a senior aide, Johnson expressed admiration for Stanton's talents, insisting he was "a most valuable man if he were not so controlled by impulses." Yet the president admitted that Stanton was a bully who "liked to get a man at a disadvantage." Another Cabinet member thought Stanton retained influence with the president by showing a fawning deference whenever he could. Plenty of advisers urged Johnson to cashier the wayward Secretary and bemoaned the failure to do so. McCulloch at the Treasury Department put the matter simply: Stanton attended Cabinet meetings "not as an adviser of the

President, but as an opponent," yet "the President lacked the nerve to dismiss him," which was "a blunder for which there was no excuse."

Though harsh, McCulloch's verdict was just. Stanton essentially intimidated his superior for months that stretched into years. Some of this mastery over the president came from Stanton's objective qualities. The war secretary's close connection to Lincoln and his war service gave him a moral stature that Johnson respected. Stanton's force of character and intellectual abilities could not be denied, not by a president who was entirely self-educated. When Stanton actually executed Johnson's wishes, the results were swift and gratifying. The Secretary's personal integrity could not be questioned, and extended to principles, as well; on more than one occasion, Stanton took political heat for official actions he might have blamed on Johnson. And Stanton commanded broad support in the Republican Congress.

Yet Stanton's ability to confound Johnson also came from his peculiar personal style. Stanton's breathtakingly bad manners could give him the initiative in conversations, shielding him from the awkwardness that a situation would create for more sensitive mortals. Stanton's infrequent fits of charm could seem all the sweeter to those bruised by his customary disdain. By whatever means, the war secretary gained the upper hand, and kept it for a long time, over the strong-willed president he was supposed to serve.

As the months marched on, even Stanton grew sensitive to the charge of disloyalty to the president, but he never loosened his hold on his office. He professed to fear any successor who might be appointed by the president, who was "led by bad passions and the counsel of unscrupulous and dangerous men." Johnson's pro-South leanings, his indifference to the freedmen's condition, his dedication to the states' rights principles that supported secession in the first place—all persuaded Stanton that Johnson was a dangerous, dangerous man. Pledging to remain at his post until he died "with harness on," Stanton insisted the nation was in greater peril with Johnson in office than it ever had been during the Civil War.

In the second half of 1866, Johnson wielded a sort of reverse Midas touch. One by one, his political schemes turned to dross until the fall elections delivered a crushing rejection of him and his policies.

First came the National Union Convention in Philadelphia. Convention managers provided high theater on the first day, August 12, when a Massachusetts delegate linked arms with a South Carolinian to lead a procession 7,000 strong. Despite the unifying symbolism, the meeting fell flat. The Republicans and Democrats could not agree on enough to support a new political party. The president blamed the failure on his old colleagues, the Democrats. They could not overlook his wartime alliance with the Republicans. Johnson realized he would have to go it alone, a man without a party in a time of intense party loyalties. To save his policies and his career, Johnson decided to break many of the prevailing rules of presidential deportment.

The president came out swinging. When the official proceedings of the Union convention were presented to him, his remarks challenged Congress yet again. "We have seen hanging upon the verge of the government," he announced, "a body called, or which assumes to be, the Congress of the United States, while, in fact, it is a Congress of only a part of the states." He predicted that "every step" taken by Congress would "perpetuate disunion" and even "make a disruption of the states inevitable." He accused a minority in Congress of seeking to establish "despotism or monarchy itself."

Having denied the legitimacy of Congress, Johnson set out on an unprecedented appeal to the people of the North. Nineteenth-century candidates for president rarely campaigned openly. Rather than stump for election, most candidates sat placidly at home while a team of agents spoke for them around the country. Even more, sitting presidents did not engage in active politicking to bring policy issues to the people. Johnson resolved to change all that. He was certain the people would support him once he explained the issues to them—the need to protect the sovereignty of the states, to uphold the "Constitution as it is." His strength as a politician had always been his power as a public speaker. He would apply that strength to the struggle with Congress.

Johnson agreed to speak at a ceremony in Illinois to honor the late Senator Stephen Douglas, the Democrat who lost to Lincoln in the 1860 presidential race. The president used the trip as the pretext for a three-week "Swing Around the Circle" through the vote-rich states of the Mid-Atlantic and Midwest. To ensure big crowds, Johnson brought along with him the reluctant Ulysses Grant, Admiral David Farragut, and Secretary of State Seward. The trainload of worthies traveled to Philadelphia and New York, across upstate New York and the Midwest, then down to St. Louis and back to Washington City.

In day after day of nonstop speechmaking, Johnson failed to rally Northern opinion to support him. Dignified and self-possessed in a conference room, Johnson was a different animal on a speakers' platform or a hotel balcony, looking out over a sea of torchlit faces. His blood rose, his language coarsened, his demeanor became stormy.

In every speech, Johnson boasted of rising through many public offices to the presidency, striking a self-congratulatory note that invited deflation. He always endorsed preservation of the Union, then accused Congress and Thad Stevens of wanting to destroy it. Reflecting his experience in the rough-and-tumble of Tennessee politics, Johnson dealt harsh blows against his enemies. One supporter, political veteran Thurlow Weed of New York, remembered Johnson at the time as "aggressive and belligerent to a degree that rendered him insensitive to considerations of prudence."

After a few stops, the president's opponents began to stage confrontations, shouting out questions and challenges that goaded him into ever more strident pronouncements. In Cleveland, he attacked "the subsidized gang of hirelings and traducers" who opposed him; he accused Congress of "trying to break up the Government." He had defeated the traitors in the South, Johnson thundered, and now would fight traitors in the North. In St. Louis, the president accused Congress of planning the New Orleans Riot (which was actually a police assault on a peaceful black assembly). In a self-pitying harangue, he railed against those who supposedly called him a Judas Iscariot, betraying Republican principles:

> If I have played the Judas, who has been my Christ that I have played the Judas with? Was it Thad Stevens? Was it Wendell Phillips? Was it Charles Sumner? These are the men that stop and compare themselves to the Saviour; and everybody that differs with them in opinion, and to try and stay and arrest their diabolical and nefarious policy, is to be denounced as a Judas.

In three weeks of speechifying, Johnson's message failed to register with much of his audience, while he did himself little good politically.

Northern voters were not yet ready to abandon the Republican politicians who had won the Civil War. Future President Rutherford Hayes of Ohio dismissed Johnson's efforts with the observation that "he don't know the Northern people." Some said the president was drinking again. For many, Johnson's speeches became an object of derision. Ulysses Grant spoke for a large section of Northern opinion when he wrote to his wife, "I have never been so tired of anything before as I have been with the political stump speeches of Mr. Johnson. I look upon them as a national disgrace." A Johnson ally estimated that the Swing Around the Circle cost the Democrats a million votes in the fall elections.

In the 1860s, many states had different election days through the autumn. Starting with Maine's vote in early September of 1866, an unmistakable pattern formed and held true in most states. By early November, the voters had elected an overwhelmingly Republican Congress. Of 226 members of the House of Representatives, 173 were Republicans. Republicans sat in all but nine of the 52 Senate seats. The president's offensive had backfired.

Johnson's acrimonious campaign in the second half of 1866 triggered powerful responses. The prospect of armed violence haunted both sides of the conflict between the president and Congress. Neither was planning insurrection, but each thought the other was.

The president's opponents feared that he aimed at a military putsch. In July, Republican Senator John Sherman of Ohio wrote his brother, General William Sherman, "I almost fear he contemplates civil war." At a Republican caucus that month, Radical George Boutwell of Massachusetts accused Johnson of being part of a conspiracy to turn the government over to the Southern rebels. Shortly after Congress adjourned in late July, the governor of Virginia reactivated that state's militia and petitioned the federal government for weapons. The prospect of armed Virginians in uniform chilled many Northern hearts. Johnson had the power to deny the request but did not do so. Wary of both Virginians and the president, General Grant dragged his feet in responding.

In the third week of August, shortly before his Swing Around the Circle, Johnson suspended martial law everywhere in the country. Charles Sumner of Massachusetts feared that the president was planning a coup d'état, which would mean "revolution and another civil war." Another Republican senator remembered that the president's supporters freely discussed the use of force against Congress, a prospect that became "rather common talk."

Rumors focused on schemes by Johnson to replace Congress. One report had him asking his attorney general whether a Congress consisting only of Northern Democrats and Southern congressmen could supplant the hated Congress of Thad Stevens. Johnson mused to General Grant about the possibility of such an alternative Congress. Versions of this alarming conversation spread like wildfire, often including a follow-up question from the president to Grant: which side would the army support in a showdown? Grant's reported response ranged from the Delphic "whichever side the law was on" to the steadfast assertion that the army would stand by the current Congress.

Republicans grew jumpy. Stanton told congressional allies that he and Grant feared an armed takeover by the president. An Ohio congressman formed a "club for watchfulness" in August of 1866, while Grant sent an aide to Tennessee to "ascertain all you can with reference to secret Military organizations that are rumored to be forming within the state." Grant sent a warning to his wartime protégé, General Philip Sheridan, then commanding troops in the South.

> I much fear that we are fast approaching the point where he [Johnson] will want to declare [Congress] itself illegal, unconstitutional, and revolutionary. Commanders in the Southern states will have to take great care to see, if a crisis does come, that no armed headway can be made against the Union.

As a precaution, Grant quietly transferred weapons away from federal arsenals in the South and canceled plans that would take him out of Washington.

The anxiety on the president's side was equally high. Reports circulated that midwestern governors met in St. Louis to commission 30,000 "boys in blue" to march on Washington as soon as Congress convened in December. Johnson suspected the Grand Army of the Republic, the new organization of Union Army veterans. In September, he dispatched an agent to investigate its activities. The agent claimed that the GAR, with arms provided by midwestern governors, would march on Washington to unseat the president by force. Citing a report from Indiana, a Cabinet Secretary insisted that "there was a conspiracy on foot to overthrow the government and set up a military dictatorship." A North Carolina newspaper suggested that Congress might need to be cleared of Radicals "at the point of the bayonet," as the police in New Orleans had used bullets to clear out the Louisiana Negroes earlier that summer.

Tensions boiled higher when the pro-Johnson governor of Maryland demanded federal troops to keep the peace during that state's November elections. A former slave state with strong Southern identification, Maryland had just revived its militia, mostly Confederate veterans. The state was angrily divided over the controversial process of deciding which ex-rebels would be allowed to vote. Though Stanton opposed the request for troops, the rest of the Cabinet supported it. General Grant refused to intervene on the side of the governor and his white supremacist party. "If insurrection does come," he wrote the president, "the law provides the method of calling out forces to suppress it." The election passed peaceably without federal troops.

By now, Grant's passive resistance to the president's initiatives had become as infuriating as Stanton's. Realizing that he could never discharge the hero of the Civil War, Johnson sought an alternative solution: to find Grant an assignment overseas and replace him with General Sherman, who was more sympathetic to the president's policies. In a series of testy exchanges in October, Johnson tried to dispatch Grant on a diplomatic mission to Mexico, where Benito Juárez was leading an insurgency against French forces under the Austrian Emperor Maximilian. The president started by asking the general to lead the mission. Grant declined. Then Secretary of State Seward ordered Grant to take the assignment. When Grant declined again, the disagreement played out in a tense scene before the entire Cabinet. Grant insisted that he was a military officer, so the president could not order him on a civil mission to Mexico. Then he walked out.

Not only was the general-in-chief intransigent, but General Sherman also refused to take Grant's place at the head of the army. "[T]he President was aiming to get Grant out of the way, and me in," Sherman wrote to his senator brother, "on the supposition that I would be more friendly to him." To his wife, Sherman wrote, "I will be a party to no such move."

Defied by his generals, the president backed down. He sent Sherman on the mission to Mexico.

Each new incident built Republican frustration with the president. Some began to cast about for a bloodless method for ridding the nation of this dangerous president, an inquiry that led directly to the impeachment clauses of the Constitution. Though no president had been impeached in the nation's first eight decades, perhaps impeachment could be the tool for removing Johnson peacefully.

Radical newspapers started impeachment talk in the spring of 1866. When he denounced Johnson's official appointments in late May, Stevens issued a menacing warning, stating that "there is a grand inquest of the nation before whom men who are guilty of malpractices in office can be brought and their cases presented to another tribunal which would try them." By the end of the summer, Stevens was wondering whether Johnson's "corrupt" patronage practices could support impeachment. Another congressman countered that Johnson should be impeached "for his attempt to [i]ncite the people to revolution" by calling Congress "a usurping & illegal body."

Perhaps fittingly, an early call for impeachment came from former Vice President Hannibal Hamlin of Maine, who had lost his job—and his chance at the presidency—to Johnson. After resigning in early September from his position as collector of the Port of Boston, Hamlin challenged Johnson's "usurpations" in creating the Southern state governments and his association with rebels and Copperheads. "Did we fight down the rebellion," Hamlin asked, "to give the South more power?"

Former General Benjamin Butler of Massachusetts, who was about to claim a seat in Congress, took up the impeachment cry with a vengeance, speaking throughout the fall campaign of 1866 on the need to remove President Johnson. Before a Brooklyn crowd of 3,000 in late November, he denounced "King Andrew the Indecent," and presented a laundry list of "charges" against him: that Johnson wrongly granted pardons to rebels, incited the New Orleans massacre, failed to confiscate Confederate property, delivered "inflammatory and dangerous harangues" (also one of Butler's favorite activities), and usurped congressional powers by unilaterally establishing state governments in the South.

The talk of impeachment reflected many factors that combined to cripple Johnson's presidency. In a decade that already featured secession and civil war, political leaders in the 1860s did not shy from extreme remedies. Extreme actions seem less extreme as they become part of the ordinary experience of life. Johnson's political messages—that the South must be left alone to define itself, and that the Constitution barred federal actions to the contrary—carried disturbing echoes of Southern political rhetoric before the Civil War. And then there was Johnson himself. For many Northerners, his most basic qualities made him seem unworthy of the presidency at that moment in history. He was a Southerner, but the South had lost the war. He was a Democrat, but that party had not supported the war. He defended states' rights theories that had supported secession and civil war. He was rigid and angry, unwilling to compromise, at a time when the nation had to be united. And many thought of him as a drunkard. It was a ruinous combination.

Passions still ran high when Congress gathered in early December. Pointing to the Republican electoral sweep, Stevens announced he had been "rather conservative last winter, but is now Radical, and expects to continue so the remainder of his days." Though some laughed at the Pennsylvanian's tongue-in-cheek conversion, Stevens meant every word. He wrote coldly in one letter that with the president "still unhung," Congress needed "to look a little after the hemp." To another Radical, he observed there was great work to do "if we are brave enough! Yes, there is the rub. And how few brave men are there?"

Despite the growing opposition, President Johnson still had no appetite for compromise. His annual statement to Congress, delivered in early December, again called on Congress to admit the representatives from the Southern states. It conspicuously failed to endorse the pending Fourteenth Amendment.

With both sides digging in deeper, the political war could only escalate.

7

FALSE START ON IMPEACHMENT

DECEMBER 1866—JUNE 1867

I do impeach Andrew Johnson, Vice President and President
of the United States, of high crimes and misdemeanors. I
charge him with a usurpation of law and violation of law:
>   In that he has corruptly used the appointing power;
>   In that he has corruptly used the pardoning power;
>   In that he has corruptly used the veto power;
>   In that he has corruptly disposed of public property of
>   The United States;
>   In that he has corruptly interfered with elections. . . .

> REPRESENTATIVE JAMES M. ASHLEY,
> JANUARY 7, 1867

WHEN THE LAME-DUCK Congress convened in early December 1866,
the nation seemed to be sliding backward. The blessings of peace
were proving disappointing. Partisan and sectional resentments seemed
to be growing. "[T]he great war of the Rebellion," a French observer
wrote, "though it is over in the military sense, still goes on in men's
minds." He added, "The hatred of the South for the North is more bitter
than ever."

In this toxic atmosphere, several Radical Republicans demanded a
special committee to investigate impeachment of the president. Meeting
resistance within the Republican caucus, Representative James Ashley

of Ohio agreed with Stevens to present an impeachment resolution to the full House. Called "a calculating fanatic" by Navy Secretary Welles, Ashley accused the president of usurpation of power by making corrupt appointments, issuing pardons to rebels, selling off confiscated property, vetoing legislation, and interfering with elections.

Stevens, persuaded that real Reconstruction was impossible with Johnson in office, provided the muscle behind Ashley's resolution. When the House referred it to the Judiciary Committee on January 7, Congress was daily receiving petitions that demanded Johnson's removal from office. The petitions, the fruits of an organized campaign, were signed by as few as three citizens or as many as three hundred. They poured in throughout 1867, mostly from the Midwest.

The new Congress mounted a furious legislative assault on Johnson and his policies. Over the president's veto, it approved Negro suffrage in the District of Columbia. Legislation admitted Colorado and Nebraska as new states—holding out the prospect of more Radicals in Congress— only to meet with presidential vetoes. Nebraska but not Colorado made it past Johnson's roadblock.

Two audacious new laws aimed to curb presidential powers. The first came from inside the president's official family. When Congress convened in December, Edwin Stanton invited George Boutwell, the Radical congressman from Massachusetts, to a private room at the War Department. Pronouncing himself more concerned about the nation's fate than he had been during the Civil War, Stanton dictated legislation that would make it a crime for the president to issue military orders that did not go through the General of the Army (Grant). Boutwell brought Stanton's language to Stevens, who placed it in the military appropriations bill for the year. Though Johnson intended to veto the bill, and with it the army's budget, his Cabinet persuaded him to sign the legislation in order to ensure military funding. The president asked Stanton for his advice on this legislation—which the secretary of war himself had drafted to hamstring the president. Stanton's reply was cool: "I approve your taking whatever course you may think best." Johnson lost power under the new law, while Grant gained it.

For some time, Stevens had been urging a second key statute, the Tenure of Office Act, which would become the centerpiece of the impeachment charges against the president. Under the legislation, the Senate would have to concur in the firing of any executive official whose appointment the Senate had confirmed in the first place.

Stevens's bill addressed one of the asymmetries of the Constitution. The Framers in 1787 required Senate confirmation of presidential appointees, but the charter was silent about who could remove those officials. With no direction from the Constitution, the power to fire executive officials could be lodged in the president or could be made subject to Congress's power to make the laws. Early statutes gave the president the right to discharge those officials without any action by the Senate. Did that mean Congress could specify different removal procedures, as Stevens now proposed to do? Or did it mean that the president always had the power to discharge executive officials? The argument had continued for decades and would be rehashed repeatedly over the next eighteen months. Indeed, it continued through the rest of the nineteenth century and into the twentieth, with parts of it unresolved to this day.

When Congress took up Stevens's statute in March, debate focused on Cabinet appointees: should the Senate have to concur when the president wanted to dismiss a member of his Cabinet? Congressional Republicans disagreed among themselves. Stevens and his allies, hoping to protect Stanton at the War Department, pressed for the statute to cover Cabinet members; others worried that no president should have to retain a department head in whom he had no confidence. In a muddled legislative sequence, the House and Senate disagreed on the issue, then adopted compromise language that did not clearly resolve it. This question, too, would be the subject of exhaustive debate during the impeachment trial.

That Johnson would veto the Tenure of Office Act was a foregone conclusion. More surprising, though, was Edwin Stanton's advice that he do so. Even though the law was partly designed to keep him in office, the war secretary was "very emphatic" that it unconstitutionally limited the president's powers. Indeed, Stanton helped draft the veto message. As was becoming routine, Congress enacted the bill over Johnson's veto.

Although the statute was intended to block the president from removing Republican officials, which it certainly did, it also shrank the powers of Johnson's successor in the White House. That *next* president would be able to appoint new Cabinet officers on his own, but he would have to seek the concurrence of the Senate in order to replace any other executive official. The perverse result of the statute would be to allow Johnson appointees to burrow deeply into the bureaucracy so long as they retained the favor of the Senate.

In addition, Stevens set an obvious trap in the statute. Section 6 of the new law stated that appointments or removals that violated the act were "high misdemeanors," echoing the "high crimes and misdemeanors" language of the Constitution's impeachment clause. Stevens and Congress were placing Johnson on notice. If he violated the Tenure of Office Act, he would risk impeachment.

Stevens pushed Congress to do away with the Johnson-sponsored governments in the Southern states. Staffed by many former rebels, those state governments maintained black codes and ignored white violence against the freedmen. Over the next several months, Congress enacted three Reconstruction laws that would sweep out those state governments after less than two years in existence. Under this new phase of Reconstruction—called "congressional reconstruction"—Southerners would again call statewide conventions to draft new constitutions. When new governments were established under the new constitutions, they could petition for readmission of their representatives to Congress. This time, many ex-Confederates would be excluded from the process. Unionists and freedmen would be encouraged to participate. The legislation also reinforced the Army's position in the South.

In this welter of political activity, the House Judiciary Committee pursued its inquiry into whether Andrew Johnson should be removed from office. This was the ultimate constitutional confrontation, one branch of government considering whether to decapitate another. All the anger and self-righteousness of the Civil War returned, but in a new garb. Instead of North versus South, now Congress was facing off against the president. There were few precedents to follow, and the committee members had difficulty defining exactly what they should be investigating. Pursuing a scattershot and often superficial course, the committee's performance would not inspire confidence, even among Republicans.

Impeachment dates back at least to fourteenth-century England. Rooted in the struggle for power between Parliament and kings, impeachment was a device for prosecuting great lords and high officials who were beyond the reach of the law courts. British impeachments carried heavy penalties, including fines, imprisonment, and beheading. Though the British mostly abandoned impeachment by the nineteenth century, the process involved charges brought by the House of Commons, followed by trial in the House of Lords.

The delegates to the Constitutional Convention in 1787 created an American version of impeachment. They wanted a peaceful means for Congress to remove judges and executive officials, including the president. Otherwise, as Ben Franklin pointed out, assassination was the only way to rid the nation of a bad president.

The Constitution devotes seven sentences—about 180 words—to impeachment. First, the House of Representatives has "the sole power of impeachment," which means that all impeachment charges must originate in that body. By custom, once the House approves those accusations (called "articles of impeachment"), it appoints several of its members (called the "House managers") to prosecute the case in the Senate.

The Senate has "the sole power to try all impeachments." To hear that trial, senators must take an oath; by its own rule, the Senate requires the oath to be a pledge to "do impartial justice according to the Constitution and laws." When the president is the target of impeachment, the chief justice of the United States presides over his trial. If two-thirds of the Senate votes to convict the accused on any single impeachment article, he is immediately removed from office. No president can absolve an impeachment conviction by granting a pardon. The removed official can also face criminal prosecution for any offenses he or she has committed.

The greatest puzzle of impeachment has been the definition of those actions that warrant its use. The Constitution authorizes impeachment for "treason, bribery, or other high crimes and misdemeanors." Treason and bribery have proved clear enough, but a crisp definition of "high crimes and misdemeanors" has eluded generations of scholars. The term was proposed in a late debate on the impeachment mechanism during the Philadelphia Convention in 1787. George Mason of Virginia complained that the draft impeachment provision was limited to treason and bribery. "Attempts to subvert the Constitution," he pointed out, "may not be treason." He proposed to add "maladministration" as a basis for impeachment. James Madison criticized that term as too vague, so Mason substituted "high crimes and misdemeanors," to the vexation of succeeding generations.

The rejection of Mason's initial proposal of "maladministration" suggests that mere incompetence is no basis for impeachment. Some have insisted that an impeachable offense must violate a criminal statute; after all, treason and bribery are crimes, and "high crimes and misdemeanors" certainly *sound* like crimes. Others have argued that "*high* crimes" and "*high* misdemeanors" refer to betrayals of official trust, what Alexander Hamilton in his *Federalist* essays called "abuse of executive authority" and "malconduct."

The uncertainty surrounding this question reflects the mixed nature of impeachment. It is fundamentally a political action. The accused suffers no consequence other than removal from office. One branch of the government (Congress) pursues it against members of the others (the executive branch or the judiciary). Yet the procedure for impeachment feels entirely judicial. The senators must "try" the impeachment charges, on their oaths. This mixture of the political with the judicial has left the most interesting question about impeachment unresolved for more than two centuries.

Little guidance on this key question could be drawn from American impeachments before Johnson's presidency. In the eighty years from the writing of the Constitution to January 1867, the House of Representatives had approved impeachment resolutions only four times, never against a president. The only brush with presidential impeachment came in 1843, when the House defeated a proposal to impeach President John Tyler. Tyler's situation bore some superficial resemblance to Andrew Johnson's. Tyler was a Southern Democrat chosen as a running mate for a western non-Democrat (William Henry Harrison was a Whig from Indiana). Succeeding to the presidency after Harrison's death, Tyler angered Whigs by vetoing bank and tariff legislation. With little debate, an impeachment resolution lost by an 83-to-127 vote.

Four judges had faced impeachment trials in the Senate, but their cases did not yield much more wisdom. In all four cases, the judge was charged with "high crimes and misdemeanors" or a "high misdemeanor"; none involved charges of bribery or treason. Two cases ended with convictions; two with acquittals.

When he entered the White House in 1801, Thomas Jefferson became intrigued with impeachment's potential to clear the federal bench of the judges appointed by his predecessor, John Adams. Jefferson started with Judge John Pickering of the New Hampshire Circuit Court. Known to be mentally unstable, Judge Pickering never appeared at his Senate trial and was duly removed from office. Emboldened, Jefferson sent his congressional hounds after Justice Samuel Chase of the Supreme Court, who was charged with misbehavior on the bench and unfairness to litigants. Defended by a lawyer who had been a delegate to the Constitutional Convention (Luther Martin of Maryland), Chase won acquittal in early 1805. Jefferson abandoned his impeachment project.

Since the Chase acquittal, two more judges had been impeached by the House. District Judge James Peck of Missouri was tried by the Senate in 1830 on a single accusation. After Peck ruled in an important land case, the lawyer for the losing side took out a newspaper advertisement denouncing the judge. Peck tried the lawyer for contempt of court and sentenced him to eighteen months in jail. The lawyer then persuaded the House of Representatives to impeach Judge Peck for imposing an excessive penalty. After a five-week trial, a majority of the Senate acquitted the judge. Finally, most congressmen in 1867 remembered the impeachment five years earlier of District Judge West Humphreys of Tennessee. The military governor of that state, none other than Andrew Johnson, recommended impeachment after Humphreys became a judge for the Confederacy without resigning from his position with the United States government. The Humphreys impeachment articles charged neither treason nor bribery, but high crimes and misdemeanors. Those offenses included giving speeches that incited secession and confiscating the property of Andrew Johnson. Humphreys, who did not appear at his Senate trial, was unanimously convicted. John Bingham of Ohio, who would play a major role in the Johnson impeachment, served as lead prosecutor for the House.

This track record should have given pause to would-be impeachers in 1867. The two successful impeachments involved a mental incompetent and a turncoat; neither had contested the charges against him. Those two convictions did not resolve whether impeachment was reserved for true crimes, or was available for abuses of office that might be called "political" offenses. Judge Pickering was convicted of conduct that was certainly no crime (mishandling his cases and being drunk on the bench), but Judge Humphreys's actions on behalf of the Confederacy likely were criminal acts, even treason. The acquittals of Chase and Peck involved charges that also did not seem particularly like crimes.

For the case of Andrew Johnson, the Constitution's failure to define "high crimes and misdemeanors" would be pivotal. The early calls for his impeachment foundered because they expressed general outrage over his "usurpation" of congressional powers; they were never framed in terms of crimes. As Senator Sumner of Massachusetts put it in January of 1867, "The President has usurped the power of Congress on a colossal scale, and he has employed these usurped powers in facilitating a rebel spirit and awakening anew the dying fires of the rebellion."

The investigation of the House Judiciary Committee got under way slowly. Democrats predicted that the effort would never begin, while one Radical grumbled that Thad Stevens was "too old and feeble to fight the great battle." Some Republican newspapers cautioned against impeachment, predicting that the effort would end up injuring those who undertook it. Through his impeachment ordeal, the president would work hard to present a calm face to the nation, but his anger over the House's inquiry was clear to intimates. One called him "cross as a cinnamon bear" over it. The rage of his navy secretary singed the pages of his diary: "There is nothing judicial or fair in this proceeding. It is sheer partisanship with most of them, a deliberate conspiracy with the few. . . . A committee is sitting in secret,—a foul conspiracy,—trying to hunt up charges and evidence against as pure, as honest, as patriotic a chief magistrate as we have ever had."

The House committee began formal (though secret) hearings on February 6. The famous detective Lafayette Baker, who had tracked down John Wilkes Booth after the Lincoln assassination, testified first. Baker described a wartime letter he supposedly carried, but no longer possessed, on a date he could not recall, from Johnson to Confederate President Jefferson Davis. The detective did not know the contents of the letter but thought it implied that Johnson would "go with them." Baker declined to state from whom he received the letter. He then described his actions the previous year to prevent Mrs. Lucy Cobb—"a disreputable woman, or, in other words, a woman of the town"—from visiting the White House. Supposedly, Mrs. Cobb disclosed to him both

President Johnson's secret methods for communicating with "his friends in the South" and her lively trade in selling presidential pardons to former Confederates. Having implicated Johnson in treason, bribery, and prostitution without producing evidence of any offense whatever, Baker retired.

The hearings never recovered, careening from unsupported allegations to nefarious innuendos, all at numbing length. The committee heard testimony that missing portions of John Wilkes Booth's personal diary might have implicated Johnson in the Lincoln assassination. It explored whether the president used intimidation or patronage inducements to block the admission of Colorado as a state. Had Johnson really asked his attorney general for a legal opinion on the legitimacy of a Congress that excluded Southern congressmen? It turned out that a newspaper correspondent fabricated that report because he "supposed" the president would want such a legal opinion and—if Johnson did want it—the attorney general was the logical person to ask for it. Had the president, the committee asked, issued pardons to West Virginia soldiers who deserted from duty? It also inquired into whether the commission for the minister to Sweden had been issued correctly.

The committee examined the sale of Southern railroads seized by the Union Army during the war, exploring the president's connection to Southerners who recovered those assets for nominal or no payment. Was this corrupt favoritism? Not according to Secretary of War Stanton, darling of the Radicals. Stanton took personal responsibility for the railroad transfers. The government did not know how to operate railroads, he told the committee; the nation's economic recovery depended on delivering them into the hands of those who did. Other testimony bounced from the New Orleans massacre to allegations of import tax frauds in New York City.

When the Thirty-Ninth Congress expired on March 3, the Judiciary Committee declined to report any findings on impeachment but recommended that the inquiry continue. When the Fortieth Congress convened the next day, a new impeachment champion entered the arena, Ben Butler of Massachusetts. As a Democrat who early supported the Northern war effort, Butler had used influence to win high military commands during the war. As a general, he showed political flair, not military skill. A smart lawyer with a jaded view of human nature and the instincts of a demagogue, Butler was a dangerous adversary. Ashley might be portrayed as a fanatic, but Butler had to be taken seriously. He would leave his mark on any enterprise he took up.

Butler immediately pushed the Republican caucus to create a special impeachment panel, but Ashley managed to keep the matter before the Judiciary Committee. Ashley darkly told the House of Johnson's "complicity in the assassination plot," of the "mysterious connection between death and treachery which this case presents," and of the need to remove Johnson, "the loathing incubus which has blotted our country's history."

Johnson and his allies grew increasingly short-tempered with an investigation that was out of control. By May, Navy Secretary Welles dismissed the impeachment inquiry in a diary entry: "No facts, no charges, no malconduct are known or preferred, for the slip-slop of Ashley was long since discarded. A more scandalous villainy never disgraced the country." When the committee subpoenaed his bank records, the president vented his wrath to an aide: "I have had a son killed, a son-in-law die during the last battle at Nashville, another son has thrown himself away, a second son-in-law is in no better condition. I think I have had sorrow enough without having my bank account examined by a Committee of Congress." Nevertheless, he produced the records. A Republican senator pronounced the investigation "a complete failure."

By early June, the Judiciary Committee had heard enough. On a 5-to-4 vote, it declined to approve impeachment articles against Johnson. Johnson had dodged the impeachment bullet.

Then he stepped back into the line of fire.

The Reconstruction Acts that passed over Johnson's vetoes that spring created five military districts across the South. The commanders of those districts had broad powers to enforce the law and oversee elections. The commanders could supersede orders of state and local governments and replace state and local officials. Southerners and Democrats denounced the system as despotic; it surely was authoritarian.

The new laws instructed ten Southern states (all the seceding states but Tennessee) to ratify the Fourteenth Amendment and to grant the vote to blacks (who in 1867 could vote in only five of the Northern states).

The goal of the legislation was to establish state governments in the South that were controlled by the few Southern Republicans and Unionists and the many freed slaves. This new leadership, unconnected with secession and rebellion, would replace the traditional Southern political structure. The reaction in the South was immediate. For the first time ever, blacks and whites mingled at political meetings as both groups tried to understand the new system.

The president abhorred the Reconstruction statutes. Their result, he warned in a newspaper interview, would be "a war of races." Because the executive branch had to implement the new system, he could obstruct it. For well over a year, he had actively undermined the Freedmen's Bureau. He reassigned Bureau personnel who displeased him. He authorized investigations that paralyzed the agency's initiatives. He reclaimed land that the Bureau had distributed to the freedmen, then returned it to former Confederates.

To drain the vitality from the Reconstruction Acts, Johnson turned to his attorney general, Henry Stanberry (who had been kept off the Supreme Court when Congress shrank that court a year before). Johnson asked for legal opinions interpreting the powers of the military commanders in the South. In late May and mid-June, Stanberry issued opinions that reached the conclusions sought by the president, over War Secretary Stanton's objections. According to the attorney general, the commanders had no powers to remove local officials who thwarted congressional policies. Stanberry also reasoned away the restrictions on voting by former Confederates. The Republican congressmen who wrote the statutes were stunned by the narrowness of their legislation when Stanberry was finished.

Johnson's use of the attorney general's opinions was daring and provocative, undermining the plain intent of Congress. Republicans in Congress, and the military commanders, grew irate. As one of General Grant's aides wrote, "The whole force of the Reconstruction measure lay in the power of the District Commanders to remove [Southern] civil officers who opposed or obstructed the new law." The attorney general had eliminated that power.

Navy Secretary Gideon Welles recognized the risks of the president's maneuver. He predicted that it would ensure Johnson's impeachment. Congress responded swiftly. The House Judiciary Committee decided to resume taking evidence on impeachment, then Congress adopted a third Reconstruction Act, over Johnson's veto, to reverse Stanberry's opinions. In yet another veto message, Johnson cried out that it was "impossible to conceive any state of society more intolerable than this." He called for a time when "the rod of despotism will be broken, [and] the armed heel of power lifted from the necks of the people." Congress immediately overrode that veto. Its leaders began to think hard about impeachment.

In the eyes of Thad Stevens, the impeachment effort had been botched. Annoyed by the committee's endless poking into corners of Johnson's financial and official conduct, he complained that "the committee are making but a mere pretense of prosecuting the impeachment. . . . I do not believe they ever intended it." He called the investigation "fussy, unnecessary, and absurd."

Stevens saw the case in simple terms. It was the president's policies, he insisted, that warranted his removal. Asked in late June what grounds existed for impeachment, Stevens instantly answered, "his unlawful usurpation of the conquered territory and his attempt to raise up states therein," which made him "as rank a usurper as was Caesar or Cromwell." Those charges could be proved without any testimony at all. Stevens predicted that impeachment would fail, complaining that too many congressmen had "no bone in their backs and no blood in their veins."

Though Congress's first exploration of impeachment had been a mess, the effort drew new life from Johnson's determined effort to thwart the Reconstruction laws. Indeed, it seemed that so long as Andrew Johnson remained in the White House, he was bound to outrage his adversaries. When Congress left Washington in late July of 1867, the president got right to work on that.

In early 1867, several leading Republican congressmen leveled the threat of impeachment at a different federal official. Henry Smythe was collector of the New York Custom House, the most lucrative public job in the nation. A New York banker with conservative credentials, Smythe supervised the 1,200 political appointees who administered the import taxes for New York Harbor, a golden river of revenue. Smythe's employees kicked back to the party in power 2 percent of their salaries, while some estimated in 1860 that the collector received more than three times his salary in "pickings and fees."

Smythe gained the plum position in 1866 by promising Johnson that he would "serve and sustain the President throughout." Smythe also agreed to pay $5,000 to Senator David Patterson of Tennessee, who was Johnson's son-in-law, and another $5,000 to a Wisconsin senator, James Doolittle, who was a loyal Johnson supporter. Though Smythe denied actually making the payments, the new collector hired Doolittle's son when he replaced almost 400 Republican employees from Lincoln's time.

In the winter of 1867, a congressional committee investigated the graft at Smythe's Custom House. In mid-March, the committee chairman declared that "corruption reigns there," calling Smythe's management "the most shameless, flagitious, disreputable, utterly disgraceful, yet deliberate system of abuse, extortion, wrong, that has been developed in scores of years." Much attention focused on Smythe's practice of leasing to private parties the government warehouses that held imported goods before they were taxed. Smythe customarily received, personally, one-fourth of the lease revenue from each warehouse; one of the lessees paid him $40,000 a year, at a time when the president earned only $25,000. (Although there are several ways to calculate the current value of a dollar from 1868, a conservative estimate would peg its worth at fourteen current dollars; by that measure, Smythe's $40,000 payoff was equivalent to $560,000 in today's dollars.)

A movement formed to impeach Collector Smythe. At the instigation of the House committee and the Radical press, a resolution denouncing him was debated in March 1867. Smythe responded with a mixture of excuses and defiance. He succeeded in riding out the storm, in large part because President Johnson stood by his crooked collector. Smythe would repay the president's loyalty during a different impeachment season.

8

THE DANGEROUS SPHINX

AUGUST—NOVEMBER 1867

The President don't comprehend Grant.

WILLIAM TECUMSEH SHERMAN,
OCTOBER 7, 1867

WALKING INTO ANDREW Johnson's White House on August 1, 1867, General Ulysses Grant had to have conflicting feelings. Johnson, who would soon offer to appoint him interim secretary of war, was his superior officer. The Constitution made the president the commander-in-chief of all military forces. But Grant's loyalties did not follow organization charts, even the one established by the Constitution, and definitely not with this president.

Despite his mild demeanor, Grant was an unusually poor subordinate. For some years, he had paid little attention to the views of his nominal superiors. Through the Civil War and since, Grant had grown used to relying on his own judgment, even to the point of disobeying direct orders. Grant's approach works only for generals who win, and not always for them, but the quiet man pulled it off with a unique combination of battlefield success and disarming modesty. When reports circulated during the war that Grant and Stanton had argued, Lincoln's secretary dismissed them, insisting, "Grant quarrels with no one." The general might not quarrel, but he also did not do as he was told.

With Johnson, Grant's personal views supported his habit of nonsubordination. The general disliked Johnson's policies toward the Southern states. During the Swing Around the Circle eleven months before, compelled to attend rally after painful rally, Grant feared being identified with the president. "I am disgusted with this trip," he wrote to his brother. "I am disgusted at hearing a man make speeches on the way to his own funeral."

That Grant was in the White House in the middle of 1867, sparring with the president on more or less equal terms, marked an astonishing personal turnaround. Eight years before, Grant despaired of being able to feed his family. Now, forty-five years old, he commanded the nation's military, was adored by the northern two-thirds of the nation, and was the presumptive Republican candidate for president the following year. Facing Johnson that day, Grant could wonder what it would be like to sit on the other side of the desk.

To Johnson, the bearded man before him had never seemed impressive. Small and quiet, puffing on cigars from breakfast until bedtime, Grant failed to impress people most of his life. As one of his senior generals observed, because Grant was "very reticent and somewhat ill at ease among strangers, . . . a first impression is never favorable." Abraham Lincoln described him as "the quietest little fellow you ever saw," then gave him command of the nation's armed forces.

In a military world filled with blustering popinjays and vainglorious peacocks, Grant stood out for his plainness and his ability (as one contemporary put it) to remain silent in several languages. If conversation was absolutely necessary, Grant chatted about horses, his passion. Ben Wade of Ohio, the president pro tem of the Senate, once complained: "As quick as I'd talk politics, he'd talk horses, and he could talk for hours on that without getting tired."

Army comrades struggled to describe how such an unassuming character rose to command the largest fighting force that ever marched in the Western Hemisphere. One called him "the most modest, the most disinterested, and the most honest man I ever knew, with a temper that nothing could disturb," adding with apparent puzzlement that Grant was "[n]ot a great man, except morally; not an original or brilliant man, but sincere, thoughtful, deep, and gifted with courage that never faltered." One of his officers during the war thought he looked "as if he had determined to drive his head through a brick wall, and was about to do it."

General-in-Chief Ulysses S. Grant.

As a West Point cadet, Grant got an early start on not impressing his peers, graduating in the bottom half of his class. "He couldn't, or wouldn't, dance," one classmate remembered. "He had no facility in conversation with the ladies, a total absence of elegance." Grant did not much care for his courses at the military academy, preferring to read novels. Evidence of Grant's unpretentious manner begins with the transformation of his name. Before West Point, he was Hiram Ulysses Grant. The congressman who nominated him to the academy mistakenly submitted his name as "Ulysses S. Grant." When another cadet saw a list featuring "U. S. Grant," he said the new student must be "Uncle Sam Grant." Thus, Grant lost his real first name (Hiram) and gained both a middle initial (S.) and his army nickname (Sam). Grant accepted all three changes without objection.

The one early hint of Grant's gift for leadership was his horsemanship. The man's intuitive connection to horses seems a symptom of the talent Grant would demonstrate for gauging the true strength of men and armies, for sensing the tide of events and of history. At final exercises for his West Point class, he electrified observers by guiding his powerful chestnut-sorrel horse over a bar higher than a man's head. During the

Mexican War, Grant purchased a stallion so wild and strong that his mates shrank from the beast. Grant had the horse blindfolded and saddled, then set off on a three-hour tear that ended with horse and rider trotting comfortably into camp. According to future Confederate General James Longstreet, "For years afterward the story of Grant's ride was related at every campfire in the country."

The Mexican War put Grant in the company of a leader he would emulate. General (and future president) Zachary Taylor was known for his informal style and casual dress, for being a fighting commander who did not hold himself above the troops he led. An officer who served under Taylor noted the similarities between Grant and Taylor, writing to his wife, "Sometimes I fancy he models himself on old Zack."

During the Mexican War—which he disdained as a colonial adventure unworthy of a republic—young Sam Grant discovered in himself the presence of mind that would bring him victory in battle after battle. When a friend asked how he felt during combat, the intuitive Grant gave a striking response: "I do not know that I felt any peculiar sensation. War seems much less horrible to persons engaged in it than to those who read of the battles."

After the war ended in 1848, Grant fell into a spiral of failure. Assigned to garrison duty on the West Coast, far from his family, he sank into despondency. Within six years he had resigned from the army, probably because he was drunk on duty. Grant was susceptible to hard drink, achieving inebriation with relatively little intake. Much of the time, he tried to stay away from liquor, fending it off with volcanic cigar smoking. Sometimes, though, drink got the better of him. Reunited with his family in 1854, little went well for Grant. He tried farming with help from his wife's family, but after a time was reduced to selling firewood on street corners in St. Louis. On such a corner in late 1857, Grant encountered William Tecumseh Sherman, another former Army officer who also was struggling in civilian life. In a brief exchange rich in portent for the nation's future, they agreed that "West Point and the Regular Army were not good schools for farmers, bankers, merchants, and mechanics." When the Civil War broke out, Grant had moved to Galena, Illinois, where he worked in his father's leather business as an indifferent clerk.

His generalship is justly the stuff of legend. After months of begging for a command, he took over a regiment of Illinois volunteers and set off to fight the rebels his way. Sometimes defying orders, and other times construing them in unintended ways, he demonstrated rare battlefield skill. Though he managed logistics well, Grant's battles were rarely pretty affairs. More than once, the enemy caught him by surprise. His distinguishing qualities as a commander were extraordinary focus in the thick of the fight, a powerful drive to strike the enemy, and a wondrously calm expectation that he would win. No one counterattacked more effectively. A staff officer remembered that in quiet times Grant "was often slow in his movements, but when roused to activity he was quick in every motion, and worked with marvelous rapidity." Another wrote home that "he is cool and quiet, almost stolid as if stupid, in danger, and in a crisis he is one against whom all around . . . would instinctively lean."

Like any great leader, Grant commanded the affection and respect of his fellow soldiers. Sherman, his right-hand man during the western campaigns, later a commanding general himself, offered a tribute every soldier would covet: "I knew wherever I was that you thought of me, and if I got into a tight place you would help me out, if alive." Sherman's dedication to Grant would prove critical in the impeachment crisis, and was captured in a remark recorded shortly after the Confederate surrender. Acknowledging their bad reputations—Grant as a drunk, Sherman as mentally unsteady—Sherman said:

> General Grant is a great general. I know him well. He stood by me when I was crazy, and I stood by him when he was drunk, and now, sir, we stand by each other always.

Despite his wartime victories, Grant was again underestimated when peacetime duties pushed him into the political arena. Sooner or later, most who underestimated Grant came to realize their error. In early 1867, Navy Secretary Welles wrote that the general-in-chief "has no political principles, no intelligent ideas of constitutional government." In August, Welles dismissed Grant as "a political ignoramus." By the end of the year, Welles had learned more respect for the "ignorant but cunning" soldier. "I am becoming impressed with the idea," he noted in his diary, "that Grant may prove a dangerous man."

In the early months of Johnson's presidency, the president and the general got along fairly well. Concerned that the Southern states needed functioning governments in order to avoid anarchy, Grant supported Johnson's early efforts to establish them. Johnson made an effort to cultivate the general. A Grant aide remembered Johnson as "trying to wheedle Grant," sending him "constant personal and familiar notes and cards—an unusual courtesy, almost a condescension, from a President." Johnson had enough confidence in Grant to send him on a short fact-finding tour of the South at the end of 1865, hoping the trip would counter reports that Southerners were still rebellious. Grant, who was moved at the end of the war by the suffering of Southerners, concluded that "the mass of thinking men in the South accept the present situation of affairs in good faith." Johnson was pleased.

Yet there were early signs of the troubles that would arise between the two men. First, and contrary to the president's wishes, Grant recommended retaining the army and the Freedmen's Bureau in the South because "the white and the black mutually require the protection of the general government." Though Grant had worked slaves owned by his wife's family, and had never been an abolitionist, the war changed his views. As he described it, he concluded "early in the rebellion that the North & South could never live at peace with each other except as one nation, and that without Slavery."

Because of that conclusion, Grant was troubled in late 1865 when former General Carl Schurz delivered a report that highlighted the violence and discrimination inflicted by Southern whites on the freed slaves. Grant directed his commanders to report to him "all known outrages . . . committed by white people against the blacks, and the reverse." This concern for Southern conditions would eat away at Grant's support for the president.

By March of 1866, after Johnson's Washington's Birthday address from the White House balcony, an aide noted that Grant was "getting more and more Radical." Fielding regular reports about the racial violence in the South, Grant could not accept Johnson's view that the Southern states should have greater power over their own affairs. Circumstances were pushing Grant into an uneasy partnership with War Secretary Stanton, a man he did not like. A Grant aide reported a "personal barrier" between the two men, observing that the general resented Stanton's "asperities." When it came to dealing with Stanton, Grant sympathized with Andrew Johnson. Noting that Stanton was "very offensive" to the president, Grant told his wife that the war secretary "would have gone and on a double-quick long ago if I had been President."

Despite his personal antipathy toward Stanton, Grant came to agree with the war secretary that Johnson's policies were encouraging white violence and imperiling both the freedmen and the military. The general-in-chief joined with Stanton to block the president's actions. When Congress asked in early 1867 for information on violence against Southern blacks, Grant wrote that he intended to "make a report showing [that] the courts in the [South] afford no security to life or property . . . and to recommend that martial law be declared over such districts." Stanton presented the evidence in February, to Johnson's great displeasure. As Congress shaped its Reconstruction legislation in the first half of 1867, Grant worked openly with Republicans to develop provisions that reinforced military authority. In a private letter, he scorned the president's veto message for the first Reconstruction Act. It was, Grant wrote, "one of the most ridiculous that ever emanated from any President." When the attorney general construed the military's powers narrowly, Grant instructed his Southern commanders that the opinions were without "the force of orders," so "I would not be controlled by them further than I might be convinced by the argument." In July, Grant and Stanton worked with Congress on legislation that would deny Johnson the power to direct military commanders on Reconstruction issues; indeed, the first draft of the bill was in Stanton's handwriting. Grant's senior aide, General Adam Badeau, summarized the rift in the government: "[The president] disregarded the will of Congress, and the officers of the army disregarded his. The situation was approaching mutiny on one side, or else treason on the other."

By August 1, 1867, when Grant sat with the president at the White House, each man viewed the other as an adversary. In Badeau's words, experience taught that with Johnson, "frankness . . . was giving away the game, and [Grant] never liked to be beaten." Keeping his own counsel came naturally to Grant and would see him through the coming conflict. Johnson, though, saw Grant as a military man who was out of his depth. In the president's mind, Stanton was the great obstacle to be removed at all costs. Without Stanton's intellectual and moral support, he reasoned, the inarticulate general could be managed. Moreover, Stanton was a far easier political target. The cantankerous war secretary was admired but not liked, and enjoyed little popular following. Grant, on the other hand, was the lion of the nation. As one contemporary described the adulation:

> Wherever Grant went he was attended by enthusiastic crowds; audiences at theatres and congregations in churches rose when he entered; the actors themselves applauded him from the stage, the preachers prayed for him from the pulpit; towns were illuminated because of his arrival; triumphal arches were built for him.

No sane politician would lightly challenge such a living icon. The president understood that. Indeed, he resolved to appeal to Grant's vanity, offering to make him the new secretary of war. That, Johnson thought, should seal the deal. In this calculation, he was wrong.

Johnson carefully selected August 1 for his move against Stanton. Congress had adjourned more than ten days before, fleeing Washington City's dread heat and humidity. For two centuries, presidents have timed controversial actions for the swelter of Washington in August, when the machinery of politics and that of news reporting are both short-staffed, and it's too hot to stay angry very long.

The general, according to notes made by Johnson's secretary, did not embrace the president's plan to demand Stanton's resignation. Those who opposed Stanton, Grant argued, had opposed the war. When Johnson offered to place Grant as interim secretary of war, the general said he would not shrink from any public duty, yet repeated "his opinion as to the impolicy" of removing Stanton.

The president also explained that he intended to remove General Philip Sheridan from command of the military district that included Louisiana and Texas. The news was not entirely unexpected. Sheridan had no patience for Southern officials who failed to embrace the Reconstruction policies of Congress. He had dismissed from office the governor of Texas, most of the elected officials of New Orleans, and Louisiana's attorney general and governor. Sheridan, in short, had been on a collision course with the president for weeks.

However foreseeable it might have been, Johnson's plan to remove Sheridan rocked the general-in-chief. The headstrong Sheridan was a favorite. Months before, when Sheridan's peremptory actions drew the president's wrath, the general-in-chief maintained that his former cavalry commander was "the same fearless, true man he [was] in the field. He makes no mistakes." An aide described Grant's feelings for Sheridan as "a story from Homer" that entailed "the friendship of chieftains, the love of strong men who had stood side by side in war." Indeed, those feelings could loosen even the wooden Grant tongue, as he "always became eloquent when he talked of Sherman or Sheridan."

Returning to his office after meeting the president, Grant composed a formal letter of protest. The Tenure of Office Act, he insisted, required Senate approval of any action against Stanton. Sheridan, "beloved by the people who sustained the Government through its trials," had served ably in the most difficult Southern military district. Dismissal of Stanton and Sheridan, he warned, would revive sectional conflict, as it was "more than the loyal people of this country . . . will quietly submit to."

The president was not interested in advice from this political novice. On August 5, Johnson wrote to Stanton that "[p]ublic considerations of a high character constrain me to say, that your resignation as Secretary of War will be accepted." Having been warned that the president was about to make his move, Stanton spat Johnson's words back at him. "Public considerations of a high character," he replied, "which alone have induced me to continue at the head of this department, constrain me not to resign."

The stalemate festered for almost a week. Johnson sat down again with Grant and asked whether "there was any thing between us" that would prevent the general from taking the job of secretary of war. In a remarkable episode of miscommunication, Grant advised the president that there was "nothing personal" between them, adding that they did disagree "respecting the constitutional amendment [the Fourteenth] and the reconstruction acts." Somehow, perhaps due to Grant's unassuming style, perhaps because Johnson had already decided to replace Stanton with Grant, the president inexplicably took comfort in the statement that the general differed with him only on the central political issues facing the nation, which were at the heart of the secretary of war's duties.

When he finally acted, Johnson made a critical choice. Rather than solely rely on his authority as president under the Constitution, his letter to Stanton on August 12 followed the requirements of the Tenure of Office Act. Instead of dismissing Stanton, the letter only suspended him and appointed Grant as interim Secretary. By proceeding this way, Johnson could not appoint a permanent secretary of war unless the Senate confirmed his choice when it reconvened in December.

When Stanton relinquished his office to Grant, Johnson expressed his satisfaction with a classical metaphor: "The turning point has at last come," he told his secretary. "The Rubicon is crossed." But who was making that metaphorical crossing—the president, or Ulysses Grant?

No doubt one of Grant's principal goals as interim war secretary was to protect Sheridan, but the general swiftly discovered he could not do it. When Johnson ordered Sheridan's transfer on August 17, Grant lodged a passionate protest "in the name of a patriotic people who have sacrificed hundreds of thousands of loyal lives, and thousands of millions of treasure." Removing Sheridan would be seen "as an effort to defeat the laws of Congress," Grant insisted, and would "embolden" the nation's "unreconstructed element." Johnson was unimpressed. Out went Sheridan.

The president then took aim at General Daniel Sickles, commander of the military district including North and South Carolina, who had aggressively squelched the resistance of local courts to Reconstruction laws. Outmaneuvered in Cabinet meetings over both Sheridan and Sickles, the general-in-chief could not contain his anger. In a bitter letter at the end of August, Grant wrote to Johnson that the nation would see the president's purpose as "the defeat of the laws of Congress," which would endanger "the quiet and prosperity of the country." Johnson recognized the letter as insubordinate and summoned the general. After a "full and free conference," Grant agreed to a tactical retreat. He withdrew his letter. Sickles, too, was gone. Like Sheridan, he was replaced with a conservative general who would allow state officials to evade the Reconstruction laws. Grant asked to be excused from future Cabinet meetings unless military matters were to be discussed.

It seemed that Johnson had routed his insubordinate general and commanded the political situation. The president followed up with a proclamation that extended the Southern amnesty he previously granted. Now he pardoned all Southerners of treason except those who had held office in the Confederate government or military, those who were on parole or in prison, and those who had served in the United States forces before secession and then renounced their duties.

The Republican reaction was swift. A St. Louis newspaper proclaimed the beginning of "the New Rebellion." Calling the president a madman, Carl Schurz wrote that he "bites at all about him like a wounded and anger-crazed boar." Another Johnson foe reported "an angry gloom" in Washington, which is "in the midst of a revolution." Fessenden of Maine reported that in New England "I meet no man who is not in favor of impeachment if any decent pretense can be found for it." Radical newspapers talked freely of impeachment, and some called for Johnson's removal. Similar demands came in letters to Republican congressmen.

But this time Johnson judged the mood of the country better than his foes did. Fatigue with the continuing conflict over Reconstruction, and a simple desire for peace, reinforced the president's position. That fall, the Democrats prospered in the off-year elections. Though the contests in twenty states were mostly local affairs, and none involved direct election of congressmen, the Democrats made progress everywhere. Seizing control of the Ohio legislature, they would soon be able to use that majority to replace Bluff Ben Wade in the Senate. The president was gratified, and as melodramatic as ever. "I have always had an abiding confidence in the people," he declaimed in a speech. "They have come, and thank God they have come, and . . . our Republic will be saved."

The Democrats' appeal in the local elections of 1867 started with raw racism, a potent political weapon in every part of the country. Though Northerners made huge sacrifices to end slavery, many agreed with Johnson that the nation should have a white man's government. The Republican Speaker of the House of Representatives, Schuyler Colfax of Indiana, stated, "I never believed in Negro equality." Voters in Connecticut, Minnesota, and Ohio defeated proposals to grant the vote to their few black neighbors. The Democratic candidate for governor in Ohio promised to fight "the thralldom of niggerism." Ben Wade, firmly committed to Negro suffrage and equality, summed up the election results: "The nigger whipped us. We went in on principle, and got whipped."

Thad Stevens read the election returns differently. "I take the occasion to thank God for our late defeat," he wrote. "The Republicans have been acting a cowardly part, and they have met a coward's fate." Win, lose, or draw, Stevens always wanted to attack. He and the president shared that quality. Still intransigent, still itching to take Johnson on, Stevens was laying plans for fresh confrontations when Congress reconvened in December.

At the War Department, Grant continued to resist Johnson's policies. He, too, did not give up easily. Johnson once more hoped Sherman would deliver him from this sphinxlike opponent. The president called Sherman to Washington and hinted that he could be secretary of war. But the ties of military comradeship between the two generals were too strong. Sherman spurned the bait and fled back to St. Louis, writing to his brother, "I cannot place myself in a position even partially antagonistic to Grant."

As senators and congressmen returned to Washington for their new session in December 1867, an escalation of the conflict seemed certain. Johnson felt revived. He had gotten rid of Stanton, Sheridan, and Sickles, yet had suffered no terrible political consequences. The election returns were encouraging. The time was right, he felt, to press these modest advantages.

Those same developments made Republicans even angrier. Despite the election results, they remained a powerful force. With overwhelming control of both houses of Congress, and led by the implacable Stevens, the Republicans would not miss the opportunity to use their majorities. Johnson himself was not popular. His ouster of Sheridan made the cavalryman an even greater hero in the North. In a triumphal procession, Sheridan was cheered by enthusiastic crowds in Baltimore, Wilmington, New York, Brooklyn, and Boston.

Both the president and congressional Republicans would have to deal with a new factor in their political calculations. Between them— really much closer to Congress than to Johnson—stood Ulysses Grant. Though new to high-level politics, he was no stranger to strategy and tactics. As Congress and the president circled each other warily, each looking to gain ground against the other, perhaps to administer a *coup de grâce*, Grant stood on the most critical ground in the fight—at the War Department, in charge of the military. Not only that, his stature with the public was too great for anyone to ignore. With Grant holding the pivot of the contest, the battle would be joined again in the poisonous political climate of Washington City.

9

IMPEACHMENT, ROUND TWO

DECEMBER 1867

> If the great culprit had robbed a till; if he fired a barn; if he had forged a check; he would have been indicted, prosecuted, condemned, sentenced, and punished. But the evidence shows that he only oppressed the Negro; that he only conspired with the rebel; that he only betrayed the Union party; that he only attempted to overthrow the Republic—of course he goes unwhipped of justice.
>
> *NEW YORK INDEPENDENT, DECEMBER 12, 1867*

IMPEACHMENT WAS DEAD. So said Thaddeus Stevens in mid-November 1867, as he planned for the session of Congress that would begin in two weeks. A few days earlier, the House Judiciary Committee had resumed its impeachment hearings, but the witnesses covered old ground: the pardoning of Union Army deserters in West Virginia; the supposed conspiracy between Johnson and Confederates during the war; and government printing contracts awarded to local printers (a rich source of patronage). Newspapers were more interested in the meteor displays that lit East Coast skies in early morning hours. "They swept through the air," one report enthused, "with almost the speed of thought and left long luminous trains in their wake."

Impeachment advocates had to choose between two approaches, neither very appealing. They could adopt Stevens's theory that Johnson had upended the constitutional structure in order to deliver power to ex-rebels. This approach had the virtue of simplicity—it involved uncontested facts about the president's policies—but it felt abstract, theoretical. Moreover, it could be challenged as not presenting a true impeachable "crime." Alternatively, the impeachers could stitch together a prosecution based on specific actions investigated by the committee. But the truly heinous actions the committee examined (Lincoln's assassination, conspiring with the Confederacy) had only vaporous connections to Johnson, while those authored by him violated no law. Stevens saw the situation clearly. The prospects for impeachment were dim.

Those prospects darkened further when the last committee witness, impeachment advocate James Ashley of northern Ohio, gave testimony that bordered on the delusional. A pharmacist whose fiery abolitionism led him into politics, Ashley had worked feverishly to tie Johnson to the Lincoln assassination. The trail led to a con man of many names—variously Charles A. Dunham, or Sanford Conover, or James W. Wallace. In jail for perjury, Dunham-Conover-Wallace offered tantalizing hints linking Johnson to Booth. The overeager Ashley visited this slippery witness in prison. Dunham-Conover-Wallace promptly accused Ashley of suborning perjury. Chastened, the Ohio congressman admitted in late November that he had no "sufficient" evidence connecting Johnson to the assassination. Pressed for what evidence he did have, Ashley disclosed to the committee that two vice presidents had murdered the presidents they succeeded in office:

> I have always believed that President [William Henry] Harrison and President [Zachary] Taylor and President [James] Buchanan were poisoned, and poisoned for the express purpose of putting the Vice Presidents in the presidential office. In the first two instances it was successful. It was attempted with Mr. Buchanan and failed. . . .

Armed with Ashley's theory of presidential demise, Johnson supporters could persuasively portray the impeachers as lunatics, or at least as entirely unreliable.

Despite Ashley's escapade, on November 25 the House committee approved an impeachment resolution, reversing its 5-to-4 vote from five months earlier. The switch came because one congressman, Republican

John Churchill of upstate New York, changed his mind. In a letter to the *New York Times,* Churchill gave his reasons for reversing his vote: Johnson's statements denouncing Reconstruction, the attorney general's opinions limiting the Reconstruction statutes, Johnson's veto of the Third Reconstruction Act, the suspension of War Secretary Stanton, and the ousters of Generals Sheridan and Sickles.

Churchill's switch pushed the impeachment resolution out of the committee, but its chances in the full House were far from robust. Committee Chairman James Wilson of Iowa and another Republican opposed it. Before the committee even issued its report, the press predicted defeat. The *New York Times* counted more than 100 votes against impeachment, with only half as many in favor. The Associated Press found but 40 proimpeachment votes, while a Philadelphia newspaper claimed 57.

Though it was largely stillborn, this impeachment resolution highlighted the central ambiguity of American impeachments: what is an impeachable offense? Until this moment, the House had impeached judges who committed indictable offenses, *and* those accused of abusing their offices so thoroughly—without committing an actual crime—that they should be removed. Leading constitutional scholars of that era agreed that impeachment applied to both types of cases. But the defeat of this resolution would tilt presidential impeachment toward requiring an indictable offense, sapping impeachment of much of its political content and beginning its transformation into a legalistic hunt for a "crime."

Stevens could have prevented the doomed impeachment resolution from coming to a vote, but he did not. No matter how poor its prospects, this resolution might present his only chance for an up-or-down count on whether to remove Andrew Johnson. Time was running out. Stevens's health was failing daily. In August, the once athletic Stevens wrote a friend that the day had come when he could "no longer attempt to hurl the discus or bend the bow of Ulysses." When he left Lancaster for Washington in mid-November, his physician sent along extensive instructions for the treatment of heart and digestive ailments.

The press followed Stevens's health closely, an early example of celebrity journalism. Daily dispatches described how frail the Pennsylvanian looked and what his friends related about his condition. On November 19, he made it to the Capitol, several men carrying him into the building from his carriage. Some reports disparaged his mental faculties. The *New York Herald* wrote that Stevens's conversation was "disconnected and broken, with frequent pauses," and showed "a great effort to confine himself to a consecutive train of thought." He could flash into coherence, according to the *Boston Post*, but then "the fire would die out, leaving him more the appearance of a corpse than a living man." Still, several correspondents thought that the political battle was reviving Old Thad. Republican politicians laid siege to his modest home near the Capitol, seeking his advice on current matters. Stevens rallied. When colleagues offered to assist him to his seat in the House chamber, he declined, snorting, "I am not as dead as some of my newspaper friends have reported me."

For Stevens, the grounds for impeaching Andrew Johnson remained straightforward. "Why, I'll take that man's record, his speeches, and his acts before any impartial jury," he boasted, "and I'll make them pronounce him either a knave or a fool." But the Senate's role was not to judge whether Johnson was a knave or a fool. It was to decide whether he should be removed from office under the impeachment clauses of the Constitution.

The House Judiciary Committee issued three reports on the impeachment resolution: the majority report, written principally by Representative Thomas Williams of Pennsylvania, and two minority reports, one by Chairman Wilson and the other signed by the committee's two Democrats, which was generally ignored. The public announcement of the committee's report was a historic moment. Many senators came to the House Chamber to view the spectacle. The galleries had neither standing nor sitting room, "nor hardly breathing room." When the report was presented, one newspaper wrote, whites in the gallery hissed and blacks applauded.

For fifty-nine pages, Williams's majority report wandered from broad denunciations of the president to disorganized factual allegations. The language was heated, depicting Johnson as claiming "more than kingly powers" and issuing "imperial proclamations." The majority report claimed that Johnson's offenses flowed from his goal of reconstructing the Southern states "in the interests of the great criminals who carried them into rebellion." In dealing with the former rebels, the majority report said, the president had "pardon[ed] their offences, restor[ed] their lands, and hurr[ied] them back [into power]—their hearts unrepentant, and their hands yet red with the blood of our people."

When it came to the president's specific transgressions, the majority report fell flat. Its review of Southern railroad transactions established only that Johnson followed the advice of War Secretary Stanton, a Radical. The majority report criticized the return of confiscated land and cotton to wealthy rebels who had been pardoned by the president. Johnson fired loyal Union men from government service, the majority report complained, replacing them with former Confederates. Also recited were corruption in Henry Smythe's New York Custom House, the New Orleans massacre (which supposedly was "encouraged" by Johnson's pro-South bias), plus dark but unproved allegations of self-dealing during Johnson's wartime service as military governor of Tennessee. The majority report argued that this hodgepodge proved Johnson had a master plan "to overwhelm the legislature and the courts, and usurp all the powers of government."

The majority report's final passages turned to the central legal question: what is an impeachable offense? The majority insisted that no indictable crime need be committed. It recited support from English legal sources, from Alexander Hamilton (who approved impeachment for "malconduct"), and from James Madison in early congressional debates, when he argued that a president could be impeached for the "wanton removal of meritorious officers." The majority report also relied on several American treatises on the Constitution. One stated, for example, that impeachment charges could properly allege that an official "has, from immorality, or imbecility, or maladministration, become unfit to exercise that office." Pointing to the four judges impeached before then, the majority report observed that most of the charges in those cases did not state criminal offenses.

The majority report also made an important point that would be submerged through much of the impeachment drama. When Johnson denied the legitimacy of a Congress without Southern representatives, Congress responded by restricting his powers as president. It shrank the Supreme Court so he could not appoint new members to it, then reduced his ability to fire underlings in the Executive Branch, then limited his ability to issue orders to the army. Rather than continue this "questionable process" of reshaping the government with a much smaller presidency, the majority report urged that the government be delivered into "the hands of those who will recognize the jurisdiction of Congress, and bow respectfully to its authority." This was an apt description of how the bitter contest between Congress and Johnson was distorting the government. Congressional Republicans were not dissatisfied with the constitutional system, but with Andrew Johnson. Yet rather than use the constitutional impeachment process to remove the man, Congress had altered the structures of government in fundamental ways. It chopped back the executive's powers, excluded Southern congressmen, and restricted the courts' jurisdiction—all to limit the mischief that one man could do. Rather than contrive fresh distortions of the government, why not simply get rid of him?

The unfocused, rambling quality of the majority report obscured its valid points. The minority statement by Chairman Wilson of Iowa was almost as long, but far more forceful. Wilson, called by one newspaper "the most business-like lawyer in the House," began by insisting that

Rep. James Wilson of Iowa, Chairman of the House Judiciary Committee and opponent of the first impeachment attempt.

impeachment could be based only on a criminal offense. He argued that the Senate acted as a court "of special criminal jurisdiction" and must follow legal forms. For Wilson, once the senators took their oaths "to do impartial justice," impeachment lost its political quality. Such a special court could consider only actual crimes. In an unsupported leap, he insisted that the Senate can try only offenses "known to the Constitution, or to the laws of the United States," and that judicial rules of evidence must apply.

Wilson scavenged through other constitutional provisions to reinforce his argument. By rough force and incomplete logic, he attempted to coax support from unpromising constitutional text. When he turned to the four American impeachment cases, which involved numerous noncriminal allegations, Wilson employed lawyerly evasions. He dismissed one as wrongly decided (Judge Pickering), avoided any conclusive statement about another (Judge Peck), and skipped over the noncriminal aspects of the remaining two (Justice Chase and Judge Humphreys). Wilson's discussion of English impeachment precedents was as murky and inconclusive as the majority's had been.

Yet Chairman Wilson effectively answered the factual charges in the majority report. Tracing the battle over Reconstruction, he denied that Johnson usurped Congress's powers, making the obvious point that Congress had overridden most of Johnson's vetoes. As for abuse of patronage powers, Wilson noted that Johnson's hirings and firings violated no laws; in fact, they followed the prevailing practices of the preceding fifty years. On pardons for Southerners, the restoration of Southern railroads, and other points, the Iowan countered that the president acted to achieve valid public purposes. Disagreement with the wisdom of a policy, he insisted, could not be the basis for impeachment.

In his conclusion, Wilson struck a resonant note. Johnson, he admitted, "deserves the censure and condemnation of every well-disposed citizen," and "we must condemn him." But Wilson denied that political considerations alone could support the impeachment: "Political unfitness and incapacity must be tried at the ballot box, not in the high court of impeachment."

The most frustrating feature of the exchange between the majority and the minority reports is the problem that has confounded impeachment scholars and lawyers ever since: the tenacious opacity of the phrase "high crimes and misdemeanors." The phrase was drawn from English impeachment precedents, but even after extended study those precedents prove incomplete, slippery, and contradictory. Each side found support in them. The American precedents supported the majority's position that impeachment did not require an actual crime, but Wilson framed important practical considerations that appealed to the politicians in the House of Representatives. If impeachment is entirely political, what is the stopping point? If a president and his policies are unpopular, is that enough to impeach him? If you do that today to a president you do not like, will your opponents do it tomorrow to a president you do like?

The majority report was a dud. *Harper's Weekly* sniffed that it did not "inspire general confidence," while even the Radical *Chicago Tribune* disparaged its charges as "inferential and circumstantial." The *Tribune* suggested that any trial covering "the score and more of accusations" against Johnson would last at least until the elections in the fall of 1868. With some glee, the *New York Times* called the report "a whitewashing" of the president, clearing him of the persistent rumors that he had conspired with Jefferson Davis and John Wilkes Booth. One Republican congressman recalled that "much of the evidence seemed irrelevant, and that which bore directly upon the question of the president's offenses fell far below the serious character assigned to it by previous rumors."

The impeachment effort did not seem to alarm the president. At his next Cabinet meeting, the discussion of impeachment centered on legislation proposed by Stevens to suspend Johnson for the period between a House vote approving an impeachment resolution and the completion of a trial in the Senate. The notion of suspending the president during the impeachment process had been afoot for some time. Johnson was on record denying Congress's power to do so, and his position was plainly correct. At the end of the Constitutional Convention of 1787, two delegates proposed that an official who had been impeached by the House should be suspended from office until tried by the Senate. The Convention rejected the proposal by a wide margin. General Grant assured the president that the army would obey his orders if Congress tried to arrest him before the end of a Senate trial. The Cabinet, including Grant, advised Johnson not to comply with any attempt to suspend him. Though Stevens continued to endorse the suspension legislation, it was never adopted.

On the eve of the House vote, the president did his customary best to enrage his opponents. Johnson's annual message to Congress defiantly challenged that body. His first sentence angrily described the "continued disorganization of the Union, to which the President has so often called the attention of Congress." Though he had hoped for reconciliation after the war, he wrote, none had occurred, a failure for which he assumed no responsibility. In apocalyptic tones, he announced, "[C]andor compels me to declare at this time there is no Union." So much for binding up the wounds.

Averting his eyes from the pandemic racial violence in the South, Johnson argued for immediate withdrawal of federal troops and the return of complete power to the Southern states. He attacked Negro suffrage as forcing Southerners to "degrade themselves by subjection to the negro race." The American republic, he declared, was "the glory of white men." To avoid having "the inferior obtain the ascendancy" over whites, Johnson rejected any effort to "Africanize" the South, which would inevitably leave it a barren wilderness.

Then the president got to the nub of the matter. How far would he go in opposing Congress? Johnson said he had "deliberated much" on the question. In such highly charged times, he observed, his opposition to Congress could "produce violent collision," which would be "simply civil war." Although civil war should be avoided, if possible, the president insisted that he might be "compelled to stand on his rights, and maintain them, regardless of consequences." Not exactly oil on troubled waters.

This time, the president's provocative and racist rhetoric failed to unite Republicans against him. Even his implicit threat of armed resistance to Congress could not muster a majority for the impeachment resolution. The telling consideration for most congressmen was the one trumpeted by Chairman Wilson: the impeachers did not claim that Johnson had committed a crime.

On December 5, crowds again jammed the House galleries, this time to hear the impeachment debate. The seats reserved for diplomats and for ladies were full. Equal numbers of blacks and whites filled the gentlemen's galleries. For the difficult assignment of justifying the impeachment resolution, the impeachers turned to Representative George Boutwell of Massachusetts. Having started his political life in the temperance movement, Boutwell brought a Puritan austerity to his labors. Small, bearded, and mostly self-educated, he had been governor of Massachusetts as a Democrat, the first commissioner of internal revenue during the Civil War, and a member of the Joint Committee of Fifteen on reconstruction. He was recognized as a man of "cool temperament, thoroughly honest mind, and sober judgment." He could be long-winded, though, having earned the sobriquet "Steady Wind Blowing Aft."

Boutwell's prim exterior cloaked a violent passion to depose Andrew Johnson. In a magazine article the year before, he pronounced that the president "conspires with the traitors in the loyal States and the Rebels of the disloyal states for the humiliation, the degradation, the political enslavement of the loyal people of the country." A young French doctor living in New York, Georges Clemenceau, who would be France's prime minister during World War I, was transfixed by this American political brawl. According to Clemenceau, Boutwell was "too much a fanatic" to win his case, but also was "too honest and sincere for his opinions to be ignored by his party." Over the next six months, the Massachusetts congressman would be a mainstay of the impeachment effort.

Saddled with a majority report that repelled more support than it attracted, Boutwell made one of the best speeches of the impeachment season. In an oration of over two hours, delivered on consecutive days, he struck a sober, restrained tone. After paying tribute to Johnson's "talents and courage in a bad cause," Boutwell rejected the legal argument pressed by Chairman Wilson's minority report. If Wilson was right that impeachment was available only for indictable crimes, Boutwell said, the resolution must fail. But he insisted that impeachment can remove from office those who fail the public trust, not solely criminals.

In addition to the usual recitation of English and American impeachment cases, Boutwell urged that the demands of government compelled his view. What if the president denied the legitimacy of Congress and ignored its enactments (positions that Johnson had flirted with for almost two years)? Congress must be able to remove him from office even if he violates no criminal statute. Any other view, he said, "is virtually the end of the Government."

When Boutwell turned to the factual allegations against the president, he confessed that he labored under great difficulties. He did not dwell on any specific incident, but listed the major actions of Johnson's tenure: constituting Southern state governments in 1865, suspending loyalty oaths in some situations, his Washington's Birthday speech in 1866, his many vetoes of legislation, his return of confiscated land and railroads to former rebels. These were all "tributary offenses," Boutwell continued, that supported his "great crime": "the restoration of the rebels to power under and in the Government of the country." In conclusion, he emphasized Johnson's failures as a leader. Two years after the nation emerged from war, "distracted, torn, and bleeding," millions of former rebels were "still bold, defiant, aggressive," while the freedmen faced constant danger. Boutwell demanded Johnson's removal not for any crime, but because he was unfit to be president.

Knowing that the impeachment resolution was a goner, Chairman Wilson spoke for only half as long. In a disingenuous opening, he denied "the slightest importance" to the question whether an impeachable offense had to be a crime. Wilson then pressed a spirited challenge on precisely that question, pointing out that although a purely political im-

Rep. George Boutwell of Massachusetts, Radical Republican
and ardent impeachment advocate.

peachment might give Boutwell the result he wanted, "can he not see that it may return to plague him?" Did Boutwell wish to give such an impeachment power to his opponents? The Iowan asked how Congress could define a political offense that warrants impeachment. "Is it," he inquired, "the doing of something that the dominant party in the country does not like?" Wilson called Johnson "the worst of Presidents," but repeated that he should be punished through "the suffrages of the people." Wilson closed with more questions, practical ones:

> If we cannot arraign the President for a specific crime for what are we to proceed against him? For a bundle of generalities such as we have here. . . . ? If we cannot state upon paper a specific crime how are we to carry this case to the Senate for trial?

No one else spoke on the merits of the resolution. After considerable squabbling, the impeachers succeeded in having a roll call vote on the resolution. On December 7, the House voted. "Yes" votes came from only dedicated Radicals like Boutwell, Stevens, Ben Butler of Massachusetts, and Ashley of Ohio. During some of the orations, Stevens had reclined on a sofa at the rear of the chamber. Rushing to his seat to cast the final vote for the resolution, he tottered unsteadily. One news account claimed that two-thirds of those voting yes would have gone the other way if their votes had been needed to defeat the measure. With Wilson and John Bingham of Ohio leading moderate and conservative Republicans into the "nay" column, the impeachers failed to command even a majority of Republicans. Fifty-seven voted in favor (all Republicans), 106 opposed (including 68 Republicans), and 22 did not vote.

The resolution's defeat flowed from its failure to identify an indictable crime. As remembered by Senator John Sherman of Ohio, the House was unwilling to use the "imposing process" of impeachment for "misconduct, immorality, intoxication or neglect of duties." Other factors played a role, too, such as the timing of the vote. Johnson's dismissal of Sheridan and Sickles, and his suspension of Stanton, were months in the past. Anger over those actions had cooled.

Presidential politics also split the Republicans. Many eagerly anticipated having Grant as the party's standard-bearer in the 1868 election. "Grant clubs" around the country supported his presumed candidacy.

Two days before Boutwell began his speech, a pro-Grant rally in New York drew a large, enthusiastic crowd. Less than a week after the vote, twenty of the twenty-three members of the Republican National Committee expressed a preference for Grant at the head of the Republican ticket. Some Radicals, though, mistrusted the general, not realizing that the silent Grant truly opposed the president. Radicals who doubted Grant saw impeachment as a way to place Ben Wade of Ohio in the Executive Mansion. Wade might divert the 1868 nomination toward a more reliable Radical, or even seize the nomination himself. That reasoning provoked a contrary feeling among conservative Republicans that it would be better to keep Andrew Johnson in the White House for fifteen more months.

Whatever the reasons for individual votes on the resolution, its crushing defeat had long-term consequences. The House, despite a three-fourths Republican majority, rejected purely political impeachment. The impeachers would have to come up with something that felt more like a criminal offense. Presidential impeachments inevitably contain a healthy dose of politics, but never again would a serious presidential impeachment proceed on the sole basis that the incumbent was not fit for the office. If that argument could not be sustained by the massive Republican majority in December 1867, which detested Andrew Johnson, it would never prevail. This result likely abandoned the initial meaning of the impeachment clauses in 1787, but Boutwell and the majority never effectively answered the practical questions that Wilson raised. How could purely political impeachments be limited? How could such a trial ever end? Wouldn't it degenerate into a standardless test of political power—in effect, a vote of no confidence—rather than a judgment of fitness to be president?

A day after the impeachment vote, Mrs. Lydia Smith admitted a deputation of Radical leaders to Stevens's house at 213 B Street. They came to sit with their leader, no matter how decrepit he might seem, and sift through the wreckage of the impeachment drive. Fired by Stevens, the group resolved not to abandon the cause. They would bring up impeachment again and again and again. As a Republican remembered their strategy, "the closest watch would be kept upon every action of the President, and if an apparently justifying cause could be found the project of his removal would be vigorously renewed." They knew that this president was prone to misadventures, particularly when flush with success. Johnson had been riding high in 1866 when he delivered his disastrous Washington's Birthday speech, then embarked on his equally disastrous Swing Around the Circle. Johnson might even, after careful deliberation, step squarely into the trap that Stevens had laid for him in the Tenure of Office Act. They would bide their time, even if time was no ally for Stevens.

With the defeat of the impeachment resolution, partisans of President Johnson could abandon one effort they had just initiated. Collector Henry Smythe of New York, threatened with impeachment himself earlier in the year, had circulated a subscription among the 1,200 patronage employees of his Custom House. The subscription stated that each employee would contribute the predetermined amount next to his name, which was proportionate to the worker's income, "for the cause of the country, and opposed to the impeachment of President Johnson." Despite some initial resistance, all employees made the compulsory contribution, beginning at $5 apiece and rising from there. No one ever accounted for where that money ended up.

10

IMPEACHMENT, ROUND THREE

DECEMBER 12, 1867—
FEBRUARY 15, 1868

I regard [the president] as a foolish and stubborn man, doing
even right things in a wrong way, and in a position where the
evil that he does is immensely increased by his manner of doing it.

SENATOR JOHN SHERMAN, MARCH 1, 1868

THE COUNTRY DID not stand still while the House of Representatives
wrestled with impeachment. The Freedmen's Bureau marshaled a
food relief effort in response to poor harvests in the South. While North
and South failed to reconcile, East and West strained to join each other.
Bold men were planning the next surge in construction of the railroad
that would tie the nation together. As soon as the spring thaw permitted,
the Chinese crews of the Central Pacific would resume laying track east
from California. Mostly Irish crews of the Union Pacific would work
west, through Wyoming. Mormon crews would pitch in when the two
lines reached Utah. In New York, financial titans Cornelius Vander-
bilt and Jay Gould fenced for control of the Erie Railway, a battle that
would extend for months. The nation was growing. In March of 1867,
Czar Alexander II of Russia had ordered negotiations to sell Alaska to
the United States. The two nations quickly agreed on a price: $7 mil-

lion. Soon Congress would have to appropriate the funds to pay for the deal.

The cultural rage of the winter season was the lecture tour of British novelist Charles Dickens. In Boston, the queue for tickets to his readings lasted from morning till night. Patient devotees warmed themselves in the street with strong drink and blazing stoves. Scalpers demanded as much as $15 per ticket (at least $210 in current values). New York newspapers proclaimed "Dickens Fever" and reported skyrocketing prices for tickets to his lectures.

By early January, Washington had its own literary lecturer in the form of humorist Samuel Clemens (Mark Twain). When he postponed an appearance, Clemens ran a notice in a local paper explaining that his manager fell ill while listening to a rehearsal of the talk. "[U]pon my sacred honor," Clemens wrote, "I did not think it would be so severe on him." To speed his manager's recovery, he pledged, "I will not read the lecture to him any more."

For ten Southern states, the reconstruction mandated by Congress was under way. (Because Tennessee reentered the Union in 1866, it avoided this stage of Reconstruction.) Under army supervision, Southerners registered once more to vote, but this time the freedmen participated, while many ex-rebels abstained or were excluded for their disloyalty.

In Virginia, for example, 105,000 freedmen registered alongside 120,000 whites. With many whites boycotting the election, Virginia's voters chose delegates for a convention to write a new state constitution, barely two years after a Confederate-dominated convention had adopted one under President Johnson's sponsorship. Of the 102 delegates to Virginia's new convention, twenty-four were blacks and a majority were Republicans. The political activity sharpened racial tensions. The army arrested a black delegate, Lewis Lindsay, for giving a speech "calculated to incite the colored against the white." Newspapers fretted over the risk of a race war.

This new Reconstruction unleashed the political energies of blacks and the fury of whites. Emancipation had brought a social revolution, but Johnson's state governments preserved white political dominance. Not anymore. Now the revolution reached into political life. State constitutional conventions for Alabama and Louisiana met in November, while five other states (Mississippi, Arkansas, North Carolina, South Carolina, and Florida) elected delegates to their conventions. Georgia's convention met in December. These conventions, disparaged by many Southern whites, turned political expectations upside down. Black delegates won elections and proudly took their seats. Because many black delegates had limited education, they often followed the lead of white Republicans, or of those blacks who traveled from the North to experience this unprecedented opportunity for political engagement.

Nevertheless, the reality of black men in public office provoked powerful feelings in both races. The state conventions wrote charters for state governments that would be elected by white and black voters. The new state constitutions incorporated guarantees of equal rights, Negro suffrage, and mandatory public education.

Under the new state constitutions, black men would serve as state officials, legislators, even congressmen. In a fitting turnabout, the Reconstruction governments of Southern states would provide the votes needed to ratify the Fourteenth Amendment. Southern whites recoiled from this political revolution, appalled by the prospect of "Negro rule." As the freed slaves entered Southern politics, white violence evolved into politically motivated intimidation.

In the White House, the president took no break from his brutal schedule. As one of his aides remembered, it was as though he wanted to do all the work of the executive branch himself. Johnson rose at dawn and reviewed papers until family breakfast at 8 A.M. Office matters consumed him from 9 until 4, though he occasionally ducked across the hall to look in on his wife, and always welcomed the grandchildren. After a break for dinner and a walk or carriage ride, he would preside over the social event of the evening. He finished his day with more paperwork and political visitors until 11 P.M., often swapping information with those newsmen he trusted. Johnson was enjoying good health, free from the painful kidney stones (he called them "gravel") that sometimes beset him. Ten years earlier, he had lost some use of his right arm when it was broken during a train derailment. The injury did not limit his political activity, though prolonged handshaking must have been a trial.

Having easily withstood the impeachment assault, and buoyed by Democratic Party advances in the 1867 elections, Johnson turned to the offensive, starting with the military. He swiftly removed two more commanders in the South—General John Pope (Alabama, Georgia, and Florida), and General Edward Ord (Mississippi and Arkansas). Southerners had complained that both men enforced Congress's Reconstruction program rather too well. Over a six-month period, Johnson had supplanted the commanders for four of the five military districts in the South. He also transferred another general serving in Alabama, for the same reason. General Pope vividly described what was at stake in the president's management of Reconstruction:

> It is a misnomer to call this question in the South a political question. It is *War* pure and simple. The question is not whether Georgia and Alabama will accept or reject reconstruction. It is [whether] the Union men and the freedmen, [will] be the slaves of the old . . . rebel aristocracy or not? Or rather shall the [Union men] be permitted to live in these states at all or the Negroes [permitted to live] as free men?

Southern whites instantly grasped the meaning of Johnson's dismissal of the commanders. "The rebels are rejoicing," complained the head of the Republican Party of Georgia, "and are now bragging that Reconstruction is a failure."

General Grant, a far more difficult target for Johnson to strike, continued to be an irritation, and worse. The new commander in New Orleans, General Winfield Scott Hancock, reversed many of the orders of his ousted predecessor, Philip Sheridan, exactly as Johnson had intended. But then Grant reversed Hancock. Unwilling to challenge the general-in-chief directly but equally unwilling to sit silent, Johnson called upon Congress to approve an official vote of thanks to Hancock. Congress, recognizing that the gesture would be a swipe at Grant, did not comply. In both Houses, according to Clemenceau, the president's message met laughter, "and neither body descended to the point of discussing it seriously."

Johnson's thorniest problem was his suspended War Secretary, Edwin Stanton, who stubbornly refused to resign. With the Senate back in session, the Tenure of Office Act required that Johnson ask that body to concur in Stanton's permanent dismissal. The president could have thumbed his nose at the statute, asserting that the Constitution gave him authority to fire Stanton. Johnson, however, judged it unwise to flout the law, which had been written by Thad Stevens himself. Alternatively, Johnson could appoint a replacement for Stanton. If he followed that course, the Senate would never vote on whether Stanton's dismissal was proper, but would simply decide whether to confirm a new war secretary. The president rejected this simple and reasonable strategy, doubting that the Senate would confirm anyone he would want to appoint. Had Johnson been willing to appoint a compromise choice for war secretary, the coming crisis could have been avoided altogether.

On December 12, Johnson sent the Senate a report justifying Stanton's dismissal. In doing so, the president accepted the procedures of the Tenure of Office Act, a course that would undercut his credibility if he ever wished to challenge that statute. He explained that he requested Stanton's resignation in August because the two men lacked "mutual confidence and general accord." Stanton's refusal to resign was "a defiance, and something more," which "must end our official relations." The president ridiculed Stanton's claim that the Tenure of Office Act protected him; Stanton himself had judged the statute unconstitutional! Johnson also detailed specific grievances. His Reconstruction policies followed the plans drawn up by Stanton for President Lincoln, yet Stanton now spurned those policies in favor of congressional Reconstruction. Johnson complained that Stanton did not relay to him a message about the New Orleans situation in late July 1866, which degenerated into the massacre. He concluded with the incontestable assertion that he could not work with this war secretary.

On January 10, a Senate committee recommended that Stanton be restored to office. A fresh confrontation between Congress and the president was under way.

Johnson thought he had a contingency plan for this turn of events. Months before, he had extracted a commitment from Grant, as interim war secretary, that he would not physically relinquish his War Department office if the Senate did not uphold Stanton's dismissal. This commitment gave Johnson some additional options. If Grant held onto the office in defiance of the Senate's action, Johnson might file a court challenge to the constitutionality of the Tenure of Office Act. Or, if Grant returned physical control of the office to Johnson—which seemed to boil down to giving the president the key to the office door—the president could try to keep Stanton out of the office by rushing over another interim Secretary. But if Stanton regained control of the War Office, Johnson's choices would be fewer and worse. Thus, the president was depending on Grant, a man he scorned as a political bumbler. Both relying on the general, and thinking him a bumbler, were mistakes. Grant would prove Johnson's match through an extended bout of maneuvering, backstabbing, and public recriminations.

Grant later insisted that his course was clear once he realized that violations of the Tenure of Office Act could be punished by a $10,000 fine and time in jail. According to Grant, he did not make that discovery until the night that the Senate committee recommended that Stanton be reinstated. (Some suspect that Stanton himself enlightened the general on this legal point.) After discussing the law's penalties with his staff and with General Sherman, Grant concluded he could not remain in the office if the Senate reinstated Stanton. He would not be lured into committing a crime, certainly not when he was expecting to run for president in a few months.

On the next morning, January 11, Grant and Johnson talked at the White House for over an hour. The dynamics of the conversation were complex. By now the two men had considerable experience with each other, little of it good. Neither liked or respected the other. Grant, the subordinate who rarely acted that way, was a man of instinct and action. He saw before him a long-winded, tricky politician. Johnson, the beleaguered president whose natural Southern constituency was still excluded from the government, saw a sullen, tongue-tied soldier with intellectual gifts below the norm. Both knew that Grant had been undermining Johnson for at least eighteen months while Johnson worked to undermine the Reconstruction statutes.

Later, Grant claimed to have told the president that if the Senate reinstated Stanton, he would give up the office. Johnson insisted that Grant said no such thing. With only those two men in the room, there is no way to know what happened. Perhaps Grant made his statement quietly while Johnson attempted to steamroller him, so the president simply missed it. By one account, Johnson offered to pay any fine Grant might face for violating the Tenure of Office Act. The full dimensions of their misunderstanding would emerge soon enough.

Consulting again with General Sherman, Grant concluded that the president should appoint Ohio Governor Jacob Cox as war secretary. Cox, a moderate Republican with a solid war record, stood a good chance of Senate confirmation. Sherman made the recommendation to Johnson, but the president did nothing about it. Grant and Johnson saw each other at a White House levee on the night of January 13, but neither mentioned the problem with Stanton. And so it festered.

While Grant and Johnson were misunderstanding each other on January 11, the Senate debated Stanton's fate in secret session. The senators voted 35 to 6 to restore him to his office, on a straight party vote. Why would Senate Republicans restore to office a secretary of war whom the president could neither trust nor work with? How could that situation serve the nation? The principal factor had to be blazing Republican anger. One observer thought the Radicals gained courage and energy during Congress's holiday recess. Certainly, Johnson had enraged his opponents anew when he removed Generals Pope and Ord from Southern commands. Many Republican senators supported Stanton solely because Johnson wanted him out.

On the morning after the Senate's action, Grant took a few mundane steps that launched the nation toward its first presidential impeachment. He went to his office at the lead-colored brick building that held the War Department, a half-block west of the Executive Mansion on Pennsylvania Avenue. After locking and bolting the door from the outside, he gave the key to his adjutant. Then he left for his other office at Army Headquarters. There, Grant sent a letter to Johnson acknowledging that the Senate had restored Stanton and thereby removed him as interim secretary of war. For the rest of the day, the general-in-chief bounced around Washington City like a pinball.

Within an hour of Grant's departure from the War Office, Stanton hurried into the building. He dictated a memo announcing his return. In his trademark peremptory fashion, he summoned the general-in-chief. For Grant, who had not expected Stanton to strike so quickly, the war secretary's return must have seemed like the recurrence of a chronic ache. Stanton spent the afternoon in his office, receiving congratulations from happy Republicans.

But the president also wanted a piece of Grant. He demanded the general's presence at the Cabinet meeting at noon. When asked for a report on the War Department, Grant replied that he was no longer head of that agency. The indignant president, maintaining his self-control, subjected Grant to a withering cross-examination over his "duplicity" in giving up the office to Stanton. Navy Secretary Welles thought that Grant, "never very commanding, was almost abject" until he "slunk away." After the general-in-chief left, all in the Cabinet, save Secretary of State Seward, agreed that Johnson should have the heads of both Stanton and the general.

The tension between Johnson and Grant was ripening into a feud that would last the rest of their lives. Johnson thought Grant's action "was that of a traitor." When other Cabinet members sided with Johnson, Grant never again spoke to them or to their families. The next two weeks featured move and countermove between the general and the president, basted with wounded pride and resentment. Sherman tried to reconcile the two bitter men, but neither wanted rapprochement. Finally, Sherman yearned only to leave Washington.

Grant was almost as angry with Stanton as he was with Johnson. At one point, the general-in-chief set off to advise Stanton to resign, only to encounter the war secretary's "loud and violent" hectoring. Stanton, master of the positive uses of bad behavior, was sufficiently unpleasant that Grant gave up on his mission, leaving Stanton's office without delivering his intended message.

The general-in-chief came up with another path out of the morass. Why not, he proposed to the president, just ignore the war secretary? Johnson could order the army to disregard directions from Stanton. Johnson agreed but then never issued the order. That failure was no oversight, but a calculated measure to discomfit Grant. As the president explained to a confidant, Grant had been glad to be rid of Stanton when the war secretary was suspended. Johnson preferred to leave the two to "fight it out."

Instead, the president again pressed Sherman to become secretary of war, a prospect that still dismayed the high-strung general. Johnson could not accept that even though he and Sherman shared political views, the general would never be adverse to Sam Grant. As Sherman had put it, they stood by each other always.

As soon as Stanton was back in the War Department, the press reported the president's unhappiness. Johnson himself showed a reporter the minutes of a Cabinet discussion of Grant's supposed double-dealing. The president gave exclusive interviews to a favored reporter from the *New York World*, complaining about his general-in-chief. Predictably, Grant grew furious, "as angry as any Hotspur in the land." The general knew how to counterattack. On January 24, he wrote to Johnson requesting in writing the order that the army should disregard directions from Stanton. When Johnson did not respond, Grant raised the stakes with a second letter. Grant wrote that Johnson had said months before that he wanted to keep Stanton out of office, whether or not that was permitted by the Tenure of Office Act. As for the Cabinet meeting on January 14, Grant denied "the correctness of the President's statement of our conversations." In short, after accusing Johnson of soliciting his help in violating the Tenure of Office Act, Grant called him a liar.

Several advisers urged the president to walk away from the confrontation. Public opinion was against Stanton, counseled one, but "by an imprudent act you may turn it in his favor." Another encouraged Johnson to end the impasse by appointing a new war secretary. Good advice fell on deaf ears.

Johnson challenged his top general with a letter asserting facts that were "diametrically the reverse of your narration." He reported that every Cabinet member, "without exception," agreed with Johnson's version of the Cabinet meeting on January 14. Grant was not cowed. Unimpressed by the massed moral power of the president and his Cabinet, Grant replied that the "whole matter, from beginning to end, [was] an attempt to involve me in the resistance of the law, for which you hesitated to assume the responsibility in orders, and thus to destroy my character before the country."

At this point, Congress demanded copies of the incendiary correspondence, which promptly appeared in newspapers across the land. The episode was fascinating and horrifying: the president and his military chief exchanging angry accusations of mendacity. Even some who disliked Johnson doubted Grant's version of events. Such doubts, it turned out, mattered little. The public was going to believe its hero general, not its president-by-accident. Early on, the *New York Tribune* distilled the calculus:

> In a question of veracity between a soldier whose honor is as unvarnished as the sun, and a President who has betrayed every friend, and broken every promise, the country did not hesitate.

Grant's successful campaign against Johnson in the winter of 1868 resembled some of his military operations. Somewhat surprised to be drawn into battle when the Senate reinstated Stanton, Grant made a swift, visceral evaluation. Whatever he might have said to the president before, he could not violate the Tenure of Office Act. Intentionally breaking a law, even a dubious one, would place him on the low ground. Worse, it would turn him into Andrew Johnson's toady. While the president dug in his heels, seething and glowering, Grant explored ways to resolve the dispute, including appointing Governor Cox as war secretary, or bypassing Stanton at the War Department. When Johnson showed no interest in resolving the impasse, Grant attacked, throwing his massive popularity against the president's checkered reputation. It had not been elegant, but it got Grant out of a tight political corner with his reputation mostly intact.

Thaddeus Stevens watched the contest closely. When the House clerk read aloud Grant's letter to Johnson of February 3—with several interruptions for spontaneous applause—the ailing congressman from Pennsylvania smelled blood. Grant, he exulted, "is a bolder man than I thought him." With this evidence, Stevens continued, "Now we will let him into the Church." Best of all, Grant gave Stevens a fresh theory for impeaching the president: that he had solicited Grant's violation of the Tenure of Office Act. Within days, Stevens was pressing that theory in another impeachment resolution.

By February 10, Stevens was ready. He persuaded the House to transfer all impeachment records to the Committee on Reconstruction, which he chaired. Now the Pennsylvanian could control the process.

The president did not sit quietly and wait for Stevens's next step. On the night before Stevens was to bring his resolution to the House, Johnson granted another interview to a friendly reporter. The president's performance had a Jekyll-and-Hyde quality. He presented himself as calm and aloof from the storm. When impeachment came up, the president "laughed as if he didn't believe the charges would ever come." Johnson shared his unusual notions of political economy, blaming the nation's economic troubles on emancipation, which converted slaves from "a good [that] increased the productive resources of the nation" into freedmen who burdened the country.

But the heart of the interview was an assault on General Grant. The general supported the president during his early months in office, Johnson stressed, and had opposed Negro suffrage. Grant's suggestion that the president order the army to ignore War Secretary Stanton was now, for Johnson, "only one of a great many instances in which [Grant] has grossly deceived me." After brandishing correspondence from Sherman to buttress his position, Johnson dismissed Grant as just another politician, the "Radical candidate for the Presidency."

But Johnson could not let go. On February 10, he fired off yet another rejoinder to the general, sputtering about Grant's "insubordinate attitude." A day later, Johnson released letters from Cabinet members supporting his version of events. Yet the president took no action against the general-in-chief, effectively admitting his mortifying political weakness. As summed up by old Thomas Ewing, General Sherman's father-in-law and longtime political power, Grant's actions "made it incumbent upon the president if he had any actual power to court martial him, but . . . he has not."

For Stevens, both sides of the Grant-Johnson correspondence established that the president tried to induce Grant to violate the Tenure of Office Act. As Stevens put it, "If the President's statement is true, then he has been guilty of a high official misdemeanor. If the General's statement is true, then the President has been guilty of a high official misdemeanor." There was enough, he insisted, to impeach a dozen men. As for "the question of veracity, as they call it," Stevens invited the two men to "go out in my back yard and settle it alone."

Stevens presented a new impeachment resolution to his committee on February 13, along with a report charging Johnson with soliciting the violation of the Tenure of Office statute. Though Stevens was "very earnest," his committee balked. "Old Thad is still firm," one reporter wrote, "but the others flinch." Moderate John Bingham of Ohio held the balance of power. He moved that the resolution be tabled. His motion won, 6 to 3.

Once more, Stevens declared the Republican Party full of cowards. Once more, he pronounced impeachment dead. Once more, Johnson had survived. No matter how many ill-advised quarrels the president picked, no matter how many apparent blunders he committed, Stevens could not find the formula for a successful impeachment. Not enough Republicans shared his view that impeachment was a political tool for removing a woeful president like Andrew Johnson. And now Stevens could not even get an impeachment resolution out of his own committee. His failure was so plain that Samuel Clemens published a labored spoof portraying Stevens and other Radicals as nurses forced finally to admit the death of "our brother, impeachment."

If he could not get rid of the man in the White House, Stevens resolved to cut off even more presidential powers. "[T]hough dying," Clemenceau wrote, Stevens "proposes more bills in one day than any of his colleagues in a month." He proposed to give General Grant unfettered control over Reconstruction in the South, a power that Grant did not want. Another bill aimed to limit the president's recourse to the courts by requiring a two-thirds majority of the Supreme Court before a law could be declared unconstitutional. Stevens's Reconstruction Committee was preparing legislation to readmit individual Southern states to the Union. Even without impeachment, there was plenty to do.

With the failure of this latest impeachment effort, Johnson's thoughts turned to revenge. After seven months of scheming, he still was saddled with Edwin Stanton at the War Department. And now he had a serious score to settle with Ulysses Grant. A reporter who visited the White House found the president looking "as if he would like to raise . . . perfect hell." Indeed, the reporter continued, "he expects to crush his enemies."

That vindictive spirit blinded Johnson to the damage he was doing to his own cause. Why not appoint a secretary of war whom the Senate would confirm? Even if such a candidate were far from his first choice, he would certainly be preferable to Stanton. But Johnson had no appetite for compromise. Indeed, he had achieved the implausible feat of making Stanton, perhaps the most disliked official in Washington, an object of sympathy. To many Americans, the president no longer seemed like the nation's leader, but rather like a man obsessed with settling personal scores.

11

SHOWDOWN ON SEVENTEENTH STREET

FEBRUARY 15–21, 1868

The President called upon the lightning and the lightning
came.

CLEMENCEAU, FEBRUARY 28, 1868

GENERAL SHERMAN PLAINLY was the answer to Johnson's problems.
Of the Union Army heroes, Sherman was second only to Grant.
After two years as Grant's senior corps commander in the West, the
general called "Uncle Billy" by his admiring soldiers had driven an army
across the South, captured Atlanta, and conducted his famously destruc-
tive and demoralizing march to the sea.

But Sherman was not only a Northern hero. He also was strongly
sympathetic to Southern whites. Before the war, while superintendent
of what is now Louisiana State University, he grew fond of Southern
ways and people. Though he was a remorseless battlefield foe whose
name would be reviled by generations of Southerners, he was a generous
victor. In North Carolina shortly after Lincoln's assassination, Sherman
accepted the surrender of the last major Confederate army in the field.
His terms were so magnanimous that War Secretary Stanton denounced

them to the press and Grant had to hurry to North Carolina to retract them.

The red-bearded Sherman was no fan of congressional Radicals or racial equality. He did not want blacks in his fighting corps, preferring a white man's war. "With my opinions of negroes and my experience, yes, prejudice," he wrote, "I won't trust niggers to fight." After the war, he thought blacks should be free, "but not put on an equality with the whites." Called a race-hater by one Northern newspaper, Sherman thought the Radicals were trying to foment a new civil war. He supported Johnson's 1866 vetoes of the Freedmen's Bureau bill and the Civil Rights Act. One Cabinet member hailed Sherman as a conservative opponent of the Radicals.

Sherman's powerful family connections would guarantee Senate confirmation of him for any appointment. His brother, John, was the junior senator from Ohio, a Republican not usually counted among the Radicals. His father-in-law, Thomas Ewing, had been a senator from Ohio, plus treasury secretary in the early 1840s and interior secretary in the early 1850s. Ewing also was Sherman's surrogate father. When

Lieutenant General William T. Sherman.

Sherman's own father died, leaving a widow with eleven children, Ewing took in nine-year-old Tecumseh Sherman, gave him the first name William, and raised him with his own children. Ewing was a Washington power broker still. Johnson's attorney general, Henry Stanberry, had been Ewing's law partner, while Ewing also sponsored Interior Secretary Orville Browning.

From Johnson's standpoint, Sherman seemed too good to be true. Which, it turned out, he was.

Many high-ranking soldiers profess a disdain for politics but are drawn to it by ambition, or by a sense of duty, or a mixture of the two. Not Sherman. His horror of the political world was unshakable. "Washington is as corrupt as Hell," he wrote to his wife in May 1865. "I will avoid it as a pest house." Moreover, Sherman would never allow himself to be used against Grant. Twice already, the volatile Sherman had deflected Johnson's efforts to raise him above Grant.

As January ground to its acrimonious close, the president contrived a new set of lures designed to overcome Sherman's resistance. Johnson offered to create a military district for Sherman—the District of the Atlantic—that would include Washington City, Maryland, Delaware, Virginia, and West Virginia. Though Sherman might dread Washington, the president knew that Mrs. Sherman longed to be in the nation's capital, close to her father and brothers. Johnson also proposed to appoint Sherman "Brevet" (or temporary) General of the Army, placing him at the same rank as Grant and making him the third officer in American history (after Washington and Grant) to hold that rank. Then Johnson would name him interim war secretary. Stanton would be gone for good, Grant would be subordinated to an officer he liked and respected, and Johnson would be able to sleep at night.

In a passionate letter, Sherman declined the offer, arguing that it would guarantee conflict among the president, Grant, and Sherman. He underscored his personal wish to be nowhere near Washington, pointing to the city's impact on Grant:

> I have been with General Grant in the midst of death and slaughter
> . . . and yet I never saw him more troubled since he has been in
> Washington, and been compelled to read himself a "sneak and de-

ceiver," based on reports of the four of the Cabinet, and apparently with your knowledge. If this political atmosphere can disturb the equanimity of one so guarded and so prudent as he is, what will be the result with me, so careless, so outspoken as I am?

Sherman closed with more sound advice for Johnson. Since Stanton had no actual power now, he wrote, Johnson could afford to leave him in office to perform empty ministerial duties. Sherman also warned Johnson not to use force against Stanton, a prospect that the president evidently had raised.

Johnson suffered a serious fit of indecision over what to do with this balky general. The president was firm to the point of obstinacy once he made up his mind, but he could hesitate before major decisions. His loyal navy secretary thought this his greatest weakness. On February 6, Johnson ordered the creation of the Department of the Atlantic with Sherman in charge. The next day, he withdrew the order. One day later, he changed course again, directing preparation of an order creating the new district but not naming Sherman as head of it. Johnson finally issued the order on February 12, directing that Sherman command the new district. On the day after, he nominated Sherman as brevet general.

Sherman was wild when he learned of the president's actions. He thought first of resigning from the army. To Grant, he likened the president's order to "Hamlet's ghost, it curdles my blood and mars my judgment." To his brother the senator, Sherman complained that Johnson "would make use of me to beget violence." He asked his brother to oppose his promotion in the Senate. Once more, Sherman pleaded with Johnson to abandon his plan. When Johnson received Sherman's protest on February 19, he finally gave it up.

Yielding to Sherman's wishes meant that the president would need another strategy for driving Stanton from the War Office on Seventeenth Street. Johnson was in a permanent state of barely suppressed rage. He had endured the disloyalty of Stanton and Grant for too many months. Twice he had watched Congress dismantle his Southern policy. He had survived thirteen months of impeachment investigation and two serious attempts to impeach him. His fury was past the bursting point. He had had enough.

• • •

On Sunday, February 16, President Johnson went to church with his personal secretary, Colonel William Moore. Back at the White House, Moore read to the president from the drama *Cato*, written in 1713 by Joseph Addison, about the Roman aristocrat who resisted Julius Caesar's grab for power. The play, with its confrontation between despotic evil (Caesar) and republican virtue (Cato), was a favorite of Americans in the colonial and revolutionary eras. George Washington fell in love with it at age thirteen. To buoy his troops' flagging spirits during the brutal winter at Valley Forge in 1778, Washington had his officers stage *Cato*. The play features little action, characters that can only aspire to be two-dimensional, and relentlessly self-righteous cant. It has slid out of favor with modern audiences. For President Johnson, it was pure inspiration.

"Cato was a man," he instructed Colonel Moore, "who would not compromise with wrong but being right, died before he would yield." Johnson pointed out that Caesar offered peace terms to Cato, "but proud old Cato folded his arms and sustained alone by his sense of duty to Rome, dictated . . . terms to Caesar." Needless to say, Cato dies at the end of the play.

Johnson, Colonel Moore concluded, "[w]ithout directly expressing the thought in words, . . . intimated a parallel between his position and that of Cato." Moore thought the president saw himself similarly devoted to pursuing the right; Johnson also could seem indifferent to the consequences of his actions, evidently wishing for martyrdom. In a newspaper interview in early February, the president made the point himself. "He said the time had arrived," the *New York Evening Post* reported, when he would be "compelled to ignore the Constitution itself or [ignore] an act of Congress [the Tenure of Office Act] clearly unconstitutional." He would not hesitate to uphold the Constitution, Johnson promised, at the risk of impeachment. Navy Secretary Welles wondered if the president courted impeachment, a glorious political death to rival Cato's.

The next day, Johnson sent Colonel Moore to see John Potts, the chief clerk of the War Department. By statute, Potts was to run the department when there was no Secretary. Moore offered Potts the chance to become interim war secretary. Potts could then demand the papers of the department from Stanton; if Stanton resisted, Potts could sue Stanton for control of the department.

"Mr. Potts," Moore recorded, "shrank from this." Understanding Stanton better than the president did, Potts pointed out that the war secretary would simply fire him as chief clerk. When Moore argued that Stanton would no longer be Secretary and thus would have no power to fire him, Potts was not convinced. He knew Stanton. Potts's refusal disappointed the president. If he could only find the proper man to replace Stanton, Johnson mused, "he would settle the matter this morning."

Anticipating that both Potts and Sherman might be unwilling, the president had cultivated a third candidate, Adjutant General Lorenzo Thomas. At a meeting with Thomas on February 18, Johnson raised the possibility of placing the adjutant general as interim war secretary. The soldier was willing. Then General Sherman's letter arrived with its plea to be spared Washington duty, and Potts scurried out of the picture. Johnson turned back to Lorenzo Thomas. Moore, the president's aide, questioned whether a Thomas appointment would "carry any weight." The president admitted it would not, but his patience was at an end.

> [Johnson] said he was determined to remove Stanton. Self respect demanded it and if the people did not respect their Chief Magistrate enough to sustain him in such a measure, the President ought to resign.

But for this unlucky intersection with Andrew Johnson in high dudgeon, Lorenzo Thomas would be remembered, if at all, as a diligent army officer for more than forty years. An 1823 graduate of West Point, he was adjutant general when the Civil War broke out. With power over the army's personnel matters, the adjutant general had to be politically deft, particularly with senior officers. Thomas did well enough in the job until Stanton took over the department in 1862. The brusque new Secretary had little patience for the avuncular Thomas, a tippler who was fond of dress uniforms. One contemporary recalled Stanton pledging to "pick Lorenzo Thomas up with a pair of tongs and drop him from the nearest window."

Stanton never flushed Thomas out of the army, but he stashed the older man out of sight for five years, beginning with an assignment to

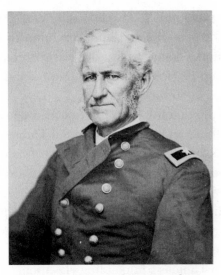

Army Adjutant-General Lorenzo Thomas.

recruit black soldiers in the Mississippi Valley that kept Thomas on the road for the last two years of the war. After the Confederate surrender, Thomas's exile included inspections of military offices and national cemeteries. His able second-in-command acted as adjutant general during his extended absence.

Thomas finally returned to Washington in late 1867 to write up his report on the cemeteries. With Stanton suspended from office, Thomas seized several opportunities to ask President Johnson for reinstatement as adjutant general. No doubt the president knew of the bad feeling between Thomas and Stanton. That hostility only commended the adjutant general to the president. Even more gratifying to Johnson, Grant also had little affection for the adjutant general, recently recommending his involuntary retirement. On February 13, the president directed that Thomas be reinstated as adjutant general, then a few days later sounded him out about the War Department appointment.

On February 20, Johnson again talked with Colonel Moore about appointing Thomas. Even though his aide continued to urge delay, the president would wait no longer. Upon arriving in his office the next morning, Johnson instructed Moore to prepare papers removing Stanton and appointing Thomas. By noon, the tall, thin Thomas was in the Cabinet Room at the White House. Johnson handed two orders to Colonel

Moore, who read them aloud. The first informed Stanton that he was removed from office and directed him to relinquish all official papers; the second appointed Thomas as interim war secretary. With conscious dignity, Johnson said he was committed to upholding the Constitution. He adjured Thomas to do the same.

Before taking this fateful step, Johnson had consulted exactly two people, Colonel Moore and Adjutant General Thomas. The list of those he did not consult is long. Not his deft secretary of state, William Seward. Not his determined attorney general, Henry Stanberry. In fact, no Cabinet member knew of this maneuver ahead of time. Equally in the dark were Johnson's allies in Congress. The president sometimes turned for advice to senior outsiders like Thomas Ewing or Jeremiah Black, a lawyer who had served in Buchanan's Cabinet. None, however, heard a whisper of Lorenzo Thomas's impending elevation.

By keeping the Thomas appointment secret, Johnson achieved several dubious results. He ensured that the news would explode into the public mind. He also insulated himself from anyone who might argue against the step. Finally, he guaranteed that his supporters would not be prepared to defend the appointment. The situation drove Navy Secretary Welles, a steadfast supporter, to wish that Johnson would "more freely communicate with his Cabinet and Friends."

Thomas went to Stanton's office at the War Department on the morning of February 21 and presented Johnson's two letters firing Stanton and appointing Thomas. Stanton reviewed the president's letters, then stalled, asking if he could have time to gather up his personal items. Here the adjutant general committed the blunder of courtesy. "Act your pleasure," he said. From that moment, Stanton steadily seized the initiative.

The dismissed war secretary requested a copy of Johnson's order. While Thomas went off to have a copy made by hand, Stanton dispatched messengers to report this stunning development to his friends in Congress. Thomas returned with the copy. General Grant entered Stanton's office and read over the president's letter. The two men conferred. Stanton ordered Grant to arrest Thomas. Grant declined. The general-in-chief added, though, that Stanton should hold his office.

Having caught his breath, Stanton could gauge his position. The Senate had voted only a month before that the president had no grounds for removing him. Stanton had done nothing in the last thirty days to alter that conclusion, so he should be able to rely on support from Congress. The president's choice to replace him, Lorenzo Thomas, enjoyed neither political support nor public reputation. Stanton likely felt insulted to be replaced by such a nonentity. By choosing Thomas, Johnson revealed his desperation to be rid of Stanton. The Secretary made up his mind. He would cross this Rubicon. Stanton told Thomas that he might not obey the president's order.

Thomas's response was to announce to the Secretary's aides that he was the new interim war secretary. Stanton directed them to ignore Thomas. Then Stanton wrote out an order commanding Thomas to stop pretending to be the secretary of war.

Flummoxed by Stanton's defiance, the adjutant general announced that he would return on Monday, three days hence, to take possession of the office. He retired to report to the president. Johnson received the news stoically, no doubt regretting that he had sent Thomas into such an uneven contest. "Very well," the president said, adding that Thomas should not wait until Monday, but should take possession of the War Office on the next day.

Johnson sent a notice to the Senate that Stanton had been replaced with Thomas. The news struck "like a thunderbolt," according to the *New York Times*. Senators converged around the desk of President Pro Tem Ben Wade, craning their necks to read Johnson's message. .

Matters snowballed beyond the president's control. Four Republican senators swept into Stanton's office to show their support, then crossed the street to deliver the same message to General Grant. Others sent messages urging the war secretary to hold his ground. The usually prolix Sumner of Massachusetts sent a one-word exhortation: "Stick."

By midafternoon, the Senate was in executive session to deliberate on the shocking event. The House adjourned in the late afternoon, after a Pennsylvania congressman submitted a fresh impeachment resolution. It was referred to Stevens's Reconstruction Committee. In the evening, one newspaper reported, "there commenced at once a search for law books." Radicals Ben Butler, George Boutwell, and others spent the night with the dusty tomes. Impeachment was on every mind.

Thaddeus Stevens remained cool, according to the *New York Her-*

ald, ready to "again try his hand, he thinks with better prospects of success." In the minutes after the electrifying news arrived from the War Department, Stevens limped from colleague to colleague on the floor of the House, delivering a single message about the president: "If you don't kill the beast, it will kill you." More ominous for Johnson, the leader of conservative and moderate Republicans, John Bingham, denounced the president for stirring up more conflict.

After seven hours of secret debate that stretched into the evening, the Senate voted 29 to 6 in favor of a resolution stating unequivocally that the president "has no power to remove the Secretary of War and designate any other officer to perform the duties of that office." When the Senate adjourned at 10 P.M., the road to impeachment lay brightly lit before Stevens and his allies. Here was an impeachable offense to hang around the president's neck, one the Senate had just declared: Johnson violated the Tenure of Office Act. Political Washington stayed up into the night, crowding into hotels and bars to digest Congress's response to what was widely described as a coup d'état by Johnson.

Stanton's office was a "blaze of light" that night. Carriages filled with congressmen arrived and left. A Methodist bishop visited. Amid the hubbub, Stanton planned his counterstrike. After conferring with Chief Judge David Cartter of the District of Columbia courts, Stanton swore out an affidavit charging Thomas with violating the Tenure of Office Act by purporting to be the interim war secretary. The papers were completed after midnight. By 3 A.M., most of Stanton's visitors had left.

While Stanton worked into the night, the adjutant general frolicked. A Senate official found Thomas at a masquerade ball at Marini's Hall. Although Thomas wore a mask, his dress uniform made him easy to pick out. (When President Johnson heard where Thomas was, he exclaimed, "Jesus Christ, a man of his years at a fancy ball!") On his way to the ball, Thomas assured two acquaintances that if Stanton attempted to bar his entry to the War Office, he would break down the doors. While taking refreshment at Willard's Hotel, he spouted similar threats. Through the night, the adjutant general celebrated with enough verve to earn a bad head in the morning. As one newspaper phrased it, Thomas "had imbibed in the true Johnsonian spirit."

Only one companion remained with Stanton through the entire night, Senator John Thayer of Nebraska. Fearing the president would attempt to evict him by force, the war secretary posted infantry on either side of the War Department building. After 3 A.M., the two men settled on sofas to rest. Less than an hour later, the Secretary, in a panic, awakened Thayer. "Senator," he said, "I believe the troops are coming to put me out."

It was a false alarm, the changing of Stanton's own guard.

In a letter to his wife on the following day, Senator William Pitt Fessenden of Maine was glum. The Senate had passed, he wrote, "a very unwise resolution, upon the strength of which Mr. Johnson will probably be impeached." Fessenden had not voted on the resolution. He deemed opposition to be pointless. The country's opinion of the president was so low, "which he fully deserves, that it expects his condemnation and removal from office." Though Fessenden shared that low opinion of Johnson, he could not support impeachment. "Either I am very stupid," he concluded, "or my friends are acting like fools."

12

THE DAM BURSTS

FEBRUARY 22–24, 1868

There was a widespread feeling among well-meaning and sober people that the country was really in some sort of peril, and that it would be a good thing to get rid of that dangerous man in the presidential chair.

CARL SCHURZ, *REMINISCENCES* (1907)

PAINFULLY HUNG OVER and awaiting his breakfast, Lorenzo Thomas answered his front door at 8 A.M. on February 22. He found an assistant U.S. marshal and a constable. They arrested him on a warrant issued by Judge Cartter a few hours earlier. Thomas persuaded his guards to stop at the White House on the way to court, though they refused to leave his side. The party of three met with the president, who thus learned of Thomas's obvious predicament. According to Thomas, Johnson said the matter belonged in the courts, then directed Thomas to stop at the attorney general's house. The arresting officers agreed to that detour as well, though Attorney General Stanberry advised Thomas to retain his own lawyer. At the courthouse, Judge Cartter set bail at $5,000. Two local merchants posted it on Thomas's behalf.

The interim war secretary retraced his steps in the company of Colonel Moore, who had rushed to help him. After reporting to the attorney general and the president that he had regained his liberty, Thomas went on to the War Department. Boldly, he strode through the main entrance and up to Stanton's second-floor office. Having been outflanked the day before, when he had the advantage of surprise, Thomas had little hope of success in a renewed confrontation.

When Thomas entered, Stanton was conversing with several Republican congressmen, one of whom seized pencil and paper to take shorthand notes of the encounter. Thomas crossed the Brussels carpet to confront Stanton. The dueling war secretaries spoke slowly, politely.

Thomas: I am Secretary of War *ad interim*, and am ordered by the President of the United States to take charge of this office.

Stanton: I order you to repair to your room, and exercise your office as adjutant-general.

Thomas: I am Secretary of War *ad interim*, and I shall not obey your orders; but I shall obey the order of the President to take charge of this office.

Stanton: As Secretary of War, I order you to repair to your office as adjutant-general.

Thomas: I shall not do so.

Stanton: Then you may stand there, if you please; but you will attempt to act as Secretary of War at your peril.

Thomas: I *shall* act as Secretary of War.

At this point, Thomas left the Secretary's office and crossed the hall to that of General Schriver. Stanton and the shorthand writer followed. With a genial laugh, Stanton asked, "So you claim to be here as Secretary of War, and refuse to obey my orders, do you?" Thomas affirmed both propositions and demanded the department's mails. The two men then abandoned their official poses. Thomas described the scene in memorable terms:

I said, "The next time you have me arrested, please do not do it before I get something to eat." I said I had nothing to eat or drink all day. He put his hand around my neck, as he sometimes does, and ran his hand through my hair, and turned around to General Schriver and said, "Schriver, you have got a bottle here; bring it out."

When Schriver's bottle turned out to be almost empty, a messenger fetched another. Pouring drinks, Stanton said, "Now this, at least, is neutral ground."

The adjutant general walked back to the White House to report his new failure to the president, who was conferring with friendly senators and Attorney General Stanberry. Johnson's response was far from helpful. As Thomas reported it, the president told him "to go on and take possession of the office, without stating how I was to do it." In the coming days, Johnson would repeat that ineffectual command, consistently telling the adjutant general to go to the War Department "and exercise those functions." Thomas never did figure out how to do so. Neither, it seems, did Johnson.

The situation had no precedent. The nation had two war secretaries. One was barricaded in his office, a half-block from the White House, gathering up the office keys and doubling the guard. The other, mockingly referred to in press accounts as "Lorenzo the Magnificent," was out on bail. After complying with the Tenure of Office Act in his earlier moves against Stanton, the president had flouted the statute. The spectacle smacked of opéra bouffe or the thrashings of a tinhorn dictatorship, not the grave proceedings of a constitutional republic.

The most pressing question was whether this was the beginning of another civil war. News reports were panicky. They accused Johnson of "thunderbolt" actions representing a "coup d'état." Some compared it to Napoléon's seizure of power in 1799. Official Washington was in a lather, more generally agitated than when the nation faced secession and war in 1861. Arriving in the midst of the uproar, one correspondent judged it "to equal that which followed the assassination of President Lincoln, and to excel that caused by the capture of Richmond and Lee's surrender."

With the tumult came fears of military conflict. Over the next few days, rumors spread like wildfire. Pro-Johnson forces were supposed to be on the march. The Maryland militia might be in Washington at any moment, along with "several hundred armed roughs" from Philadelphia. Offers of armed support swamped the president: he could have 1,000 men from New Jersey and a regiment of Kentuckians, or 30,000 Virginians, 2,000 men from Louisiana, and 100,000 from Missouri. The New

York police reported finding a cache of nitroglycerine as part of a "Guy Fawkes conspiracy" to blow up Congress. A number of congressmen fled the Capitol on hearing the report, which then was dismissed as a dubious promotional gambit by the manufacturer of the explosive.

Martial ardor surged on the congressional side as well. Pennsylvania's governor announced that "the spirit of 1861 seems again to pervade the Keystone State," with Union Army veterans offering their services to support Congress. The *New York Herald* reported that "if violence is used in ejecting Mr. Stanton[,] 100,000 men are ready to come to Washington and put him back." The Grand Army of the Republic, the leading veterans' organization, urged Congress to stand firm. Its commander-in-chief, Congressman John A. Logan of Illinois, sent an astonishing handwritten note to the GAR's administrator on February 22, the day after Lorenzo Thomas's failed "coup":

> I hope you will quietly and secretly organize all of our boys, so that they can assemble at a signal that you may agree upon . . . ready to protect the Congress of the U.S. . . . This must be done quietly, and no indiscreet persons must understand or know anything about it. . . .
>
> All of this must be done by verbal communication, as no official orders must be made on the subject at present, until a necessity might arise to protect the Government against traitors to it.

Organized into battalions, the GAR veterans formed a private security force throughout Washington City. Logan posted them, in civilian dress, as round-the-clock sentinels, concentrating them near the White House and the War Department. Sleeping on a cot in Stanton's office, Logan was in position to call out his forces "at a moment's notice." He offered to assign 125 GAR veterans to the War Department as a praetorian guard, but Stanton rejected any use of force. No blood, he directed, should be shed on his account. The Secretary chanced an excursion to the curb in front of his building to explain events to his wife on the afternoon of February 22. That evening, a reporter found him "calm and determined."

Alarming rumors swept through the city, ricocheting off the credulous and the fearful. Any development seemed possible. The frenzy bubbled through a sarcastic report in the *New York Herald*:

During the evening the President was arrested nineteen times. Grant was put in arrest five times, dismissed [from] the army eight times, relieved from duty three times, ordered to Alaska once, sent on a tour of inspection once, a court martial convened for his trial four times, and assassinated twice. Stanton committed suicide once, was arrested six times, had an indefinite number of quo warrantos, mandamuses and other awful things served upon him. Nine different files of marines were marching to eject him from the War Office, and the President, in a fit of rage, had gone over personally and unceremoniously pitched him out of the window of the War Office. As for [Lorenzo] Thomas, it was impossible to keep track of the number of times he had been seen drunk. . . .

Though the tempest had a comic side, the confrontation was in deadly earnest, particularly in a nation with more than a million experienced soldiers—Confederate and Union—spread through every state. General Grant, head of the real army, canceled a scheduled trip to New York. He shunned the public spotlight, a prudent course for the man expected to be the Republican candidate for president later in the year. One day, he was seen "pleasantly engaged guiding his favorite team [of horses] on an afternoon drive and smoking his immortal cigar." Early in the crisis, when visited by a delegation of anxious Republican senators, Grant maintained his customary silence: "He may have smoked, but he said nothing."

Johnson worried about the loyalty of the army, and of General Grant. The president's greatest risk, however, was constitutional, not military, and it centered on that relentless, crippled old man, Thad Stevens. Soon the newspapers would be speculating over who would be appointed to the Cabinet of new President Ben Wade, after Stevens finished up the impeachment trial.

Stevens saw the moment clearly. This was his best chance yet to impeach Andrew Johnson.

While Thomas and Stanton were playing low farce at the War Department, Stevens and his Reconstruction Committee prepared for high drama. Committee members gathered at Stevens's house at ten-thirty on the morning of February 22. The Republicans were unanimous for impeachment. The two dissenting Democrats interposed objections but were ignored. By noon, the committee adjourned to gather certified copies of the president's orders dismissing Stanton and appointing Thomas. During an hour's recess, George Boutwell of Massachusetts led a subcommittee that prepared an impeachment resolution. It was strong on conclusion, weak on details: "That Andrew Johnson, President of the United States, be impeached of high crimes and misdemeanors."

By noon, excited spectators clogged the Capitol. Hundreds were turned away from the House galleries. At 2 P.M., the Reconstruction Committee was ready. Stevens's entrance caused a sensation, then the crowd grew so quiet that even he, weakened by his many ailments, could be heard. The old man seemed invigorated. One reporter wrote that "the atmosphere and excitement of a *coup d'état* is to him the elixir of life." Stevens called for the committee report. When it had been read, he offered to take an immediate vote, or to allow debate. The Democratic leader, James Brooks of New York City, sprang up with a speech in hand. Stevens yielded the floor, reserving the right to close the debate. He settled back for speeches that extended into the night and then for much of the following Monday.

In private, some Democrats expressed relief that Johnson had erred so badly that he would not be a contender for their party's presidential nomination later in the year. In public, though, they defended him. Brooks warned that Americans were on the verge of reliving the French Revolution, "baptized in blood." He struck a threatening note by claiming that four-fifths of the Army's soldiers were Democrats who would "follow the Democratic instinct and stand by the Constitution and laws of his country." (Because so many soldiers were black, however, Brooks's claim was highly implausible.) When he reached the impeachment resolution, Brooks offered a preview of Johnson's defense at trial.

Though these defenses would be described over the next three months in orations of enervating length, they could be stated simply. First, that the president had the constitutional power to remove members of his own Cabinet, no matter what the Tenure of Office Act said. Second, that the first several Congresses acknowledged that constitutional power by enacting laws granting him the same power. (This argument was not exactly airtight; if the Constitution truly granted the power to the president, why did Congress have to enact laws to achieve the same result?) Third, that the Tenure of Office Act did not cover Cabinet members—like Stanton—who had been appointed by President Lincoln.

House Republicans vied to see who could denounce the president in the most hysterical language. Johnson was capable of "any extreme of madness," according to John Bingham. Called an "incubus and a disgrace," the president was compared to Nero, Torquemada, and Emperor Louis-Napoléon, held to be guilty "of the nameless crimes which have been inflicted upon the freedmen of the South," and labeled "the great criminal of our age and country." An Indiana congressman was not surprised that "one who began his presidential career in drunkenness should end it in crime." A Tennessean won the prize for oratorical frenzy by denouncing the president as "the worst tyrant and usurper that history was ever called on to record."

Democrats responded in kind. A New Yorker proclaimed that "Robespierre, Marat, and Danton were less vindictive than [the Radicals]; and the bloody rule of the Jacobins was mild compared to that which is sought." Democrats accused their opponents of prolonging the Civil War, overthrowing the Constitution, and supporting Negro supremacy. The Republicans were "blind with rage," charged a Kentuckian, and would take "the fatal plunge into the sea of revolution."

While the bitter debate raged, both camps—Johnson and his supporters on one side, and Stevens and the Republicans on the other—feared bloodshed in the streets. Navy Secretary Welles hurried to the White House on the morning of February 22 to deliver news learned from his son. At a social event the night before, army officers were twice commanded to return to their barracks. First came a summons for officers of the Fifth Cavalry, then one for officers of the Washington garrison. Was this a military rising? Would troops march down Pennsylvania Avenue to seize the president?

Troubled, Johnson summoned the commander of the Washington garrison, General William Emory. In an exchange that would become the basis for the least persuasive impeachment charge against him, Johnson asked the general whether there had been any changes in the disposition of his troops. Emory described some reassignments over the preceding several months, which were of no interest to the president.

He meant any changes in the last twenty-four hours. Assuring Johnson that there had been no troop movements so recently, Emory added that by statute he could receive orders only through General Grant, not directly from the president.

Rumors continued to swirl through the agitated city. General Emory, a Marylander, was feared to be under the influence of South-leaning relations and friends. Navy Secretary Welles was supposed to have offered to march 500 marines to the White House to defend the president. Maryland's governor visited the White House, renewing fears of the Maryland militia. Senator Ben Wade of Ohio, next in line for the presidency, was reported to be "vibrating between the War Department and General Grant's headquarters, with an air of profound and ominous distraction."

The president gave another placid interview to a pet reporter, professing utter indifference to the prospect of impeachment. In private, Johnson betrayed intense anxiety. Twice the president sent a junior secretary to the floor of the House to gauge the likely vote on impeachment. Johnson insisted that his course was the right one, that "if he cannot be President in fact, he will not be President in name alone."

The president conferred with Attorney General Stanberry and Navy Secretary Welles, urgently seeking a way out of the tempest. Stanberry suggested another candidate to be war secretary: Thomas Ewing, his former law partner and father-in-law to General Sherman. Ewing, a conservative Republican in his late seventies, known to everyone in Washington, might win Senate confirmation. Johnson, desperate, agreed. Colonel Moore tried to deliver Ewing's nomination papers to the Senate, but the chamber had closed. More than two-thirds of the senators were watching the debate in the House. The Senate never did take up the Ewing appointment, which dropped from sight after a few days.

With the battle lines drawn between the president and Congress, Johnson entertained two visitors who were unknown to the public and have remained obscure since. In different ways, Sam Ward of New York and Perry Fuller of Kansas exemplified that Washington species that thrives at the intersection of power and money. Never holding office themselves, they represented pools of wealth whose fortunes were tied to the continuation of Johnson in office. Joining with a passel of like-minded political fixers, Ward and Fuller would help apply money—the universal lubricant of politics—to save the president.

As an historical figure, Sam Ward ranks somewhere between implausible and preposterous. Born to an aristocratic banking family in New York City, by his mid-forties he had burned through two marriages (one to an Astor heiress), several careers (including spells as literary agent for Henry Wadsworth Longfellow), and a fortune. Wealth, in any event, was a temporary condition for someone with Sam Ward's rich tastes and narrow attention span.

In middle age, Ward started anew as a Washington lobbyist. Always a pro-South Democrat, he flourished in the Johnson years and was acclaimed as the "King of the Lobby." Ward's client list featured foreigners worried about tariffs, bankers and gold traders eager to anticipate Treasury policies, and the kingpin of New York's gambling and lottery businesses. He won greatest fame as the host of brilliant dinners. Ward's European education and savoir-faire added to his luster, as did the salacious reports of his cross-dressing mistress, or "protégé," back in New York. He charmed Washington with his grand style, quick wit, and amiable rotundity. One newspaper gushed that Ward "has been all over the world," had mastered multiple languages and published poetry, "shipped before the mast, and knows every considerable public man in the country. He drinks only champagne, buys gold at the rate of fifty thousand at a stroke, [and] wears good clothes. . . ."

Yet Sam Ward was no mere bon vivant, guilelessly amusing his guests at ever more extravagant meals. He understood how cash and patronage eased the gears of government, particularly for the horde of crooked federal tax collectors in New York, where the thriving seaport and flourishing whiskey business generated waves of bribes and kickbacks. One newspaper acknowledged Ward's worldly side, proclaiming that the New Yorker had "a peculiar faculty of coming in at back doors and by private staircases."

At dinner with a group of Democrats on February 22, 1868, Ward learned of Johnson's failed attempt to place Lorenzo Thomas in charge of the War Department. Ward immediately prevailed upon the secretary of the treasury, Hugh McCulloch, to give him an introduction to the president.

The president received Ward late that evening. Johnson had endured a stressful day, capped off with a diplomatic dinner and reception. In their late-night interview, according to Ward, he advised the president "to secure the ablest counsel, half Democrats and half Republicans." Though this was surely good advice, Ward's true contribution to the president's defense was yet to come.

Perry Fuller of Kansas spent the following evening, February 23, at the White House with the Democratic National Committee. Fuller had nothing like Sam Ward's refinement, but a lot more money. In the Kansas of the 1860s—ten years before Wyatt Earp cleaned up Dodge City—politics was a bare-knuckled fight for prime feeding spots at the public trough. Perry Fuller had staked out some of the best.

Fuller stole most of his wealth from Indian tribes and from government programs to help them. He sold bad liquor, cut timber pilfered from Indian land, and supplied beef rustled from reservations. He also helped tribes sell their land to railroads at bargain basement prices while his trading company grew fat on Indian supply contracts that federal officials denounced as "outrageous swindle[s]." Cherokee Chief John Ross accused Fuller and his partner of "corrupting everything on that [Kansas] frontier."

Once he grew rich, Fuller purchased enough votes in the Kansas Legislature to elect both of the state's senators. (Senators were chosen by state legislatures until the Seventeenth Amendment was adopted in 1913.) As one Kansas trader wrote dryly, when it came to the two Kansas senators, plus one from Nebraska, Fuller "by some mysterious influence can get them to favor all of his projects." Fuller was "the virtual gatekeeper of the Indian office" at the Department of the Interior. In a Supreme Court case, a clerk in the Indian office could not explain how he came to have $45,000 (at least $630,000 in present value), alleged to be bribes from Fuller. Fuller had big ambitions. He was pressing Johnson to appoint him as commissioner of internal revenue, a mouth-watering opportunity to sit atop the pyramid of crooked tax collectors. To prove his dedication to Johnson's cause, Fuller had paid $7,000 (more than $100,000 in today's dollars) to underwrite the abortive National Union Convention in August 1866 and was pledging to support the struggling pro-Johnson newspaper in Washington City.

"Smooth faced, shrewd, large, 'paunchy,' . . . repulsive at a second

147

examination," Fuller left behind no record of his conversations at the White House on February 23. Such a large affair would afford few opportunities for intimate talk of sensitive matters. In any event, Fuller did not like to leave tracks. Like Sam Ward, the Kansas Indian trader had skills that would prove useful during the next ninety days of hand-to-hand combat over who would be president, and what course the nation would follow.

With the House of Representatives in recess on that Sunday, February 23, passions ebbed slightly. Cold temperatures kept many indoors, though sensational rumors continued to rocket through barrooms and lobbies. Stanton received adherents at the War Office, while letters and telegrams of support poured in. Adjutant General Thomas, feeling ill after two difficult days, chose not to drop by.

Johnson huddled at the White House with Attorney General Stanberry and Secretary of State Seward, exploring schemes to divert the confrontation into the courts. Perhaps Stanton had outsmarted himself by having Thomas arrested. Maybe Thomas's case could be a vehicle for a court ruling on whether the Tenure of Office Act was constitutional. Attorney General Stanberry prepared a response to the Senate resolution that had denied the president's power to fire Stanton.

On Monday morning, the excitement returned with a wet and gloomy snow. Guided by military patrols, crowds converged on the Capitol early. The building's rotunda filled with sightseers. From ten in the morning until six at night, the House galleries bulged with citizens eager to know the president's fate. Though a somber decorum prevailed during debate, the harsh jeremiads against the president continued, occasionally interrupted by fierce challenges to the impeachers. Incendiary language, delivered with dignity, was the order of the day.

Stevens, who sat through the day's proceedings in a special chair next to the Speaker's podium, rose after the sun had set. Stepping unsteadily into the well of the House, supported on a cane, Stevens paused with a showman's assurance, allowing the silence to gather weight. Congressmen sidled closer to him. Every ear in the gallery strained to hear. Stevens struggled to begin his speech. As an observer noted, he plainly ached to "perform a duty which he felt belonged to himself alone." After a few words that almost no one could hear, Stevens gave up. He handed his speech to the House clerk to be read for him.

The speech insisted that impeachment was a political remedy and recited Johnson's violation of the Tenure of Office Act. Stevens added a unique charge against the president, accusing him of attempted bribery when he offered to pay any fine levied on General Grant for violating the statute. God, he told his colleagues, would hold them responsible for their votes. They were choosing between a continent "filled with free and untrammeled people" and one that was "a nest of shrinking, cowardly slaves."

The vote overwhelmingly favored impeachment, 126 to 47, with 17 not voting. No Republican voted "no"; no Democrat voted "yes." When the tally was announced, the onlookers exchanged whispers and meaningful looks, awed by the gravity of the moment.

The House Speaker, Schuyler Colfax, appointed Stevens and John Bingham of Ohio to deliver the resolution to the Senate. He also named a committee to prepare articles of impeachment. Stevens, Boutwell, and Bingham were on it, along with James Wilson of Iowa (the Judiciary Committee chairman who led the fight against impeachment ten weeks before) and John Logan of Illinois (and of the GAR).

The president received the news calmly. It was no surprise. Stanton rejoiced over the bulletin, but all was not well in the Stanton family. Realizing he might be living in his office for some time to come, the secretary sent a sergeant to his home for food, clothes, and bed linen. Mrs. Stanton refused to provide any of it. She instructed the sergeant to tell her husband to resign immediately and come straight home.

Thus obstructed to an extent that Lorenzo Thomas had never managed, Stanton asked the sergeant to retrieve the necessaries from the sergeant's home. They prepared an Irish stew in an office fireplace, but the dish burned when they fell asleep. On the following afternoon, a pleading note from the war secretary brought Mrs. Stanton back to the curb outside the War Office. Seated in her carriage, they continued their quarrel until she drove off in a renewed rage. Not for several more days would Mrs. Stanton be reconciled to her husband's self-imposed exile from home.

Personal problems aside, the impeachers were riding high, while Johnson loyalists were heartsick. Sam Ward predicted the president's immediate ouster. "Make your calculations upon having Ben Wade for president by the 30th of March," he wrote. "There is more volcanic danger today than when South Carolina seceded."

For now, the action would be in the House of Representatives. Three days after Lorenzo Thomas tried to take control of the War Department, the House had voted to impeach Andrew Johnson. Now the congressmen had to decide what they were impeaching him for.

13

THE WATERLOO STRUGGLE

FEBRUARY 24–MARCH 4, 1868

If he was impeached for general cussedness, there would be
no difficulty in the case.

SENATOR WILLIAM PITT FESSENDEN,
MARCH 1868

EVERY EYE FOLLOWED Thad Stevens as he limped down the center
aisle of the crowded Senate chamber on February 25, 1868.
Stevens's countenance was stony, his gaze defiant. His mission that day
was unique. He was about to announce that the House of Representatives had voted to impeach the president. Though sick and stooped at
seventy-five, Stevens could radiate a fearful intensity, a "will of inherent
and uncommon might." His "brilliant eye," wrote one correspondent
that evening, "spoke of a strength within equal to the Waterloo struggle
before him." Stevens's resolve to oust Johnson hardened daily. The president, he intoned with extravagant hyperbole, "is guilty of as atrocious
attempts to usurp the liberty and destroy the happiness of this nation, as
were ever perpetrated by the most detestable tyrant who ever oppressed
his fellow men."

The Senate galleries overflowed with spectators as snow swirled outside. Most of the 54 senators and 185 congressmen wedged themselves
into the chamber. An eerie silence descended at 1 P.M. as Stevens and
John Bingham of Ohio made their way toward the podium, then stopped.

151

For a long breathless moment, the anxious throng watched the pair standing before Ben Wade of Ohio, president pro tempore of the Senate. The rough-hewn Wade would take over the White House if Andrew Johnson were deposed. Stevens and Bingham wore somber black, contrasting with the flaming reds and yellows of the Senate's decor. The falling snow dimmed the skylight overhead, but the glow from gas jets was bright.

It was a moment for reflection on the nation and its president. Having begun in the tragedy of Lincoln's assassination and the euphoria of victory over the Confederacy, Andrew Johnson's term in office seemed a freakish catastrophe. Years of public truculence and private intransigence had led him, and the nation, to this point. Now the House would prosecute him before the Senate for high crimes and misdemeanors. If the upper house convicted by a two-thirds majority, Johnson would be the first president ever ejected from office.

Stevens and Bingham deliver the impeachment resolution to the Senate, February 25, 1868.

Recognized by Senator Wade, Stevens surprised the crowd by answering in a strong voice. He invoked the authority of the House of Representatives and the people of the United States, then announced, "We do impeach Andrew Johnson, President of the United States, of high crimes and misdemeanors in office." With no trace of embarrassment, Stevens added that the House "in due time" would deliver "particular articles of impeachment and make good the same." In other words, Johnson had committed high crimes and misdemeanors, but the House had not yet decided which ones to pursue. Wade appointed a committee to receive specific charges when the House adopted them.

Stevens and Bingham withdrew. The old man rode in a chair, carried by two brawny attendants, back to the House side of the Capitol. There the two congressmen reported what they had done. Then Stevens lay down to rest in a nearby room.

The House impeachment committee was already working, having first met the day before. The committee members braved a Washington snowstorm that the *Chicago Tribune* interpreted politically as a reminder that "there is a North, pure, bright, and cold as justice." A subcommittee of the usual impeachment hands—Stevens, Boutwell, Bingham, and Wilson—began to assemble the evidence and draft articles of impeachment.

Taking over the Capitol room of the House Judiciary Committee, the subcommittee set a brisk timetable: articles to be released in two days, then approved by the House and presented to the Senate in six days. As described by Stevens in an interview, the subcommittee's procedure reflected the egotism of its members. Each was preparing his own impeachment articles, which the subcommittee would sort through and aggregate. This approach, Stevens admitted, risked disagreements over each member's favorites, but he hoped for the best. Asked if he still despised moderate Republicans as cowards, Stevens declared, "No, they are not cowards now because they have been pushed to the wall and are fighting like brave men."

The collision in the Capitol, one correspondent recalled, riveted the nation and "stirred the whole North to its very depths."

[T]here was not a moment when men's opinions were not hot; not a moment when rumor and rancor were not in the air; not a moment when hearts did not tremble for the Republic. Day by day the people hung on the news from Washington and constantly hungered and thirsted for more.

With political momentum on their side, the impeachers leaned into the task. On Wednesday, February 26, they took testimony from Lorenzo Thomas, from General Emory, head of the Washington garrison, and from Emory's second-in-command. The facts, though, were not in dispute. The principal arguments would be legal ones: What did the president intend when he sent Lorenzo Thomas to the War Office? Did his actions, combined with his intent, constitute an impeachable offense? What did the Tenure of Office Act really mean?

The subcommittee struggled to reach agreement. Some wanted only three impeachment articles. Others proposed five or six. A visitor to their deliberations found Stevens and Bingham arguing. "Both are profane," the visitor recorded in his diary, "but Stevens is especially so." Looking thin and haggard, the Pennsylvanian sipped wine or brandy through every drafting session, pushing the work along, the "ruling spirit" of the group.

The pressure to add articles grew stronger. The list reached six, then eight. They would not include any charges from the November impeachment report that the House had rejected. Reviving those claims, the *New York Times* reported, was deemed "fatal to the moral and legal effect of the prosecution."

Johnson had one last ploy for avoiding impeachment: He hoped to take the starch out of the Republicans by submitting key legal issues to the courts, starting with the constitutionality of the Tenure of Office Act and whether he had the constitutional power to remove Stanton. Shouldn't the Supreme Court, rather than the partisan Senate, decide those issues?

The press filled with predictions that the attorney general would file a lawsuit raising those questions, but the problem with this strategy was time. A lawsuit would take too long. It would start before a single district court judge in Washington City, followed by an appeal to the full district court, which could not act until May. That court's decision would not be reviewed by the Supreme Court until December. No one thought the proceedings could be expedited, which meant that no decision could issue until after the presidential election, a few months before Johnson's term of office expired. The Senate impeachment trial would end long before then.

Johnson's team figured out a shortcut, one that could take advantage of Stanton's lawsuit against Thomas. If Judge Cartter kept the adjutant general on bail, or under any form of restraint, Thomas could demand a writ of habeas corpus directly from the Supreme Court. Then the eight justices—at least five of whom were reckoned favorable to the president—could decide the constitutionality of the Tenure of Office Act. With luck, that decision would come before a Senate trial ended.

Edwin Stanton, barricaded in the War Office, performed the same legal analysis. Though Stanton doubtless had enjoyed the spectacle of Thomas under arrest, the war secretary was not sentimental about legal strategies. If prosecuting Thomas could thwart impeachment, he would abandon the case.

Thomas appeared in Judge Cartter's chambers at 10 A.M. on Wednesday, February 26. When his lawyer asked for a writ of habeas corpus, Stanton's lawyer moved to drop the prosecution. After all, he explained, the adjutant general no longer threatened to take the War Department by force. The ploy forced Thomas's counsel to insist that the prosecutor must proceed against his client, an awkward argument for any defense lawyer. The judge had no trouble dismissing the matter. When Thomas called for his mail at the War Department a day later, he complained he had been "euchred . . . again."

Thomas's days took on a depressing routine. He presented himself to the president in the morning. If Johnson was feeling combative, he directed Thomas to demand control of the War Department. The adjutant general would trudge over to Stanton's office, make the demand, be denied, report his failure to the White House, and return home. If the president felt less aggressive or was involved in other business, Thomas was allowed to call quietly at the War Department for his mail and then head home. Sometimes he stopped to confer with his lawyers. As the Radical *Philadelphia Press* wrote with glee, he "receives for this arduous duty the salary of a brigadier general." Stanton had locked the adjutant general's office at the War Department, denying Thomas the key until he agreed to perform that job, and that job only. Thomas, Johnson's pawn in the game, could not accept those terms.

Thomas sued Stanton for wrongfully denying his right to be interim war secretary, demanding $150,000 in damages. The case was destined for that limbo where insincere lawsuits drift. Johnson could not shift into the courts the fight for his political life. The battle would be in the Senate, on impeachment articles approved by the House of Representatives.

When George Boutwell of Massachusetts rose in the House on Leap Day—Saturday, February 29—the novelty of impeachment was wearing off, but the thrill remained. Once more, the galleries overflowed with fascinated citizens of both races and both sexes. Again, the House of Representatives was poised to do something for the first time in history: it would debate what specific charges should be lodged against a president it already had impeached.

Boutwell presented ten articles of impeachment. As the clerk read them aloud, confusion spread. The articles were a jumbled horror. Having failed a few months before with broad and amorphous impeachment allegations, the impeachers had careened to the other extreme, keeping their focus painfully narrow and obscurely legalistic.

The first nine articles addressed only the Thomas-Stanton confrontation, dissecting it into overlapping allegations of "high misdemeanors" and "high crimes." The House would not deploy impeachment as a political remedy, but would pursue it as an ersatz criminal prosecution. As *The Nation* observed, Johnson was impeached because he had finally "committed a distinct and palpable violation of the law," though the offense of firing Stanton was not "by any means the worst in a moral point of view."

This strategy raised problems. Shrinking the scope of the articles seemed to cheapen the enterprise. The impeachers were reduced to charging the "great criminal of the age"—the man who betrayed the sacrifice of Union soldiers while abandoning the freed slaves to lives of want and oppression—with misapplying a personnel statute. To make these small-gauged articles seem proportionate to Johnson's enormous crimes, the impeachers charged his misstep as nine separate violations that grew more mystifying as they multiplied. The strategy was unnecessarily complex. It would take only one successful impeachment article to remove the president. Having many overlapping allegations would do the prosecution no good.

The first article charged Johnson with violating the Tenure of Office Act when he dismissed Stanton; the second alleged that he violated the same law by appointing Thomas as interim war secretary. Those two articles might seem redundant—mirror images of the same violation—but at least they could readily be understood. The real trouble started with the third article, which charged Johnson with unconstitutionally appointing Thomas to a position that was not vacant. Only unadorned hairsplitting could distinguish this allegation from the one before it.

Serious incoherence set in with the next five charges, all alleging conspiracy between Thomas and Johnson. Article IV alleged that Johnson violated the federal conspiracy law when he agreed with Thomas to drive Stanton from office, while Article V charged that the same conspirators attempted to use *force* to the same end, in violation of the Tenure of Office Act. The sixth stated that the same conspiracy violated both statutes; Article VII alleged a conspiracy to violate the Tenure of Office Act *without* using force. Citizens in the House galleries had to be scratching their heads.

The eighth article repeated the conspiracy motif, this time charging that Johnson and Thomas conspired to seize the *property* of the War Department. Article IX charged the president with firing Stanton for the purpose of gaining control over War Department funds. The modern mind paces nervously around these last two articles. Isn't the president *supposed* to have control over government property and funds?

Happily for those in attendance, the final article was on a different subject; unhappily for the impeachers, it had no foundation. Article IX concerned President Johnson's meeting with General Emory on February 22, just the week before, during which he asked about the disposition of federal troops in Washington City. The article charged Johnson with instructing Emory that the Constitution invalidated the statute requiring all army orders to pass through General Grant. That Emory's testimony would not directly support the allegation, and that the president might be entitled to state his opinion on the subject, had not deterred the impeachers.

Boutwell betrayed no embarrassment over these unfortunate impeachment articles, which one Senate aide thought "savor of the attorney too much." Modestly, Boutwell invited the House to revise or replace the articles as it saw fit: "We have no special attachment," he said, "to the particular words and phrases employed." They had little enough reason for such attachment.

The House debate was scheduled for all day Saturday and the following Monday. Seeing the impeachment articles for the first time that afternoon, several congressmen urged the House to slow down. Radical Republicans bemoaned the narrowness of the articles, which addressed only two episodes of Johnson's many misdeeds. They ached to charge the president with his *real* crimes, all of them. A Democrat denounced the charges as trifling, while another observed that "ten articles have been presented, or rather ten specifications of one article."

Another theatrical moment arose when Stevens closed debate on Monday, March 2. His words were bitter. Increasingly gaunt and pale, he began to read his speech from a seat facing the House. "Never," he began, his voice weak, "was a great malefactor so gently treated as Andrew Johnson." The House began to fall silent. Congressmen again strained to hear the words. This time strength came to the Pennsylvanian. He kept speaking. He complained that the committee, "determined to deal gently with the President," had omitted many crimes from the impeachment articles. The articles covered, he lamented, only "the most trifling crimes and misdemeanors."

Years began to fall away as the old man justified each article in turn. Stevens stood up. He began to gesture and his voice reached the gallery. Though trifling, he said, the articles should be approved so the nation could finally be rid of this pestilence in the White House. "Unfortunate man!" Stevens said to the rapt chamber, "thus surrounded, hampered, tangled in the meshes of his own wickedness—unfortunate, unhappy man, behold your doom."

Boutwell brought forward revised impeachment articles, which now numbered only nine, one of the conspiracy articles having been blessedly dropped. The House rejected motions to add articles. Ben Butler of Massachusetts presented a lengthy new charge. After reciting several of the president's stump speeches denouncing Congress, Butler's article accused him of the high misdemeanor of bringing the presidency "into

THE LAST SPEECH ON IMPEACHMENT—THADDEUS STEVENS CLOSING THE DEBATE IN THE HOUSE, March 2.—[Sketched by T. R. Davis.]

Stevens, closing debate on impeachment, March 2, 1868.

contempt, ridicule, and disgrace." Here was a political offense pure and simple. Butler argued that his article tracked one presented against Supreme Court Justice Samuel Chase more than sixty years earlier (one that was rejected by the Senate). Butler's proposal was defeated—for the time being. The House then approved by overwhelming margins each of the nine articles proposed by the committee.

The House turned to designating those members who would act as prosecutors during the Senate trial, preparing the case and presenting the evidence. They would be the public face of the impeachment effort, standing in the Senate chamber and demanding the conviction of Andrew Johnson. The Republican caucus had designated seven "managers," beginning with Boutwell (a leading Radical) and Bingham and Wilson (leading moderates). In a poignant turn, the caucus on its first ballot passed over Stevens. Many doubted he was strong enough to be an effective prosecutor. On a second ballot, those doubts yielded to respect for his relentless opposition to Johnson.

Three more Radicals were less obvious choices as managers. Dash-

159

ing John Logan of Illinois commanded the Grand Army of the Republic, but was no great shakes as a lawyer. Thomas Williams of Pennsylvania was a respected lawyer, but was extreme in his hatred for the president. He had written the ineffective majority report for the impeachment resolution rejected by the House only ten weeks before.

And then there was Ben Butler of Massachusetts. Though he had served in Congress for less than a year, Butler would become the lead prosecutor. The *New York Times* explained that Butler was chosen as a House manager because of "his great ability and fertility of resource as a criminal lawyer." The *Chicago Tribune* offered the jest that Butler "was one of the greatest criminal lawyers in the country, and Johnson the greatest criminal." Few men in public life have overcome such memorably odd physical attributes. Touching lightly on Butler's bald pate, drooping eyelid, and severe case of strabismus (cross-eyes), a Civil War officer left this description:

> With his head set immediately on a stout shapeless body, his very squinting eyes, and a set of legs and arms that look as if made for somebody else, and hastily glued to him by mistake, [Butler] presents a combination of Victor Emanuel [King of Savoy], Aesop, [and] Richard III, which is very confusing to the mind.

One more crafty lawyer in a Congress that teemed with them, Butler had energy and intelligence that propelled him through a tumultuous public career. A lifelong Democrat, in 1860 Butler supported Jefferson Davis of Mississippi for president. He nimbly switched to the Union side when Southern guns fired on Fort Sumter. Securing a military command for which he had no qualifications, Butler became a Northern hero by welcoming escaped slaves into his camp. His army service mixed political triumphs with military failures. The popularity of "Old Cockeye" grew in the North when Southerners named him "Beast" for his heavy-handed occupation of New Orleans, then spiked again when he was christened "Spoons" for pilfering the silver from the Louisiana mansion where he made his headquarters. One war-derived nickname—"Bottled-Up Butler"—was less welcome, reflecting a military campaign during which his "bottled up" army was useless. According to the Massachusetts general, he declined Lincoln's offer of second spot on the 1864

Republican ticket, the place that went to Andrew Johnson. Many, how-ever, doubt the tale.

By the time Butler crashed into the House of Representatives in March of 1867, the former Democrat had become a full-fledged Radical Republican. One Republican was not surprised by the transformation, noting that "it never was General Butler's habit to be moderate." Thought by many to be the political heir to Stevens, Butler was already driving his finger into the eye of moderate John Bingham within three weeks of arriving in Congress. Observing Bingham standing on the Democratic side of the House, Butler declared the Ohioan had "got over to the other side not only in body, but in spirit." Bingham, thin-skinned in the best of times, answered by denouncing Butler as a man "who recorded his vote more than fifty times for Jefferson Davis, the arch-traitor of this rebellion, as his candidate for President of the United States." Then they took the gloves off.

Referring to one of Butler's military failures, Bingham rejected with "scorn and contempt" the remarks of "the hero of Fort Fisher not taken, or Fort Fisher taken." Butler replied that during the war "the only victim of [Bingham's] prowess that I know of was an innocent woman hung upon the scaffold, one Mrs. Surratt" (one of the Booth conspirators). Drawing on the rich store of Butler nicknames, Bingham rejoined that the general's accusations were "fit to come from one who lives in a bottle and is fed with a spoon."

Remembering that and other encounters with Butler, John Bingham pitched a fit when the House Speaker announced the seven managers on March 2. Bingham was incensed to find his name in third position on the list, after Stevens and Butler. By reading the names in that order, the Speaker seemed to imply that Stevens would be chairman with Butler as his second. "I'll be damned if I serve under Butler," Bingham exploded. "It is no use to argue, gentlemen. I won't do it."

The House sidestepped Bingham's flare-up by electing the manag-ers without designating a chairman. The Ohioan was gratified to com-mand the highest total vote, but was affronted anew when the managers themselves chose George Boutwell as their chairman. Intolerable! Bing-ham promptly announced his resignation as manager. To make peace, Boutwell declined the chairmanship in favor of the touchy prima donna from Ohio. Because Bingham led the moderate and conservative Republicans, the managers could not afford to lose him from the prosecution team.

The managers quickly approved two more impeachment articles, starting with Butler's "stump-speech" article. The full House was restrained in its enthusiasm for that one, with eleven Republicans actually voting against it. No such diffidence applied to the final article. Adopted by a wide margin after no debate, Article XI would play a large role in the trial to come.

Proposed by Stevens and Wilson of Iowa, this last article was a clever mélange of complaints about the president: that he declared in 1866 that Congress represented only some of the states and had no power to propose amendments to the Constitution; that he had removed Stanton as war secretary in violation of the Tenure of Office Act; that he evaded the statute that required him to deliver military orders through General Grant; and that he thwarted the first Reconstruction Act. Article XI thus mixed a criminal offense (the Stanton question) with political ones. By lumping several theories together, it aimed to sweep up the votes of senators who accepted one or another of those theories, combining them all (the drafters hoped) into a two-thirds majority for conviction.

There was no precedent for such a "catch-all" impeachment article, which sharply tilts the odds against the impeached official. The accused cannot challenge allegations one at a time, but must confront several at once. In its one-sidedness, Article XI bears the handprint of Stevens's unabashed drive to remove Johnson from office. Regrettably, it became a model for future impeachments, which similarly lumped a range of charges into single impeachment articles. The technique is designed to make it easier to vote for conviction. If satisfied that at least one of many allegations has been proved, a senator is justified in voting to convict. Even if there is no two-thirds majority on any single allegation, a catch-all impeachment article may bring conviction as some senators are persuaded by allegation "A," others by allegation "B," and so on.

To deliver the impeachment articles on Wednesday, March 4, the entire body of House Republicans marched in a sober column from their chamber, through the Capitol rotunda, and into the Senate. Leading the column, the seven managers gave no hint of their rocky relations with each

*Members of the House of Representatives march through
the Capitol rotunda to the Senate.*

other. Inside the Senate, Bingham and Boutwell led the procession, arm in arm, followed by Butler and Wilson, then Logan and Williams. Stevens came last, slowly passing down the Senate's center aisle, no longer carried in his chair but with a friend supporting him on either side. Because of his still fierce visage, because his grip on life seemed so slight, because he remained the soul of the impeachment, the Pennsylvanian took central place in the tableau even without a speaking part.

Bingham rose after the managers sat in cushioned armchairs at the front of the chamber. The other congressmen stood in a semicircle behind the senators' desks. Bingham read through the eleven impeachment articles, a tedious journey through dense legal undergrowth that nevertheless commanded the chamber's full attention. Those present had to marvel at the speed with which the House had acted. Less than two weeks had passed since Lorenzo Thomas tried to claim Stanton's office.

As it moved from one side of the Capitol to the other, the impeachment story was changing in important ways, starting at the White House.

The reality of impeachment sobered the president. He had thrown caution to the winds when he placed his political hopes on the slight shoulders of Lorenzo Thomas. The impeachment stampede had a salutary effect on Johnson's decision-making. For the next ninety days, he seemed to remember the skills that had served him through a long political career. He stopped issuing enraged and enraging proclamations, or flinging antagonistic barbs in extemporaneous statements. In the words of one congressman, he became "guarded against the folly of talking, which was his easily besetting sin." A committee from Baltimore presented him with a resolution of support in late February. Johnson's short remarks were dignified and determined. With his office on the line and the prospect of permanent disgrace yawning before him, Johnson also would discover compromise, an act he had mostly foresworn since becoming president.

The president turned to advisers and began to listen to them. Johnson looked first to Attorney General Stanberry, who was designated lead counsel for the defense. The president also consulted with Jeremiah Black, longtime Democratic power in Pennsylvania and a fixture in Buchanan's Cabinet. An important early recruit to the defense team was former Supreme Court Justice Benjamin Curtis, who contributed stature and unquestioned legal skills. Curtis brought political assets, as well. He was a Boston Republican, though a conservative one, and had dissented from the hateful *Dred Scott* ruling, which had helped precipitate the Civil War.

Surveying the field before them, Johnson's team faced daunting challenges. The Republican majority in the Senate was overwhelming. Of the 54 senators, only 9 were Democrats. The Democrats could be counted on to oppose impeachment even if they did not care for Johnson. Three Republican senators consistently voted for Johnson's policies and were solid for him. That made 12 votes for the defense. To avoid conviction by a two-thirds majority, Johnson needed 19 votes, so he had to win over 7 more Republicans. That number—7 Republicans—would dominate impeachment strategies, press speculation, and backroom maneuvering.

At this early stage, an aide proposed that the president use his power over patronage to secure support from individual senators. Johnson was irate. "I will do nothing of the kind," he stormed. "If acquitted, I will not owe it to bribery. I would rather be convicted than buy acquittal." He would change his mind on that point.

Changes also loomed on the prosecution side. Stevens could take pride in having finally, on his third try, steered a presidential impeachment through the House. No other man had done that. But the Pennsylvanian had reached his limit. He might rally his dwindling powers to deliver a speech for twenty minutes, but he could not manage a grueling, weeks-long trial. He was too weak and too sick. The voting for the seven House managers, which nearly omitted him entirely, recognized this reality. Of the impeachment articles, only the last one (Article XI) reflected Stevens's views. He might still contribute insights and stratagems. He could be the living, barely breathing symbol of Radical virtue, and of Radical vengeance. But younger men would have to do the hard work. Who would do it? Could someone, or a team of two or three, make up for the loss of Stevens's leadership?

For the next ten weeks, the national government largely stopped functioning as its officials and workers were transfixed by the inexorable impeachment process. "Nothing is being done because of impeachment," the *New York Times* reported from Washington City. "Nothing else is noticeable; neither the price of coal, nor the budding of the crocuses in the Capitol Grounds, nor the coming of Arkansas quietly back into the fold of the Union." In Philadelphia and Cincinnati, in New York and Chester County, Pennsylvania, marchers demonstrated in support of the president or of Congress.

Yet Americans were learning to live with the prospect that the president would be ejected and replaced by Ben Wade of Ohio. The nation's financial market, which involved mostly trading between gold and currency in New York, was reasonably stable. There was room on the front pages for news of a fire in New York that consumed most of the animals in P. T. Barnum's circus; survivors included an elephant, a giraffe, a leopard, and a kangaroo.

Mrs. Mary Logan, wife of the House manager from Illinois, remembered Washington's winter of 1868 as socially brilliant. The president's daughters mounted fine events at the White House. Through the week when the House was impeaching him, Johnson presided over a dinner for senators, another for Supreme Court justices, and greeted guests at receptions. Ben Butler staged the party of the season for the debut of his daughter, Blanche, in his mansion at the corner of I and 15th streets. Decorated with thousands of delicate camellias, Butler's house filled up with everyone of distinction. Wherever society met, Mrs. Logan recalled, "General and Mrs. Grant were the recipients of much attention."

Charles Dickens's speaking tour reached Washington in early February. The novelist spent an entire evening with Senator Charles Sumner of Massachusetts and Edwin Stanton (before he locked himself in his office). The war secretary, ever the pedant, regaled Dickens by reciting from memory long passages from *The Pickwick Papers*.

By early March, fears had receded of armed battles in the streets. The nation would allow the impeachment process to proceed, to perform its intended function as a peaceful means for deciding whether to remove a bad president. A sure sign of reduced tensions was Stanton's appearance on the sidewalk in front of the War Department, unguarded, consulting with a subordinate. His continuing occupation of that building required a critical adjustment, since President Johnson refused to have any contact with him, or with General Grant. The faithful assistant adjutant general, Edward Townsend, became the "neutral ground" for the three sulking principals: Each sent his orders to Townsend, he recalled, "and by a little tact I managed to avoid any question of jurisdiction or other difficulty." As for the reports that Stanton and Grant ordinarily would have sent to Johnson, those went to Congress instead. Such rickety communication links might not have served in a military crisis, but they held up for the next three months.

Senate President Pro Tem Ben Wade, faced with the possibility of moving into the Executive Mansion in a matter of weeks, was in an awkward spot. The press speculated on the members of his Cabinet, while office-seekers laid siege to him. He was widely mentioned as a possible running mate with General Grant in the fall. In an early newspaper interview, he tried to avoid unseemly eagerness for the presidency, insisting, "I do not covet the position." Yet the specter of Wade in the White House, a ripsnorting Radical as chief executive, would figure prominently in the outcome of the trial.

Wade's future, and that of the nation, now lay in the hands of the fifty-four men of the Senate. And, of course, in the hands of the lawyers who would wage the impeachment battle and the political operatives who would use every tool at their disposal to influence the verdict.

14

SEND IN THE LAWYERS

MARCH 5–29, 1868

We are all nervous about delay in the impeachment case. That
is the overshadowing all-absorbing question with the country
just now. Like an aching tooth, everyone is impatient to have
the old man out.

JOSEPH MEDILL, *CHICAGO TRIBUNE*,
MARCH 18, 1869

THE TEAM OF House managers boasted deep legal talent and wide
experience. Stevens had defended fifty murder cases and claimed
he lost only one. Ben Butler was a feared courtroom advocate with an
extensive criminal practice. He had argued (and lost) the leading Supreme Court case on the military's wartime powers to detain civilians.
John Bingham led the 1862 impeachment of Judge West Humphreys,
the court-martial of the Army's surgeon general, and the prosecution of
the Booth conspirators. Wilson and Boutwell were intelligent lawyers.
Williams and Logan were determined ones who accepted their supporting roles. Yet when it came time for the team of House managers to
perform, the whole proved to be far less than the sum of its parts. They
made a hash of the most important case of the nineteenth century.

Building a team of trial lawyers is no easy task. Courtroom advocates
have strong personalities, healthy self-esteem, and an affection for speaking at length. Balancing robust egos requires tact, judgment, and leader-

ship. Only one singer can perform each aria, and each show can feature only so many lead singers. The balancing act grows more challenging when the lawyers are also politicians with long habits of self-promotion and interpersonal manipulation. Indeed, there is something odd about confiding a critical prosecution to congressmen rather than to professional advocates, though doing so underscores the political nature of impeachment.

Of the managers, only Stevens could have led the team effectively. As the emotional heart of the quest to be rid of Andrew Johnson, Stevens could have commanded the senators' respect. As an acute strategist who understood how weak Johnson was politically, he could have pressed for a streamlined case and an early vote. But Stevens was too frail. He missed meetings of the committee managers, while the press continued its ghoulish reports on his cadaverlike appearance. Visibly clinging to life, he could not prosecute the case he cared more about than anything else on earth.

For all the talents of the House managers, none could effectively take over for Stevens. Bingham was too waspish. Boutwell was too aloof. And Butler—well, Butler became the lead prosecutor so the failure fell mostly on his bullish frame.

The managers' failures were not due to lack of effort. Within three days of delivering the impeachment articles to the Senate, they were taking testimony in closed session. In the first week, they heard twelve witnesses. With Butler posing most of the questions, they heard from twelve more witnesses before the trial began at the end of March. The effort was largely misplaced. But for Lorenzo Thomas, the witnesses were peripheral or routine. The committee heard from stenographers who recorded the president's public tirades in 1866. They asked a Western Union official about the president's telegrams. Clerks explained the paperwork for the Stanton firing. The managers quizzed Colonel Moore, the president's closest aide, but mostly asked him whether Thomas was performing any functions as secretary of war, not a central question for the impeachment. Even with Stanton offering ideas and assistance from his pied-à-terre at the War Department, the fact-gathering was not particularly productive.

After being summoned to the committee room as a witness, a news-

The House managers (seated, l. to r., Ben Butler of Massachusetts, Thaddeus Stevens and Thomas Williams of Pennsylvania, John Bingham of Ohio; standing, James Wilson of Iowa, George Boutwell of Massachusetts, John Logan of Illinois).

paper reporter sketched a peculiar portrait of the managers. Stevens sat with his club foot resting on a table before him, his eyes closed and his brown wig askew. Butler stood before a fire, studying a sheaf of papers and smoking furiously. Bingham, Boutwell, Williams, and Wilson, immersed in law books, each occupied one side of a table. And so they all remained, silently, for ten minutes.

Without opening his eyes, Stevens posed a languid question about a recent letter from Chief Justice Salmon P. Chase, who was presiding over the trial. After a minute passed without a response, Stevens directed the question to Wilson. The Iowan briefly disparaged Chase's missive. Stevens called the chief justice "a damned political trickster," then recounted a tale from the beginning of the Civil War, when Chase argued that the North should let the Southern states secede without a fight. Distracted from their studies, the other managers joined a general discussion of Chase's qualities.

The managers did not spend all their time together in the committee room. They had other political interests. As chairman of the Reconstruction Committee, Stevens pushed through a bill to set the terms for readmitting Alabama as a state, then released a public letter announcing that the Declaration of Independence contemplated Negro suffrage. Butler issued a lengthy statement on how the nation's heavy war debts should be repaid.

By sheer energy and industry, Butler seized leadership of the group. The burly, cockeyed former Democrat, whose charisma somehow overcame his mismatched features, was an outrageous, polarizing figure. "No man in the broad land," observed one of the few female correspondents of the day, "is so fearfully hated." A Shakespearian denunciation chastised Butler as

> hell's blackest imp . . . the unclean, perjured, false-hearted product of Massachusetts civilization; the meanest thief, the dirtiest knave God ever gave breath to; total depravity personified; that baggy-faced fruit of perdition, Beast Butler!

General Ben Butler during the Civil War.

Even Butler's enemies admitted his substantial gifts, including a powerful speaking style and a fearlessness that resembled audacity. He was quick in debate, well read, and could be disciplined in his reasoning. Perhaps as important, he had a capacity for hard work.

Butler proposed which witnesses should be summoned, dominated their questioning, and set the managers' agenda. He handled his colleagues with finesse. When Bingham demanded to be chairman of the committee, Butler kept his head down. He was after power, not titles. Then Butler angled to make the trial's opening speech. He suggested that the chore usually descended upon the "youngest counsel, and that is myself." His colleagues fell for it.

Early on, Butler made two contradictory judgments about the prosecution strategy. First, he proposed to try the case at "railroad speed," taking advantage of then modern technology (railroads and telegrams) to assemble and present the case quickly. When the defense asked for forty days to prepare for trial, Butler scoffed that the flood destroyed the world in that time. The national crisis required a speedy trial to remove the president. Also, a relaxed pace might provide too much time for second thoughts, especially as the natural end of Johnson's term drew ever closer.

Butler's commitment to railroad speed was thwarted, however, by his second strategic decision. For a short time, the managers dithered over the tone to strike before the Senate. They were unsure of the proofs that would be required in this unique form of trial. Butler resolved to try the case "upon the same rules of evidence, and in the same manner as I would try a horse case"—that is, a case of horse-stealing. And so he did, putting on a display of pettifoggery that reflected the range of technical arcana that prevailed in nineteenth-century courts. Butler haggled over every jot and tittle of proof. He badgered witnesses, belittled opposing counsel, and made himself the central figure of most trial days. It was a blunder, extending the trial and alienating moderate and conservative Republicans whose votes he needed.

THE TRIAL TEAMS

The House Managers (Prosecutors)

Benjamin Butler	Controversial Civil War general and Radical congressman from Massachusetts, in his first term in Congress.
John Bingham	Leader of Republican moderates in the House and nominal chair of the House Impeachment Committee.
Thaddeus Stevens	Chairman of the House Ways and Means Committee and the leader of the Radicals, but too sick to take a major trial role.
George Boutwell	Radical congressman from Massachusetts and leader of the failed impeachment effort in December 1867.
James Wilson	A moderate from Iowa and chair of the Judiciary Committee, Wilson opposed the impeachment drive in December 1867.
Thomas Williams	From Pennsylvania, a violent opponent of President Johnson.
John Logan	An Illinois Radical, former Civil War general and head of the Grand Army of the Republic (Union Army veterans).

The Defense Lawyers

Henry Stanberry	An Ohioan, Stanberry resigned as attorney general to lead Johnson's defense.
Benjamin Curtis	Massachusetts Republican and former Supreme Court justice.
Jeremiah Black	Pennsylvania Democrat and former Cabinet member for President Buchanan; resigned before the trial began.
William Evarts	A Republican added at the last minute; a New York associate of Secretary of State William Seward.
William Groesbeck	A former Democratic congressman from Ohio.
Thomas Nelson	A former Tennessee adversary of the president, then an ally.

The president built his defense team incrementally, starting with the sixty-five-year-old attorney general, Henry Stanberry. Having spent most of his life in southern Ohio and Kentucky, the tall, lanky Stanberry came to Washington in 1866 to serve as Butler's co-counsel in the Supreme Court dispute over the powers of military commissions. Though he lost the case, Stanberry impressed the president, who wanted to appoint him to the Supreme Court. In eighteen months as attorney general, Stanberry earned Johnson's confidence. He resigned that post on March 11 to stifle any grumbling that he could not faithfully serve both as attorney general and as the president's chief defender.

As lobbyist Sam Ward had recommended, the defense team reflected political balance as well as legal acumen. Former Justice Curtis and Stanberry were Republicans. Jeremiah Black was a Democrat. Two more Democrats were signed up: William Groesbeck of Ohio and Thomas Nelson of Tennessee, a familiar face from the president's home state. The last lawyer to join the team, Republican William Evarts of New

York, would prove the most important one, even though there was disagreement over whether to add him at all.

The defenders faced formidable challenges. In a very short time, they had to master the legal arguments surrounding impeachment and to anticipate the prosecution's factual presentation. Fortunately for them, the managers announced most of their strategies through the newspapers, so there would be few surprises at trial. The president's lawyers also needed to get control over their client. Johnson could damage his own case more than anyone else could. Every public statement and action posed risks, and the headstrong Johnson had a long track record of unwise public utterances. For a defense lawyer, few terrors rival those posed by a client who likes to swap stories with newspaper reporters into the night.

Sure enough, on the evening of March 9 the president unburdened himself to a favored reporter from the Democratic *New York World*. Insisting that he was unfazed by the impeachment effort and labeling Stanton "a marplot in this administration," Johnson unveiled a detailed defense that included precedents from the days of John Adams. He noted bitterly that he was facing trial in the Senate, but former Confederate President Jefferson Davis still had not been tried for treason. On the very next day, Stanberry made his first demand on his client. The newspaper interviews had to stop. Those conversations, the lawyer insisted, "injure your case and embarrass your counsel." Taken aback, Johnson attempted an apology. No one in the room supported him. All had gnashed their teeth over the president's nocturnal conversations with the press. One Cabinet member called them "unaccountable and inexcusable."

The first defense chore was to draft an answer to the impeachment articles. Jeremiah Black was in the middle of a week-long argument before the Supreme Court, while Stanberry was still attorney general. With the other defenders en route to Washington, the job fell to Curtis. Writing alone in his room at Willard's Hotel, the former Supreme Court justice felt the burden of his responsibility. He sought help from his brother, a legal scholar (George Ticknor Curtis). Buoyed by his impressions of the president's "calm, honest sincerity," Curtis finished in time. Though long and weighed down with every technical defense the Curtis brothers could contrive, the thrust of the president's case remained clear:

Stanton was not protected by the Tenure of Office Act; the president had constitutional power to remove him regardless of that statute; and Johnson had no intent to violate the law but had wished only to elicit a judicial decision of the legal questions involved.

Stanberry was eager for battle. On March 16, he announced to Johnson that he was "in regular training, like a prize-fighter," including twice-a-day rubdowns. "Don't lose a moment's sleep," he advised the president. "You will come out of it brighter than you have ever shone." The lawyer added that if he could stay healthy for the trial, "I will be willing to be sick during the balance of my life." Stanberry had no idea, of course, that he would soon fall seriously ill.

The White House library was set aside for the lawyers. Johnson met with them for hours on end. As a client, he was a handful. He declared one day that unless the defense was conducted as he wished, he would present it himself. Nine days later, he repeated the threat. The lawyers, Colonel Moore noted laconically in his diary, "were unanimous in the opinion that he should not attend [the Senate] in person." Dissatisfied with the draft answer to Stevens's Article XI, Johnson prepared a package of materials to explain how to challenge it. Johnson's focus on impeachment curtailed his time for public business. In Cabinet meetings, he seemed uncertain, anxious, and distracted.

As the trial date neared, the president's agitation subsided. He became "quite philosophic," according to one aide. "I think he believed firmly he would be convicted, that nothing could avert his expulsion, and he submitted calmly as to a decree of fate." Johnson turned aside an embarrassing demand from Jeremiah Black, the Democratic lawyer. In a crude attempt to take advantage of his position as the president's defender, Black sought help for clients involved in a contest over guano deposits on the Caribbean island of Alta Vela. He asked that an American warship be sent to support his clients. Without such intervention, the lawyer insisted, he could not handle the impeachment trial. Johnson bade Black farewell, telling Colonel Moore that the lawyer had "made a pretty record—one which will do him far more injury than it can me."

The remaining defense lawyers dug into their case with enthusiasm and mutual respect. Their task may have been eased when a recurrence of kidney stones sidelined the president in the last week of March.

• • •

To mount the first presidential impeachment trial, the senators had to address many practical issues, starting with the physical arrangements in their chamber. They set up tables at the front of the room for the House managers and the president's counsel, adding two hundred cane-seat chairs in the rear for visiting congressmen. Seven telegraph wires were installed to ensure speedy transmission of press reports to a waiting nation. The Senate resolved to issue tickets for admission to its galleries. Each senator received six tickets for each trial day, with smaller numbers going to other officials. One consequence of the ticket system was to exclude blacks, who had avidly watched the impeachment in the House but lacked the connections necessary to acquire Senate tickets. This limitation was unmistakable when the Senate first convened as a court in mid-March: the House members marched from the House to the Senate, two abreast, through the Capitol rotunda, between "two dense lines of blacks, forming a corridor from door to door." The blacks in the rotunda lacked tickets to enter the Senate.

A more difficult problem arose when Chief Justice Chase entered the Senate on March 4 to administer to each senator the oath required by the Constitution. When Ben Wade of Ohio rose to take the oath, an Indiana Democrat objected. Because a conviction would vault Wade into the White House, he said, the Senate president pro tem should be disqualified from voting on the impeachment articles. After all, his pow-

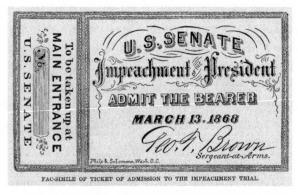

FAC-SIMILE OF TICKET OF ADMISSION TO THE IMPEACHMENT TRIAL.

Impeachment trial ticket.

erful self-interest would disqualify him from sitting on a jury if the trial were held in court.

The Senate plunged into a three-hour debate on the objection. Angry Republicans insisted that the people of Ohio were entitled to have both of their senators vote on the impeachment. They added that Wade had no greater interest in the trial than did Senator David Patterson of Tennessee, a Democrat married to the president's daughter. The comparison to standards for jurors, they insisted, was irrelevant. As public officials, senators might have made public statements that would disqualify them from a court jury (as indeed many had). The Senate was a political body and its members could not be disqualified on political grounds. The debate blew itself out the next day and Wade took the oath, but discord on the question continued in the press and in Washington lobbies for the next seven weeks.

Equally challenging was how to frame Chief Justice Chase's role at the trial. The Constitution directs that the chief justice shall preside over a presidential impeachment trial, but offers no further enlightenment on the subject. What were his powers? Could he admit or exclude evidence, as a judge would in court? The Senate ordinarily governs itself and Chase was a stranger there. What if there were a tie vote on a procedural point? When the vice president presides over the Senate on nonimpeachment matters, he casts tie-breaking votes. Could the chief justice exercise the same power?

Chase took an expansive view of his authority. The Senate did not. When the chief justice addressed questions of procedure in an early letter, he triggered a violent reaction. The reaction was amplified because many senators had political reasons for not trusting him.

Beginning in the 1830s, the tall, handsome Chase won a national reputation as an abolitionist lawyer in Ohio, earning the epithet "Attorney General of fugitive slaves." After serving as senator and governor of his home state, he sought the Republican nomination for president in 1860. When Lincoln won the presidency, Chase agreed to serve as secretary of the treasury. His financial creativity helped keep Union armies in the field. His unquenchable ambition led him to place his own image on every dollar bill printed by his department, transforming the money supply into political handbills. In December 1864, Lincoln made him chief justice.

This unbroken progression through public office masked Chase's limitations. The chief justice's self-importance wore out many supporters. A nonsmoking teetotaler who rarely laughed, Chase had a short supply of charm. His poor eyesight could make him seem rude. Too vain to wear eyeglasses in public, he often failed to recognize friends at events. Many respected him. Few liked him. As one friend wrote, Chase was "born an old man" and was ignorant of human nature. A particular enemy was Ben Wade, the man who would be president if Johnson was convicted. Chase's "theology is unsound," Wade once said. "He thinks there is a fourth person in the Trinity."

Chase desperately wanted to be president. Indeed, he held the dangerous opinion that he *deserved* to be president. Chase's undisguised lunge for the Republican nomination in 1864 persuaded Lincoln to accept his resignation from the Cabinet in July of that year. (Chase had been a serial resigner, sending several earlier withdrawal letters that Lincoln did not accept.) After becoming chief justice, no sense of judicial propriety restrained his ambition. He offered political advice to Presi-

Chief Justice Salmon P. Chase.

dent Johnson and corresponded freely with operatives about his own prospects for the presidential nomination in 1868. Chase was not fussy about which party elected him president. During the trial, his agents worked to elect Chase delegates to the Republican Convention scheduled for the third week of May. With Grant the prohibitive favorite for that party's nomination, Chase hedged his bets, flirting with Democratic leaders, too. A Republican contemporary captured the general disillusion with Chase:

> He has an unhappy way of too plainly exhibiting his presidential aspirations, so that those who really mean well by him are denied the privilege of warming up to him. . . . His position of chief justice, which to another would be the fulfillment of highest ambition, merely makes him a martyr. The presidential fever is a deadly malady.

Because of his hostility to Wade and his own aspirations, Chase would never appear to be the impartial judge that the occasion demanded. As early as October of 1867, Chase had urged congressmen and senators to oppose impeachment. Every decision he made would be analyzed for political motivation and impact. Republican senators, convinced that Chase would tilt the scales to favor the president, resolved to keep him on the shortest possible leash.

Chase took the podium on March 13 to begin the pretrial phase of the impeachment. The month's most lurid rumors had proved false. A teacher of Johnson's granddaughter had reported that the family would leave soon for Tennessee. It was not true; the president would not resign. And Thaddeus Stevens, contrary to persistent gossip, still was not dead.

The trial carried powerful cachet in Washington society, with women making up two-thirds of the gallery that day. Stanton's mother-in-law was there, along with Senator Trumbull's mother and Kate Chase, the chief justice's glamorous daughter (wife of Senator William Sprague of Rhode Island). Washingtonians snapped up books recounting earlier impeachment trials in Britain and America. "People who never could be brought to comprehend the simple process of habeas corpus," one account wrote, "now talk learnedly upon the nice points of law involved in a trial of impeachment."

The peaceful attempt to remove the American head of state commanded international attention. Baron Gerolt, Prussia's envoy, sat in the Senate gallery with Baron Wetterstadt of Sweden and Norway, Mr. Rangabee of Greece, Señor Sarmiento from Argentina, and representatives of France, Denmark, Russia, and Spain.

The newspapers reported breathlessly on the proceedings. Lawyers were graded on appearance: Bingham, resembling a frenzied poet or fanatic preacher, was decreed less untidy than usual, but "never looks well shaved"; Butler preened in a swallowtail coat with an extra exposure of linen; Logan glowered dark and handsome behind heavy mustaches, while Stevens, with a face of dried parchment and features of marble, was "the very embodiment of fanaticism, without a solitary leaven of justice or mercy." Speaking styles were scored, too. A tall, commanding figure, Stanberry had a "peculiar sliding manner of delivery," while Bingham seemed "a first class spouter from the country." Evarts, small and neat, employed a sweet tenor that pleased the ear. Curtis was barely audible. Details were noted reverently. During a recess, Stevens polished off a plate of oysters while Stanberry leaned his head on his hand.

The president's lawyers asked for more time to answer the articles, as defense lawyers have done since the beginning of contested proceedings. In response, John Bingham demanded that their answer be filed immediately, stressing an important point for the managers—that the senators "are a rule and a law to themselves." The president was given ten more days. To show how eager they were to proceed, the House managers filed their reply one day after the president's answer arrived. Another defense request for delay drove Manager Logan to cry out in frustration. Johnson, he warned, retained the power to trample the laws and the Constitution; justice must be swift! The Republican senators agreed. They set the trial's opening day for March 30.

15

INFLUENCE AND EDMUND COOPER

MARCH 1868

I told him, I thought if he had the nerve we could make $25,000, or $50,000 out of these fellows. . . . I had become satisfied there was a good deal of money floating around or being gathered up. . . . I concluded I would see if I could not get hold of some money.

POSTAL AGENT JAMES LEGATE, MAY 22, 1868

FROM THE FIRST, a favorite pastime of the impeachment season was "counting to seven." With nine Democrats and three Johnson Republicans bound to vote for the president, which seven Republican senators might save Johnson from conviction by a two-thirds majority? While the lawyers planned to sway the senators with persuasive presentations, practical men focused on other means of influence. All of the political arts—from appeals to party solidarity to threats of retribution, from pledges of patronage jobs to negotiations over cash bribes—would be on display from March to the end of May.

Potential Republican defectors were identified early and the list was refined daily. Even before the House adopted impeachment articles, one Radical newspaper counted six Republican senators who might support the president. A week later, the same newspaper predicted that Kansas Senator Edmund Ross was lost, along with Fessenden of Maine and Sprague of Rhode Island. The mistrust of Sprague arose largely because

Chief Justice Chase was his father-in-law. Many doubted Fessenden because he so disliked Ben Wade. A Baltimore paper reported that six Republicans would vote to acquit, while eight more were on the fence. Newspapers across the country repeated the report.

Attention focused early on Republican Senator Joseph Fowler of Tennessee, who had stood with Johnson during the secession crisis of 1860 and throughout the war. By January 1868, having soured on Johnson's Reconstruction policies, Fowler called for Johnson's impeachment. Once impeachment proceedings began in the Senate, though, he began to sit with the Democrats, winning a place on the list of the "doubtful."

Both sides used every political tool at hand. The impeachers, who needed only to maintain party discipline in order to convict the president, combined demands for party loyalty with warnings of dire consequences for those who strayed from the Republican fold. Promises of positions in a Ben Wade Administration filled the air. Ben Butler developed a network of agents and spies to keep track of the doubtfuls. Butler wanted to know who those senators spent time with and what they were saying.

The president's friends—both in and out of office—organized themselves to support his cause with patronage jobs and even bribes. These tools were familiar to experienced traffickers in influence like New York Collector Henry Smythe, Indian trader Perry Fuller of Kansas, and Sam Ward, King of the Lobby. But someone had to coordinate those efforts, to make sure that the correct inducements were offered to the correct senators, and also that they were offered only once to each. No reason to pay twice. The president's team marshaled at least three separate efforts to offer cash to senators in return for votes for acquittal. All three ran through the hands of Edmund Cooper of Tennessee.

Cooper was the type of upper-class Southerner that Andrew Johnson often resented. Born into a wealthy cotton-trading family in middle Tennessee, Cooper attended Harvard Law School. Family connections (the Coopers were close to President James Polk) smoothed Edmund's way. Contemporaries celebrated Cooper's polish. One gushed over his "good breeding, gentlemanly instincts, and sense of honor," calling him a "talented, artful man." Andrew Johnson enjoyed none of these advantages. He came from a very different Tennessee.

Yet Cooper stuck by the Union in 1861 when two of his brothers joined the Confederates. Despite a period of detention by Southern forces, Cooper became private secretary and "confidential agent" for the military governor of Tennessee, Andrew Johnson, who was thirteen years his senior. Through their shared experience of danger and public service in wartime, the two men formed a strong bond.

After the war, Cooper served as one of Johnson's personal secretaries in the White House before being sworn in as a congressman from Tennessee. Cooper's fierce dedication to Johnson surfaced on the House floor when a Pennsylvania Radical referred to the president as a "usurper." Cooper artfully called his colleague a liar, which prompted the accusation that Cooper had assisted Johnson as "the paid confidential agent of the usurper, and knew all the secrets of the usurpation."

Cooper sought the president's advice on political matters: whether he should run for governor of Tennessee, and how he possibly could win reelection to Congress after 5,000 blacks registered to vote in his district. After imploring Johnson to appoint him to a position that would take him out of Tennessee politics, Cooper pleaded, "Write to me! Tell me what to do!"

When Cooper lost his reelection bid, he signed on again to be Johnson's aide, arriving in Washington City in the early autumn of 1867, as the battle over Reconstruction raged. Cooper shared the president's combative instincts. "The more boldly you fight it out," he advised Johnson, "the better for the country." The president's opponents, he warned, "intend to destroy you, if they can. They will hesitate at nothing." Cooper pledged himself to the president's service:

> I would forego all personal and private considerations if in your estimation I can be of any service in aiding you in the great struggle for the preservation of the Government.

Back in Washington City, Cooper told Navy Secretary Welles that he would serve "as a companion and friend to the president." Welles applauded the development. "The President needs such a friend," he wrote in his diary, "and it is to be regretted, if Cooper is such, that he was not invited earlier." Johnson welcomed this familiar partisan during his time of many troubles. Cooper bubbled excitedly about the experience in a letter to his father, citing the "universal approval given of my course since I have been in close proximity with the President" and the "good effect" he was having. Cooper lauded the "quiet and self-reliant courage with which the President now meets all threats or charges," concluding, "It is a good thing that I am with him."

The president soon determined that the loyal Cooper could be even more useful at the Treasury Department. Johnson never quite trusted his treasury secretary, Hugh McCulloch, a holdover from Lincoln's time. Periodically questioning McCulloch's loyalty, he considered replacing the Indiana banker but never did. Instead, he decided to appoint Cooper, his home-state acolyte, to the second position in the department. When the Senate refused to confirm Cooper for the job, Johnson left him there on an "interim" basis. Cooper's "interim" posting would endure until the last day Johnson was in office.

From his perch at Treasury, Johnson's "companion and friend" became the hub for schemes to influence Republican senators to vote for acquittal. The polished Southern gentleman engaged in hard-nosed bargaining with rascals and senators (groups that could overlap), acting as an unsung coordinator of the president's most practical defense measures.

Cooper's first opportunity to play this role came from Kansas and its rugged political culture.

Shortly after the House sent its impeachment articles to the Senate, several Kansans began to explore the crudest methods of influencing senators' votes. The outlines of the scheme are unmistakable, though accounts of it include a forest of half-truths and undisclosed facts.

As a special agent for the Post Office Department, James Legate had a large geographic responsibility—Kansas and the New Mexico Territory. Despite those official duties, the Kansan was ordered to Washington City by the commissioner of Indian affairs, Nathaniel Taylor, a powerful patronage appointee. Taylor, formerly a congressman from President Johnson's home region of East Tennessee, was close to the president. While in Washington, Legate performed no duties for the Post Office. Instead, he spent his time negotiating over bribes for the impeachment vote. When his leave was about to expire, it was extended upon the request of Thomas Ewing, Jr., an influential lawyer, and Sena-

Postal agent, and bribery conspirator, James Legate of Kansas.
(The Kansas State Historical Society)

tor Edmund Ross of Kansas. These powerful men took a surprising interest in a mere postal agent from Kansas. Did Taylor arrange Legate's
official leave—and did Senator Ross arrange its extension—for the sole
purpose of working out bribes for impeachment votes? The available
records are silent on this point.

Shortly after Legate arrived in Washington City, Commissioner Taylor summoned him to discuss the case before the Senate. Impeachment,
the commissioner explained, "was rather a question of brute force than
otherwise; [and] if the President had brute force, enough to overcome
the power against him, he would be acquitted." A day later, the commissioner told Legate he "might make some money" from the impeachment,
then turned the conversation to the Kansas senators, Ross and Samuel
Pomeroy, both Republicans. The superintendent wanted to know, Legate testified later, "if there might not be some way invented by which
through me [Legate], they [Ross and Pomeroy] might be induced to vote
against impeachment."

Recognizing an opportunity, Legate sought guidance from Thomas
Ewing, Jr., a former Kansas Supreme Court justice who also was brother-
in-law to General Sherman and the son of the pending appointee as sec-

retary of war. Both Ewing and his father served as informal advisers to President Johnson. Ewing sent Legate to Indian trader Perry Fuller. After all, Fuller had bribed Kansas state legislators to secure Senate seats for both Pomeroy and Ross. Who would know better how to influence those two senators? Fuller also had a personal connection with Senator Ross. While in Washington City, Ross lived at the home of Robert Ream, who was Fuller's father-in-law.

The crafty Fuller made a proposal to the postal agent that was round-about, almost subtle. Legate, Fuller said, should organize a movement to support Chief Justice Chase's presidential longings. This "Chase movement" could receive funds that then would be diverted to pay senators for their votes to acquit the president. Legate replied that in return "for $50,000, $25,000 down and $25,000 after acquittal," Pomeroy could direct four Republican votes for acquittal. Legate urged that the funds be paid to a reliable third party who would hold them for the "Chase movement." After the senators voted to acquit the president, the third party could deliver the funds to the senators' agents.

Under this scheme, Legate and Fuller intended not only to bribe senators, but also that the middlemen (them) would help themselves to some of the "Chase movement" funds. To this end, Legate joined up with another opportunist who dwelt in the shadows of government. Willis Gaylord, a New Yorker who was Senator Pomeroy's brother-in-law, had acted for Pomeroy in earlier payoff schemes involving land grants to Kansas railroads and treaties to acquire Indian lands. Gaylord, again acting for Senator Pomeroy, angled to be the stakeholder of the $50,000 in bribe money.

Perry Fuller took Legate to see Edmund Cooper, the president's man at the Treasury. Jointly, Cooper and Fuller instructed Legate on a key political consideration. The president, they boasted, could call on the vote of Kansas Senator Ross if needed, but that could be controversial for Ross in Republican Kansas. To limit Ross's political risk, they wanted the other Kansas Republican (Pomeroy) also to vote for acquittal. They were willing to pay for Pomeroy's vote.

The courtly Cooper instructed Legate on how the bribe money could be raised. Tax collectors in New York and New Jersey had seized large amounts of whiskey on which federal tax had not been paid. Cooper, showing Legate a list of the seizures, said that Legate could earn commissions by helping to settle those cases. Those commissions could pay for bribes to senators, with some money left over for themselves. Two days later, Legate took the train to New York to complete this mission. Lists of whiskey seizures in the New York area were prepared. Within a few days, however, Treasury officials cooled on the project. Legate returned to Washington City empty-handed, resolved to renew his scheming with Gaylord and Cooper. He became a regular visitor to Cooper's room in the Metropolitan Hotel as he pressed the Treasury official to find another way to conclude a bribery deal.

The resumed negotiations advanced to the point of concrete proposals about specific sums. Gaylord promised that $40,000 would ensure the pro-Johnson votes of Pomeroy and four other Republican senators. Cooper authorized Perry Fuller to offer $40,000 for the "Chase movement," with the money to be paid if the Senate acquitted Johnson. In one version, Cooper met with Gaylord and counted out most of the money in cash, then added a check drawn on a Washington bank. Gaylord declined the payment, in this account, because he would not accept the check.

Though the schemers admitted engaging in extensive bribery foreplay, they tended to deny that there was any consummation. Cooper claimed that during negotiations over the payment to Gaylord, he began to suspect that the New Yorker's overture might be a trap, that Cooper's efforts to purchase senators' votes could be revealed publicly to embarrass Johnson.

THE KANSAS CABAL

Senator Samuel Pomeroy	Radical Republican who proposed Cabinet changes to President Johnson to defeat impeachment, and whose agents negotiated for bribes for several Republican senators.
Senator Edmund Ross	Radical Republican who (like Pomeroy) owed his Senate seat to bribes paid to Kansas state legislators.
Perry Fuller	Indian trader who bribed Kansas legislators to win seats for Pomeroy and Ross, and sought to head the federal tax agency. Assisted Legate in a proposal to bribe senators to vote to acquit.
James Legate	Postal agent detailed to Washington; negotiated with Treasury official Edmund Cooper for bribes to Republican senators.
Willis Gaylord	New Yorker and brother-in-law of Pomeroy; negotiated with Cooper on behalf of Pomeroy and others for bribes.
Robert Ream	Landlord of Senator Ross; father-in-law of Perry Fuller.
Thomas Ewing, Jr.	Adviser to President Johnson and Senator Ross, former Kansas Supreme Court Justice, and brother-in-law of Gen. Sherman; helped Legate advance a scheme for bribing senators.

Perhaps the most remarkable part of the Kansans' saga is that their scheming reached into the White House, into Andrew Johnson's office. In late March, postal agent Legate persuaded a representative (probably Fuller or the younger Ewing) to deliver a message to a Johnson aide: If the aide would ask Senator Pomeroy for his opinion of Legate, the ensuing conversation "would open up the way of securing half a dozen radical votes for the President." When the aide described Legate's message to the president, Johnson understood its significance immediately. He replied that he preferred conviction with a clean conscience to acquittal by nefarious means.

That was what the president said. But Senator Pomeroy made a similar overture to the White House and met a different reception. Pomeroy sent a message to Johnson: If the president would change his Cabinet, impeachment would halt. "Impeachment," Pomeroy's message insisted, should be viewed "as a *political*, not a *legal* question." Johnson again reacted indignantly, announcing to his staff, "I will have to insult some of these men yet." The president's huffy response may have been due to the source of the proposal. Pomeroy, a Radical and hardly a Johnson ally, had a noisome reputation for mixing corruption with sanctimonious Christian piety. The Kansan's hypocrisy was so notorious that he served as the model for Mark Twain's avatar of venality, Senator Dilworthy, in his novel *The Gilded Age*.

Despite his pious protestations, the president met with Pomeroy early the next morning. He did not use the occasion to insult the senator. Afterward, Johnson related an innocuous version of this meeting. According to the president, the Kansas senator said nothing of changing the Cabinet, but offered a few tepid comments about current Cabinet officers. After a "very friendly" talk, Pomeroy supposedly departed with the wish that Johnson give him "suggestions that might tend toward producing a good effect in the present condition of affairs."

Johnson's bland account of his conversation with Pomeroy concealed far more than it revealed. In the midst of the impeachment crisis, two such veteran politicians were not likely to pass the time exchanging vague niceties about Cabinet officers. Certainly not when, as Johnson admitted, "several persons" had urged him to talk to Pomeroy. (Was Cooper one of those urging him?) The Kansas senator had a definite agenda for the meeting, and no doubt pursued it. Perhaps he pressed for changes in the Cabinet. Perhaps the proposal for a Cabinet shakeup morphed into a bold demand for control of federal patronage jobs in Kansas, or an even bolder demand for a bribe. Though the president had protested that he would not bargain for votes, for the next two months Senators Ross and Pomeroy would figure in many discussions of what type of bargain might bring them to vote for acquittal.

. . .

The Kansans were the first, but they were not the only ones thinking about how to use money to influence the Senate's verdict. A second plan came from more august sources. Three of Johnson's Cabinet members established a war chest for bribing Republican senators. Once more, the scheme ran through the hands of Edmund Cooper at Treasury, Johnson's trusted supporter.

This plan originated with Secretary of State Seward, Treasury Secretary McCulloch, and Postmaster General Alexander Randall. The three high officials fretted that the president might well be convicted and removed from office. They convened a conference with an expert on corruption, printing executive Cornelius Wendell. A Democrat who performed all federal printing contracts in the 1850s, Wendell was a notorious figure in Washington City. He operated a political slush fund in the years before the Civil War, using excess payments from his government contracts to support Democratic newspapers and make contributions to Democrats around the nation. In a six-year period, Wendell received $3.8 million for public printing (at least $50 million in current dollars), more than half of which was pure boodle. That arrangement, directed by President Buchanan himself, led another Democrat to call Wendell "that most corrupt of all men." In but one example, in 1858 Wendell spent $40,000 (at least $560,000 in current dollars) to push legislation through Congress.

Although Wendell's graft and bribery were exposed in congressional hearings in 1860, President Johnson made him Superintendent of Public Printing. One Wendell sponsor said he had recommended the scoundrel to Johnson "as Gen. [Andrew] Jackson employed Lafitte the pirate. He knew the intricacies of the mouth of the Mississippi and would be able to detect the approaches of the enemy." That sponsor later recanted his recommendation, admitting, "Wendell has joined the knaves whom he supplanted."

The three Cabinet officers had a pressing question for this infamous character: how much would it cost to assure the president's acquittal? After some hedging, Wendell estimated that $150,000 (over $2 million in today's money) should do the job, though he refused to handle the funds himself. After the impeachment trial ended, Wendell recalled that the entire amount was raised and placed in an acquittal fund. Some came from Postmaster General Randall, some from Treasury Secretary McCulloch. Much was raised by "outsiders."

Contributors to the acquittal fund doubtless included the many government contractors and patronage employees whose livelihoods depended on the continuation of the Johnson Administration. Some came from employees of the custom houses in Baltimore and Philadelphia. More came from whiskey distillers who evaded taxes by bribing Johnson's tax men. Collector Henry Smythe, who presided over the golden river of revenue at the New York Custom House, was eager to help. He sent a deputy to the White House to inquire about the best way to pay the president's defense costs. After all, three months earlier Smythe had collected funds from every employee in his domain for the stated purpose of helping the president with impeachment. Moreover, Smythe was now after a foreign posting, the plum position of minister to Great Britain. A man seeking high appointment will want to be useful. Colonel Moore, Johnson's aide, referred Smythe's man to William Evarts, the president's lawyer from New York, so they could arrange money matters "in a quiet way." Moore warned that "extreme caution was necessary."

The acquittal fund was assigned to the care of Cooper and Postmaster General Randall, who jointly controlled it. The inconspicuous Cooper thus coordinated a second major scheme for buying impeachment votes. Before the trial ended, at least one more corrupt intrigue would land on his desk.

While the fixers plotted, the trial loomed as a momentous event in the nation's life, nowhere more so than in the South. Southern Unionists and freedmen, outnumbered and beleaguered, held their breath. "The impeachment of the President," wrote an Alabama Republican, "will be a death blow to the rebellion, still strong with life." An army commander in Kentucky reported that the "rebels" were alarmed by the impeachment. "Here in the South," he added, "we cannot calmly think of the failure of impeachment and the long train of evils that would follow in its wake."

As each day passed, every participant in the trial could feel the lens of history beginning to focus. The House managers went to Mathew

Brady's gallery to sit for a group photograph, a grim affair in which some resemble avenging angels, others seem befuddled to be there at all, and only James Wilson looks like a potentially pleasant dinner companion. Stevens learned that teenage sculptor Vinnie Ream had completed a statuette of him. Ms. Ream, the precociously talented daughter of Senator Ross's landlord, Robert Ream (and thus sister-in-law to Indian trader Perry Fuller), was eager to show the work to Stevens, who doted on her. Ben Butler worked feverishly on his opening speech in the Senate, his opportunity to frame the constitutional contest. Through three days of preparation, he slept only nine hours, refusing to meet his many callers, aided by a team of stenographers and an Ohio congressman. No other manager lent a hand.

The troubled president sought solace in history and in familiar things. He read and reread Addison's *Cato*, committing parts to memory and comparing present-day senators to those portrayed in the play. He reflected at length on a sermon he heard at St. Patrick's Church, observing that there was nothing more depressing than "to labor for the people and not be understood. It is enough to sour [a man's] very soul." Then he was back to ancient Rome, comparing his situation to that of the Gracchi brothers, tribunes of the people who were murdered at the instigation of the Roman Senate. "This American Senate," he insisted, "is as corrupt as was the Roman Senate." Johnson dug out a weathered collection of political speeches, the first book he ever owned, given to him before he learned how to spell. He turned to the speeches of Lord Chatham (William Pitt the Elder), denouncing British policy toward the American colonies. Johnson lingered over Chatham's statement that "no tyranny is so formi[d]able as that assumed and exercised by a number of tyrants." For Johnson, the parallel to Thad Stevens's Congress was unmistakable.

Johnson's closest adherents expected the worst. Navy Secretary Welles judged that every member of the Cabinet thought the president would be convicted.

But the unexpected can happen in a trial, and in politics. Everyone was nervous. Everyone was excited. The battle was about to be joined.

16

BEN BUTLER'S HORSE CASE

MARCH 30—APRIL 8, 1868

[The impeachment committee] put in the forefront of its battle
a lawyer whose opinion on high moral questions . . . nobody
heeds . . . and whose want . . . of decency, throughout the case
gave the President a constant advantage.

THE NATION, MAY 21, 1868

E VEN BRASH BEN Butler felt intimidated. Waiting to give the opening
statement on the first full day of trial, Monday, March 30, "I came
as near running away then as ever I did on any occasion in my life."

Rising to address the Senate, Butler was not a commanding figure.
One observer described him as "short, broad-shouldered, short-legged,
fat, without much neck, but with a good many flaps around the throat,
standing as if a trifle bow-legged . . . [with] a great cranium of a shining
pink color." Another complained of his raspy voice, like a cross-cut saw.
A third deprecated his enunciation as "neither silvery nor distinct." On
this day, Butler lost his usual swagger. Cowed by the significance of the
moment, he clutched his papers close to his face while nervously reading
a three-hour speech.

Crowded to suffocation, the Senate galleries bloomed with bright
feminine costumes. Many remarked on Butler's daughter Blanche, her
youthful beauty contrasting with her father's singular appearance.
Equally lovely were Chief Justice Chase's daughter Kate, whose hus-

Ben Butler delivers the opening statement for the prosecution, March 30.

band Sprague was at his desk on the Senate floor, and the notorious former Confederate spy, Belle Boyd, with "very black eyes and a very blue veil." Only two "Africans" were there, as was British Ambassador Edward Thornton.

The managers sat at the table to the left of the chief justice, facing him. The table for the defense team was to the right. Butler regretted that the prosecution was "too weak in the knees" to demand that Johnson attend the trial. The Massachusetts Radical had argued for compelling his appearance, forcing him "to stand until the Senate offered him a chair." In truth, Johnson ached to gratify Butler's wish. That morning, he felt again "strongly impelled" to attend the trial. His lawyers once more dissuaded him from being Exhibit A in a spectacle managed by Ben Butler and Thad Stevens. Allowing himself to be dragged into the Senate would diminish the presidency, they argued. Johnson should remain above the battle.

Though many listeners were disappointed by Butler's restrained presentation that day, the speech was as solid as the ill-constructed prosecution permitted. Eight impeachment articles focused on the confrontation between Stanton and Thomas, and the Tenure of Office Act.

Butler emphasized those articles, charging that the president claimed a "most stupendous and unlimited prerogative" to ignore the statute when he replaced his war secretary. The manager admitted that the last three articles—the General Emory charge, Butler's own stump-speech article, and Stevens's catchall Article XI—were diminished by the "grandeur" of the first eight. Butler thus created a logical inversion, calling the eight narrow articles (thought "trifling" by Stevens) truly grand, and disparaging the three broad ones as slight. To justify all eleven articles, the manager had to define an impeachable offense expansively; it was, he said, any act that subverted a "fundamental or essential principle of government or [was] highly prejudicial to the public interest." The question before the Senate, he contended, was whether Johnson, "because of malversation in office, is no longer fit."

In a passage that drew much criticism, Butler told the Senate that it was "bound by no law, either statute or common." The senators, he continued, were "a law unto yourselves, bound only by natural principles of equity and justice."

Without an explicit constitutional provision granting or denying Congress the power to adopt the Tenure of Office Act, Butler marshaled the historical precedents that supported the statute. In *The Federalist*, Alexander Hamilton had insisted that the Senate's consent would be necessary under the Constitution "to displace as well as to appoint." Not only had Congress in the 1790s defined the president's power to remove high officials, but it again asserted its power over the question in 1863 when it set a term for the comptroller of the currency, and in 1866 when it directed that military officers could be removed only by impeachment. Johnson himself signed the 1866 statute. Johnson followed the procedures of the Tenure of Office Act when he suspended Stanton the prior August. The House manager agreed that Johnson could challenge the constitutionality of a law by violating it, but only at his peril. "[T]hat peril," Butler continued, "is to be impeached for violating his oath of office." Butler botched his discussion of Article XI, stating incorrectly that acquittal on the other charges would require acquittal on the catchall article.

Butler offered the customary comparisons between the president and despots of yore (Caesar and Napoléon). He described Johnson as "thrown to the surface by the whirlpool of civil war," and acceding to the

presidency as "the elect of the assassin, . . . and not of the people." Butler blamed Johnson for Southern murders of freedmen and white Unionists, "encouraged by his refusal to consent that a single murderer be
punished, though thousands of good men have been slain." On the
Senate's verdict, he warned, the welfare and liberties of Americans "hang
trembling."

Managers Wilson and Bingham then read into the record the prosecution's first evidence, the presidential oath of office and the president's
December letter justifying his removal of Stanton under the Tenure
of Office Act. Having sat from 12:30 until 5 P.M., the Senate called it
a day.

The prosecution's case took five days to present, with the Senate sitting
as a court from noon to five, through Saturday. In the unseasonably warm
weather, it seemed longer. Throughout the week, attendance declined in
the galleries and among the congressmen. Ladies brought knitting and
novels to their seats. Senators wrote letters at their desks. The fourth day
was the nadir, according to one newspaper, "intensely dull, stupid, and
uninteresting." By Saturday, April 4, senators had to be herded back into
the chamber after a recess, and the galleries were half-empty. Fewer
than fifty House Republicans showed up for the hearings on Friday and
Saturday, some playing hooky to catch the afternoon show of Dan Rice's
traveling circus. (The circus included a political element befitting the
season; the animal acts were interspersed with pro-Johnson monologues
by Mr. Rice.) When Butler announced the end of the prosecution case,
impeachment supporters were deflated.

Some sense of anticlimax was unavoidable. No one could sustain the
fevered emotions of the early impeachment days. Moreover, the taking
of factual evidence is mostly a businesslike affair. Even in the Senate
Chamber, the rhythmic catechism of question and answer offers few opportunities to cry out for justice or to compare adversaries to legendary
tyrants.

Also, everyone already knew the interesting facts. Newspapers had
printed complete accounts of the confrontation at the war office, plus
summaries of the testimony taken by the House managers in their prep-
arations. President Johnson's unfortunate addresses in 1866—the basis

for the stump-speech article—had circulated around the nation. Compelling testimony might have come from Edwin Stanton, but the managers had good reasons not to present him. If Stanton left his office for an afternoon, Lorenzo Thomas could slip in and change the locks, undermining the case. Also, Stanton could be a disaster as a witness. He would have to explain why he should remain in office against the wishes of the president he had assiduously disserved. A skilled cross-examiner might goad Stanton into revealing his native arrogance, an unattractive quality in a witness. Butler likely was content to leave the war secretary undisturbed at his bivouac.

Left with mostly dull testimony, Butler did the best he could. The first meaty witness was the fourth one, a Republican congressman from Niagara County, New York. Burt Van Horn, one of the group in Stanton's office when Thomas arrived on February 22, was the shorthand writer who jotted down on an envelope the exchange between dueling war secretaries. Another Republican congressman who was then in Stanton's office echoed Van Horn's testimony.

With the sixth witness, the congressional delegate from the Dakota Territory, Butler began to take the wheels off his own case. Walter Burleigh was a friend of Adjutant General Thomas. Butler wanted Burleigh to relate Thomas's statements on the evening of February 21, before the adjutant general attended the masquerade ball at Marini's Hall. Stanberry objected that the testimony was irrelevant. When a senator requested that the objection be submitted to the Senate for decision, the chief justice demurred. Referring to himself in the third person, Chase announced that "the Chief Justice is of opinion that it is his duty to decide preliminarily upon objections to evidence." If a senator disagreed with the chief justice's ruling, he could ask the Senate to overrule it.

On every possible ground, Butler objected. Chase's procedure would bias evidentiary rulings during the trial, he argued, since the Senate would defer to the chief justice's initial decision on an issue. Worse, the House managers could not themselves appeal for a Senate vote, but would have to rely on some friendly senator to do so. Reciting seventeenth-century English precedents, Butler expressed concern that Chase's procedure could be abused by a future chief justice who would not be as admirable a jurist as Chase: "We have had a Johnson in the presidential chair," he warned, "and we cannot tell who may get into the chair of the

Chief Justice." Having sat quietly for almost two days, Managers Bingham and Boutwell chimed in. Then Butler popped up with a few more choice remarks.

The Senate's response was utter confusion. After wrangling through five inconclusive roll-call votes on procedural motions, the senators retired for an executive session on the subject. Then the Senate adopted a rule that followed Chase's proposed procedure. Adjournment at 6:30 P.M. was a blessing.

That evening, the defense team must have chuckled all the way back to the White House. Defense lawyers ordinarily yearn for procedural snarls and quibbles over motes—anything that will distract the court from the prosecution case. With only slight provocation from the imperious Chase, the managers and the Senate had sunk into the sort of contentious squabble that the defense craved. What a capital sight, watching the managers climb over each other in their eagerness to derail their own case with indignant speeches on a not very important dispute! After battling manfully over the Senate's procedure for resolving evidentiary issues, what senator could even remember Burleigh's testimony, much less that the fate of the Republic hung in the balance?

The next morning, the managers, at their regular pretrial meeting at 11 A.M., fumed over the Senate's failure to adopt a rule that would bar the chief justice from casting a tie-breaking vote (as the vice president does in legislative matters). Butler proposed that the managers withdraw from the trial in protest. They should, he said, ask the House of Representatives for instruction on the question. Though supported by Stevens and Boutwell, his proposal lost 4 to 3. After the managers trooped into the chamber, Senator Charles Sumner proposed a rule to bar such a tie-breaking vote by the chief justice. The motion lost.

At this point, the advocates settled in for two more hours of debate over whether Delegate Burleigh should be allowed to relate his conversation with Lorenzo Thomas. Finally, by a margin of 39 to 11, the Senate said yes. The payoff for this stupefying exercise was Burleigh's description of the adjutant general's presumably inebriated pledge to take control of the War Department Office, to "meet force by force," and to break down any doors that were barred to him. Butler had used more than four hours of the Senate's time to secure a few minutes of mildly titillating testimony that would sway not a single vote.

The Senate Chamber during the impeachment trial.

The president's lawyers recognized the opportunity before them. They started to use the evidentiary procedures to have some fun. William Evarts interposed frequent objections to Butler's questions, triggering the same excruciating sequence. If Butler rephrased the question to meet the objection, Evarts raised a new one. And another. Finally, in exasperation, Butler would write out his question and hand it to the chief justice to read to the Senate. The lawyers then exchanged volleys over the virtues and vices of the written question, and a roll-call vote would decide whether the witness had to answer. If the Senate allowed Butler to press that question, Evarts protested the next one.

The prosecution threatened to become a Dickensian satire of itself. The ratio of procedural scuffling to actual testimony was soaring. Topping off the chaos was the weird vision of Adjutant General Thomas buzzing around the building in his full dress uniform. Having been advised that he might be called as a prosecution witness, Thomas restlessly wandered the Senate Chamber, flitting from the gentleman's gallery to the ladies' gallery to the press gallery.

At the end of the second day of evidence, Butler caught a small break. His witness was an ingratiating gentleman from Delaware, George

199

Karsner, who had encountered Thomas at a White House reception on March 9. Butler summoned Karsner to testify that Thomas promised to kick Stanton out of the War Department, a shred of evidence of barely marginal interest. Karsner explained that he exhorted Thomas (a fellow native of Delaware), "General, the eyes of Delaware are on you!" The phrase brought a roar of delight from the entertainment-starved chamber. The chief justice laughed until he shook. It became a catchphrase for the impeachment season, somehow capturing the contrast between the trial's quotidian reality and its epochal significance.

After Karsner, Butler's case slid downhill. A powerful thunderstorm rattled the Capitol building on Thursday, April 2, blowing dust through its corridors. Black clouds darkened the Senate's skylights, leaving the chamber dramatically lit by gas lamps during the daytime. Another congressman testified about the faceoff between Thomas and Stanton. General Emory of the Washington garrison and his senior aide gave testimony that did not really support the ninth impeachment article. Then the managers began a parade of ever more dreary witnesses. Some testified about the form of commissions issued to executive officials. More described their shorthand practices in recording the president's speeches. Butler's attention to such minute points reflected the practices of a time when most documents were handwritten. Forgery and misrepresentation were constant risks. Still, with defense lawyers launching objections at will, the case slowed to a crawl. This was not the "railroad speed" promised by Butler; it was tedium. As one Radical wrote in dismay, "What bores us, disgusts us."

Butler even offered evidence surrounding the unsuccessful appointment of Edmund Cooper as assistant treasury secretary. Noting Cooper's close ties to the president, Butler offered a convoluted motivation for Cooper's appointment. According to the House manager, Johnson wanted to place "his man, his Secretary" at Treasury so Cooper could approve expenditures to be incurred by a future war secretary whom Johnson would appoint illegally to replace Stanton. Butler insisted that Cooper's appointment violated the Tenure of Office Act. The president's lawyers replied that Cooper's appointment had nothing to do with the offenses described in the impeachment articles. The Senate agreed.

Like every trial lawyer, Butler wanted to end his case on an upbeat note. His final crescendo came from a letter sent by Treasury Secretary Hugh McCulloch in August of 1867, when Johnson suspended Stanton. The letter stated that Stanton was suspended under the Tenure of Office Act, directly contradicting the assertions of the president's lawyers that Johnson had acted under his constitutional powers. The defense, caught flat-footed, reacted with a consternation that had to delight the managers. With this modest flourish, the direct evidence against Andrew Johnson was closed.

The Senate adjourned until the next Thursday, giving the president's lawyers three extra days to prepare their defense.

Republican newspapers declared victory. The managers, according to the *Philadelphia Press*, "demonstrated beyond doubt or cavil the truth of every assertion contained in the impeachment articles." Other newspapers disagreed. "It is very generally conceded," the *New York Herald* reported, "that the evidence in the impeachment trial is too weak to hold water." Stanberry, maintaining the defense position that an impeachable offense must be a crime, claimed that a court would dismiss the managers' case for failing to prove the president had criminal intent when he sent Thomas to replace Stanton.

Even Democrats acknowledged that Butler had proved to be a quick-witted and tenacious advocate. Perhaps, on the whole, too tenacious. Many expressed surprise at the near-total eclipse of the other House managers. "Mr. Butler looms up as the one managing brain," a correspondent observed, "while the unfortunate Mr. Bingham and Mr. Wilson are proportionately dwarfed." Thad Stevens, who "uses stimulants [liquor] constantly, and is failing every day," was declared "practically defunct."

Butler had been everywhere, doing everything. He gave the opening statement, questioned every witness, and argued most of the legal issues. In the mornings, before the Senate convened, he took informal statements from potential witnesses. These sessions explored the Treasury Department's gold-trading practices and the president's opposition to the Fourteenth Amendment. Butler fired off a letter complaining that Treasury workers were helping the defense by searching records through the night, an effort that was risking fire in the archives. His spies prowled the city. One rummaged through William Evarts's wastebasket in his hotel room—a ploy Butler boasted about.

Butler's whirlwind of activity produced not very much. What facts, after all, had his twenty-three witnesses proved? That Lorenzo Thomas had acted foolishly and said foolish things? Few would have disputed that proposition before the trial began. In truth, Butler was banging through the evidentiary trees, moving from one to the next with panache, but without much sense of the forest. As he had promised, he performed as though he were trying a simple case of horse-stealing, according to judicial rules, but this was a presidential impeachment trial in the United States Senate. The verdict was going to be a political one. Well over two-thirds of the senators did not like Johnson and wished for an end to his presidency. Butler's fine legal points were of no importance to the political calculations each Republican senator would make. The prosecution needed to give those senators reasons to vote the way their hearts told them they should—for conviction.

Stevens's Article XI offered a road map of such arguments: the president usurped congressional powers in 1865 when he created Southern state governments; he was undermining the Reconstruction laws. These were arguments with visceral appeal to Republican senators. Instead, Butler achieved only delay, frustrating his supporters in the Senate. It was a miscalculation that the managers would compound in the coming weeks.

Butler participated in a very odd moment at a dinner the night after he closed his evidentiary case. It was a high-toned affair, including the British ambassador and House manager Boutwell. Also present was the urbane defense lawyer from New York, William Evarts, who had tormented Butler through much of the week. Mellow with good food and strong drink, Butler observed to his fellow gladiator that he rather wished he was on the opposite side of the trial, defending the president. Evarts matched Butler's whimsical mood, suggesting that he, too, would happily change sides in the case.

As Evarts's remark implied, it was not all hearts and rainbows on the defense team. The major problem continued to be the client. Johnson's feelings were raw, his temper short. He was beset by fears of all sizes, from the apocalyptic to the trivial. The times matched the biblical prophecy, he told Colonel Moore, "when the devil was to be let loose and would roam among the people." He complained when his lawyers requested help from the White House staff, pointedly asking Colonel Moore why "some people" wanted others to do their work for them? The sight of a crew of blacks working on the White House grounds triggered an eruption. Johnson demanded to know whether any whites still worked on the White House staff. Moore despaired of his employer's "morbid distress and feeling against the negroes."

The president's anxiety would not go away. He compulsively reviewed with his aides the characters of various senators, predicting grim consequences that would befall certain of them if the impeachment succeeded. Johnson assigned an aide to prepare a summary of the ghastly fates suffered by the English judges who signed the death warrant of King Charles I of England in 1649. He seemed to take comfort in their hideous ends.

Falling back on old habits, Johnson disobeyed his counsel and granted two interviews to a favored reporter. On the Sunday night before Butler's opening address, the reporter found the president to be despondent. Four nights later, presidential spirits had revived. He was "not only confident, but combative."

The president used the occasions to offer his own testimony on the facts in the case, free from the awkwardness of being under oath or facing cross-examination. Notably, he savaged his own appointee as war secretary, then turned on his bête noire, General Grant.

Lorenzo Thomas, Johnson told the reporter, "seems to be a queer old gentleman." Twice the president implied that the adjutant general's taste for liquor was the problem, describing Thomas as "refreshed" and "elated" over his appointment as interim secretary of war. "You know how it is with these military men," he added, "how much style they like to put on, and how much fuss they like to make, and how they like to show their authority." Johnson insisted he was not responsible for Thomas's statements or actions "independent of my orders."

The discussion of inebriation led the interviewer to question Johnson's own condition when he gave the extravagant speeches during the Swing Around the Circle in 1866, which were the basis for the tenth impeachment article. The president denied being drunk during those addresses, adding, "I didn't drink half as much as one or two others, about whose condition nobody dares to say a word." The reporter pressed Johnson. Was he referring to the person who had left the tour to go to Detroit (General Grant)? That was exactly who he meant, Johnson replied, adding that Grant "wasn't in a condition to know much about politics just then." Indeed, on occasion that same man had been in Johnson's office "so drunk that he couldn't stand."

In any event, Johnson continued, he could not be held responsible for anything he said during those speeches. He had answered hecklers in the crowds. "If I used any rough expressions," he protested, "they were put into my mouth by my enemies."

When the interview was published, Johnson was chagrined, first saying it should not have been published. Then he blamed the reporter, claiming he had been misquoted. The presidential temper was stirred by another press report. The Radical *New York Tribune* stated that General Grant viewed the president's conviction as "the only hope for the peace of the country." Unless Johnson was removed, the general-in-chief supposedly predicted, there would be "determined resistance to law" in the South. The president derided the notion that the opinion of a soldier could matter on impeachment. He finally concluded that Grant probably had not made the statements (as indeed he had not).

While the president stewed, one of his supporters started a very productive conversation. As assistant secretary of the navy during the Civil War, Gustavus Fox had been a catalyst in the development of the Union's first ironclad ship, the *Monitor*. On the night after Butler closed his case, Fox visited Senator James Grimes of Iowa, one of the Republicans fingered as a potential crossover vote for acquittal. When the conversation turned to the trial, Grimes shared some political insights.

Any Republican thinking of voting with the president, the Iowan pointed out, must fear that Johnson would greet acquittal as an occasion for wreaking vengeance on his foes. That fear alone could cause senators to vote against Johnson. In a recent public letter, Speaker of the House Schuyler Colfax of Indiana raised that concern, warning that an acquitted Johnson would cashier General Grant and refuse to obey any law he deemed unconstitutional. Was there some way, Senator Grimes wondered, for Johnson to provide reassurance that he would act moderately if retained in office? The Iowa senator also observed—as Sherman and Grant and Thomas Ewing had before him—that if only the president would appoint a politically acceptable war secretary, he might extricate himself from this mess.

Fox carried Grimes's messages back to his former chief, Navy Secretary Welles. Within a day, Welles delivered them to Johnson. This time, Johnson was almost ready to listen to reason.

17

DEFENDING THE PRESIDENT

APRIL 9–20, 1868

The president either did or did not violate the Tenure of Office Bill. Mr. Curtis makes out that (1) he did not violate it, and (2) he set out to violate it, but that in doing so he acted with the best intentions in the world. I leave to someone more clever than I the task of finding some connection between these two propositions.

GEORGES CLEMENCEAU, APRIL 10, 1868

SITTING AT THE defense table when the Senate convened at noon on Thursday, April 9, Benjamin Curtis gazed over piles of law books and manuscript sheets. The clean-shaven lawyer—of medium height and meaty build, with a large head—somewhat resembled his client, the president. He waited as Butler presented inconsequential testimony from two final prosecution witnesses. Then the fifty-nine-year-old former Supreme Court justice rose to give the opening statement for the defense. He cautioned his audience that his legal analysis would be "dry work." He was as good as his word.

Curtis's manner was judicial and restrained, even "monotonous," according to one observer. Many ladies fled the gallery during his opening hour, disappointed by his lack of flair. He used few vivid metaphors, indulged no personal recriminations, predicted neither glory nor doom for the Republic. In short, his stiff presentation contrasted in every way with

Benjamin Curtis, former Supreme Court Justice.

Butler's splenetic posturing, a contrast that made the defense seem more professional and more reliable. Even Butler acknowledged Curtis's effectiveness. After Curtis's speech, Butler wrote in his memoirs, "[N]othing *more* was said in [Johnson's] behalf, though . . . much *else* was said."

The Boston lawyer dove directly into the Tenure of Office Act, which was the basis for the first eight impeachment articles. He seized on a vexing ambiguity in the law. As initially approved by the Senate, the statute did not apply to Cabinet-level officers (the secretaries of war, state, interior, agriculture, and navy, and the postmaster general and attorney general). The House of Representatives then adopted a version that specifically covered Cabinet officers. A conference committee of senators and congressmen hammered out new, compromise language. A House sponsor declared that the new language covered Cabinet members (the House position); a Senate sponsor told the Senate that the new provision excluded the Cabinet (the Senate position). Thus reassured with diametrically opposed descriptions of the revised bill, both houses approved it, then enacted it over Johnson's veto.

The critical passage was deceptively simple. It stated that Cabinet officers "shall hold their offices respectively for and *during the term of the president by whom they may have been appointed*, . . . subject to removal by and with the advice of the Senate." Curtis stressed two ambiguities in applying this passage to Edwin Stanton. First, he argued, Johnson did not appoint Stanton to be war secretary. Lincoln did, and he did it in 1862. After Lincoln's death, Johnson merely permitted Stanton to continue in office. In addition, Curtis continued, Lincoln's term of office had been over since April 1865, since Lincoln was dead. "Death is a limit," he stated bluntly. Stanton, Curtis concluded, was now serving during the "term" of a president (Johnson) who had not appointed him. Accordingly, the Tenure of Office Act did not protect him, so Johnson had been free to cashier the war secretary.

There were two effective responses to the defense lawyer's argument. It was true that President Johnson did not appoint Stanton to the Cabinet, but by retaining him there, the president demonstrated the intent to have him in office. In many circumstances, the law would view Johnson's conduct as constituting the effective appointment of Stanton to that position. In addition, wasn't Johnson filling out Lincoln's "term" as president? Johnson had never been elected president in his own right. If Lincoln's term continued until March 4, 1869, then Stanton was still serving within the term of the president who appointed him.

Recognizing that there were rejoinders to his arguments, Curtis did not press them too hard. He sought only to establish that he had raised "a very honest and solid question" about whether the statute applied to Stanton. If reasonable minds could differ on the point, he asked, then how could the prosecution show that Johnson had intentionally violated the law? If Curtis could persuade senators that the statute was not clear, then the president's actions were not "so willful, so wrong" as to be a high misdemeanor warranting conviction by the Senate.

Speaking for three hours on the opening afternoon, and then another hour the next day, Curtis showed lawyerly ingenuity. He not only contended that Johnson never meant to violate the Tenure of Office Act, but also insisted that the president had the constitutional power to fire Stanton and so had no duty to respect the statute. Curtis shrugged off the inconvenient fact that Johnson had several times complied with the Tenure of Office Act without seeking a judicial ruling on its constitutionality. The president followed the statute's procedures when he first suspended Stanton, and when he fired four other officials. Holding the president to have thereby abandoned his constitutional powers would be, in one of Curtis's rare flights of rhetoric, "a spectacle for gods and men."

Curtis then spun around to take an entirely different position. Johnson's intent to replace Stanton was irrelevant, the lawyer insisted, because he had not actually removed the war secretary. In urging this surprising proposition, Curtis chose to ignore the president's refusal to transact business through Stanton, as well as Lorenzo Thomas's regular attendance at Cabinet meetings as the supposed interim war secretary. Curtis also denied that Johnson had *appointed* Thomas as interim war secretary at all, calling the president's action the temporary filling of a vacancy—a distinction of bewildering subtlety.

On Curtis's second day, Friday, April 10, the weather was wet and grim. Inside the Senate, he had some uncharacteristic fun with Butler's stump-speech article. The Boston lawyer called the attack on the president's blustery speeches the equivalent of turning Congress "into a school of manners, selecting from its ranks those gentlemen whom it deems most competent . . . to teach decorum of speech." After Butler's performance before the Senate, the thrust was a fair one.

Despite his dry work and dry oratory, Curtis successfully launched the president's case. His thoughtful demeanor had a positive impact, which was reinforced by his stature as a former Supreme Court justice. Curtis brought a dignity to the defense that Butler could not match. It was not, after all, a case of horse-stealing, and no one could think so after listening to Curtis.

Curtis's legal analysis had the power to persuade, particularly his dissection of the Tenure of Office Act and his insistence that the president did not have to be correct that Stanton was not covered by the statute. So long as Johnson's interpretation of the statute was not unreasonable, Curtis had argued, then a senator should vote to acquit. How could a president be deposed for applying an ambiguous statute in a reasonable manner? By the time Curtis completed his speech, all but one Cabinet member changed his view of the trial, suddenly agreeing that the president would be acquitted. Though many other factors played into the final vote on impeachment, Republican Senator Fessenden of Maine awarded Curtis the highest accolade: "Judge Curtis gave us the law and we followed it."

The galleries were looking forward to the testimony of the first defense witness. Jaunty Lorenzo Thomas did not disappoint. With disarming insouciance, he related how the president designated him interim war secretary, then described his efforts to seize control of that department. Thomas beguiled listeners with his tale of Stanton's gentle response to the news that Thomas was arrested before breakfast. The image of Stanton stroking Thomas's hair, "as he sometimes does," then pouring out whiskeys for the two of them, seemed to dissolve the risk of a second civil war. "No two cooing doves ever met on milder terms," crowed the *New York Herald*. Managers Butler and Bingham attempted to shatter the warm feelings with almost an hour's worth of objections to testimony about the president's statements to Thomas, but the Senate overwhelmingly voted to hear out the adjutant general.

Butler fricasseed Thomas during cross-examination. The adjutant general gamely insisted that it was his idea, not the president's, to use force to take over the War Department. Thomas maintained he did not even tell Johnson of his intention to use force. Then, Thomas testified, he changed his mind about using force, though he could not explain why he did, or why he failed to share that decision with the president. Finally, he said that Johnson never told him how to take charge of the War Office. Butler struck pay dirt when he secured Thomas's admission that he was attending Cabinet meetings as the war secretary, and that the president took the position that Stanton was out of office. That testimony contradicted Judge Curtis's claim that Stanton never had been removed as war secretary. Butler's sarcastic questioning elicited frequent laughter. When Thomas left the stand, Butler bade him a cheery farewell: "We shall always be glad to see him."

If Thomas brought laughter to the Senate Chamber, the next witness contributed star power. General William Sherman strode forward to take his oath. He chose to testify while standing, his strong voice reaching each corner of the large hall. The galleries, with opera glasses trained on the red-bearded soldier, leaned forward for a better look. Sherman answered Stanberry's preliminary questions briskly, his formal demeanor almost thrilling after Thomas's genial bumbling.

The defense, as Butler knew, wanted Sherman to testify that the president's every step was designed to secure a court decision on his power to remove Stanton. Stanberry asked whether Sherman had interviews with Johnson over Stanton's status. "I had," Sherman answered. The House managers erupted with objections. Sherman retreated to a seat to wait out the lawyers.

The managers protested any testimony about the president's statements to Sherman. If the defense wished to present Johnson's statements, Butler insisted, they should produce the president himself. The defense lawyers replied, and Chief Justice Chase agreed, that the Senate had allowed Adjutant General Thomas to offer exactly such testimony. The Senate promptly reversed that ruling and refused to hear the testimony from Sherman. Stanberry struggled to get around the ruling and elicit from his witness the desired statements by Johnson, but without success. Stanberry brought Sherman back the following day for another try, but had no better luck.

The defense contrived a new tactic. On the following trial day, Monday, April 13, General Sherman took the stand for a third time. Senator Reverdy Johnson, a Maryland Democrat and ally of the president, posed a question. Did the president explain to General Sherman why he offered to appoint him as secretary of war? By a single vote, the Senate allowed Sherman to answer. Sherman gathered his thoughts for a moment, now that he finally would be permitted to share them.

Astonishingly, the general did not give the testimony the defense had labored for three days to present—that the president wished the dispute over the Tenure of Office Act to go to the courts. Johnson "did not state to me," Sherman said, "that his purpose was to bring [the dispute] to the courts directly; but [said it was] for the purpose of having the office administered properly in the interest of the Army and of the whole country." According to Sherman, when he asked Johnson why the matter was not before the courts, the president replied that it could not be. Wisely, the managers saw no need to cross-examine Sherman.

The general had confounded the defense lawyers and helped the prosecution by describing Johnson as uninterested in going to court. Sherman had undermined one of the president's principal defenses. On

the other hand, the Senate's rulings on the admission of evidence per-
plexed everyone. The Senate allowed Thomas to testify about the president's statements, then refused to hear such testimony from Sherman,
then reversed itself again. These arbitrary changes in direction raised
questions about the fairness of the trial.

On the night when Sherman's testimony ended, another misfortune
struck the defense. Stanberry, who had trained like a prizefighter for the
trial, fell ill. It was pleurisy, a dangerous lung infection. The Senate
granted the defense a one-day recess, but the president's team would
have to persevere without the lawyer Johnson trusted most. Stanberry
would not be able to answer the bell for the next round.

The president brooded over his fate. Every night, he greeted an aide
who attended the trial, William W. Warden, with the words, "Well, what
are the signs of the zodiac today?" The news rarely cheered him. On
Sunday, April 12, he heard a sermon on Chapter 12, third verse, of the
First Book of Samuel, in which an old king walks among his people and
self-righteously demands, "Whose ox have I taken? Or whose ass have I
taken? Or whom have I defrauded? Whom have I oppressed? Or of
whose hand have I received any bribe to blind mine eyes therewith?"
Dwelling on the application of that verse to his situation, Johnson pulled
from his shelf a Bible he had brought with him from Tennessee. He
studied the passage. Colonel Moore, who sat with him, was struck by
how keenly Johnson felt the injustice of the trial.

That night the president's defenders met in the White House. A
visitor recorded the scene. With Nelson, the Tennessee lawyer, sitting
to one side, Curtis and William Evarts reviewed possible trial exhibits.
Each time they turned to a document, they fretted that it could do as
much harm as good. After a lifetime in courtrooms, Judge Curtis said, he
"feared every new witness," since the House managers "were fishing for
evidence." Evarts concurred.

The next day, when Sherman unexpectedly damaged the defense
case and Stanberry took to his sickbed, the president was gloomy. The
official events of his days only reinforced the nation's troubles, both from
the war and from the current struggle over Reconstruction. On April 15,
the third anniversary of Lincoln's death, Johnson presided over the ded-

ication of a monument to the late president. Perched on a thirty-five-foot pedestal, the life-size statue stood in front of Washington's City Hall. The ceremony was not entirely harmonious. General Grant declined to join Johnson on the platform, but stood on a nearby sidewalk. In Lincoln's memory, War Secretary Stanton directed that a cannon be fired every half hour from sunrise to sunset. Demonstrating his control over the department, Stanton closed it at noon that day. The closing did little to disrupt a city that was transfixed by impeachment. Department heads reported that never before had government workers performed so few duties.

On April 16, Johnson greeted a Union Army veteran, Sergeant Gilbert Bates, who had executed a personal project to unite the country. As a gesture of reconciliation with Southerners, Bates walked 1,400 miles from Vicksburg, Mississippi, to Washington City, carrying an American flag. He gave Johnson the flag along with messages he collected along the way. The sergeant reported that he was received warmly throughout the South. In North Carolina and Virginia, he recounted, "I had a bouquet in my hand every hour of the day." Bates told the president that thousands of former rebels would gladly fight for the Union now.

At the same time, and despite raw weather, blacks in Washington celebrated the anniversary of the Emancipation Proclamation. From a White House window, Johnson bowed to salutes from the marchers, who gathered to hear speeches on a field south of the mansion. Johnson complained that a military display was part of the ceremony, fearing that it aligned the federal government with the blacks.

The new Ku Klux Klan was growing at astonishing rates across the South, gaining virtual control of whole counties in Tennessee, whipping black people in the night and burning homes and courthouses. The Klan took credit for the murder of a leading Unionist in Georgia. With the spread of the Klan and other paramilitary organizations dedicated to white supremacy, the prospect rose again of guerilla warfare that could bloody the South for years.

The Klan delivered its verdict of hate directly to the House managers. Logan, Stevens, and Bingham received messages in red ink, festooned with skulls and coffins, pledging death to traitors. Butler, due to his prominent trial role, was the target of multiple threats: A message on a window shutter in the House Reporters' Gallery stated BUTLER PREPARE

TO MEET THY GOD. THE AVENGER IS ABROAD ON YOUR TRACK. AFTER DEATH COMES
JUDGMENT. HELL IS YOUR PORTION.

The managers were not deterred. Butler summoned people from
around the country as possible rebuttal witnesses. He asked a former
Confederate general for information about any "pro-secession proclivi-
ties" of Lorenzo Thomas during the war. He brought General Sherman
in for more questioning, along with the publisher of a pro-Johnson newspaper in Washington.

With several managers preparing closing speeches for the trial's end,
the prosecution was irate over the Senate's rule that only two final speakers could appear for each side. There were, after all, *seven* managers.
They agreed among themselves that Butler would give no closing address and that Bingham and Boutwell would. That raised the alarming
prospect that the other four managers would never step into the trial's
spotlight. Stevens, John Logan, and Thomas Williams had devoted considerable effort to preparing closing orations. The managers demanded
the right to deliver at least five closing speeches, or maybe more. When
the issue was raised by motion on April 12, Stevens supported it with his
first public words of the trial. The Senate ducked the question until April
22, when it finally yielded, allowing an unlimited number of closing
statements by both sides.

With the trial entering its third week, War Secretary Stanton began
to relax. Visiting the War Department in early April, General Sherman
had been surprised by the heavy guard around the building. Stanton, he
remarked, was better protected than Sherman had been when riding
through Indian country. By the middle of the month, Stanton was stray-
ing from his post. He and Mrs. Stanton, evidently reconciled, slipped
away for a weekend in Baltimore, leaving his son Eddie (who was his
personal aide) to guard the fort. After that, the Secretary started going
home in the evenings for dinner and a rest. Stanton continued to provide
advice to the impeachers.

After General Sherman's testimony, the proceedings languished. For
most of Wednesday, April 15, the defense bored the Senate near to
death. Benjamin Curtis, master of bloodless presentation, submitted
documents reflecting the methods of appointing and removing officials

through the life of the Republic. Curtis covered interim appointments of postmasters, naval officers, and every Cabinet-level official from 1829 to 1860. He was proving an uncontested point: that previous presidents routinely discharged executive officials without the participation of the Senate, even when the Senate was in session. Because those dismissals came before the Tenure of Office Act was adopted, they had little bearing on the issue before the Senate.

The following day brought unexpected fireworks. Ben Butler's temper frayed through an afternoon of battling to exclude testimony about statements made by Johnson. In this instance, the Senate chose to hear the testimony. The Senate's inconsistency was maddening. When William Evarts proposed to adjourn early, Butler pitched a fit. Every minute the trial dragged on, he warned, meant that white marauders would slaughter more law-abiding citizens in the South. "The moment justice is done on this great criminal," he thundered, "these murders will cease." He warmed to his subject:

> While we are being courteous [to Johnson's lawyers] the free Union men of the South are being murdered, and on our heads and on our skirts will be their blood.

Butler delivered the emotional words with passion. One observer depicted the stout Massachusetts manager moving "every muscle and limb of his body, like a frog in the pangs of vivisection." Defense lawyer Evarts calmly disparaged Butler's speech as a "harangue," and won his early adjournment.

Though many applauded Evarts's unruffled response to Butler, President Johnson despaired over its mildness. Evarts, Johnson complained, missed the chance to "administer a rebuke that would not only have told upon the Senate but upon the whole country." With Stanberry ailing, the president was "particularly dissatisfied" with Evarts. He considered telling the New York lawyer that he had mismanaged the case.

Despite his client's feelings, Evarts was playing an increasingly central role. He took charge of the final evidentiary push for the defense. From the beginning, Johnson's lawyers planned to present testimony by Cabinet members. Trailing the dignity of high office, they would describe how Stanton himself had condemned the Tenure of Office Act as unconstitutional. They also were expected to fill the evidentiary hole left by General Sherman; they would testify that the president intended to challenge the Tenure of Office Act in court. That argument over the president's intent was a red herring, since Johnson had taken no step to challenge the law while complying with it in several instances.

Evarts began to play the Cabinet card in the early afternoon of Friday, April 17. He started with Gideon Welles, secretary of the navy through the full terms of both Lincoln and Johnson. Principally remembered for the sharp-edged entries in his daily diary, Welles was a strong Johnson loyalist. With a tart New England outlook and a beard even more ebullient than Stanton's, Welles walked ramrod-straight to the front of the Senate, brandishing a pair of gold spectacles.

Evarts asked Welles about Johnson's disclosure to his Cabinet that he had fired Stanton. Butler sprang to his feet, objecting that Welles learned of the president's action after it happened, so the conversation was irrelevant. After a lengthy argument between lawyers, the Senate voted 26 to 23 to hear the testimony. Soon Butler was objecting again, this time to evidence that the Cabinet thought the Tenure of Office Act was unconstitutional. The defense, he protested, wanted to "have the ministers shield the king." If Johnson could hide behind his Cabinet's

Gideon Welles, Secretary of the Navy.

advice, then he need only select Cabinet officers who would advise him "as he wants to be advised." Evarts fell back on the defense mantra: if the president thought the statute unconstitutional, then he had no intention to commit an illegal act when he replaced Stanton.

The dispute spilled over to the next day, when Manager James Wilson took over the argument. In his sober and ingratiating manner, Wilson explained that even if Cabinet members thought the Tenure of Office Act unconstitutional, they did not advise Johnson to ignore it, so the offered testimony was irrelevant. Though Curtis tried to counter Wilson's reasoning, the Senate once more changed its standard for receiving evidence. By a 20-to-29 vote, it refused to hear Welles testify about the Cabinet Secretaries' views of the statute, and by a wider margin refused to hear evidence of their wish for a court challenge to the law. Though other Cabinet members, including Secretary of State Seward, were waiting to testify, the defense lawyers gave up the effort.

The dispute, at one level, was pointless. Every senator knew that Johnson's Cabinet thought the Tenure of Office Act was invalid. Indeed, the Senate had accepted into evidence documents reciting the Cabinet's view. Yet the defense won a considerable victory by losing on this question. The exclusion of the Secretaries' testimony made the Senate seem high-handed, even unconcerned with justice. To many, the Senate had demeaned the distinguished members of the Cabinet. By muzzling some of the most prominent men in the nation, it seemed more interested in covering up than revealing the truth, while denying the president a fair opportunity to present his case. In the end, the episode only emphasized the evidence that the Senate supposedly excluded.

This last fight magnified a negative impression that had built through the trial: that the case was a lawyer's frolic, an exercise in legal formalism that was divorced from the momentous question of who should run the country. By several counts, the evidentiary squabbles consumed roughly one-third of the trial. Every minute of sparring over evidence made the case seem more like Butler's horse case and less like a constitutional confrontation of historic importance. In Butler's hands, the case became small. The managers—particularly Butler—should have known better. They talked too much about too little.

Evarts announced the end of the defense case on Saturday, April 18. Two days later, the House managers offered a few scraps of rebuttal, notably a list of 41,000 federal jobs. If acquitted, the managers argued, Johnson would claim unbridled discretion to fill every one of those jobs with his cringing dependents. Nothing in the rebuttal materials made much impression. Indeed, the trial had performed little practical function beyond the theatrical. "[T]he evidence sheds absolutely no light on the case," complained an editorial in *The Nation*. "It might all have been dispensed with on both sides."

Most European observers found the spectacle confusing, a distasteful example of America's rambunctious politics. The *Times* of London was puzzled. Congress had passed its legislation over Johnson's veto. What need was there to remove him? For Frenchmen living in the Second Empire of Louis-Napoléon, the impeachment demonstrated the wisdom of limiting the power of representative assemblies.

Two steps yet remained to the contest. First, the combatants would give their closing statements. Then the Senate would vote. Though those two steps sound simple, it would take a month to complete them, longer than the trial up to then. It took so long because the fight grew ever more fierce.

18

COUNTING TO SEVEN

APRIL 1868

[I]t is certain that no man has the least confidence in the [House of Lords'] impartiality when a great public functionary, charged with a great state crime, is brought to their bar. They are all politicians. There is hardly one among them, whose vote on an impeachment may not be confidently predicted before a witness has been examined.

THOMAS BABINGTON MACAULAY, 1841

ON SUNDAY, APRIL 19, Colonel Moore asked the president how he thought the impeachment vote would turn out. It was all conjecture, Johnson replied, declining to say more. Despite his demure response, the president was devoting careful attention to the question. With the trial nearing its end, counting the votes in the Senate became an obsession throughout Washington City. The arithmetic remained simple. The president could rely on the votes of nine Democrats and three "Johnson Republicans." That left him seven votes short of the nineteen he needed to block conviction. Judgments varied on whether and where he could find those seven additional votes.

On April 11, the *Chicago Tribune* predicted that Johnson would be convicted; six days later it reported that gamblers were betting large sums on acquittal. After another five days, the *Springfield* (Mass.) *Republican* explained that conviction was certain because only three Republicans would vote to acquit. The *New York Times* agreed with that prognosis in early May. The *New York Independent* wrote, "The President's intimate friends abandon all hope, and report him to be dejected and silent." At the same time, the *New York Herald* found that the president's acquittal was expected. The *Petersburg Index* in Virginia confessed that it could not predict how the vote would turn out.

Some of these conflicting reports reflected the wishful thinking of writers and editors. News reporting in the 1860s often included a strong dose of bias. But the contradictory reports also reflected reality. The forecast changed from day to day as rumors were sifted with incomplete reports of offhand remarks by senators. Samuel Barlow of New York, a lawyer and Democratic power broker, struggled to reconcile the reports from Washington. On April 4, he was told that Johnson could not be saved by all the money available for bribes from "the whiskey Ring together with all the Political Influence and Political trickery of [Secretary of State] William H. Seward and [New York Republican boss] Thurlow Weed." Two weeks later, he heard that Johnson would win with eight additional Republican votes. Barlow remained skeptical.

At the end of the first week of trial, Judge Curtis estimated that between twenty-two and twenty-five Republican senators "began the trial with a fixed determination to convict" and would never change their minds. That left more than a dozen Republicans whose votes he could not predict. "What will become of them I know not," he wrote, "but the result is with them." Senator James Grimes of Iowa was more generous in his estimate of how open-minded the Senate Republicans were. Grimes insisted that at least thirty of his colleagues "intend to hear the evidence and weigh the law before they pronounce judgment."

As the trial wore on, many tried to ferret out which way the uncommitted senators were leaning. Senator William Sprague of Rhode Island was judged an uncertain vote until a newspaper story related his conversation on a train between New York and Washington. The senator told a companion that, unlike his father-in-law, Chief Justice Chase, he believed Johnson should be removed. Sprague thus ended, for a time, active speculation about his vote.

Schuyler Colfax of Indiana, the Republican Speaker of the House, counted votes carefully. In a note to the editor of the *New York Herald*, he despaired that Fowler of Tennessee not only was sitting with the

Democrats, but also was voting for the defense on evidentiary questions. Grimes of Iowa appeared to be lost, Colfax added, along with Fessenden of Maine. Senator Ross of Kansas was suspiciously intimate with the pro-Johnson Ewing family, while Colfax was anxious about the other Rhode Island senator, Henry Anthony. Colfax named four more Republicans who were mistrusted by others, but he refused to believe they would betray the party on this crucial vote.

Colfax, like several newspapers, stressed that gamblers were betting heavily on Johnson's acquittal. The role of gamblers in the impeachment troubled many. By linking private profit with this pivotal public event, the widespread wagering created the same motivations for bribe-paying (and bribe-taking) that arise with gambling on sporting events. Most obviously, betting could be used as a vehicle for payoffs. For example, to bribe a senator to vote for conviction, a person could bet on acquittal with an agent of that senator; if the president were then convicted with that senator's vote, the briber could pay off on the bet and the senator's agent could share the winnings with the senator. The same device could be used to acquire votes for acquittal. Indeed, one correspondent reported that abundant funds were available to buy an acquittal. A half-million dollars supposedly was offered for the influence of one man.

A good deal of the impeachment betting, along with rumors of bribery, was tied to the "Whiskey Ring." The whiskey ring of the 1860s—a shorthand reference to regional groups of distillers—demonstrated how tax policy can warp private and public conduct. Untaxed until 1862, whiskey then sold for about 24 cents a gallon. To finance the war effort, Congress levied whopping excises on alcoholic spirits, which finally reached $2 per gallon in 1865. Each tax increase took effect after a grace period, which created a powerful incentive to distill huge quantities of whiskey before the higher tax rate applied. As a result, the nation's distillery capacity tripled and whiskey inventories skyrocketed.

After 1865, many distillers bribed officials not to collect the huge taxes on their product. The corruption of revenue officers was so rampant that whiskey often sold for less than the amount of the tax, an impossibility without crooked tax collectors. As New York political boss Thurlow Weed wrote to Secretary of State Seward, the Whiskey Ring came to prefer the high tax because it "affords a larger margin for plunder." Between January and March of 1868, the House Ways and Means

Committee conducted hearings on whiskey tax frauds in New York. Bent collectors were prosecuted in New Orleans, Philadelphia, and New York, but the cases only scratched the surface of the corruption.

During the impeachment season, the Whiskey Ring loomed as a powerful force for retaining Johnson in office. Any change at the Treasury Department could disrupt the pervasive cheating that was the lifeblood of the industry. After the trial, public attention would focus on how the whiskey interests might have influenced Senate votes.

The doubtful senators faced nonstop advocacy wherever they turned. Republicans from around the country descended on Washington to urge their senators to convict the president. They emphasized the cause of the party. Losing the impeachment vote, their argument went, would reveal Republicans as weak and divided, thereby ensuring Democratic victories in the fall elections. "There are a thousand Thad Stevenses in Washington shaking their fingers in the faces of the Senate," wrote the *New York Times*, "and daring any member to vote otherwise than Thad Stevens desires." Republican governors of Pennsylvania, Wisconsin, and Minnesota were in town on April 17 to support the impeachers. Colonel Moore at the White House worried that home state officials were arriving "to manage Senators who are suspected of leaning to the side of the President."

Much of the advocacy, in those days before civil service reform, was distinctly mercenary. With every position in the federal government a political appointment, a change in presidents meant a bounty of job opportunities. Republicans nattered eagerly about jobs that would flow to the party faithful when Ben Wade of Ohio took over the Executive Mansion. Though Wade mostly refused to discuss appointments he might make as president, he was beset by office-seekers. His mail bulged with requests for positions. "The worst class of political cormorants," wrote future President James Garfield, "are thronging the lobbies and filling the hotels in high hopes of plunder when Wade is sworn in." Wade's disposition, "not the most agreeable" under ordinary circumstances, soured under the onslaught.

Though Wade's term as president would last for less than a year if Johnson were convicted, the Tenure of Office Act gave extra value to any executive appointment by Wade. Under the statute, any president elected in the fall of 1868 would not be able to remove Wade's non-

Cabinet appointees without the concurrence of the Senate. Consequently, a Wade appointee with strong Senate sponsors might look forward to lengthy public service. Newspapers routinely speculated about which Cabinet offices would go to which Republican worthies in a Wade Administration. Many thought that Ben Butler's hard work on the trial would win him the Treasury Department. Speaker Colfax deplored this crass response to the impeachment. "The set of men who assume to speak for Wade," he wrote at the end of April, "and who are making Cabinets and pressing patronage openly . . . don't help with the doubtful men."

The pro-Johnson forces pointed with horror at the prospect of Ben Wade in the Executive Mansion, an eventuality that might be only days away. On April 25, the *Chicago Tribune* predicted that the Ohio senator would be sworn in on May 1. A Democratic newspaper warned that Wade's elevation would raise the "constant danger of a bold committal to woman suffrage [and] some novelty in the financial system." Wade also would gain the inside track on the Republican vice presidential nomination. For Republicans who preferred someone else on the ticket with General Grant, that was one more reason not to convict Andrew Johnson.

William Pitt Fessenden of Maine topped the list of "doubtful men" in the Senate. The acerbic New Englander made no secret of his distaste for impeachment, and for Ben Wade. Playing cards during the trial, he remarked that he would soon be one of the most unpopular men in the nation. He confided to a cousin that the impeachment was "most unwise and can result only in disaster." He added, "I prefer tar and feathers to lifelong regret." Though Fessenden was a senator of stature, having served as chairman of the Joint Committee of Fifteen and as treasury secretary, his support for acquittal was apparent early enough that it did not prove especially influential. Moreover, his vote for Johnson was dismissed as resulting from his antipathy toward Wade.

More significant was the potential defection of James Grimes of Iowa, also an alumnus of the Joint Committee of Fifteen. In the spring of 1868, Grimes not only left the Republican fold on impeachment, but also paved the way for others to follow.

A New England expatriate, the burly lawyer rose to prominence on the Iowa frontier as an antislavery man. A year earlier, Grimes wrote to his wife that President Johnson was "guilty of many great follies and wickedness," but his misdeeds were not enough to justify the "shock" of impeachment. Two more years of misrule by Johnson, Grimes added, were a short time in the life of a nation. The botched effort to place Lorenzo Thomas as war secretary did not change the Iowan's views. In early April, while speaking with Gustavus Fox, the former Navy official, Grimes had raised two crucial points facing every Republican considering a vote for acquittal: how Johnson would behave if he were acquitted, and the need to have only one secretary of war. Fox had passed the message back to the White House.

Impatient with the slow response to Fox's message, Grimes waylaid Reverdy Johnson on the Senate floor. The Maryland Democrat, who was close to the president, was meeting nightly with a White House aide to report on the scuttlebutt passing among senators. Grimes pressed the Marylander to broker a meeting between him and the president. Republicans might vote for acquittal, Grimes said, but only if they believed that the president would engage in no rash acts that would "encourage rebels." Skittish Republicans had to know they would not regret letting Johnson off the hook. The president, Grimes urged, could provide those assurances informally, at a social encounter. Reverdy Johnson agreed. He proposed that Grimes and the president drop by his rooms at the Arlington Hotel at 9 P.M. the following evening.

Here was an opportunity for Johnson to try a new approach: conciliatory words and deeds. Looking down the barrel of impeachment, he could win support by offering the sort of commitments that can make governing possible. Had he been willing to take such conciliatory steps earlier, he might have avoided impeachment altogether.

The next night, the president visited the Arlington Hotel and joined Grimes in Reverdy Johnson's drawing room. After some social banter, the host raised the question that had brought them there. How would Johnson deport himself if acquitted? The president answered that the alarmists had no reason to fear him: He would comply with the Constitution in all matters. As much by his willingness to meet as by any particular statement, the president persuaded the Iowa senator that acquittal would not release floodgates of partisan retribution. Thus armed, Grimes assured doubtful senators that he knew Johnson's intentions and there would be no postacquittal reign of terror. The president, he assured them, "has no thought of wrong or rash doings."

That still left Grimes's second concern, the standoff at the War Department. The situation was ridiculous. No one in North America—not even the president, based on his recent newspaper interview—thought Lorenzo Thomas should be head of that department. Nevertheless, Thomas attended Cabinet meetings as part of the charade that he was the interim Secretary, while Stanton occupied the War Office but had no contact with the president. After weeks of stalemate, with the nation convulsed over impeachment, Johnson still had offered no viable alternative as war secretary. To win acquittal—to show that he could govern—the president had to resolve the situation. Johnson could be acquitted, wrote one correspondent, if only he "would quit his foolery with Lorenzo Thomas."

Prodded by Grimes's message, Johnson consulted his inner circle, which certainly included the canny secretary of state, William Seward, who took care to preserve cordial relations with political friends and opponents alike. A compromise candidate for war secretary emerged: General John Schofield. The thirty-seven-year-old West Pointer was not a renowned combat leader, but he was politically adept. Of the five generals first appointed to command Southern military districts under the Reconstruction laws, Schofield was the only one Johnson had not fired for enforcing those laws too vigorously. The president did not care for the plump and balding general from upstate New York, calling him a "cold and selfish man." Republicans also were tepid on Schofield, who opposed the Fourteenth Amendment. In short, neither side liked him, but both could live with him: exactly what the situation required.

Although William Evarts held no government position, the president's lawyer (and Seward confidant) played a central role in the Schofield nomination. On the afternoon of April 21, a recess day after the defense closed its evidence, Evarts invited the general to his rooms at Willard's Hotel. The lawyer explained that the president was prepared to appoint him as secretary of war. A note from General Grant interrupted them. The general-in-chief had business with Schofield, who was

William Evarts, New York lawyer, who led the president's defense inside and outside of the Senate.

staying at the Grants' home while in Washington City. Schofield excused himself, but not before gaining Evarts's agreement that he could talk to Grant about the offered appointment as war secretary.

Schofield kept a level head. He needed to be sure that his elevation would not rile the general-in-chief. He would fail as war secretary if he were caught in a cross fire between the president and Grant. After dinner that evening, the two generals went for a walk. Schofield described the proposition from Evarts. Grant, who viewed Schofield as a friend, had no objection to the appointment. With that assurance, Schofield returned to Evarts's hotel room at 8 P.M.

Evarts explained that although there was no factual basis for impeachment, some Republicans would not vote for acquittal unless the War Department was restored to normal. Schofield had been selected, Evarts said, because Grant would accept him (which Schofield knew was true), which would satisfy Republicans. The appointment was not a personal matter for the president, the lawyer went on, because "he really had no friends."

When Schofield returned to the Grants' home at 11 P.M., Grant insisted he would never believe a pledge by Johnson of future good conduct, then added that the president should be removed from office. Yet Grant still thought it proper for Schofield to accept the appointment. Next morning, Schofield told Evarts that he could go forward if the president abandoned the "annoying irregularities" in War Department matters that had developed during months of struggle with Stanton. When Evarts objected that Johnson could make no such commitment, Schofield replied that he would assume that his condition was acceptable if the president went through with the nomination.

Evarts kept tight control over the announcement of Schofield's nomination. The president sent Colonel Moore to deliver it to the Senate on Thursday, April 23, but Evarts waved the colonel away. The moment was not right. On the next day, the third day of closing arguments, Moore was back at the Senate with the nomination in hand. This time, Evarts nodded yes, and the paper was delivered. It created, Moore wrote in his diary, "considerable interest." Judge Curtis gave Moore a cheering message to carry back to the president. "[D]uring the last twenty-four hours impeachment had gone rapidly astern."

The press reported the Schofield nomination as an olive branch extended to doubtful Republican senators, and noted that Grant did not object to it. That last point was the most important one. Grant could have scuttled the maneuver by advising Schofield not to take the appointment. Partisans like Stanton and Stevens doubtless would have preferred for Grant to do so, denying the president any advantage in the trial. The general-in-chief did not, however, consult political advisers on the question. He decided on his own. Every day, he knew, the standoff over the War Department snarled the military. Even though the appointment might save Johnson, Grant would not obstruct resolution of that standoff. The Schofield nomination represented a surprising act of mutual forbearance between Johnson and Grant, whose dislike for each other had not abated. If Johnson would swallow his pride enough to appoint a secretary of war whom the Senate could confirm, Grant would not stand in his way.

A couple of days later, though, the general-in-chief changed his mind. On April 25, he dashed off a one-sentence note to Schofield suggesting that he decline the promotion to war secretary. Grant may have come to regret Schofield's nomination as it began to seem like a lifeline for the president. In reply, Schofield pointed out that he had already agreed to accept the position.

Despite the conciliatory gesture, Andrew Johnson still hungered for revenge against Grant. On the day after the Schofield nomination was announced, the president mused over ways to get at Grant "when this trouble is over." He had an idea. Because Grant's commission as General of the Army did not award him command of the army, and because Johnson had never appointed him to that command, Johnson thought he might still "get hold of him after a while."

• • •

As closing arguments filled the Senate Chamber, the head-counting gained in intensity. The president learned that Stanton was complaining that Fessenden, Grimes, and other Senate Republicans "had gone back on him." The news must have given Johnson hope.

Lyman Trumbull of Illinois, who had sponsored fourteen Reconstruction statutes, was leaning toward acquittal. In late February, when Johnson tried to appoint Lorenzo Thomas as war secretary, Trumbull had been "earnest for impeachment." During the trial, though, his doubts increased. Though he deplored Johnson's opposition to Congress on Reconstruction, Trumbull was not inclined to convict the president on any of the eleven impeachment articles.

In the tumult that followed the final impeachment votes, Fessenden, Grimes, and Trumbull received grudging credit for having expressed their doubts early. Few challenged the integrity of those three early defectors. Others of the doubtfuls did not receive a similar benefit of the doubt.

For example, Senator Edmund Ross of Kansas, protégé of Indian trader Perry Fuller, inspired little respect. "A great and insidious influence is operating upon Ross," wrote one observer, "who is a weak man and may be artfully operated on without his apprehension of the fact." Joseph Fowler of Tennessee was still sitting with the Democrats, so his inclinations were a source of Republican anxiety. Uncertainty also surrounded Peter Van Winkle of West Virginia, who often voted without regard to party.

Though the final outcome could not be predicted, by the last week of April the president had made progress toward securing the Republican defections he needed. The work of corralling votes would continue behind the scenes. Onstage, the stars of the show, the lawyers, were eager to deliver closing orations so brilliant, so incisive, so inspirational, that they would change history. If they fell short of that goal, it would not be for lack of effort.

19

AN AVALANCHE OF TALK

APRIL 22—MAY 6, 1868

[W]e have been wading knee deep in words, words, words. . . .
[T]here are fierce impeachers here, who, if [faced with] the
alternative of conviction of the President, coupled with their
silence, and an unlimited opportunity to talk coupled with his
certain acquittal . . . would instantly decide to speak.

REP. JAMES A. GARFIELD, APRIL 28, 1868

THE EXCITEMENT WAS back. On Wednesday, April 22, crowds flocked to the Senate chamber to hear closing arguments. The president was still in the White House. Secretary Stanton was still camped out in the War Department. One of them would be moving very soon. Spring temperatures brought ladies and gentlemen to the Capitol in their finest outfits, eager to hear soaring rhetoric about the fate of the Republic. This day, however, fell short on that score.

The session began with a ninety-minute dustup over how many speeches could be delivered on each side. Finally acceding to the House managers, the Senate grudgingly allowed an unlimited number of speakers. Manager John Logan of Illinois submitted his remarks in written form. In view of their great length, the Senate had cause to be grateful. Manager James Wilson of Iowa was even more gracious, offering no statement at all. Despite these self-denying gestures, the final speeches would consume almost two weeks. Four lawyers would speak for each side, in an alternating pattern: a House manager would begin, then two defense lawyers, followed by two managers. The last two defense lawyers would speak, and then a final House manager would conclude the ordeal. Americans in the 1860s were accustomed to long addresses, often treating oratory as a spectator sport. Nevertheless, the number and length of the closing arguments would wear down both the senators and the public.

Manager George Boutwell of Massachusetts opened for the prosecution. Having worked doggedly for more than a year to remove Andrew Johnson from office, Boutwell had to take some satisfaction in the moment. His address consumed three hours, until the Senate called it quits for the day.

The compact Boutwell, then fifty years old, did not electrify audiences. His solemn delivery could grow wearisome. Senators became distracted after the first thirty minutes. The galleries began to rustle. The ladies turned their opera glasses on one another, with even the occasional "telescopic flirtation."

Whatever his rhetorical limitations, Boutwell presented a thoughtful analysis. The president, he argued, had no innocent intent in the War Office episode. Johnson knowingly violated the Tenure of Office Act

The Ladies' Gallery in the Senate during the trial.

without taking any step to test the statute in court. Reviewing the legislative history of the statute, Boutwell challenged the defense view that it did not apply to Stanton. He made deft use of learned allusions, deploying a passage from *Hamlet* to compare Johnson's Cabinet to the simpering servility of Polonius. He also offered the most obscure classical analogy of the trial, equating the president's performance in office with the disastrous administration of Sicily by Caius Verres in 80 B.C.

Boutwell's bland demeanor cloaked a white-hot rage against Andrew Johnson. The anger burned through on the second day of his peroration. He denounced Johnson for delivering to Southerners the power "they had sought by rebellion," condemning the region to "disorder, rapine, and bloodshed." Then he offered an astronomical interlude, describing a part of the night sky where no heavenly body could be seen. That "dreary, cold, dark region of space," Boutwell continued, was the only proper destination for the president:

> If this earth was capable of the sentiments and emotions of justice and virtue, . . . it would heave and throw, . . . and project this enemy of two races of men into that vast region, there forever to exist in a solitude as eternal as life. . . .

Most press accounts ignored this powerful image of a convulsing planet ejecting the horror that was Andrew Johnson, but defense lawyer William Evarts was paying close attention. He would make the managers regret Boutwell's astronomical curse.

The press neglected Boutwell's moment of excess because the next speaker, defense lawyer Thomas Nelson of Tennessee, offered nothing but excess. A Whig from East Tennessee, Nelson had opposed Johnson politically for many years. The two reconciled in the dangerous days of 1861, when both opposed secession from the Union.

The outline of Nelson's speech made sense. By showing the president's human side, the Tennessean aimed to tear down the monstrous image created by the Radicals' perfervid rhetoric. Nelson's manner, though, was ill suited to the task. After his opening, shouted question, "Who is Andrew Johnson?" Nelson rapidly lost his listeners' attention. He was loud and confrontational, denying that the Senate could legitimately conduct the trial without Southern senators present. One observer thought Nelson "mistook the Senate for a set of Tennessee sinners, and appealed to its feeling instead of its judgment." Another described his oration as "a great impassioned appeal to defend the President without strict regard to time and place, the rules of logic, or the nicer distinctions in grammar and philology." When Nelson ended his seven-hour speech on Friday afternoon, April 24, most seats were empty. Of the managers, only Butler remained. Judge Curtis drowsed alone at the defense table.

Nelson also inserted a distraction: the Caribbean guano island of Alta Vela. Boutwell had referred to the withdrawal of Jeremiah Black as one of Johnson's defense lawyers. Black abandoned the president when Johnson refused to intervene in favor of his clients' claim to bird waste on Alta Vela. In answer to Boutwell, Nelson revealed a letter to the president, dated six weeks earlier, in support of Black's clients. Drafted by Ben Butler, the letter was signed by three other managers (Bingham, Stevens, and Logan), and several more Republicans. These impeachers thus petitioned the president on behalf of guano claimants as they attempted to remove him from office. In truth, the letter had nothing to do with impeachment, but those who signed it suffered deep embarrassment.

The next defense lawyer, William Groesbeck of Cincinnati, elicited a far different response. Groesbeck had been to Washington City before. He had served a single term as a Democratic congressman and attended the "Peace Convention" that met in Washington in early 1861 to try to head off war. Still, he appeared before the Senate as a tall, lanky unknown. He had not spoken during the trial. The beaky lawyer not only finished his address in a single day but also bewitched his audience. One listener claimed that Groesbeck gave the finest speech ever heard in the Senate.

In contrast to Nelson, Groesbeck was not combative. In contrast to Judge Curtis, he was not dry. Groesbeck impressed his listeners with a careful description of the historical precedents for presidential removal of subordinates. Instead of denouncing the impeachers, he expressed dismay that Johnson could be ousted based on "these miserable little questions." He drew a sympathetic portrait of his client. Johnson, Groesbeck insisted, "trod the path on which were the footprints of Lincoln," seeking only reconciliation.

William S. Groesbeck of Cincinnati, counsel for President Johnson.

Ah, he was too eager, too forgiving, too kind. The hand of conciliation was reached out to him and he took it. It may be that he should
have put it away, but was it a crime to take it? Kindness, forgiveness,
a crime?

Groesbeck thus reinvented the congenitally angry president who had
demanded that traitors be hanged, who had accused the Radicals of
seeking his assassination, whose dedication to states' rights prevented
him from compromising with Congress, and who had abandoned Southern Unionists and freedmen to brutal violence. In Groesbeck's version
of the world, Andrew Johnson's only crime was excessive kindness.

After a Sunday of what must have seemed like golden silence, the
week began with the much anticipated address by Thad Stevens for the
prosecution. Throughout the spring, the press had been transfixed by
the Pennsylvanian's decline, meticulously charting his progress to the
grave. His daily attendance at the trial was compelling stuff. "He seems
to breathe with difficulty," reported the *Cincinnati Commercial*. "His
voice has that dreadful low, grating sound that we hear from deathbeds."

On the Senate floor, Stevens sipped brandy and port while eating raw eggs and terrapin. He limped unsteadily on his club foot or rode in a chair hoisted by powerful porters. His gaunt face and empty gaze seemed to summon judgment from the world beyond.

For twenty-five minutes on Monday, April 27, Stevens gave it a try. He read from foolscap sheets, his voice steadily weakening until almost no one could hear him. Stevens accepted Ben Butler's offer to read the final half of the address for him.

Acknowledging that the Senate trial was no place for "railing accusation," Stevens could not help himself. He demanded that Johnson "be tortured on the gibbet of everlasting obloquy." He insisted that impeachment was the correct remedy for the president's political offenses. Stevens tried to widen the Senate's focus, to show that the case against Johnson could turn the nation toward a society based on equality. Brushing past the Tenure of Office Act, Stevens deplored Johnson's creation of Southern state governments in 1865 and his opposition to Congress's Reconstruction laws. If the president was unwilling to enforce the laws, Stevens said, he should "resign the office . . . and retire to his village obscurity."

Following the sepulchral Stevens, Manager Thomas Williams delivered a speech that emptied the chamber until the next day. When he was done, the galleries filled in anticipation of the address of defense lawyer William Evarts. The arrivals included Anthony Trollope, the novelist, who sat with the British ambassador. The ruddy, gray-bearded writer used an ear trumpet to follow the proceedings while accepting cards from ladies in the gallery who were eager to praise his books. During a recess, Trollope's contempt for the impeachers led him into a spirited argument with a young Republican who found the novelist rude and violent.

Before Evarts could speak, Ben Butler was on his feet. Guano was on his mind. He attacked defense lawyer Nelson for his "insinuated calumny" in revealing Butler's letter supporting the Alta Vela claimants. The Massachusetts manager stressed that his involvement with the guano claims predated the impeachment and was unrelated to it. Nelson scornfully answered with an implied challenge to a duel. After their squall erupted again the next day, it receded to its proper insignificance, leaving behind one of the better jokes of the spring: Nelson and Butler supposedly fought their duel, the story went; after Nelson was shot through the brains and Butler through the heart, both of them walked back to the Capitol, uninjured.

Unruffled by Butler's outburst, Evarts began an immense oration. A slim figure of less than medium height, the lawyer spoke with few notes, one hand in his coat pocket while the other gestured with clutched eyeglasses. Putting in an hour on Tuesday, Evarts carried on for most of the Wednesday session, all of Thursday's, and much of Friday's. In all, his argument consumed more than ten hours. Even in 1868, ten hours was a long time to listen to one man. Evarts hoped to make his speech immortal, John Bingham jeered, by making it eternal. (Bingham would soon have to eat those words.)

Despite his prolixity, Evarts held his audience in the palm of his hand. As one observer noted of the address, "although it seems interminable, it is not tiresome." Evarts presented clear, earnest reasoning with an easy grace and a pleasing voice. The substance of his remarks varied little from those offered by Judge Curtis and Groesbeck. The difference was that Evarts understood the power of humor, and the power of ridicule.

On his second day, Evarts scored heavily with his lighthearted review of Manager Boutwell's wish for Johnson to face "astronomical punishment" in the coldest, darkest place of the heavens. The defense lawyer noted that Boutwell thought the Constitution allowed the removal of Johnson but "has put not limits on the distance." In an extended fancy, Evarts imagined Boutwell bearing the president on his shoulders to the top of the Capitol dome and flinging the apostate "upon his flight, while the two houses of Congress and all the people of the United States shall shout, '*sic itur ad astra* [thus do we reach the stars].' " Joined by Boutwell himself, the listeners roared with laughter as the chief justice strained to gavel them to a more decorous state.

The next day, the merriment returned when Evarts discussed Butler's stump-speech article (the tenth one) and its accusation of "crimes against rhetoric." "We are speech-makers," the defense lawyer observed with a shrug befitting a man in the third day of a speech. Evarts argued that no spoken words could ever warrant impeachment. He then illustrated his point by comparing Johnson's admittedly intemperate remarks with some of Butler's own extravagant rhetorical adventures. The exercise brought the Senate to a state of sustained hilarity. In slightly over two pages of the lawyer's remarks, the stenographer noted "[Laughter]" eleven times. Evarts's marathon performance transformed the New York lawyer into the darling of the trial, heaped with praise and adulation.

When Evarts concluded on the afternoon of Friday, May 1, the defense surely should have stopped. Everything that could be said in the president's defense had been said, several times. But former Attorney General Stanberry had recovered enough from his illness to return to the fray, and he needed to add more words. So the Senate endured hours more of the same legal arguments. Forced by lingering weakness to have an aide read the final half of his remarks, Stanberry offered his personal attestation that the president sought only to comply with the Constitution, and had acted with "sublime patience." Evarts, however, was a difficult act to follow. Stanberry made little contribution to the cause beyond his personal assurance that the president—"more sinned against than sinning"—would not act vindictively if acquitted.

Only one speaker stood between the Senate and the finish line, House Manager John Bingham. After ceding to Butler the principal role in the evidentiary phase of the trial, Bingham had labored for weeks on his address. He had apologized to his daughters in Ohio for how brief his letters to them were, explaining that the trial was filling his days and nights. Once more, the crowds surged back to the Capitol, eager to be present at a crossroads of history. Some onlookers had to perch on the steps of the galleries.

Bingham's oration might be the most important moment of the trial. Since late February, when Republican moderates joined with Radicals to demand Johnson's removal, impeachment had suffered a slow leak of enthusiasm. Ejecting Johnson from the Executive Mansion had seemed so obviously necessary during those first heady days. Some deflation of those initial spirits was inevitable, especially when the president adopted the simple ploy of committing no fresh outrages. Then, with time for reflection, the impeachment articles began to wear thin. In the flesh, Lorenzo Thomas was more clownish than scary. In contrast, Stanton's defiant encampment at the War Office became more unsettling to anyone who might expect presidential appointees to act at the direction of the president. And what about Johnson's putative successor, Ben Wade? Would the gruff Radical be enough of an improvement to justify convicting Johnson? Would he be an improvement at all?

Bingham aimed to revive the prosecution case with a magnificent effort that would win for him the hero's mantle. Sporting a new black coat, the usually disheveled House manager was attired "with unusual neatness." He was lean and of average height, with side whiskers that met under his chin. In a stern voice, he framed the decision before the Senate: "Yesterday the supremacy of the Constitution and laws was challenged by the armed rebellion; to-day the supremacy of the Constitution and laws is challenged by executive usurpation."

Bingham announced that he hoped not to be "a mere eater-up of syllables, a mere snapper-up of unconsidered trifles," but then he matched Evarts in length, delivering his oration for twelve hours over three days. Recognizing that Evarts had delivered the principal defense of the president, Bingham took on the New Yorker directly, challenging each of Evarts's principal assertions. To the accusation that Congress sought omnipotence in the government, Bingham replied that Congress must answer to the voters every two years. The House manager lingered over the defense claim that the president need not enforce an unconsti-

John Bingham of Ohio, who gave the final argument for the prosecution.

tutional law. Until the courts declare a law void, he insisted, the executive must respect it. Of the defense contention to the contrary, "There never was a balder piece of effrontery," Bingham roared, "since man was upon the face of the earth."

Bingham's style contrasted with Evarts's beguiling mixture of wit and insight. The Ohioan was sharp and declamatory, attitudes that fit his prosecutorial message. He ranged far beyond the narrow legal questions presented by the Tenure of Office Act, making emotional appeals to the memory of Lincoln that left spectators weeping. Bingham attacked Johnson's claim that Congress was not legitimate without Southern representatives; the president's position, he said, was "arrogance and impudence." Johnson's opposition to the Fourteenth Amendment was, for Bingham, an attempt to revive the Civil War. In his closing crescendo on Wednesday, May 6, Bingham appealed for impeachment as the last, essential battle of that war:

> We stand this day pleading for the violated majesty of the law, by the graves of a half million martyred hero-patriots who made death beautiful by the sacrifice of themselves for their country, the Constitution, and the laws.

Bingham's conclusion loosed cheers from the galleries. Many rose from their seats and ladies waved their handkerchiefs as the Ohioan mopped his brow with a red bandana. When Chief Justice Chase called for order, the crowd laughed and hissed. Senator Grimes demanded that the police clear the galleries, prompting spectators to regale the Iowan (whose opposition to impeachment was known) with a song predicting his imminent demise. Chase directed that all spectators be removed. With only senators and lawyers left in the chamber, the Senate agreed that its further deliberations on impeachment would occur in secret session, then adjourned.

Though Bingham's speech pleased the galleries—perhaps because Republicans passed out most of the admission tickets—he advanced his cause very little. His address had become flat and repetitive on the second day. One Radical called it overprepared. The anti-Johnson *Chicago Tribune* sniffed that the Senate listened to Bingham placidly, "its withers unwrung." Bingham was humble about his effort. "God knows I have tried to do my duty," he said. "It is in the hands of the Senate now. The great work of my life is done."

For almost three weeks, William Evarts had been maddeningly confident of his client's acquittal. How could he be so certain? Was he simply putting up a brave front? Did he know something? Speaker Colfax, diligently counting noses, thought impeachment was losing steam. "We are not as strong or as confident," he wrote on April 28, "as last week."

With the lawyers silenced for good, the struggle over Andrew Johnson's fate moved away from center stage. Much would happen now in private rooms where powerful men could speak frankly with one another, and in silent rooms where wavering senators calculated their public duties and their private interests. If there was a way to persuade a senator to vote one way or another, this was the moment to do it.

20

THE DARK MEN

MAY 5–9, 1868

We should go through barring corruption—money is here to be used like water.

BENJAMIN BUTLER, MAY 12, 1868

O N TUESDAY MORNING, May 5, before John Bingham began the second day of his closing argument, three groups of powerful men met privately to discuss the impeachment vote. Two of the meetings were in Washington City. The House managers gathered for their daily pretrial session at 11 A.M. They carefully reviewed which way each senator might vote, along with the reasons why. With the outcome uncertain, they doubtless vowed to redouble their efforts to persuade or compel Republican senators to toe the party line.

High spirits infected the second meeting, Johnson's Cabinet session. The department heads assembled at the Executive Mansion at noon. Secretary of State Seward, supremely confident, taunted a colleague who was uncertain of the verdict. Seward offered to wager a basket of champagne on the president's acquittal. When the bet was declined, Seward offered two-to-one odds. Treasury Secretary Hugh McCulloch was equally optimistic.

The third meeting took place two hundred miles to the northeast. Thurlow Weed, for more than three decades a newspaper editor and powerful political boss, welcomed four political professionals to his plush suite at the Astor House hotel in New York. The hulking Weed, at age seventy still "altogether massive," with shaggy eyebrows and great natural strength, had assembled men with the experience to evaluate a proposal to bribe Republican senators to vote for the president's acquittal.

Johnson's supporters were already working on at least two bribery schemes, both of which passed through the hands of Edmund Cooper of Tennessee, the interim assistant treasury secretary. Along with Postmaster General Alexander Randall, Cooper was managing the president's $150,000 acquittal fund. Cooper also was negotiating over bribes with several Kansas-based connivers, including postal agent James Legate, Indian trader Perry Fuller, and Willis Gaylord, the brother-in-law of Senator Pomeroy. Now Weed had assembled several of Seward's closest allies, along with the postmaster general, to review a third bribery scheme.

Though they tried to conceal their activities, the five men of the Astor House group left behind a web of circumstantial evidence that includes coded telegrams, murky messages, and striking intersections with the efforts of other Johnson operators like Edmund Cooper, Perry Fuller, New York Collector Henry Smythe, printer Cornelius Wendell, and lobbyist Sam Ward. Taken together, the surviving evidence leaves the indelible impression that dark men undertook dark deeds to keep Andrew Johnson in office.

The proposal that prompted the May 5 meeting at the Astor House came from an unsavory source, General Alonzo W. Adams. A native of upstate New York, Adams left a trail of chicanery behind him when he crossed the nation. After army service during the Mexican War, he joined the California Gold Rush in the late 1840s, ending up as a collector of that state's tax on foreigners wishing to prospect for American gold. Adams won election to the California State Senate in 1850, but soon was under investigation for failing to turn over to the state some $5,000 in taxes he had collected. A State Senate investigating committee recommended Adams's expulsion from the legislature, but he was allowed to resign. In early 1851, as a local newspaper put it, Adams "quietly slipped away from the Capitol, to avoid the earnest greetings the Sheriff had in store for him." He evidently left behind a wife; at least that was the claim in the bigamy lawsuit filed by a New Jersey woman whom he later married.

When the war came in 1861, Adams signed on with the First New York Cavalry. His second round of military service included numerous disputes with brother officers, as Adams liberally used political connections to advance his career. By war's end, Adams commanded the regiment and could point to a distinguished battlefield record. He then cashed in on that record. According to a niece who lived with him in New York, Adams labored as "a Lobbyist of the worst type, doing all the dirty work of parties who are vile enough to employ him." Adams boasted of buying senators' votes, she continued, including during the impeachment trial.

In late April of 1868, Adams approached Henry Smythe, the collector of the New York Custom House. Smythe, who himself had been threatened with impeachment only the year before, was still seeking diplomatic appointment, now as the American minister to Austria. Adams's overture resembled the tale spun two weeks earlier by James Legate, the postal inspector who joined Perry Fuller in a bribery scheme focused on Senators Pomeroy and Ross of Kansas. General Adams told Smythe that for $30,000 he could guarantee three additional Republican votes for the president's acquittal. (Adams named at least two of the senators to be bribed.) Adams wrote Smythe a letter explaining that he already had arranged to pay the bribes but needed funds to conclude the scheme. Smythe promptly introduced Adams to Thurlow Weed, a man who surely would know how to manage this opportunity. Although Weed later said that he told Smythe to ignore Adams's proposal, that claim rings particularly hollow since Weed convened the Astor House meeting to review the Adams scheme and thereafter received a half-dozen telegrams on the same subject.

Weed's guests on May 5 were political mechanics of distinction from the principal centers of government patronage and corrupt dealing. Weed himself had unquestioned credentials as a political fixer. The longtime sponsor of Secretary of State Seward—one Cabinet member described Seward as "part of Weed"—the boss assembled a large fund for Seward's presidential bid in 1860. In return, donors to Weed's fund received franchises to provide trolley and local railway service in New York City. When Seward lost the nomination to Lincoln, Weed used the fund to pay "floaters" to travel to southern Illinois and vote Republican there. During the Civil War, Weed arranged government contracts in return for 5 percent of the take. As pay for supporting a land grant request in Minnesota, Weed received $750,000 worth of shares in a railroad (the equivalent of at least $10 million in current dollars). He had long followed a practice in the New York legislature of buying the votes he needed.

Preeminent among Weed's guests was Postmaster General Randall, who took a train up from Washington the night before. Not only did the former governor of Wisconsin preside over the largest trove of federal jobs—postmaster positions in every town and village—but he also comanaged with Edmund Cooper the $150,000 acquittal fund that had been proposed by Cornelius Wendell and approved by Seward and Treasury Secretary McCulloch. If there was bribing to be done, Randall had the wherewithal to do it.

Then there was Weed's righthand man, Sheridan Shook. As chief federal revenue collector in New York, Shook was implicated in congressional investigations of whiskey tax frauds. He also served on the New York Board of Supervisors with the notorious William Marcy Tweed, better known as "Boss" Tweed. Erastus D. Webster, an official in Shook's graft-ridden revenue district, represented the secretary of state, whom he had served as personal secretary. For the impeachment trial, Seward gave Webster the delicate task of canvassing the votes of senators.

No meeting about bribing senators would have been complete without a representative from the Whiskey Ring. The fifth man in the room was Charles Woolley, a Kentucky lawyer closely identified with liquor interests. To support his taste for fast horses and the finer things of life, Woolley concentrated his law practice on Cincinnati distillers and their disputes with the federal tax authorities. Though Woolley was the least prominent figure in this worldly group, and the only one lacking a close connection to Seward, soon he would be more notorious than all the others combined.

THE ASTOR HOUSE GROUP, AND ALLIES

Thurlow Weed	New York editor and political boss, longtime sponsor of Secretary of State Seward.
Alexander Randall	Postmaster general and former Wisconsin governor; cocustodian of "acquittal fund" with Edmund Cooper.
Sheridan Shook	Trusted Weed associate and chief revenue collector for New York district.
Erastus Webster	Revenue official in New York and former personal secretary to Seward.
Charles Woolley	Lawyer from Cincinnati and Kentucky, represented Whiskey Ring interests.
Henry Smythe	Collector of Customs for New York City and aspirant for diplomatic appointments.
Sam Ward	"King of the Lobby," New York-based bon vivant who worked with the Astor House group.
Alonzo Adams	Former Union cavalry officer and source of proposal to purchase Senate votes to acquit the president.

Through long careers in this heyday of political manipulation, these five men had encountered each other before. Political and financial interest united them in support of President Johnson and his power to appoint every postmaster, every custom house employee, and every tax collector. No president could manage all of those appointments, so he had to rely on men like Thurlow Weed to screen applicants. Those advisers ensured that lucrative positions went to reliable men who would remember to be grateful to their benefactors. Even though Johnson had less than a year left in office, there were plenty of jobs to protect and hand out during that time. Indeed, the Tenure of Office Act could have the unintended effect of increasing the value of Johnson's more senior patronage appointments. As long as that statute was in effect, the next president would need the concurrence of the Senate to remove each Johnson appointee below Cabinet rank.

The purpose of the Astor House session, Thurlow Weed admitted later, was to secure his support in raising still more funds for bribing senators. After reviewing General Adams's proposal, the Astor House fixers set off in a determined fashion. Much of their story unfolds through elliptical telegrams—some coded, many sent under aliases, all carrying the distinctive scent of skullduggery. Edmund Cooper at the Treasury now became the single point of intersection for all three schemes to purchase Senate votes for Johnson's acquittal. As soon as the Astor House meeting ended, Webster (the tax official and Seward confidant) fired off a message to Cooper in Washington City. "All's well," he reported. Webster's telegram promised a meeting with Cooper in the morning, no doubt to report fully on the Astor House session. Webster joined Woolley and the postmaster general on the evening train back to Washington. Weed set off in another direction, seeking the aid of a longtime factotum, Albany editor Hugh Hastings. Weed's telegram told Hastings he was needed in Washington. Hastings was needed, Weed later confirmed, to deal with the impeachment.

Woolley, the Whiskey Ring lawyer, wrote to Sheridan Shook from Washington in the late morning of the next day, May 6. "My business is adjusted," he announced. He asked Shook to place $10,000 to his credit at a New York bank. For what purpose did Woolley need that $10,000, just the day after the Astor House meeting, now that his "business" was "adjusted"? Where did Shook get the money? Woolley then withdrew $10,000 from a Washington bank in ten $1,000 bills. In whose pocket did those $1,000 bills end up?

Shook simultaneously received a terse message from Erastus Webster, who had just met with Cooper at the Treasury: "All right," Webster wrote, with admirable brevity. *What* was all right? Had Cooper approved the plans of the Astor House group? Webster sent a second message to Thurlow Weed. This one was heavier with unexpressed meaning, yet almost as light on detail: "He will do it; telegraph Hugh Hastings to come here right away." *Who* will do *what*? And how did Hugh Hastings figure in this event?

Whatever the Astor House group was up to, it seemed to bear immediate fruit. A "Wall-street operator," who had offered to share with

Johnson's men his special access to certain senators, announced in a telegram that day that there had been a shift in the trial's prospects: "Radical change in favor of the President. Bets are offered five-to-one against conviction." Sam Ward, the King of the Lobby, agreed that the president's prospects had improved suddenly. At the same moment on May 6, he telegraphed to New York, "All OK—I think twice eleven sure"; Ward later explained that his message meant that he then counted twenty-two senators who would vote for acquittal. Was this dramatic change the doing of Cooper and Webster, and of Woolley and Shook?

The definitive answers to these questions lie buried with the men of the Astor House group, and with Edmund Cooper and their allies. None of them ever completely described what they did to pursue General Adams's proposal, or the scheme of postal agent Legate, or any other plan to buy senators' votes. Indeed, the few statements they later made about their vote-buying often involved polite refusals to comment, sometimes bald-faced lies.

Still, their activities were directed from the highest levels of government. Weed, Shook, and Webster had close ties to Secretary of State Seward. Seward himself authorized the acquittal fund, as had Treasury Secretary McCulloch and Postmaster General Randall. Every scheme led to Cooper, who had been called to Washington to serve as Johnson's "companion and friend" and was the second-ranking official at Treasury.

By early May, the president had a copy of an odd letter, dated the year before, from Senator Pomeroy of Kansas to postal agent Legate. The provenance of this letter has been disputed, mostly because its substance was incendiary. In the letter, Pomeroy authorized Legate to assert that the senator supported his bid to be postmaster for Leavenworth, Kansas. If Legate is appointed, the letter promises, Pomeroy will support future postal appointments *and* will vote against any impeachment of the president.

In some respects, the letter seems dubious. Why would the Kansas senator make such sweeping promises to gain a single postmaster's job? Moreover, the promise of a vote on impeachment seems out of place in April 1867. Even though the House Judiciary Committee was then investigating impeachment, the prospect of a Senate trial was remote. Still, possession of the letter, Colonel Moore wrote in his White House diary, contributed to the president's "excellent spirits."

Other mysterious epistles concerned New York Collector Henry Smythe. In late April, Colonel Moore received a report that Senator Pomeroy, now supporting impeachment, claimed to have a letter from Smythe "showing expenditures on behalf of the President," adding that the letter "might do Smythe great harm." A troubled Smythe sneaked into Washington that evening, avoiding the main hotels. Despite his stealthy entrance, Smythe was immediately accosted by an agent of Ben Butler. Butler's man hustled the New Yorker to a meeting with the Massachusetts congressman. Butler accused Smythe of trying to buy senators' votes, and backed up his accusation with letters acquired, according to Smythe, by "stealth and trickery." Smythe's account so alarmed Colonel Moore at the White House that he begged Smythe to determine whether the stolen letters came from Moore's desk in the Executive Mansion, or perhaps his wastebasket.

A day later, Smythe was back at the White House, reporting that the stolen letters (now in the possession of War Secretary Stanton) were torn, so they probably came from Moore's wastebasket. Because the letters mostly damaged Smythe, not the president, they were never released publicly.

As the Senate vote neared, the Kansas postal agent (Legate) continued to press his bribery scheme with the help of Willis Gaylord, Senator Pomeroy's brother-in-law. For at least a week during the beginning of May, Legate was in regular contact with Cooper at Treasury. At the same time, Gaylord demanded $10,000 from Indian trader Fuller to "negotiate for votes." Gaylord still offered to sell the votes of Pomeroy and four other senators, in return for cash.

As a matter of simple politics, Gaylord's persistence was puzzling. By this point in the trial, Pomeroy was acting as a whip for the impeachers, pressing senators to vote for conviction and maintaining a running tally of likely votes. Indeed, after his initial flirtation with the president's camp, Pomeroy seemed to have struck a deal with Ben Wade, the Senate president pro tem, which would grant the Kansas senator control over Kansas patronage in a Wade Administration. It would take a prodigious contortion for Pomeroy now to vote for acquittal. Perhaps, for the right price, the Kansas senator was prepared to perform such a gyration. His graft-ridden career suggests that he might not have blanched at doing so. Perhaps Pomeroy proposed to sell the votes of other senators, but not his own. Or perhaps Gaylord and Legate intended to steal the supposed payoff money themselves and did not much care what Pomeroy planned to do. Once they had their hands on any bribe money, what could anyone do to get it back? Whatever the explanation, the Kansans persevered.

After the trial's closing arguments finally ended, Legate told Cooper that he would leave Washington City unless their business was arranged by 3 P.M. the next day. When the Treasury official responded coolly, Gaylord and Legate tried a different approach. At a meeting with Cooper, Gaylord presented yet another letter from Pomeroy. This one authorized Gaylord to act on the senator's behalf. "I will, in good faith," the letter stated, "carry out any arrangement made with my brother-in-law, Willis Gaylord, in which I am a party." After the meeting, Gaylord tore up Pomeroy's note. As a precaution, Legate retrieved the scraps, reassembled the letter, and took photographs of it. Just in case. Shortly thereafter, Cooper claimed to Legate that he did not close the deal with Gaylord because the president's men already "had votes enough to acquit."

The Astor House group pressed on. By May 7, two days after the gathering in Thurlow Weed's suite, Astor House conspirators in Washington were sending urgent messages for assistance.

General Adams, the source of the initial bribery proposal, telegraphed Collector Smythe: "To be decided next Tuesday [in one week]. Come on yourself immediately."

A clamor arose from Washington for Hugh Hastings of Albany, Weed's man. Woolley, the Whiskey Ring lawyer, and Seward aide Erastus Webster both demanded Hastings's presence in Washington City. After a day of anxiety, the reassuring news came that Hastings would arrive in the morning, with an essential letter in hand. What was the letter? Was it a tool for blackmail? Would it trigger the release of funds? How did Hastings get it?

Sam Ward, the King of the Lobby and now an ally of the Astor House group, asked a New York client whether the president's supporters had a plan if the vote went against Johnson. Not to worry, came the answer. One hundred thousand dollars (at least $1.4 million in today's values) had been raised against that contingency. The president's lawyers would be paid from that fund, with the balance to go to Johnson "for faithful service." If Johnson was not convicted, he would still receive $50,000. Money for this purpose—again managed by the assistant treasury secretary, Edmund Cooper—came in part from employees at the Baltimore and Philadelphia custom houses. At the trial's end, the defense lawyers (Stanberry, Curtis, Groesbeck, Nelson, and Evarts) each received $2,125, an amount raised by Seward, Cooper, and Postmaster General Randall. The lawyer fees totaled less than $11,000. No one has traced the rest of that $100,000. After the trial, Ben Butler noted the contrast between the modest fees paid to the president's lawyers and the large sums raised for the supposed purpose of paying them. "Raising money for the President's counsel," he concluded, was "only a means to procure the acquittal of the President" by bribery.

The efforts of the dark men were no secret to Butler and his operatives. The House manager resolved to uncover and reveal the bribery schemes. Searching for a weak spot in the President's team, Butler entered a high-stakes chess match with Cornelius Wendell, the corruption professional who had designed the president's acquittal fund.

Convinced that Wendell knew about all the plots to bribe senators, Butler offered through intermediaries to pay Wendell $100,000 to disclose the perfidious details. The negotiations reached a critical point. Butler drove in a closed carriage to a location near Wendell's home on F Street, behind the Patent Office. The Massachusetts congressman waited in his carriage while his agents tried to persuade Wendell to join him. After two hours of palaver, Wendell demurred, objecting that he had no witnesses to back up his story.

Butler rode home with disappointment as his companion. He may have wondered whether Wendell had wanted to trap *him* in an overt act of bribery. For all of his spies and suspicions, Butler failed to expose the corrupt schemes of the president's defenders—not the workings of the Astor House group, not the cabal of greedy conspirators from Kansas, and not the acquittal fund assembled by the three Cabinet secretaries. Knowing there were evil deeds afoot, he still needed proof.

21

SCRAMBLING FOR VOTES

MAY 6–12, 1868

> There is much the same feeling here in reference to impeach-
> ment that there is in the army the night before a battle. The
> same fluctuation in feeling, of hope and fear. I don't see how
> we can lose, and yet we may.
>
> REP. JAMES A. GARFIELD, APRIL 28, 1868

FIVE LONG DAYS passed between the end of Bingham's closing argument and May 11, the date when the Senate would meet in executive session and senators could explain their intended votes. Until then,
the suspense and anxiety would only build.

The impeachers met directly with wavering senators to cajole, reason with, and threaten them. "Butler and Stevens," wrote one correspondent, "have not attempted to restrain their pugnacious tendency to
anti-impeachment Senators; they have given full vent to their feelings."
More Republican officials came from around the country to agitate for
the president's conviction. According to some reports, doubtful senators
were receiving death threats. Wherever they went in Washington, they
were watched and overheard, every ear alert for a whisper of commitment to one side or the other.

Republican newspapers applied their own pressure. Horace Greeley
of the *New York Tribune* pledged to Stevens that his paper would "keep

up a steady fire on the impeachment question till the issue is decided." He asked Stevens to supply him with "any fact or suggestion . . . that seems calculated to aid us." Senator Fessenden of Maine complained that because he was widely understood to favor acquittal, "[a]ll imaginable abuse has been heaped upon me by the men and papers devoted to the impeachers." The other Republican senator from Maine wrote a passionate letter to Fessenden urging him to vote for conviction. If he went the other way, his colleague warned, "the sharp pens of all the press would be stuck into you for years, tip'd with fire, and it would sour the rest of your life. . . . You cannot afford to be buried with Andrew Johnson."

Anti-Johnson forces congregated in the offices of General Grant and War Secretary Stanton, where they traded information and coordinated their efforts. Grant had emerged as the impeachers' most potent asset. Republican senators had many reasons to accede to the general's wishes, not solely out of respect for the man. With the Republican convention only two weeks away—it was scheduled for May 20 in Chicago—Grant would soon be the head of the national party and the likely next president. If elected, he would control the reservoir of federal patronage that the Astor House group was fighting so hard to hold on to.

The general-in-chief met quietly with individual senators. He visited the Indiana Avenue home of Frederick Frelinghuysen of New Jersey, who agreed to remain true to the Republican cause. Grant had less luck with William Fessenden of Maine and John Henderson of Missouri. While riding with Henderson on a streetcar, Grant sputtered that Johnson should be removed from office "if for nothing else than because he is such an infernal liar." Henderson later recalled his own reply: "On such terms, it would be nearly impossible to find the right sort of man to serve as President."

With the vote shaping up as extremely close, the impeachers turned their attention to Senate President Pro Tem Ben Wade, who would succeed Johnson if the Senate convicted. Wade had taken the juror's oath, ignoring objections that his interest in becoming president should bar him from deciding the case. Since then, however, Wade had not voted on any procedural and evidentiary question. Now, the impeachers argued, he could no longer afford to be so concerned with appearances.

His vote was essential. Ohio was entitled to be represented in the final tally, they added, and the nation was entitled to be rid of this president.

Some Republicans contrived a ploy for preserving Wade's integrity while increasing their chances of winning a conviction. Wade could resign as president of the Senate just before voting against Johnson. If Johnson were convicted, House Speaker Schuyler Colfax would move into the White House as the next official in the line of succession to the presidency. Wade, though not president, would preserve his reputation and serve the nation. As an inducement to take this self-denying step, Wade was offered the Republican nomination for vice president. Best of all, the switch would make it easier to convict Johnson. The amiable Colfax (nicknamed "Smiler") would be a less alarming successor to Johnson. Senators who feared Radical Ben Wade in the White House would not have the same anxiety about Colfax.

Wade said no. Plans went forward to swear him in as the new president as soon as Chief Justice Chase announced a "guilty" verdict on any impeachment article.

Yet the prospect of a Wade presidency continued to drag down the drive for conviction. Wade supported an immediate increase in the tariff on imported goods, an emotionally charged position that dismayed many Republicans. "The gathering of evil birds about Wade (I refer to the tariff robbers)," wrote the editor of the Radical *Chicago Tribune*, "leads me to think that a worse calamity might befall the Republican party than the acquittal of Johnson."

On May 9, a Saturday, two ceremonies marked the horrors and consequences of the late war, reflecting the strains that lay just below the surface of the impeachment trial. Groups of Virginians visited the nearby battlefields at Bull Run, decorating the graves of rebel soldiers who fell there. They planned a Confederate memorial for the site. Simultaneously, the General Conference of the African Methodist Episcopal Church convened in Washington. Two Union generals from the Civil War gave speeches to the delegates.

The president, beyond the power of his lawyers to restrain him, granted another exclusive press interview. This one was with the correspondent of the *Boston Post*, who conveniently enough was Johnson's own secretary, William Warden. Writing on May 10, Warden found that

Johnson "has never looked better than he does to-day, and his fine flow of good humor indicates anything but a troubled mind." After expressing confidence in the Senate's judgment, and his willingness "cheerfully" to bow to its authority, Johnson's gorge rose when questioned about House Manager Bingham's suggestion that Johnson might refuse to vacate his office if the Senate convicted him. Bingham's suggestion was "base," the president said, though "in perfect harmony with the charges and suggestions contained in the eleven articles of impeachment." If Johnson had to leave his office "according to the forms and requirements of the Constitution," he said, he would be pleased to do so.

Talking with another correspondent a couple of evenings later, Johnson pointed to a list of the fifty-four senators and asked his guest to indicate how each would vote. The president showed "a cool, deliberate interest" in the tally. Though he liked to portray himself as unconcerned with the trial, the president—like everyone else in Washington City—was counting the votes very carefully.

On the mild morning of Monday, May 11, the Capitol hummed with excitement. The atmosphere mingled, according to one observer, the elements of a presidential election, a public execution, and a lottery drawing. After weeks of listening to witnesses and lawyers, the senators themselves would be able to talk about whether Andrew Johnson should be convicted. Their speeches could reveal the fate of the president, and of the nation.

At Manager Stevens's home, the day began with a poignant visit from officials of the African Methodist Church. After a minister praised him, Stevens told them of his joy that the black men were now his fellow citizens. He did not deserve their flattering remarks, he continued, but would "try to deserve them in the few years he had left to live." Ever partisan, the congressman reminded his guests that it was the Republican Party that ended slavery.

The Senate session began at 10 A.M. and lasted into the night. Though it was an executive session, the senators were free to describe the speeches to outsiders, and so they did. Whenever a senator left the chamber, he was cross-examined by House managers, reporters, and agents of both sides, all desperate to know how the numbers were sorting out. The Astor House group was well represented. Charles Woolley, the Whiskey Ring lawyer, described himself as in the "look out chair." Collector Smythe and Indian trader Fuller were there, too.

Predictions about Johnson's chances continued to shift with the rumors of the hour. A week earlier, Republicans had been eager to bet on conviction, even offering odds to Johnson supporters. By May 11, the betting line had shifted to even, with a suggestion that the pro-Johnson money was holding back to avoid moving the line further.

Only about a third of the senators spoke during the May 11 session, and several were more confusing than enlightening. A few questions were answered. Grimes, Trumbull, and Fessenden openly declared for acquittal. In private remarks, Fowler of Tennessee dashed the hopes of impeachers. He, too, would vote to acquit. George Edmunds of Vermont said he would support conviction on the first three articles, but not on

IMPEACHMENT—REPORTERS AND CITIZENS IN THE SENATE LOBBY SEEKING INFORMATION DURING THE SECRET SESSION.—[SEE PAGE 350.]

"Reporters and Citizens in the Senate Lobby
seeking information about the secret session."

the conspiracy articles. John Sherman of Ohio left more than a few heads shaking. He announced he would oppose Article I, which charged that the firing of Stanton violated the Tenure of Office Act. Because Sherman had chaired the committee that produced that statute, his views on that question might have persuaded other senators. But Sherman also said he would support Articles II and III, which alleged that the appointment of Lorenzo Thomas violated the statute. Sherman's reasoning was elusive at best. John Henderson of Missouri declared he would vote against the first eight articles. Maddeningly, time expired before he could announce his view of the last three. Several doubtfuls sat silent, not committing themselves one way or the other.

As the afternoon progressed, the impeachers in the lobby grew dismayed. With the confirmation of Republican defections, one Radical recalled, "An indescribable gloom now prevailed among the friends of impeachment." Another described the experience as being like "sitting up with a sick friend who was expected to die." In the crowd outside the Senate Chamber, Managers Boutwell and Wilson were steadfast. John Logan was downcast. Bingham talked with friends while Butler stalked the rotunda and corridors with anxious defiance. Thad Stevens, ailing, had stayed home. When the dinner recess arrived, Republican hearts sank at the sight of several doubtfuls trooping off to dine with Chief Justice Chase, who was known to oppose conviction.

By evening, though, the impeachers' spirits rallied as they dissected the opinions in the Senate Chamber. Some doubtfuls, they realized, were still uncommitted and might yet come through. Even doubtfuls who opposed most of the impeachment articles might vote for a single article, helping the impeachers reach the magical two-thirds total on at least one charge. Conviction on a single article would remove Johnson from the White House. The nervous energy grew until the Senate adjourned at 10 P.M. The vote would take place on the following day. The final moment was nigh.

The impeachers took stock that night. With five Republican defections seemingly confirmed (Grimes, Fessenden, Trumbull, Fowler, Henderson), the president's expected vote total stood at 17. He needed only two more. The momentum was definitely in his favor, but maybe he still could be ousted. Maybe Fowler or Henderson could be lured back into the Republican fold. The contest was not over.

The House managers adapted their tactics to the shifting opinions of key senators. Sherman of Ohio and Henderson of Missouri doubted that the Tenure of Office Act applied to Cabinet officers, so they were skeptical of the articles based solely on that statute. That could make it impossible to convict on the first eight impeachment articles. Prospects were even worse for the ninth and tenth articles—the charges based on the president's consultation with General Emory on February 21, and Butler's stump-speech article. Those articles were widely disparaged. That left Article XI, the catchall set of accusations sponsored by Thad Stevens. Because of its mix of political charges with alleged crimes under the Tenure of Office Act, Article XI seemed to have the best chance of commanding a two-thirds vote.

On May 7, the managers had decided to propose inverting the articles so the Senate would vote on the last one first. The senators' speeches on May 11 reinforced this strategy. Senate Republicans agreed that the balloting should start with Article XI. In a countermove, Johnson supporters proposed that the Senate should vote separately on each subpart of Article XI. Chief Justice Chase rejected that motion. The separate allegations in the article, Chase ruled, charged a single high misdemeanor. Stevens no doubt smiled at this vindication of his judgment in assembling Article XI.

As the impeachers braced for the final push, the Johnson forces were optimistic. Charles Woolley sent bullish telegrams on May 11. He proclaimed Johnson's "stock above par," and "Impeachment gone higher than a kite." Collector Smythe was more measured. "Matters look well," he telegraphed, "though still some doubt." By the next day, Woolley was again demanding money from Sheridan Shook, Thurlow Weed's right-hand man. "The five should be had," Woolley wrote. "May be absolutely necessary." He also drew $5,000 from a Washington bank, plus another $20,000 from Cincinnati sources. For the big day, Woolley would carry in his pockets the equivalent of $350,000 in current dollars.

Johnson spent the day of May 11 quietly, receiving breathless reports from those collecting information outside the Senate Chamber. In the afternoon, he walked the White House grounds with the daughter of Collector Smythe. The evening took him to a ball at the National Theatre with his daughter (the First Lady's health kept her from such events).

Smelling presidential victory, the crowd at the ball cheered lustily when Johnson entered.

The tension of the moment was fearful. Johnson's partisans painted the struggle as a last-ditch defense of the Constitution. Those seeking to remove him insisted that only conviction would redeem the terrible sacrifices of the Civil War.

The night of May 11 was an agony for the contestants, who schemed and harangued into the wee hours. Some slept not at all. Three Radical senators worked one more time down the list of doubtfuls, focusing on three whose votes they needed—Henry Anthony of Rhode Island, Waitman Willey of West Virginia, and Frederick Frelinghuysen of New Jersey. They also were not sure of Peter Van Winkle of West Virginia. At 5 A.M., a fellow Radical wrote urgently to General Grant's closest political adviser, begging that Grant meet early in the day with all four of those doubtful senators!

A lovely late spring morning greeted the crowds at the Capitol. They arrived hours before the Senate would convene at eleven-thirty. Telegrams poured in for the senators, begging for conviction or for acquittal.

Early that morning, six Missouri Republicans cornered one of their senators, John Henderson, in his rooms. The conversation started Henderson down a strange road of vacillation over his impeachment vote.

Henderson's visitors, who included congressmen and state legislators, were troubled by his announcement the day before that he would vote to acquit the president on the first eight impeachment articles. Henderson told them that he could not change his course on those articles; he agreed, however, that he could vote to convict on the eleventh, catchall article, and that it would be better for the nation if Johnson were removed from office. Henderson, skeptical that the president would be convicted at all, offered to consult with other doubtful senators. If there were sufficient votes to convict, he would vote against Johnson on Article XI. Eager to gratify his visitors, Henderson added that if his proposal did not satisfy them, he would resign so the state's governor could appoint a senator more to their liking. Some of his visitors worried that his resignation might disrupt federal patronage in Missouri. Why didn't they, he asked, put in writing what they wanted him to do? The Republicans drafted a letter insisting that Henderson vote to convict or abstain from voting. The senator responded with a slightly different assurance: he said he would either withhold his vote on impeachment, or would resign. Henderson's vote, it was clear, was now in play.

As noon approached, the scene inside the Senate Chamber was tense. When the gallery doors opened, men and women rushed to grab seats. To suppress the sort of outburst that followed Bingham's closing speech, three policemen stood in each aisle, batons drawn, giving the galleries the look of a civil detention facility for the well dressed. Senators and illustrious visitors patrolled the chamber's floor, standing in anxious knots, speaking loudly or softly as the conversation warranted. Three Radical senators buttonholed Willey of West Virginia. Other doubtfuls—Anthony, Van Winkle, Ross, Fowler—were magnets for attention. Stevens and the House managers were there with Stanberry and Evarts for the president. Ex-senators, generals, editors, all had gathered for the great moment.

But it did not happen.

A senator announced that Jacob Howard of Michigan, a Radical stalwart certain to vote for conviction, had fallen ill overnight. Not able to spare a single vote, the Republicans postponed the balloting until noon on Saturday, May 16. Deflated, the murmuring spectators filed out, cheated of the great moment in history.

The delay guaranteed more agitation, more plotting, more recrimination, but it also provided a pause for reflection as the nation teetered for a few more days on the constitutional precipice. Would the Senate exercise its power to remove the president, or would it desist? The most striking aspect of the situation was that the war over impeachment was one of words, not bullets.

The impeachment process certainly had the power to confuse. Was impeachment a political event or a judicial one? What was a high crime? How about a high misdemeanor? Could Johnson be removed for leading the country so poorly, or only if he had committed crimes that could be prosecuted in court? Who could sort through the meaning of the Tenure of Office Act and whether the secretary of war was covered by it?

Yet, for all its medieval peculiarities, impeachment had channeled into a peaceful forum a potentially deadly confrontation between Congress and President Johnson, one that carried heavy overtones of the sectional war that had so recently raged across the continent. The reason for having a constitutional method for removing the president, Ben Franklin had explained eighty years before, was to preserve peace in times of crisis. The impeachment clauses were allowing, albeit imperfectly, the nonviolent resolution of the demand, heartfelt and widespread, that the nation's leader must go.

The *Chicago Tribune* credited impeachment with calming the nation's political storms. Since the effort began, the newspaper commented, the president "with hands upon his breast, has been upon his best behavior." Indeed, Reconstruction in the South had proceeded at the same time as the impeachment trial. Through almost three months of impeachment drama, six Southern states adopted new constitutions under the new Reconstruction laws, then elected new state governments. Within weeks those states would be readmitted to the union, a result the newspaper attributed to the "sudden and severe check given to Andrew Johnson's reckless proceedings by the impeachment." Even if Johnson were not removed from office, the impeachment had greatly reduced his ability to oppose Congress.

The vote could not be delayed beyond May 16. Many senators would attend the Republican National Convention in Chicago on May 20, and the nation would not wait longer than that. Western Union made arrangements to transmit the Senate's verdict as soon as it was announced, warning its operators that the bulletin would preempt all other traffic on its nationwide network. By the end of the week, the verdict would be in.

22

DESPERATE DAYS

MAY 12—15, 1868

Have been the rounds. Room for plenty of work. Other side desperate.

WILLIAM W. WARDEN to HENRY SMYTHE,
MAY 14, 1868

NOBODY KNEW WHAT to believe. Predictions of the verdict, and of individual senators' votes, fluctuated constantly. Around the nation, people waited and wondered, argued and rallied. On May 12 in Lewiston, Maine, the brother of Senator William Pitt Fessenden helped sponsor a rally opposing the senator's support for the president. In Philadelphia and St. Louis, telegraph bulletins announced that acquittal was certain, then that conviction was possible. Johnson supporters in Baltimore planned bonfires and a parade for the moment the Senate returned a verdict of acquittal. Newspaper offices, political clubs, and barrooms teemed with people eager for the latest. The uncertainty triggered a new wave of betting. Business activity dwindled.

The impeachers urged citizens to press their senators to convict. "Great danger to the peace of the country," warned a telegram sent to Republicans around the country. Before Saturday, the recipients should send senators "public opinion by resolutions, letters and delegations."

The response was overwhelming. A "perfect avalanche" of telegrams, according to the *Baltimore Sun,* fell on those favoring acquittal, or deemed doubtful. The governor of Maine sent "indignant denunciations" of the president. The *Philadelphia Press* applauded the outpouring of messages, as well as those "friends of law and order" who came to Washington to demand that the president be convicted.

Though calumny still occasionally rained down on the initial Republican defectors—Fessenden of Maine, Grimes of Iowa, and Trumbull of Illinois—most concern focused on four additional senators deemed likely to defect. These last four could provide the votes that would keep the president in office for another ten months. Republicans had to dissuade at least one of them from acquitting the Great Criminal.

Fowler of Tennessee, written off a week earlier as pro-Johnson, drew fresh attention. Republicans recalled anew that Fowler had advocated impeaching Johnson before the debacle at the War Department. How could Fowler have changed his view after the Lorenzo Thomas fiasco, which created even greater reason to remove the president? The Tennessee General Assembly adopted resolutions supporting conviction. The governor and every Tennessee congressman entreated Fowler to vote against the president, as did a delegation of "loyal men" from his home state. By one account, he was offered a seat on the state Supreme Court if he voted to convict. A pro-Johnson newspaper feared that Fowler might yield to the pressure.

Besieged, Fowler made conflicting statements. He led a group of congressmen to believe he would vote to convict, then told another group he could never do so. Finally, Fowler was through listening. He cut short a meeting with the statement that he would hear no more arguments for the prosecution. The impeachers gave up on him.

Peter Van Winkle, a former railroad executive who had helped found the state of West Virginia five years before, was an independent sort. He voted "about as often with one party as the other," a home state newspaper wrote, "without much reference to the wishes of his constituents or the requirements of party discipline." Moreover, the sixty-year-old Republican did not plan to seek reelection, so he cared little when the West Virginia legislature demanded Johnson's removal. With a phlegmatic personality and no political aspirations, Van Winkle drew the least attention among the potential defectors. One report called his vote uncertain. Before the final ballot, Van Winkle declared he would support the president.

In contrast, handsome, bearded John Henderson of Missouri proved a magnet for controversy. Then forty-two years old, Henderson had been orphaned at ten, though he inherited enough wealth to secure an education. He rose quickly in Missouri politics. After a brief spell in the Union Army, he began serving in the Senate in 1862. Henderson often voted with the Radicals and supported black suffrage, yet maintained cordial relations with President Johnson.

While Evarts and Bingham were delivering their gargantuan closing arguments, Henderson made time for romance. In the first week of May, he announced his engagement to Mary Foote of upstate New York. His fiancée came from a family of prominent Democrats; her father, Elisha Foote, would soon be a candidate to head the Patent Office, no doubt with support from his prospective son-in-law. Indeed, political Washington cynically assessed the blending of love and impeachment. "The vote of Henderson of Missouri is relied upon," wrote Navy Secretary Welles, "through the influence of Miss Foote."

After the Senate vote was put off to May 16, Henderson was a prime target for the forces of influence. He had spoken against the first eight impeachment articles on May 11. On the next day, he promised a delegation of Missouri Republicans that he would vote "guilty" on Article XI if he thought there were enough votes to convict Johnson. If there were not, Henderson said, he would either abstain on the impeachment vote or resign. This complicated matrix of positions made Henderson look indecisive, even unprincipled.

At this point, James B. Craig of Missouri stepped forward. A former Democratic congressman and ally of the Astor House group, Craig headed the Hannibal & St. Joseph Railroad, which was then expanding into Kansas. Craig was politically close to the president, to Henderson, and to Senator Edmund Ross of Kansas. Henderson was known as the senator who looked after Craig's railroad, while Johnson had appointed Craig to a revenue collector position. In May 1868, Craig was working with both senators and with the president to win approval of a Cherokee treaty that would give his railroad 800,000 acres in southeastern Kansas.

After meeting with Sam Ward in New York, on May 13, Craig hurried to help Henderson through the tumult created by the senator's complex set of promises on the impeachment vote. Craig urged the senator to retain his Senate seat and support the president down the line. When he left Henderson, Craig pronounced him solid for acquittal, a message that was instantly sent to Treasury official Cooper. "The Henderson matter all right," Cooper relayed to President Johnson. "Lacy has been to see him with Craig—all right—so says Evarts."

What elixir, or reasoning, did Craig apply to calm the senator's nerves and bring him to support acquittal? Neither man ever said. But that same day Henderson fired off a telegram to Missouri stating, "Say to my friends that I am sworn to do impartial justice according to law and the evidence, and I'll try to do it like an honest man." When Henderson's message was released to the press, it triggered a celebration at the Executive Mansion. Henderson had entered the president's camp. The next day, he wrote to the Missouri Republicans who had previously stampeded him into pledging to convict or abstain or resign. Abstention, he pointed out, would have the same effect as a vote for acquittal, since in both instances the impeachers would lose his vote toward the needed two-thirds majority. Henderson deplored resignation as shirking his duty "to follow the dictates of my conscience." He promised to "throw myself upon the judgment of a generous people for my vindication."

Sniffing the air for wrongdoing, House manager Ben Butler found something pungent about Henderson's vacillations. The Massachusetts manager seemed to have spies everywhere; the black servants who cleaned the Executive Mansion sent him discarded papers that might be of interest. Somehow Butler acquired the note about Henderson that Edmund Cooper had sent to the president. Intrigued, Butler promptly issued subpoenas for White House aide William Warden and for defense lawyer William Evarts. Butler wanted to know why the president was receiving early reports about how senators intended to vote. Butler was curious, too, why Senator Grimes's clerk and one of Senator Trumbull's sons were betting against conviction. Though Warden came to the Capitol in response to the subpoena, he did not testify. Possibly someone pointed out to Butler that senators could disclose their voting intentions to whomever they wished, even to the president.

For all of his dithering, Henderson managed to decide how he would vote and to communicate that intention widely. By doing neither, one remaining Republican senator, Edmund G. Ross of Kansas, placed himself in the middle of a political firestorm.

• • •

Born into an antislavery family in Ohio in 1826, young Edmund Ross bounced from printing job to printing job through the Midwest. In the early 1850s, he married and settled in Milwaukee. The young printer led a party of antislavery emigrants from Wisconsin to "Bleeding Kansas," which was then the front line of the struggle against slavery. By 1859, Ross and his brother were publishing an antislavery paper in Topeka, mingling politics with journalism. When the war came, Ross fought for the Union with a Kansas regiment, rising to the rank of colonel.

Ross adjusted readily to the rough-and-tumble of frontier Kansas. At the beginning of the war, he and two competing printers agreed to inflate their bids on contracts with the state. The conspirators decided which contracts each would bid on, ensuring that the winner would receive double the competitive price. Ross unwisely complained when a fourth printer won a contract at half the price Ross had quoted. State investigators were more interested in Ross's bid-rigging than in his complaints about the low bidder, but the investigation of Ross was overtaken by the pending impeachment of the Kansas governor for other misdeeds. Ross was not charged.

In the spring of 1866, a scandal broke over ties between Indian trader Perry Fuller and Kansas Senator Jim Lane. News reports charged that Lane had "a pecuniary interest" in Fuller's businesses and government contracts. Lane hotly proclaimed his innocence until he was confronted with documents showing his ownership in one Fuller operation, as well as a canceled check to him for $20,000 (or almost $300,000 in current dollars) from another Fuller firm. On July 1, Lane put a pistol in his mouth and pulled the trigger. Ten days later he died.

The Kansas governor could fill the vacant Senate seat until the state legislature could meet in January 1867 and choose Lane's successor. The governor startled many by selecting Ross, who had never held public office. Perhaps the printer seemed a safe choice, with a good war record, not too many enemies, and reliably Radical views, like most Kansans. By the time the legislature convened five months later, Fuller was sponsoring Ross. For $42,000 in bribes, Fuller purchased Ross's reappointment for the last four years of the Senate term, plus a full term for senior Senator Samuel Pomeroy.

Kansas Senator Edmund G. Ross.

In the Senate, the small, bearded Ross was an inconspicuous back-bencher. He took a room in the Capitol Hill house of Robert Ream and became one of many sponsors of Ream's improbably talented daughter, Lavinia (known as Vinnie). Combining artistic gifts with a knack for charming politicians, Vinnie Ream acquired several public commissions while still in her teens, along with a studio in the Capitol itself. In January 1868, Ross urged the State of Wisconsin to award a commission to the nineteen-year-old sculptress, who stood less than five feet tall. (Ben Wade also sponsored her Wisconsin application, while Thad Stevens sat for her during the impeachment trial.) To complete the circle of Kansas connections, Vinnie Ream's sister had married Perry Fuller, who lived nearby.

During the impeachment trial, Ross voted with the pro-Johnson senators on many evidentiary issues, but his position on the verdict was unclear. Some newspapers projected him as doubtful. Others pegged him as proconviction.

In mid-April, with trial evidence still being presented, a letter to Butler accused Ross of being "owned by Perry Fuller." The Kansas senator, the letter continued, helped Fuller "push his frauds through the

Teenage sculptress Vinnie Ream, with her bust of Lincoln.

Indian Bureau and Quartermaster Department" and was sponsoring Fuller's campaign to become commissioner of internal revenue. The letter also accused Ross, married and the father of three, of being "infatuated to the point of foolishness with Miss Vinnie Ream, Fuller's sister-in-law." Butler sent a copy of the letter to Ross, with a disingenuous cover note: "I never allow slanderous communications against gentlemen of position to be sent me," Butler wrote, "without transferring them to the party injured so that he may be able to protect himself." Butler thus put the Kansas senator on notice: he was being watched. Despite the warning, Ross would dangle his vote provocatively before both sides of the case, inviting exactly the sort of political bargains that Butler suspected.

Ross tested the strength of his position during John Bingham's interminable closing argument. On May 4, he sent Perry Fuller on a mission to Interior Secretary Orville Browning. The Reconstruction conventions in Southern states were sending their new constitutions to the president's office, as was required. Though Johnson was supposed to convey them to Congress, he was slow to do so. Fuller told Browning he was speaking on behalf of Ross and that

> if the President would send [to Congress] the constitutions of South Carolina and Arkansas, which were now before him, without delay, it would exert a salutary influence upon the trial now pending, and that he [Ross] and others would then vote against impeachment.

Browning, in turn, urged the president to send the state constitutions to Congress. Here was an opportunity to redeem the president's commitment to Iowa Senator Grimes that he would not embarrass Republicans who supported him. Johnson sent the constitutions to Congress. The incident also tested the president's willingness to bargain for acquittal votes. The answer was plain. Johnson would bargain.

Ross's approach to Johnson grew out of a political problem the senator faced with his Kansas colleague, Samuel Pomeroy. Although Pomeroy's agents (Legate and Gaylord) were still trolling for bribes to acquit the president, Pomeroy himself had plunged into the effort to win a conviction, possibly in return for control over Kansas patronage appointments in the (presumably) incoming Wade Administration. A deal between Wade and Pomeroy would leave Edmund Ross out in the cold, politically neutered in his home state. If Pomeroy had locked up the Wade connection, the smart move for Ross would be to keep Andrew Johnson in office and get very, very close to him.

In the days leading up to the impeachment vote, Ross played a double game. With each side trying to pin him down, Ross dallied with both.

On May 12, Senator Pomeroy saw Ross closeted in a Senate office with defector Lyman Trumbull of Illinois. When Pomeroy entered, the other two were discussing the impeachment. They fell silent. After Trumbull left, Pomeroy confronted Ross with a tally sheet that recorded how each senator would vote on each impeachment article. Pomeroy had listed Ross as a "guilty" vote on several articles. He now asked Ross if the listings were correct. "He [Ross] said they were right," Pomeroy recalled later, "with the exception of the eighth [impeachment article]." Ross said he was undecided on that one. Ross confirmed that Pomeroy's sheet properly recorded him voting to convict on four of the impeachment articles.

Meeting a newspaper correspondent and another senator a day later (May 13), Ross said he would vote to convict Johnson on four impeachment articles—the first three and Article XI. Ross's position seemed slightly softer on the next evening, May 14, when he told a fellow Kansan that the impeachment vote should be postponed, but "the next best thing was conviction."

Later in the evening of May 14, Ross joined a conclave of doubtful senators in the rooms of Van Winkle of West Virginia, at the National Hotel on Pennsylvania Avenue. Once more dropping in where he was not wanted, Senator Pomeroy knocked on Van Winkle's door. In the awkward conversation that followed, Henderson of Missouri predicted that the impeachers would fail by four votes. Pomeroy replied that his tally showed the president would be convicted on Article XI. At that point, the doubtfuls began to urge postponement of the vote. If the vote were put off, Henderson insisted, the president would overhaul his Cabinet. Henderson himself might be under consideration for a Cabinet slot. Ross broke in with a warning. Without being specific, he told Pomeroy that "he desired to notify me that he was doubtful on some of the articles."

Yet another factor confused those trying to predict Ross's vote. His brother, William W. Ross, was in Washington City. Formerly his brother's business partner, the younger Ross now lived in Florida as one of the "carpetbaggers" of lore, who are generally denounced for trying to profit from Southern hardships. Supposedly offered $20,000 to reveal his brother's vote, William insisted that Edmund would support conviction.

Back in Kansas, reports that Ross might defect created a furor. On May 14, the editor of the *Leavenworth Times*, D. R. Anthony (brother of suffragist Susan B. Anthony) fired off a telegram on behalf of "1,000 others." "Kansas has heard the evidence," Anthony wrote to Ross, "and demands conviction." On the day of the vote, Ross's reply denied that his constituents could dictate his vote. "I have taken an oath to do impartial justice," he answered. Unimpressed, Anthony fired back: "Your motives are Indian contracts and greenbacks. Kansas repudiates you as she does all her perjurers and skunks."

Through the afternoon and evening of Friday, May 15, less than eighteen hours before the vote, Ross continued to string both sides along. At the end of the day, he called at Pomeroy's home on H Street to acquire a copy of Anthony's telegram. Joining the Pomeroy family at dinner, Ross said he favored conviction, and that Article XI was the strongest of the charges. Ross added that the vote should be postponed, arguing that they could control Johnson by holding impeachment over his head. He left the Pomeroys at 6:30 in the evening.

Ross also was seen at Dubant's restaurant on Pennsylvania Avenue, where he sat with fellow doubtfuls Henderson and Van Winkle. Encountering an acquaintance from Kansas, Ross said again that the vote should be postponed. Back at his rooms at the Ream house, Ross received a late night visit from fellow Kansan Thomas Ewing, Jr. Ross showed him the telegram from Anthony, the editor, and the reply Ross had drafted. Ewing urged Ross to send the reply right away. Ross agreed. At midnight, the two men set off on foot for the Western Union office a mile away.

This moonlight expedition with the younger Ewing, who was closely tied to the president and had been Ross's commanding officer during the war, certainly could have included a visit to some other destination. At that moment, Washington City was bursting with men eager to bribe Republican senators to acquit the president. Edmund Cooper was there, as were Sheridan Shook of New York, Postmaster General Randall, and Charles Woolley of Cincinnati. All of them had ready access to piles of greenbacks. Out in the early morning hours, Ross had a notable opportunity for clandestine negotiations over his vote, and to close a deal for it. Whatever happened on that stroll, by morning Ross would be with Johnson.

Because of his foray with Ewing, Ross missed an uninvited visit from General Dan Sickles, who had gone for months without a military assignment since Johnson removed him from a command in the South. Ross and Sickles were friendly. During the trial, Sickles had hunted Ross down when he heard that Johnson's allies were "tampering" with the Kansan. Ross then assured Sickles that he would vote for conviction. Late in the evening of May 15, Sickles heard an alarming report about Ross. This time, the Kansan supposedly had been swayed by the temptress Vinnie Ream to vote for Johnson. Some impeachers were convinced that the sculptor held Ross in a form of sexual thrall. Earlier, a Radical congressman had accused her of influencing the Kansan to vote for acquittal. When young Vinnie denied the charge, the Radical demanded that she employ her wiles to induce Ross to vote for conviction.

Sickles, who lost a leg at the battle of Gettysburg, gathered his crutches and called a cab. After some blundering through unlighted streets, the driver found the Ream house. The sculptor admitted the one-legged general to the parlor but told him that Ross was not in. Years later, Sickles claimed that he waited there until 4 A.M., but Ross—walking the streets with the younger Ewing—never materialized. Sickles's florid recollection depicted the young woman playing the piano and singing for him, then bursting into tears over Senator Ross's quandary. Miss Ream differed over several details in Sickles's narrative, and denied she had ever discussed the impeachment case with Ross, but she confirmed that Sickles visited that night. In any event, Sickles and Ross never met in those early morning hours. Failing in his mission, the general crutched dejectedly back to his waiting cab.

On the morning of the vote, Ross breakfasted at Perry Fuller's nearby house. A Democratic senator joined him and Fuller. By the time Ross arrived at the Senate, his course was set. Ten minutes before the roll call began on Article XI, Senator Pomeroy approached Ross. This time, with Thad Stevens stopping to listen, Ross said he should be counted doubtful on every impeachment article.

The Astor House group kept up its pressure through all four days before the Senate vote.

On the same day that James Craig met with Senator Henderson—Wednesday, May 13—the railroad man sent an urgent message to Sheridan Shook, who was then in New York: "Come on by first train—very important." Craig reinforced that dispatch with a follow-up, also to Shook: "You must come here and untangle a snarl between friends at once." Woolley, the Whiskey Ring lawyer, sent a similar message to New York: "There are serious differences among your friends. Shook . . . should come immediately." A third voice, a former Democratic congressman working with the Johnson forces, echoed the demand for Shook. Leaving nothing to chance, Woolley sent another message, the fifth of the day, to another New York contact: "Please go to Shook's house and ask him to come here immediately." Shook came to Washington on the day before the vote, joining Woolley at Willard's Hotel, parlor no. 6. Visitors to the suite included Perry Fuller, Sam Ward, and railroad man Craig.

Woolley was in touch with Fuller, confidant to Senator Ross, on May 12. He then reported to one Cincinnati client, "We have them by the throat," and advised another, "The fight is bitter beyond description."

A New York client supported Sam Ward's efforts with the Astor House group. Referring on May 12 to that alliance, the client insisted that "[t]ogether you can do anything you need." On May 15, the day before the vote, he wrote to Ward that an unnamed person "has been waiting all day for a telegram which so far has not come and he infers that he is not needed. The arrangement was perfect that he should be sent for if required."

Despite the intense activity, the Astor House group took a cheery view of the president's prospects. Tax official Erastus Webster, Seward's vote-counter, advised Weed on May 13 that acquittal was "a fixed fact." In a message on the next day, Woolley wrote of his opponents, "We have them [the impeachers] demoralized and bitter." A presidential aide struck a similar tone in a May 14 message to Collector Smythe: "Other side desperate." Sam Ward sent two confident messages on May 15, promising "result as predicted." Colonel Moore at the White House shared the optimism. He instructed Collector Smythe not to release the letter from 1867 in which Senator Pomeroy promised to oppose impeachment if his man (James Legate) were named postmaster of Leavenworth, Kansas. They did not need it.

On the night of May 15, a few hours before the big vote, the Astor House group staged an early celebration. In his dinner invitation to defense lawyer Evarts, Sam Ward wrote that Woolley, the Whiskey Ring lawyer, would be there and "has been steadfast and useful." The celebrants met at Ward's favorite eatery, Welcker's, where Ward had instructed the chef in the preparation of a wide range of delicacies, including ham, Chicken Sauté Sam Ward, and terrapin. Ward's table was ringed with happy Johnson loyalists, from lawyers Evarts and William Groesbeck to Edmund Cooper, the hub of the bribery schemes. Woolley and Sheridan Shook were there, along with railroad man James Craig and two others. While Senator Ross of Kansas dined awkwardly at the Pomeroys', the president's defenders luxuriated in the lavish wines and delectables for which Sam Ward was justly famous.

The impeachers knew they were in trouble. Controlling neither patronage jobs nor government contracts nor tax collection, they had fewer tools for influencing senators. They could pledge advantages in the future Wade Administration, but the Ohio senator himself often undercut that approach. Most of the rumored commitments by Wade involved appointments for staunch Republicans who should have supported impeachment anyway. Beyond the case of Senator Samuel Pomeroy of Kansas, there is little evidence that Wade used promises of patronage to secure votes for conviction. Republicans had to find other tools for building the two-thirds majority they needed.

General Grant gave a press interview. The soldier offered a wishful prediction that the president would resign rather than face the Senate's vote, adding that he had bet Stanton a box of cigars on that outcome. Removing Johnson, Grant said, was the only hope for restoring peace to the South. Paradoxically, the future president promised that once Johnson was replaced with a man who would enforce the law in the South, many federal troops could be withdrawn from the region; if the troops left, who would enforce the law?

The impeachers toyed with a dubious gambit for expanding the Senate itself. Seven Southern states (Arkansas, Louisiana, Georgia, Alabama, Florida, and the Carolinas) had completed the steps prescribed in Congress's Reconstruction legislation of 1867. Allowing the freedmen to vote, those states had elected statewide conventions that drafted new constitutions. Now senators and representatives from those states were poised to join Congress. The new senators, fourteen of them, were Republicans, elected with black votes and intimately familiar with the violence besetting Unionists and freedmen in the South. They were certain to support impeachment. Better yet, many of the new Southern senators were already in Washington City, eager to be sworn in.

Some Radicals argued for delaying the impeachment vote until the new senators could be seated. Then the Southerners could provide the margin of victory. It would be an excruciating irony. After more than two years of demanding that Congress take no action without the full participation of Southern senators and congressmen, the president would be removed from office by the votes of senators from the South.

Stevens went so far as to threaten the ploy. His Reconstruction Committee reported legislation to restore those seven states to full representation. The House approved the bills by May 14, two days before the scheduled impeachment vote. The Southern senators "are standing waiting at the door," thundered the *Philadelphia Press*. "Bring on, if you need them, patriot senators from Florida, Georgia, Louisiana, and the Carolinas." But not even Stevens was willing to pack the impeachment jury this way. In debate on the day of the *Philadelphia Press* editorial, he said that the legislation would not take effect before the impeachment votes were cast.

On the night before the vote, a group of Republican senators converged on Senator Pomeroy's house shortly after Ross had left it. Ben Wade, the president-in-waiting, joined them. He had visited Grant earlier in the day, showing the general-in-chief the list of Cabinet members he intended to appoint. Wade did not want to name anyone his probable successor would not like. For hours, the Republican senators reviewed each likely vote in the Senate and agreed again that the balloting should start with Stevens's eleventh article. Pomeroy assured them that Ross would vote for conviction.

For black Americans, still at the margins of national life, the vote loomed especially large. In the North, blacks could vote in only five New England states. Most blacks were in the South, only recently released from bondage and suddenly given the vote at the point of federal bayonets. They knew Johnson did not support their rights, that his removal could only be good for them. On its last day in Washington, the conference of the African Methodist Episcopal Church declared that May 15, the day before the vote, should be a day of fasting and prayer that the Senate be guided by the Holy Spirit.

Beginning at 9 A.M. on the fifteenth, the Negro churches in Washington City offered prayers for the president's conviction. In one sermon, the minister called on the Lord to stiffen the backbone of the doubtful senators so they would remove from office "the demented Moses of Tennessee."

Prayers were in order for the health of key senators. Radicals cheered the news that Michigan Senator Howard, whose illness delayed the May

12 vote, was recovering. Two other Republicans were struggling with gastric fever. Some suspected poisoning. A warning went out for senators to avoid water pitchers at the Capitol. More shocking, James Grimes of Iowa, the first Republican defector to declare for Johnson, suffered a stroke on May 14. Weak and partially paralyzed, Grimes reassured his anxious visitors. He would not miss the vote, no matter what the state of his health.

23

FREE AGAIN

MAY 16—26, 1868

Glory enough. We all get on a big drunk to-night. Open a
bottle and drink to the health and long life of "Andy."

S. TAYLOR SUIT, MAY 16, 1868

M R. SENATOR ANTHONY, how say you?" The question from Chief Justice Chase filled the Senate Chamber at 12:30 P.M. on Saturday,
May 16. "Is Andrew Johnson, president of the United States, guilty or
not guilty of high misdemeanors as charged in this article [Article XI]?"

The bearded Rhode Islander stood at his desk. The silence in the
Senate Chamber was perfect. "Guilty," he said. The gallery let out its
breath. One vote for conviction. Thirty-five to go.

The morning had been a mixed one, clouds and sun taking turns in
the warm Washington sky. Senate Republicans caucused at the Capitol
at 10 A.M., but Edmund Ross was not there. Someone went to double-
check how Ross would vote. The message came back. Ross was solid for
conviction. The Republicans resolved to go forward with the balloting.

Outside, carriages and horsecars rumbled up to the Senate entrance.
Lush green lawns and colorful flower beds highlighted the spring dresses
of the women spectators, which featured billowing polonaise overskirts.
Inside, the marble halls echoed with footfalls and low voices. The atmosphere felt threatening to a young Radical as the "ghosts of managers and
impeachers stalked gloomily through corridors." The young man suc-

cumbed to "a state of unusual, not to say painful excitement." Ignoring reporters, impeachment advocates stared through a doorway at senators who talked eagerly in an anteroom. Inside the chamber, other senators stood and sat in groups, waiting for the voting to begin. Leaning on his crutches, General Dan Sickles cornered Ross on the Senate floor, having missed him at the Ream house the night before. Sickles urged conviction. Ross turned to his desk.

For this final scene of the impeachment drama, House members packed into the rear of the chamber. Many observers held long tally sheets listing the fifty-four senators, pencils poised to mark down each vote as it was cast.

The clerk called the Senate to order and the chief justice took the podium. The quiet gave the moment an almost religious feeling. The Senate started with the question whether to vote on the eleventh article first. The margin in favor of that motion was not quite the two-thirds that would be needed to convict on an impeachment article. Ross of Kansas voted against.

In the corridor, Senator Howard of Michigan arrived on a stretcher. Leaning on two friends, he entered the chamber and unsteadily made his way to his desk. Though it was a warm day, he wore an overcoat with a shawl around his shoulders.

The partially paralyzed Grimes of Iowa appeared at another door. He supported himself with a cane, his other arm leaning on a Senate official. Pale and shaky, Grimes did not try to make it to his desk. He sank into a chair next to the door. Henderson of Missouri found the tension unbearable. "All turns on Ross' vote," announced a noon dispatch to the *Cincinnati Gazette.*

After Anthony of Rhode Island cast the first vote, each ear listened for the names of the doubtfuls, paying little heed to the votes of those partisans whose loyalties had long been known. The first Republican defector in the alphabet, Fessenden of Maine, voted as promised: "Not guilty." Next came Fowler of Tennessee, who wore black kid gloves for the occasion. With his head cast down, Fowler spoke in a soft voice. The crowd buzzed. Had he said guilty? What did he say? Simultaneously, Chief Justice Chase and Charles Sumner of Massachusetts asked Fowler to speak up. He said, clearly this time, "Not guilty."

Grimes was next. The chief justice told him to vote from his seat, but

Grimes would not have it. Leaning heavily on his cane, he strained to rise. "Not guilty."

Henderson of Missouri also voted to acquit. The rhythm was steady. The clerk called the name of a senator. The senator rose. The chief justice posed his question. The senator voted as expected. There was no other sound. A congressman on the floor could hear breathing in the galleries. Colleagues around him looked pale and ill. The clerk reached the name of Senator Patterson of Tennessee, the president's son-in-law. He stood quickly and shouted out, "Not guilty." Many smiled and would have laughed but the chief justice instantly called for order.

Silence returned, then became more profound as the clerk neared the name of Ross. Sitting at his desk, the Kansan shredded paper into smaller and smaller bits. His lap and the floor around him were covered with white scraps. He was the fulcrum on which the president would stand or fall. Ross rose for the chief justice's question, paper bits on his fingertips, his face white. Aware that every eye was trained on him, Ross felt as if he "looked down into my open grave."

With no hesitation, he answered, "Not guilty."

An urgent sound passed through the crowd. Some heard it as a long sigh of disappointment. That was that. Impeachment would fail. Trumbull of Illinois and Van Winkle of West Virginia voted not guilty, as expected. By the time Ben Wade's name came up, it no longer mattered whether he voted or not. He cast his ballot for conviction. The final count was 35 guilty, 19 not guilty. Andrew Johnson had been acquitted by a single vote, that of Edmund Ross.

There was no cheering from the gallery, no applause. Some suppressed glee, others rage. The prosecutors had to swallow their failure. Ben Butler's bald scalp flushed red. John Bingham leaned his forehead against the table before him. Stevens, who had predicted failure the day before, bit his lip. John Logan spat tobacco juice at a spittoon, missed, and spattered the carpet.

Dismayed, unsure what to do next, Republicans played for time. They adjourned the Senate for ten days, until May 26, without voting on the ten remaining impeachment articles. It was a stall. Going forward meant certain defeat. Maybe something would come up. Maybe something could be done to change votes on another article.

Stevens rode in his chair, borne by two porters, above the river of humanity that streamed from the Senate. Men in the corridor called for news of the vote. What had happened? "Black with rage and disappointment," according to one observer, Stevens shouted, " 'The country is going to the devil.' "

A Johnson aide ran the sixteen blocks from the Capitol to the White House. Bursting into a presidential meeting, he delivered the news, which had already arrived by telegram. As Johnson accepted congratulations, tears ran down his face. Whiskey came out with sandwiches. Johnson and his men drank a toast.

The *New York Times* correspondent also bolted from the Senate. Vaulting into a waiting hack, he raced to the White House. His carriage passed Chase on the street, then novelist Anthony Trollope, then the crowds waiting for news in front of the National Hotel and Willard's Hotel. The correspondent's carriage entered the White House drive behind one carrying the president's lawyers, former Attorney General Stanberry and Thomas Nelson of Tennessee. With sweat pouring down his face, Nelson rushed up the steps to Johnson's office and plunged in. "Well, thank God, Mr. President," he announced, "you are free again."

When the *Times* correspondent wedged his way into Johnson's office, he found the president in high spirits, though cautious. The impeachers had not given up entirely, the president said, though they should. "Men's consciences are not to be made harder or softer," he said. Senators "will not know any more about the law and the evidence on the 26th instant than they know to-day."

Secretary of State Seward, whose intimates had been deeply involved in the bribery schemes, greeted the news with aplomb. May 16 was also his birthday. He was sixty-seven. After congratulating the president, he returned to his office and stretched out on the sofa with a cigar and a volume of Rousseau.

Later that day, a Republican congressman saw Senator Ross walking on the White House grounds. "There goes the rascal," he said sourly, "to get his pay."

The Astor House group was elated but not surprised. Hours before the ballots were cast, Whiskey Ring lawyer Charles Woolley sent telegrams announcing victory. To Hugh Hastings of Albany, in care of Sheridan

Shook, he crowed, "We have beat the Methodist Episcopal church north, hell, George Wilkes [a Ben Butler operative], and impeachment." Another message was more succinct: "Andy all right." After the votes were in, Shook and Woolley hosted a party in a suite at the Metropolitan Hotel. They were still drunk the next day.

One of Ben Butler's agents monitored the night's celebrations. Johnson threw open the Executive Mansion to well-wishers, an event that included "much whiskey drinking and jollification," plus a band serenade at 10:30 P.M. The president also attended a party for the diplomatic corps at Seward's house.

Butler's interest in the celebrations was not a casual one. Less than three hours after the Senate vote, John Bingham pushed a resolution through the House of Representatives that authorized an investigation of whether "improper or corrupt means have been used to influence the vote of the Senate." Before the day was over, a committee led by Butler approved summonses for eight witnesses, including Edmund Ross, Indian trader Perry Fuller, and several of the Missourians who tried to persuade John Henderson to vote for conviction. The committee started hearing testimony that evening. The first witness was Senator Ross's brother, William. He denied knowledge of corruption in the voting but was disappointed with his brother's vote.

Butler was certain, as were many Republicans, that the president's men had purchased the votes of Ross, Henderson, Fowler, and perhaps Van Winkle. "How does it happen," the Massachusetts congressman wrote, "that just enough & no more Senators are convinced of the President's innocence[?] . . . Is conscience confided to only enough to acquit the President?"

Across the nation, the president's adherents rejoiced. Hundred-gun salutes sounded in Boston, in Hartford, Connecticut, and in Titusville, Pennsylvania. Demonstrations massed in New York, St. Louis, Memphis, Kansas City, Cincinnati, and Alexandria, Virginia. In several southern cities, though, the reaction was muted. Richmond received the news quietly, as did Savannah, Georgia. With new state governments elected under congressional Reconstruction laws, and with Grant the likely next president, Johnson's acquittal might not mark much change in Southerners' political realities.

At first, many Republicans denounced the seven defectors. The *New*

York Tribune posted a list of them under a sign that screamed "TRAI-
TORS." Henderson was burned in effigy in Missouri. Ross received a
telegram from an enraged Kansan: "Probably the rope with which Judas
hung himself is lost, but the pistol with which Jim Lane committed suicide is at your service." The West Virginia legislature passed a resolution
deploring a world in which a senator from that state (Van Winkle) had
kept the president in office. Those supporting impeachment reviled
Chief Justice Chase, who was suspected of inciting defectors to vote for
acquittal.

Then came recriminations against the impeachment enterprise itself. The Radical *Chicago Tribune* offered a pithy summary of the reasons why Johnson was still in office:

1. Bad articles.
2. Lame Managers.
3. Doubtful consequences [that is, Ben Wade as president].

For Republicans, though, impeachment took a back seat for several
days. The faithful repaired to Chicago to nominate their candidate for
president. The anointing of General Grant went off without a hitch. For
vice president, the Republicans passed over Ben Wade, who now looked
like damaged goods, in favor of House Speaker Colfax.

When May 26 rolled around, Chief Justice Chase reconvened the
trial. Ten impeachment articles still loomed, but there was little reason
to expect a conviction. Not much had changed in ten days. Butler's committee had been taking testimony at a feverish pace, but it could issue
only a preliminary report that featured implications of bribery without
enough direct evidence. Two House managers, Stevens and Thomas
Williams of Pennsylvania, anticipated that the last ten articles would fail;
both congressmen had prepared new impeachment articles, but the
committee rejected them. Despite rumors of possible vote shifts, only a
miracle would produce a different outcome on any remaining article.
Nevertheless, Republicans hoped for a miracle. Despairing of bringing
Ross back to the impeachment cause, Butler sputtered, "Tell the damned
scoundrel that if he wants money there is a bushel of it here to be had."

The Republicans skipped over Article I again, concerned that Sherman of Ohio would not support it. Instead, they called for a vote on Ar-

ticle II, the charge that the appointment of Thomas as interim war secretary violated the Tenure of Office Act. The vote was exactly the same, 35 to 19, with the same seven Republican defectors.

The chief justice moved on to Article III, which also focused on the appointment of Thomas. Same vote. Same Republican defectors. The impeachers threw in the towel. They adjourned the trial for good. The Senate never voted on the remaining eight articles.

At the War Department, Edwin Stanton knew the game was up. In the afternoon, he instructed his assistant adjutant general to take charge of the department "subject to the disposal and directions of the President." The officer delivered a letter from Stanton to the White House. The war secretary, querulous to the end, did not admit that the president had removed him; rather, he wrote that he relinquished the office.

Around the nation, the impeachment bets were settled up. William Warden, the Johnson aide who doubled as a newspaper correspondent, collected thousands from other gentlemen of the press. Much of his booty came from a correspondent for the *New York Sun* who doubled as an adviser to Ben Wade.

Only one step was left for the formal impeachment process. By rule, each senator could file a public statement of the reasons for his vote. Five of the Republican defectors provided such statements.

Trumbull of Illinois and Grimes of Iowa stressed how much they disliked Johnson. "If the question was, is Andrew Johnson a fit person for President?" Trumbull wrote, "I should answer, *no*." He adopted the argument of Judge Curtis: he could not remove the president for misconstruing a doubtful statute, the Tenure of Office Act. Grimes called the incumbent "an unacceptable president," but insisted that he would not disrupt the "harmonious working of the Constitution" to get rid of him. Fessenden of Maine coolly analyzed each impeachment article, stumbling slightly over Article XI. Impeachment, he concluded, should be used only "in extreme cases, and then only upon clear and unquestionable grounds" that raise "no suspicion upon the motives of those who inflict the penalty." Henderson's explanation also struggled briefly with Article XI, the one on which he had promised to vote for conviction only four days before the final ballot.

The explanation filed by Senator Peter Van Winkle embraced a range of hair-splitting niggles. He objected that the firing of Stanton did not violate the Tenure of Office Act because the articles failed to state that Stanton actually received the removal order from the president. As to the appointment of Adjutant General Thomas, Van Winkle triumphantly pointed out that the word "appoint" appeared nowhere in the president's letter designating Thomas as Stanton's successor. Therefore, the West Virginian concluded, the designation was not an appointment "in the strict legal sense of the term." Van Winkle did not explain what Johnson had done other than appoint Thomas. Finally, the senator denied that the president prevented the execution of the laws, as charged in Article XI. Johnson, he said, merely devised a plan to do so, a mere "mental operation."

Van Winkle was one of the targets of a countervailing eruption from Massachusetts Senator Charles Sumner against the "technicalities and quibbles" arrayed in the president's defense. Calling them "parasitic insects, like vermin gendered in a lion's mane," the disappointed Radical challenged history for an instance of "equal absurdity in legal pretension."

An explanatory letter from Tennessee's Fowler appeared several weeks later. Decrying the impeachment effort as a "scheme to usurp my Government," Fowler insisted, "I acted for my country, and have done what I regard as a good act."

In a letter to his wife, Ross predicted that the nation would thank him: "Millions of men are cursing me today, but they will bless me tomorrow." In remarks in the Senate on May 27, he admitted he had changed his mind before casting his impeachment vote, asking, "Who among you . . . was at all times free from doubt?" He had been singled out, Ross charged, as the "scapegoat for the egregious blunders, weaknesses, and hates which have characterized this whole impeachment movement, itself a stupendous blunder." He denied that his vote reflected any improper influence.

Though the seven defectors have ever since received credit, or blame, for thwarting the first presidential impeachment, they may not have been Johnson's last line of defense. Substantial evidence suggests that the president had in his vest pocket several other Republican senators who would have voted for acquittal if their votes were needed. An ally of the Astor House group, New York broker Ralph Newton, telegrammed Collector Smythe a few hours after the vote, "Twenty-two

were sure on other articles, and twenty-one on that [Article XI] if necessary." Sam Ward made the same claim. The *Chicago Tribune* reported
that Johnson's advocates claimed they had at least four more votes if they
needed them. Over the next years, reports named several senators as
having been willing to support acquittal in a pinch: Waitman Willey of
West Virginia, William Sprague of Rhode Island, Edwin Morgan of New
York, and James Nye of Nevada. The listing of Nye, a former New Yorker
with ties to Thurlow Weed, is intriguing; he was one of the senators
listed by postal agent James Legate when he offered to sell votes to Edmund Cooper.

There could have been others. On the day after the vote, Johnson
expressed surprise that an Oregon senator did not vote for him. That
man, the president explained, had "financial relations" with Treasury
Secretary McCulloch and had said he would vote as McCulloch directed.
The president blamed McCulloch for not giving the senator proper direction. Johnson also had expected to win the vote of Rhode Island's
Henry Anthony.

Only nineteen votes, though, were needed. Despite the speculation
about other senators, only the seven who did vote for acquittal would be
the principal targets of Butler's investigation into corruption. No matter
what the Senate thought or the nation wished, the impeachment saga
would not be over until Ben Butler said it was.

24

---·•·---

SEARCHING FOR SCANDAL

MAY 17—JULY 5, 1868

People here [in Washington] are afraid to write letters, and I must
be a little cautious at present. Spies are, really, everywhere.

JEROME STILLSON to SAMUEL BARLOW,
MAY 22, 1868

PARTS OF BUTLER'S investigation started while the trial was still going
on. As the Senate received evidence, Butler's agents reported to
him about suspicious characters and shady conversations. He knew
about printer Cornelius Wendell, the architect of the president's acquittal fund. Thurlow Weed's minions had been in Washington City for
weeks, so the New York boss was high on Butler's list, along with Sheridan Shook, Sam Ward, and Collector Henry Smythe. Butler knew about
the corrupt Perry Fuller and his hold over Edmund Ross—that cried out
for a closer look. Missouri Senator John Henderson's erratic course certainly seemed fishy. And then there was the Whiskey Ring, America's
political bogeyman, and its lawyer, Charles Woolley. Equally important,
Butler knew the subjects he had to keep concealed. It would not do to
reveal some of his own activities, or those of his allies.

Tips poured in from around the country. What about the doctor from
Paterson, New Jersey, who claimed he was in the president's bedroom when
Woolley revealed a $20,000 payment for Ross's vote? Another source claimed
that Ross received $150,000. A New Hampshire man was convinced that a

cousin of Ross's delivered bribe money to the Kansas senator. The niece of General Alonzo Adams pleaded for an investigation of her uncle and his boast that he bought senators' votes for the verdict. Volunteer informants urged Butler to question an honest revenue agent in Chicago who could reveal all. What about the businessman in Troy, New York, who supposedly sent $100,000 to aid the president, or Vinnie Ream with her female charms, or a former army colonel with ties to the Whiskey Ring, or a tax collector who gave 10-to-1 odds that Johnson would be acquitted?

Butler's most prolific source of leads was a raffish New Yorker, George Wilkes, who published the scandalmongering *National Police Gazette*, a crime magazine. Sometimes accused of blackmailing the subjects of his stories, Wilkes only once was convicted of criminal libel. He turned that jail sentence into profit by publishing an exposé of the prison system. Wilkes sponsored prizefights and acquired a sporting weekly, *Spirit of the Times*. Politically, he became a Radical Republican during the war, then joined Butler in a scheme to colonize Baja California. Avid for impeachment, Wilkes shared with Butler his expertise in the world of detectives and law enforcement. Wilkes and Butler were accused of keeping the doubtful senators under twenty-four-hour surveillance for the week before the vote on May 16. Wilkes was on the Senate floor several times during May, engaging in informal advocacy with individual senators. Like many sporting men of the day, the New Yorker bet heavily on the trial's outcome.

Wilkes developed a confidential informant who was close to Sam Ward. According to this source, Ward paid Senator Ross $12,000 for his vote. The money supposedly came from John Morrissey, the prizefighter-turned-congressman who ran both Tammany Hall and New York's biggest lottery business, and also was one of Sam Ward's clients. In a salacious twist, Wilkes speculated that the payoffs were handled by "Charley Morgan," Sam Ward's cross-dressing mistress who supposedly was having a simultaneous affair with Congressman Morrissey's wife. Charley Morgan, Wilkes pointed out, "has the singular advantage of being able to change himself into a handsome young woman for one purpose or another."

In the middle of Butler's investigation, the young woman posing as Charley Morgan was arrested in New York. Identified in the *New York Times* as "Julia H," she pleaded guilty to the misdemeanor of "indecency," telling the court that she had not worn women's clothes for four years. Butler assured Sam Ward that he had nothing to do with Morgan's arrest, protesting that he had resisted pressure to "mortify" Ward by calling her as a witness. Butler never proved that Sam Ward had bribed Senator Ross.

The impeachment committee took testimony for six weeks after the vote on May 16. While the committee made its inquiries, workmen replaced the heavy carpets of the Capitol with white matting for the heat of summer; they retired cushioned chairs in favor of wooden ones. The committee—which soon shrank to Butler and John Logan of Illinois, with only Butler present on some days—heard over a dozen witnesses, several for more than one day. Four members of the Astor House group appeared: Weed, Shook, Erastus Webster, and Woolley. Butler questioned Treasury official Edmund Cooper, New York Collector Henry Smythe, Indian trader Perry Fuller, railroad man James Craig, and Sam Ward. Although it offended the dignity of the Senate to be investigated in this way, two senators agreed to testify. Missouri's Henderson appeared early in the investigation, while Pomeroy of Kansas testified four times in a frantic effort to straighten out his crooked story.

From the first day of the investigation, Butler zeroed in on Woolley, the Whiskey Ring lawyer. Butler may have understood that he could only get so far with wily political alligators like Thurlow Weed and Cornelius Wendell. They gave the testimony they intended to give, no more and no less. They did not get embarrassed or flustered. Weed, for example, admitted to having conversations about bribing senators and receiving numerous coded telegrams following up on those conversations. When pressed for details, the New York boss lamely insisted that he knew only that the messages "related to impeachment," but did not recall what they meant—even though all of the events had occurred within the previous two weeks! In another notable exchange, Butler began to abuse Wendell for refusing to answer a question. "If I tell anything," Wendell responded coolly, "I shall tell all I know. Do you wish me to do so, General?" Butler, acutely aware of his own attempt to pay $100,000 for Wendell's testimony against the Astor House group, changed the subject.

Butler did not back down with Charles Woolley, the Whiskey Ring lawyer who handled large piles of cash during the last two weeks before the vote. Through two committee appearances, Woolley used evasions, objections, assertions of the attorney-client privilege, and other delaying tactics. The committee tried to "follow the money" in Woolley's possession— employing the tactic that became a mantra in the Watergate investigation a century later—particularly Woolley's withdrawal of $20,000 from a Washington bank during the trial. Where had the money gone? The next day, Woolley argued that his prior testimony was void because he took the oath from a mere committee member, not from the nominal committee chairman, John Bingham. After hours of testifying, Woolley claimed he gave most of the money ($16,000) to his hotel suite-mate, Sheridan Shook, for safekeeping. The rest, according to Woolley, went for high living. Unfortunately for Woolley, Shook denied receiving any money from him.

When Woolley was summoned for a third day of testimony, the Whiskey Ring lawyer lost his appetite for the process. First he pled illness, providing a letter from a physician who said Woolley could not leave his hotel because of "irritation from sequellae of gastric derangement." Woolley accompanied that message with an affidavit challenging the committee's power to seize his papers or ask him about his private business. Miraculously recovering his strength, he fled to New York. Stalling was a shrewd tactic. Butler was under impossible time pressure. The second round of voting on the impeachment articles was scheduled for May 26. If the corruption investigation were to make any difference in the outcome, Butler needed results before then. Only Butler signed the committee's interim report, which issued on May 25. That report admitted there was no proof yet of corruption in the Senate's vote but demanded that the House compel Woolley's testimony.

On the evening of May 25, the sergeant-at-arms of the House seized Woolley, who had returned to Washington. Hauled before the House the next day, Woolley had to explain why he would not answer the committee's questions. The proceeding was interrupted so the congressmen could trudge to the other side of the Capitol to witness the death rattle of the impeachment case: the Senate's acquittal of Johnson on Articles II and III. Reconvening, the House ordered Woolley to answer the committee's questions. Protesting that he had not tried to corrupt any senators, Woolley told the House he would not answer questions about actions unrelated to the trial. The House found him in contempt and authorized the sergeant-at-arms to detain him until he testified. Woolley was held in the hearing room of the Committee on Foreign Affairs, which was fitted out with a bed. Meals came from the Capitol restaurant.

The jailing of Woolley was a sensation. Democrats flocked to see the new celebrity, who passed the time in his elegant prison with his wife

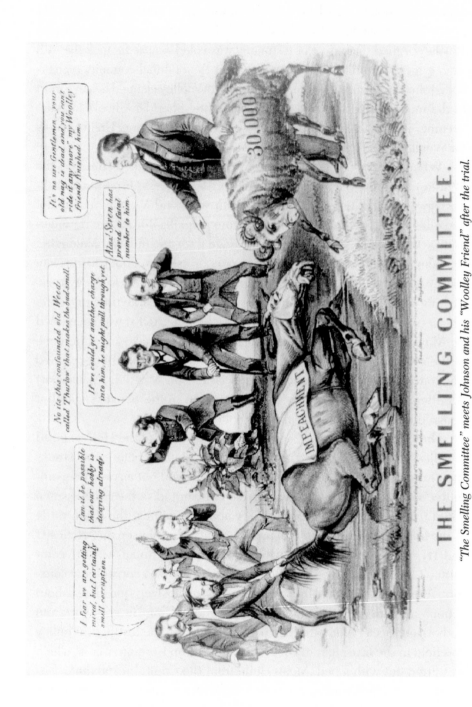

THE SMELLING COMMITTEE.

"The Smelling Committee" meets Johnson and his "Woolley Friend" after the trial.

and child. House Democrats staged confrontations over Butler's high-handed tactics. As the lawyer's detention dragged on, he was moved to the studio of Vinnie Ream in the Capitol basement. She was forced to shift her sculptures into the corridor.

While Woolley battled Butler, his Astor House allies scrambled to back him up on the unexplained $20,000. Another Seward intimate, who served as the secretary of state's agent in several matters, stepped forward with an unlikely alibi. After the committee first questioned Woolley about the money, Cornelius Wendell and Woolley's new alibi witness took the noon train to New York, polishing a story through nine hours of jostling over the tracks. They met Sheridan Shook late that evening (May 20) at the Astor House, whereupon the alibi witness pulled a wad of currency out of a pocket and claimed it was Woolley's money. Or so Wendell testified.

The alibi witness, who carried the aristocratic name of Ransom Van Valkenburg, told Butler's committee that on May 17 (the day after the first impeachment vote) he and Woolley made a $10,000 bet on the 1868 election. The bettors supposedly asked Shook to hold the stakes, but Shook refused. Portraying Shook and Woolley as blind drunk at the time, Van Valkenburg said he picked up Woolley's money and placed it in the safe at the Metropolitan Hotel, where it remained undisturbed for three weeks. In one of the most convincing passages in his final report, Butler wrote, "[Y]our committee believed no part of this stupid fabrication."

The committee questioned the imprisoned Woolley on May 27, after his first day under arrest, rejecting his request for a lawyer. Finding the lawyer still unresponsive, Butler sent Woolley back to his detention. However much Woolley might dislike being detained, Butler was the one who could not wait. Eleven days later, Woolley managed to place his dilemma before the House. This time, Woolley assured the House that he would answer Butler's questions. Butler accepted those empty assurances. The committee brought in Van Valkenburg, who produced a package of greenbacks totaling $17,000 and a hotel manager who said the package had, indeed, been in his hotel safe. Stymied by this "mass of corruption," unable to distinguish Van Valkenburg's cash from any other cash Woolley may have had, Butler released the Cincinnati lawyer after seventeen days of confinement.

Butler had other leads. He brandished a statement by seven congressmen that in January 1868, Senator Fowler of Tennessee demanded the impeachment of President Johnson to end "the sufferings of Southern

Union men and the murder of so many of them." Butler recited other examples of Fowler's previous support for impeachment. What, he demanded, converted the Tennessean to a key vote for acquittal? John Bingham and the governor of Tennessee were certain Fowler had been bribed. And what about Henderson of Missouri and his mystifying changes in position? In each case, Butler could not get his hands on definitive proof of bribery.

Butler got closer with Senator Ross and his sponsor, Indian trader Perry Fuller. Fuller admitted that he offered $40,000 to Senator Pomeroy's brother-in-law Willis Gaylord for the "Chase movement," and that he did so on the authority of Edmund Cooper at Treasury, the president's devoted supporter. Even more damning, Fuller acknowledged that in late May, in the midst of Butler's investigation, he paid off the home mortgage of James Legate, the Kansas postal agent who had spilled the beans about Fuller's involvement in vote-buying. Fuller also arranged for Legate to collect pay from the Post Office for his many weeks of scheming in Washington and then paid for Legate's passage back to Kansas. In return, Legate gave Fuller all his papers about the bribery scheme, which Fuller promptly incinerated. The Indian trader's purpose in all these steps, he admitted, was "drying up the investigation." Despite the sinister implications of these deeds, Butler did not uncover the final link, the one that traced Cooper's cash to the pocket of a senator.

In at least one instance, Butler seems to have missed key evidence. After a two-hour appearance before the committee, Sam Ward, the King of the Lobby, shared his fine cigars with the House manager. Ward admitted later that he had "trembled about that d——d telegram of Monkhood [an alias used by Ward] & Harry Smythe which would, if interpreted, have brought [railroad man James] Craig's business in . . . which I have steered clear of." What had Butler overlooked while savoring Ward's cigars? Was there another ring of corruption around the impeachment, one connecting Collector Smythe with the Missouri railroad man and the King of the Lobby? Because Butler never found out, neither have we.

Ward was so elated by his escape from Butler's clutches that he wrote an audacious letter proposing that Butler drop the investigation, apologize to Woolley, and introduce legislation to pay the president's legal fees. Whatever Butler missed, it may have been why Ward said that in his whole life, he was "proudest of the part I took in defeating the impeachment of Andrew Johnson."

For all of Butler's industry, though, he seemed to pull some of his punches, chasing less promising leads while failing to follow up on others. To begin with, he concentrated on securing the testimony of Woolley, the least well-connected member of the Astor House group. He meticulously traced Woolley's financial transactions during those critical weeks of the trial, ultimately placing some $45,000 in Woolley's hands. Other witnesses declined to answer questions, were evasive, or were contradicted by competing evidence, yet Butler gave those other witnesses a pass. The House manager freely allowed witnesses to revise their testimony after the fact, sometimes in significant ways. Some witnesses were questioned informally, not under oath. General Alonzo Adams, who originated one bribery scheme, claimed he could not even recall when he had become a General of the Army. He was deemed by the committee "utterly false and untruthful." Yet Butler took no action against him.

Was Butler merely putting on a show of pursuing the truth? He likely realized soon enough that he could not gain great political advantages from the investigation. Neither the House nor the Senate intended to deal with impeachment any more. Johnson's term in office would end on March 4, 1869, which was drawing ever closer.

Butler evidently sought to uncover only certain truths, those that would serve his political goals, which involved inflicting the maximum possible damage on the president and the Democratic Party, while reinforcing the Grant-Colfax ticket for the fall election. Also high among Butler's priorities was any development that would increase his own power and influence. With these goals, Butler found it awkward, at best, that so much evidence seemed to implicate Kansas Senator Pomeroy, who had been a firm vote to convict the president but also had a most checkered reputation. Butler's ability to attack others was limited by his need to whitewash Pomeroy, despite evidence so incriminating that the Kansan testified four times in a desperate search for a satisfactory narrative for his conduct. Postal agent Legate went through a three-hour preparation session in Pomeroy's committee room to ensure that he did not irretrievably implicate his fellow Kansan.

In the final committee report, Butler cried out in frustration that the only senators named by the Astor House group as potential bribe-takers were Republicans who voted "guilty," including Pomeroy, Nye of Nevada, Anthony and Sprague of Rhode Island, and Morton of Indiana. What else did Butler expect his political enemies to say? After all, he spent no effort investigating allegations about those other Republicans and chose to focus on Woolley, the only Democrat in the Astor House group.

Butler hurried the report into print on July 3. He wanted to thwart President Johnson's quest for the Democratic nomination for president. That party's convention was meeting in New York the following week. The report, though, was an anticlimax. As with the preliminary report, only Butler signed it. The proof still failed to place dollars in the pocket of any senator. In a letter to his father, Thomas Ewing, Jr. scorned the committee's claim that it lacked only a link or two in proving that Charles Woolley bribed Senator Ross: "That is, they can't tell who got [the money] from Woolley or who paid it to Ross!"

Still, Ross, Henderson, and Fowler—the defectors most suspected of selling their votes—blistered the report in speeches on the Senate floor. Ross's denunciation was particularly vigorous, referring to Butler's "well-known groveling instincts and proneness to slime and uncleanness." Denials, most politicians learn, have less force than accusations. Though that truism can be unfair, it also reflects human experience. As Henderson himself argued several years later, when he was prosecuting Whiskey Ring defendants, anyone capable of committing a crime is capable of denying it.

For eighteen months after the impeachment trial ended, one newsman fitfully tried to answer the questions that Butler's report raised. A native of Massachusetts, Henry Van Ness Boynton was not a man to trifle with. Made a general of Ohio Volunteers during the Civil War, he earned the Congressional Medal of Honor at the battle of Missionary Ridge, where he was severely wounded. Writing for the *Cincinnati Gazette*, Boynton quickly established himself as a leading Washington correspondent. Though a firm Republican, he was nonpartisan in ferreting out official misconduct.

In reports published in late December 1869, Boynton identified three schemes to use cash to influence the impeachment vote. The first involved an offer that agents of certain Republican senators should wager $50,000 (at least $700,000 in today's dollars) that the president would be acquitted. Once those senators voted to ensure acquittal, the bet would be paid off. Though this proposal was supported by two Cabinet members (Seward and Postmaster General Randall), Boynton concluded that the scheme was not implemented. The second plan was the one designed by Cornelius Wendell at the request of Seward, Randall, and Treasury Secretary McCulloch. Boynton found that $150,000 (over $2 million in current value) was raised for payoffs, but he could not establish that the funds were paid to senators. Most likely, he thought, middlemen like Fuller and Legate siphoned off most of the money. The third scheme, according to Boynton, was Butler's attempt to induce Wendell to reveal scheme number two in return for $100,000 (worth at least $1.4 million today).

To Boynton, Ben Butler was the worst rascal in the crowd. Butler's pursuit of Charles Woolley, the correspondent concluded, was a smokescreen behind which all other scoundrels were able to retreat. Boynton was disgusted by Butler's failure to publish key testimony from the investigation (only a few transcripts survive from Butler's inquiry). Wendell, Randall, and Seward aide Erastus Webster all gave testimony that was never disclosed. Boynton did not know what Butler was hiding but was sure the congressman was hiding something. Having expected to prove the perfidy of the president's defenders, Boynton concluded that Johnson's pursuers were no better.

In response to Boynton's articles, Cornelius Wendell gave an intriguing newspaper interview. He confirmed Boynton's reporting about the proposed wager on the verdict, and the acquittal fund. In a public exchange with Senator Ross, Wendell said he did not know of money that was paid to Ross. Wendell added that several thousand dollars had been offered to Perry Fuller to influence Ross, but Fuller declined it.

Boynton's investigation certainly reinforces suspicions of corruption in the Senate vote. So does a letter that Wendell wrote the day before Johnson left office in March of 1869. In it, Wendell requested the president's help in recovering $10,000 paid for "expenses attending the impeachment trial." The costs, Wendell explained, were incurred "at the instigation and by the direction of [Postmaster General] A. W. Randall, E[dmund] Cooper, and E[rastus] D. Webster." Randall and Wendell had managed to raise $1,500 of the amount, but the balance remained unpaid. Without directly asking for payment, Wendell told the president, "You can judge the object of this note."

With evidence that is both untidy and incomplete, definitive pronouncements are difficult to make about bribery and the impeachment vote. Operating without modern tools for investigating public crime—such as coercive grants of witness immunity, ready access to sophisticated banking records, or the threat of long prison terms for perjury and official misconduct— Butler still turned up intriguing evidence, significant chunks of which can be confirmed. That Butler was not exclusively interested in the truth makes the historical riddle yet more challenging. Still, some points can be stated.

The president's partisans assembled at least one war chest, and probably more, to buy senators' votes. They entered into substantive negotiations with numerous parties claiming to represent senators interested in selling their votes—General Alonzo Adams, postal agent James Legate, Indian trader Perry Fuller, Willis Gaylord (Pomeroy's agent), Senator Pomeroy himself, and possibly others who managed to cover their tracks more effectively. Legate described a concerted effort to sell senators' votes, which Fuller confirmed in substantial part. Indeed, Legate claimed eighteen months after the trial that John Henderson of Missouri received $50,000 at New York's Astor House for his vote, and that Gaylord received $25,000 that had been raised for the impeachment but was diverted to a futile attempt to purchase Collector Smythe's confirmation as American minister to Austria. Sixty thousand dollars, Legate explained, was paid for yet another senator's vote, and $25,000 went to Senator Waitman Willey of West Virginia, who double-crossed his bribers by voting for conviction but keeping the money. Though many elements of Legate's tale are not confirmed, Perry Fuller had to have very good reasons for paying off Legate's mortgage in return for the postal agent's papers and his hasty departure from Washington. And then Fuller burned Legate's papers.

Were any votes actually sold? With no solid proof, only probabilities can be offered. A number of clever and powerful people worked hard to purchase votes. Virtually all contemporaries defended the honor of Senators Fessenden, Grimes, and Trumbull. In doing so, most made clear that they were not so sure about the other four defectors. At least three of those others—Ross, Fowler, and Henderson—cast votes that were contrary to their prior statements and to their immediate political advantage as Republicans. And what of the two or three additional Republicans who were expected to vote for acquittal if their votes were needed? Were arrangements (that is, payments) made with them, also?

Then there was Ross's double game before the May 16 vote. The Kansan argued that he should not be suspected of corruption merely because he changed his mind about how to vote. That's a fair point. His actions might be explained as reflecting genuine uncertainty. But they are explained equally well, even better, as the efforts of a man holding out for the best offer. For a man whose companions in the hours before he voted were Perry Fuller, the embodiment of corruption in 1868, and Thomas Ewing, Jr., another leading political manipulator, that explanation has great power.

Selling a vote in the first presidential impeachment would have been a dazzlingly craven act, but not inconsistent with the ethics of the era. House Speaker Colfax and a fistful of congressmen took railroad stock in return for supporting the Union Pacific Railroad. A secretary of war, William Belknap, would be forced to resign in 1872 for taking kickbacks from military contractors, while President Grant's chief of staff would be linked to the Whiskey Ring. Were senators' votes purchased to preserve Johnson's presidency? Admitting a lack of certainty, the verdict here is that it is more likely than not.

Though he kept some distance from the grimy details of the campaign to save Johnson by all possible means, Secretary of State Seward plainly inspired and set in motion much of the effort. Many of the schemers who planned the political deals, bribes, and patronage payoffs were Seward men, from Thurlow Weed to William Evarts, from Sheridan Shook to Erastus Webster to Ransom Van Valkenburg. Seward, who had accepted Johnson as Lincoln's true heir, drew no ethical lines in the desperate battle to preserve Johnson's presidency.

Then arises the more modern question: What did President Johnson know and when did he know it? Was he aware of the war chests assembled to buy senators on his behalf? Did he know of the bargaining with supposed agents for senators willing to be corrupted? The president's men were generally careful to absolve Johnson of having any knowledge of their activities in trying to buy

Secretary of State William Henry Seward, staunch Johnson loyalist.

295

impeachment votes. Johnson made several statements to staff members that he would not buy senators' votes. Are they, and he, to be believed?

Here again, only probabilities can be stated, but they are strong. Edmund Cooper of Tennessee, Johnson's friend and companion, touched every corrupt scheme. Other senior officials were deeply involved in the vote-buying efforts. From the Cabinet—Secretary of State Seward, Treasury Secretary McCulloch, and Postmaster General Randall. From the White House staff—Colonel William Moore and William Warden. Is it possible that all of them engaged in such high-risk activity without telling the boss? Is it possible that none of them ever mentioned their activities to the president with a passion for micromanagement, who kept a list of senators on his desk and reviewed with newspaper correspondents how they would vote? A truism for corruption investigations in the modern era is that when there is widespread cheating, the top official knows. Indeed, the corruption cannot happen unless that person approves. People are not so foolish as to undertake high-risk behaviors like bribery without being certain that their superiors approve. That lesson rings even more true for powerful people like Cabinet members who are jealous of their public reputations. President Johnson knew.

For those who accept the proposition that a vote can be corruptly purchased with patronage, as well as with greenbacks, the evidence on these questions is stronger still.

On May 14, two days before the Senate vote, Willis Gaylord sent a message to postal agent Legate. "As matters stand now," Gaylord wrote, "the money to be made is on the other side by appointments, etc. Keep watch of good places and let me know." By referring to "the other side," Gaylord may have been counseling an attempt to secure promises of patronage jobs in the (presumably) incoming administration of Ben Wade. Gaylord's focus on patronage was apt. Fortunes could be amassed in a short time as a revenue collector or Indian agent.

As soon as the Senate votes were tallied, those who had conducted the bribery schemes swamped the president with demands for lucrative positions. On May 18, Edmund Cooper urged a tax collector position in New Orleans for Andrew Lacy, who assisted Woolley and the Astor House group. "I have been saved by so many men," Johnson remarked, "that I am often accused of ingratitude because I can't help them all." He did, however, help a lot of them.

When it came to converting the president's acquittal into lucrative patronage, Edmund Ross was at the head of the line. For Ross, the biggest prize was making Perry Fuller the commissioner of internal revenue, a position Fuller had pursued for six months. On June 23, while Butler's committee was hearing witnesses about vote-buying, Ross sent Johnson a letter urging him to name Fuller to the position, referring to their earlier conversation on the matter. Three days later, the president did just as Ross asked.

The negative reaction to Fuller's nomination was immediate. Press reports referred to Fuller as "that notorious Indian trader and lobbyist," a man whose "reputation is bad," a name "associated with corrupt contracts, and with a ring of western adventurers who have been implicated in many of the inequities notorious at Washington." When the Senate Finance Committee recommended against Fuller's nomination, Johnson withdrew it.

In response, Fuller set his sights a bit lower. In late August, Johnson appointed him collector at the Port of New Orleans, through which passed the heavy Mississippi River traffic to and from foreign destinations. Because the Senate was in recess, Fuller could take office immediately, without being confirmed. One correspondent wrote disgustedly that Fuller's appointment resolved any nagging doubt that perhaps Johnson was not so bad after all: "The man who can give the country such public servants has come to posterity and been judged already."

Fuller arrived in New Orleans in September and set straight to work. He fired 65 Republican employees of the custom house, replacing them with no fewer than 150 worthies, all his creatures. Fuller's overhaul caused the treasury secretary to fret that expenses "will be considerably increased by Mr. Fuller while those of all other Custom Houses are being reduced." But Fuller was just getting started.

He appointed Vinnie Ream's father—Senator Ross's landlord in Washington—to be superintendent of the warehouses that held imported goods before they were taxed. Goods sent through one of those warehouses, however, were never taxed. Though Fuller served as collector in New Orleans for only seven months, he was arrested in September 1869 and charged with using this scheme to defraud the government of $3 million in tax revenues. A grand jury in New Orleans returned a nineteen-count indictment against him. Fuller won release on a bond that was guaranteed by two United States senators: Edmund Ross of Kansas and an Arkansas senator whose brother was Fuller's business partner. When Fuller failed to appear on his bond, Ross was called upon to produce the fugitive. The senator never answered in court. According to a later report, Fuller's New Orleans scam generated more than $50,000 in kickbacks for him. The criminal charges against Fuller were never pursued.

But Perry Fuller's was only the most lurid name on Senator Ross's shopping list. According to one Radical newspaper, the president yielded to Ross the control over all patronage appointments in Kansas and the territories of Colorado and New Mexico. In early June, Ross requested the appointment of a friend as superintendent of Indian lands in Kansas and the neighboring Indian Territory (the future Oklahoma). Ross's letter to Johnson was blunt. "There is a large amount of patronage connected with that office," he wrote on June 6, "making it very valuable to the possessor." The appointment was "vital," the Kansan continued, to maintain his political position after "my action on the impeachment." The president made the appointment.

A week later, Ross demanded that the president approve a treaty with the Osage Tribe. On the same day, Johnson sent the treaty to the Senate. Two weeks later, Ross wanted his brother appointed a special mail agent in Florida. Shortly after that, the Kansas senator requested three appointments, including the surveyor general of Kansas and two Indian agents. Acknowledging that he was asking much of the president, Ross wrote that he felt warranted in doing so "by the many assurances of kindly personal regard that I have received from you." Only the candidate for surveyor general was nominated as Ross requested. Undeterred, the Kansas senator also asked the president to grant public lands to a Kansas coal company. Ross's demands made an impression on Johnson's bodyguard. The Kansas senator, the guard recalled, "was at the White House a good deal during the last months of Mr. Johnson's administration," pursuing "appointments in Kansas."

Johnson's patronage largesse was not confined to Senator Ross. Van Winkle of West Virginia, Fowler of Tennessee, and Grimes of Iowa all sent the president requests for appointments, albeit on a more modest scale. Cornelius Wendell, the corruption consultant who designed Johnson's acquittal fund, received a lucrative sinecure as a government director on the board of the Union Pacific Railroad.

John Henderson of Missouri was not appointed to the Cabinet, despite reports that his vote was purchased with promises of such a spot. In late June, he wed Mary Foote in a Washington ceremony. The president attended the wedding, where Senator Fowler of Tennessee served as a groomsman. With an impressive lack of concern for appearances, Johnson provided a unique wedding gift, appointing the senator's father-in-law, Elisha Foote, to be commissioner of patents. The Senate promptly confirmed the appointment.

On the same day as the Henderson-Foote nuptials, the president nominated Collector Smythe to be U.S. minister to Austria. The nomination embarrassed so sturdy a Johnson loyalist as Navy Secretary Gideon Welles. It was, Welles noted tersely in his diary, "an appointment that should not have been made." Welles's judgment was vindicated ten weeks later when an investigation of the New York Custom House placed the collector under temporary arrest to secure his testimony. One historian estimated at "sixfold" the corrupt overcharges imposed on imports by Smythe's Custom House. When the Senate would not confirm Smythe for Austria, Johnson nominated him to be minister to Russia. Smythe ran afoul of two more political hazards. The Custom House investigation ripened into criminal prosecutions alleging the theft of $700,000 of tax revenue during Smythe's watch, while the collector was excoriated for placing on the public payroll the former editor of the *Richmond Examiner*, a prominent Confederate during the war. Despite Johnson's dogged efforts, Smythe never did join the diplomatic service.

Was this parade of patronage nothing more than the standard act of rewarding one's friends? The actions of 1868 should not be judged by the standards of the twenty-first century. Plainly, though, the most generous view of Ross's actions must acknowledge that he strained every muscle to cash in on the president's sense of obligation after the impeachment vote. Indeed, that surely was one of his expectations when he and Perry Fuller consulted over breakfast on the morning of May 16, and when he and Thomas Ewing, Jr., went on their midnight ramble the evening before. Were those patronage deals reached before Ross saved the president? Did the president know the extent of his obligations to Ross before the Kansan cast his vote? No sporting man would bet against it, not without the benefit of very good odds.

25

THE CARAVAN MOVES ON

JANUARY 1, 1869—

[Acquittal] leaves him less hopelessly in the wrong than he seemed six months ago, and it leaves him in possession of the honors of the field. His escape, to be sure, has been very narrow, but in politics, as in war, an inch of a miss is as good as a mile.

THE NATION, MAY 21, 1868

T HE FIRST DAY of 1869 brought cold drizzle and sleet to Washington City, but callers at the White House found a profusion of fresh-cut flowers and a buoyant Andrew Johnson. The president betrayed no sadness that his time in the Executive Mansion was coming to an end, even though the despised Ulysses Grant would succeed him in office, having defeated the Democratic candidate, New York Governor Horatio Seymour, in the fall election. Supported by his two gracious daughters, Johnson greeted official guests in the Blue Room for an hour. At noon, the doors opened to the public. With the Marine Band playing, visitors left their dripping umbrellas in the anterooms and piled in to offer New Year's greetings to Johnson. The dapper president smoothly took the hand of each visitor, exchanged a quick word, and turned to the next.

For Johnson, the holiday season had been a good one. On Christmas Day, he issued a proclamation granting amnesty to every former rebel, including Jefferson Davis, something he had wanted to do for months. December 29 might have been his most carefree day in the White House. To celebrate Johnson's sixtieth birthday, his family invited four hundred children of their friends to a dancing party in the East Room. The children joined in square dances, waltzes, polkas, and the Virginia reel before enjoying refreshments. Mrs. Johnson came downstairs to admire the event, only the second function she attended at the White House.

At the New Year's Day reception, two guests drew special attention. Noble Hurdle, an aged resident of Georgetown, announced that he had shaken the hand of every president since the Republic began and was happy to shake Johnson's, "the last President, but by no means the least!" The president thanked Mr. Hurdle for the compliment, muted though it was.

Yet more remarkable was an earlier visitor, Ben Butler of Massachusetts. Despite all his tirades against the Great Criminal in the White House, despite his relentless efforts to remove Johnson from office, Butler delivered a robust two-handed greeting to the president. The two men, recently bitter adversaries, held up the reception line for five minutes while they chatted and beamed happily at each other. What accounted for such a change in political relations? Did this fraternal feeling reflect the realism of experienced politicians who were moving on to the next chapter? Or had the president respected his promise to Senator Grimes during the trial, pulled in his horns, and behaved himself following the dramatic acquittal?

Johnson had indeed honored the most specific commitment he made to Grimes: after seriously considering backing out on the appointment of John Schofield as secretary of war, the president went through with it. The Senate confirmed Schofield's appointment in late May. On June 1, Johnson thoroughly enjoyed a visit to the War Office, finally rid of Edwin Stanton. With a laugh, the president observed, "It is some time since I was in this room!"

By many measures, though, Andrew Johnson did not change his political course after the acquittal. Not only did he nominate dubious figures like Perry Fuller and Henry Smythe to high positions, but he also kept on vetoing legislation. On June 20, Congress adopted a bill to readmit Arkansas under its new state constitution. The president vetoed; to do otherwise, he explained, would accept Congress's power to exclude

Arkansas's representatives in the first place. Five days later, Johnson vetoed a law readmitting six other Southern states (all but Virginia, Mississippi, and Texas). Congress enacted both bills over his vetoes.

Johnson continued to support white conservatives in the South. He appointed new military commanders who would take little action to curb violence against blacks. Pleas for military intervention against white violence came from Republican governors in Georgia and Mississippi and the military commander in Tennessee. Johnson did not respond. Using terror tactics to drive the freedmen from the polls, Democrats in Georgia and Mississippi posted gains in the fall elections.

Estimates of the election-year carnage in the South were staggering, though often imprecise. The House Committee on Elections found that in Louisiana more than 1,000 blacks and white Unionists were killed and an equal number wounded, more than 600 killed in Kentucky, and dozens more in South Carolina. From August to October, the Freedmen's Bureau reported, Georgia saw 31 killings of blacks and white Unionists, 43 nonfatal shootings, 5 stabbings, and 63 beatings. A Republican congressman from Arkansas was assassinated for political reasons. Fifty armed men attacked a plantation owned by a Unionist in Texas, killing seven freedmen. The Ku Klux Klan claimed credit for murdering leading Republicans in Alabama, in Georgia, in Texas, and in South Carolina.

Southern Republicans wrote anguished letters to Northern colleagues, pleading for assistance. From Vicksburg, Mississippi, came the report that "organized bands of desperadoes, cut throats and murderers [are] at large in this state," driving Republican voters from the polls. Bribery, threats, and force were used for the same purpose in Kosciusko, Mississippi. Many freedmen were blocked from voting. Others were compelled to vote for Democrats.

Much of the worst violence continued to be in Texas. A former governor reported in May 1868 that 250 "union men" had been murdered in the state in the preceding six months. For a price, gangs would kill blacks, Republicans, or federal soldiers. Efforts at self-defense by the poorly armed freedmen often brought catastrophe. Civil war broke out in Brazos County, with whites and blacks forming militias. Twenty-five freedmen died in a battle that drove most blacks and Union families from the area.

Over the summer of 1868, the new legislatures of Louisiana, Alabama, and Tennessee requested more federal troops to reduce civil violence. The response from Washington was halting and reluctant. War Secretary Schofield issued instructions that military force be applied only upon the president's order. The attorney general lectured army commanders that the duty of maintaining order "belongs to the civil authorities of the States," not federal officials. If the man in the White House cared about the mayhem across the South, there was little evidence of it.

In early July, the president grew edgy while Democrats gathered in New York City to pick their candidate for president. Edmund Cooper and other Johnson agents headed to the convention. One of Johnson's defense lawyers at the trial, Thomas Nelson of Tennessee, placed his name in nomination. The president paced the Executive Mansion awaiting word, his ambition gnawing at him, considering resignation if he was not nominated. After the first ballot, Johnson stood second among the Democratic hopefuls. He was so close to vindication.

Amid the smoldering ruins of his presidency, Johnson could see no reason why the Democrats would not choose him. His administration had been marked by unprecedented conflict with Congress, by unprecedented rates of vetoes and veto overrides, and by an impeachment effort that barely failed. Nevertheless, the president fumed that he had bested General Grant, the Republican candidate, in every confrontation over the last several months, including the impeachment trial. Having been "successful in every single issue heretofore," Johnson railed that giving the Democratic nomination to anyone else would be "an abandonment of our cause." Why shouldn't the Democrats nominate him, he demanded of Colonel Moore: "They profess to accept my measures: they say I have stood by the Constitution and made a noble struggle."

The prospect of vindication proved to be a mirage. On the twenty-second ballot, the Democrats selected Governor Seymour of New York.

Shortly afterward, the Fourteenth Amendment to the Constitution was ratified despite Johnson's opposition. On July 20, 1868, Secretary of State Seward certified that twenty-eight states—three-fourths of the thirty-seven states—had approved the amendment. He issued a further certification eight days later after receiving notice of ratification by Alabama and Georgia. Seward's decision to issue the second certification reflects just how messy the ratification process was.

When Congress sent the amendment to state legislatures in 1866, some argued that ratification could be based on approval by three-fourths of the twenty-seven states then represented in Congress (that is, not counting the ten Southern states excluded from Congress). That position never prevailed. Two Northern states (Ohio and New Jersey) ratified the amendment but then attempted to rescind their ratifications after Democrats won control of their state legislatures. Seward concluded that those rescissions were invalid, and so signed the first certification that the amendment had been ratified. Seward issued his second certification because the intervening ratifications by Alabama and Georgia meant that twenty-eight states had ratified without attempting to rescind (that is, excluding Ohio and New Jersey). When Oregon's legislature purported to rescind its ratification three months later, Seward took no further action. Although Seward did not recognize the attempted rescissions, three Southern states (the Carolinas and Louisiana) were permitted to change their course in the other direction. While ruled by the state governments sponsored by Johnson, all three states rejected the amendment. The new state governments formed under the Reconstruction laws of 1867, however, approved it.

Of the provisions of the Fourteenth Amendment, the guarantees of due process of law and equal protection would prove most enduring. The reach of the due process clause changed over time, ultimately becoming the source of many personal rights now taken for granted by Americans. The equal protection clause lay mostly dormant until the middle of the twentieth century, when civil rights lawyers persuaded the courts to breathe life into it, making it central to American political and social life.

By the fall of 1868, the end was in sight for the Johnson Administration. The president's annual message to Congress in December included his familiar denunciation of congressional Reconstruction, which he described as failed and pernicious. Though Johnson's pledge of better conduct had produced few changes in his behavior, he did become less and less important as his term ran out. By New Year's Day, 1869, with Ulysses Grant poised to occupy the White House in two months, Ben Butler could pass a few pleasant moments with Andrew Johnson because, finally, Johnson no longer mattered very much.

• • •

Thaddeus Stevens never gave up. On July 7, 1868, six weeks after the last votes acquitting Johnson, he presented five new articles of impeachment. Knowing that his days were dwindling, the Pennsylvanian made no effort to cloak the political nature of his accusations. Johnson, Stevens charged, had betrayed Republican principles and replaced Republican officeholders in an effort to build a personal political party. The president had unilaterally created state governments in the South in 1865, usurping the powers of Congress to make the laws. He induced Colorado officials to perjure themselves to defeat statehood, pardoned Union Army deserters so they could vote for Democrats, and returned confiscated property to ex-rebels. In a long speech that he submitted for publication but did not read in person, Stevens ignored the recent impeachment trial, choosing instead to warn his countrymen "not to place our trust in princes." He ended with an exhortation from graveside:

> My sands are nearly run, and I can see only with the eye of faith. . . .
> If you and your compeers can fling away ambition and realize that
> every human being, however lowly-born or degraded by fortune, is
> your equal, that every inalienable right which belongs to you be-
> longs to him, truth and righteousness will spread over the land. . . .

Representative Thomas Williams, also a former House manager, submitted fourteen more impeachment articles on the same date. The House took no action on any of the new impeachment proposals.

By early August, the newspapers resumed the death watch on Stevens, running daily bulletins on his health. For ten days, he could not leave his room. In bedside chats, Old Thad regretted that when the war came he became "so radical that I had no control over anybody." His only satisfaction, he said, came from his time in Pennsylvania's state government, especially the creation of free public schools in the 1830s. When a caller commented on his appearance, Stevens's wit flashed briefly. He was not concerned about his appearance, he replied, but his disappearance.

As Stevens grew weaker in this lingering public death, he admitted fewer and fewer visitors. On his final evening, he was attended by an aide, a nephew, his sister Loretta, and Mrs. Smith. Two black clergymen prayed with him and left. Late that night, two Sisters of Charity from a nearby Catholic hospital visited. With the consent of Stevens's nephew, they baptized the dying man. In Stevens's final moments, his nephew held his hand while Mrs. Smith knelt at the foot of his bed.

On the next day, citizens of Lancaster who lived in Washington carried his casket to the nearby Capitol, where his body lay in state overnight, surrounded by dignitaries and a detachment of Negro soldiers. Mourners came to pay their respects until midnight. The next morning, a crowd watched the funeral party's progress, the hearse drawn by four white horses, to a special train. When Stevens was buried in Schreiner's Cemetery in Lancaster, more than 15,000 people overflowed the surrounding streets. Before his death, Stevens had sold two plots in a white-only cemetery, then acquired a space at Schreiner's because it accepted people of all races. His headstone reads:

> I repose in this quiet and secluded spot,
> Not from any natural preference for solitude,
> But, finding other Cemeteries limited as to Race
> by Charter Rules,
> I have chosen this that I might illustrate in my death
> The Principles which I advocated through a long life;
> EQUALITY OF MAN BEFORE HIS CREATOR

That fall, Lancaster Republicans nominated a dead man, Thaddeus Stevens, as their candidate for Congress. He won easily.

For the other House managers, the failure of impeachment proved no obstacle to advancement. No one who saw Ben Butler joking at the White House on New Year's Day could be surprised by his future success. Butler settled a bitter wartime feud with General Grant and became a political adviser to the new president. He lost his House seat in 1874 but won another term two years later. In 1879, Butler was elected governor of Massachusetts with Democratic Party support. After an unsuccessful run for president on the Greenback Party ticket in 1884, Butler retired from politics.

John Bingham of Ohio stayed in the House until 1872, when President Grant appointed him ambassador to Japan, a post that Bingham held through three presidential terms, retiring in 1885. He lived long enough to see a distant cousin, William McKinley, elected president in 1896. George Boutwell of Massachusetts served in the Grant Administration as secretary of the treasury, then was chosen senator from his home state. In his final years, Boutwell led the Anti-Imperialist League in opposing the Spanish-American War and the acquisition of overseas colonies. John Logan, serving in the House and then the Senate until his death, was the Republican candidate for vice president in 1884. As head of the Grand Army of the Republic, the veterans' group, Logan led the movement to create Memorial Day to honor the nation's war dead.

Fewer honors awaited the president's defense team. Johnson tried to appoint Benjamin Curtis as his attorney general, but Curtis turned down the position. The president then picked Henry Stanberry. Showing more than a little spite, the Senate rejected him. One more time, William Evarts benefited from Stanberry's bad luck. Johnson nominated Evarts and the Senate confirmed him. Despite his loyal service to Johnson, Evarts later was welcomed back into the Republican Party. In 1876, his legal work was critical during the months-long dispute over the presidential election. Evarts's client, Rutherford Hayes, rewarded Evarts by making him secretary of state. Evarts later was a senator from New York. Stanberry returned to private law practice, becoming a leading courtroom defender of the Ku Klux Klan.

Edwin Stanton left the War Office in miserable health, his asthma tormenting him. He tried to resume his law practice in Washington City. President Grant nominated him for the Supreme Court, and the Senate confirmed Stanton in December 1869. Four days later, on Christmas Eve, Stanton died after taking the oath of office in bed. Ben Wade's Senate term expired in early 1869. He stayed in Washington as a lobbyist. Grant appointed him to the board of the Union Pacific Railroad and sent him as a special envoy in unsuccessful negotiations to acquire the Caribbean land of Santo Domingo.

• • •

One of the enduring myths of the Johnson impeachment involves the fates of the seven Republican defectors who supposedly chose principle over party, sacrifice over self-advancement. Each of them, according to the myth, ended his life a broken man, crushed by vindictive Radical Republicans. "Not a single one of them escaped the terrible torture," wrote John F. Kennedy in *Profiles in Courage*, "of vicious criticism engendered by their vote to acquit." It is a myth.

All seven defectors supported Grant's candidacy in the fall of 1868. Grimes of Iowa, despite his stroke in May, returned to the Senate the following year. He pronounced that his influence in the new Congress was greater than it had been before the impeachment. Poor health forced his resignation at the end of 1869. Only a few months earlier, Fessenden of Maine died during a summer recess, still in office. Peter Van Winkle of West Virginia reported in July 1868 that the "stir" over his impeachment vote "died away very suddenly." Soon, he found, "I am invited to and attend all the Republican caucuses." He retired from the Senate in 1869, as he had intended. None was a victim of postimpeachment retribution. Indeed, their careers were not wildly different from those of the thirty-five senators who voted to convict Andrew Johnson: only seventeen of those senators won reelection as Republicans, while one crossed the aisle and won with support from Liberal Republicans and Democrats.

Missouri's John Henderson did not seek reelection to the Senate when his term expired in 1869, but he stayed true to the Republicans, and they to him. In 1872, he was the Republican candidate for governor of Missouri, and for senator the next year, though his impeachment vote still could draw negative comment. Failing in both campaigns, Henderson secured appointment as United States attorney in Missouri, where he prosecuted alleged members of the Whiskey Ring. In the most formal recognition of Henderson's good standing among Republicans, he was the presiding officer at the party's national convention in 1884. He moved to Washington a few years later and built a thirty-room mansion on Meridian Hill, a platform from which his wife startled the city with her advanced social views. In the early twentieth century, Mary Foote Henderson mounted vegetarian and nonalcoholic dinner parties, as well as weekly dancing classes in the style of Isadora Duncan. On a memorable evening in 1906, Mrs. Henderson and her temperance ladies pillaged her husband's wine cellar, smashing into the gutters of Sixteenth Street more than a thousand bottles of wine, brandy, and whiskey.

Three of the defecting senators did move away from the Republican Party, though at different speeds. Of the three, Lyman Trumbull of Illinois lingered the longest. Following Grant's election, he continued to chair the Senate Judiciary Committee and still received Republican Party honors. Like many other Republicans, Trumbull soured on the Grant Administration. In 1872, he campaigned for reelection on the Liberal Republican ticket, but lost. He later ran for governor of Illinois as a Democrat, losing that race, too.

Fowler of Tennessee chafed at criticism of his acquittal vote. In the days following the trial, he moved his seat permanently to the Democratic side of the Senate to escape "Radical whisperings." He lost his committee assignments the following year. Fowler did not seek reelection, anticipating that Tennessee Republicans would not support him. In 1872, he campaigned against Grant, then largely retired from public life.

Between his impeachment vote and his deals with Johnson, Edmund Ross's prospects were poor when the Grant Administration arrived in March 1869. Only weeks later, Grant threw the Kansas senator out of the White House after a heated argument over patronage. Ross claimed he told the new president to "go to hell." Ross sought a full term in the Senate from the Kansas legislature in 1871. Fittingly, the legislators chose a rival who paid them $60,000 in bribes, even more than Perry Fuller paid for Ross's seat in 1867. The bribery was so blatant this time that his successor was forced to resign in 1873. Ross started two Kansas newspapers that failed, then in 1880 ran unsuccessfully as the Democratic candidate for governor. Two years later, Ross moved to New Mexico, where he ran a printing business. When the Democrats won the White House in 1884, President Grover Cleveland named Ross the territorial governor of New Mexico. In his final years, Ross was the major source of the legend of the seven martyrs, defending his impeachment vote in correspondence, magazines, and a book.

Thus, of the seven defectors, five either retired from the Senate voluntarily, died in office, or left because of health. Henderson remained a Republican in good standing for the rest of his life. Trumbull chose to leave the party years later, while Ross remade himself as a Democrat. Hardly the trail of suffering and despair that has been depicted.

Samuel Pomeroy of Kansas ended his Senate career in disgrace. In January 1873, he paid a $7,000 bribe to a Kansas state legislator to support his bid for a new term. The legislator marched into the state Capitol building, denounced Pomeroy's bribery, and delivered the cash to the legislative clerk so it could be used to educate the children of Kansas. A state investigation found Pomeroy guilty of bribery; but the United States Senate found insufficient evidence to reach that conclusion. Pomeroy retired to Washington, then Massachusetts. He ran for president in 1884 for the American Prohibition Party.

The Astor House group and its allies showed remarkable resilience, though Perry Fuller was not the only one to collide with the law. Postal agent James Legate of Kansas was appointed governor of the Washington Territory in 1872. Within a year, he was under investigation for his time as a Kansas state legislator, this time for taking a bribe to vote for Ross's successor in the Senate. A decade later, reports claimed that Legate paid $25,000 to dissuade a Kansas governor from running for president for the Prohibition Party. Eight years after that, Legate was mired in another scandal, this one involving the use of Whiskey Ring money to buy the votes of Kansas legislators to support a lottery.

Sheridan Shook, the New York tax official and right-hand man of Thurlow Weed, was indicted in September 1869 on charges of mishandling public funds. After winning dismissal of the charges, Shook became a prominent theater and brewery owner, remaining active in Republican politics until his death in 1899.

Shortly after President Grant ousted Henry Smythe as collector of customs in New York, an investigation found longstanding frauds in that operation. Smythe argued that the fraudulent practices started before he took office, adding that the Johnson Administration had been too distracted by the impeachment to combat the frauds. Smythe again escaped formal charges. Only low-level employees were prosecuted.

After the impeachment trial, Charles Woolley of Cincinnati worked closely with Democratic leaders, then ran into controversy following the bitter Hayes-Tilden election of 1876. According to charges trumpeted by the *New York Tribune*, Woolley was part of a Democratic program that paid $50,000 in bribes to Florida election officials. Coded telegrams between Woolley in Florida and senior New York Democrats were splashed across front pages with sinister-sounding translations. Woolley, who was then president of the National Trotting Association, was never charged with any crime.

Sam Ward gave up lobbying by the middle of the 1870s and returned to the financial world of New York, where he handled—among others—the accounts of William Evarts. Unable to meet margin calls several years later, Ward fled to Europe to escape his creditors. In his remaining years, he befriended Oscar Wilde, published a book of poems, and settled in Italy, where he died.

Only one of the dark men of the impeachment season lost his resilience; indeed, he suffered a form of capital punishment for his inveterate scheming. In November 1890, Willis Gaylord, Senator Pomeroy's brother-in-law and business agent, landed in a Philadelphia jail, charged with swindling an investor in a Southern railroad. Confined for weeks to cell 143 of Moyamensing Prison, Gaylord hanged himself from the bars over the cell window.

Ulysses Grant's victory in the 1868 election was not as overwhelming as Republicans had hoped. Though his margin in the electoral college was wide (214 to 80), he won only 52.7 percent of the popular vote, a 300,000 vote cushion out of almost 6 million votes cast. At forty-six, the president-elect was the youngest man yet to win the office.

Southern participation in the election was spotty. Three states (Texas, Mississippi, and Virginia) were not yet readmitted to the Union and were excluded from the canvass. Florida had no popular election, so its legislature cast that state's electoral votes. Grant lost Georgia and Louisiana, where terrorist attacks by white Democrats kept freedmen from the polls. In St. Landry Parish, Louisiana, Grant received not a single vote even though the Republican candidate for governor had won 2,500 votes there a year earlier. As many as 300 blacks were murdered around New Orleans, and a like number in Caddo Parish, where Grant received one vote out of 2,000 recorded. The Grant voter in that parish was then killed, according to a witness, "for voting the Grant ticket." One hundred sixty-two blacks were killed in riots in Bossier Parish. Of 1,500 eligible blacks in Americus, Georgia, only 137 voted.

Grant's campaign slogan was "Let us have peace," but there was no peace between the outgoing and incoming presidents. Rather than attend Johnson's White House reception on New Year's Day, Grant found business to attend to in Philadelphia. Johnson appointed a new minister to Mexico knowing that Grant detested the man. Grant struck back by helping to scuttle an agreement with Great Britain over shipping losses inflicted by Confederate privateers that had been outfitted in British ports.

With the approach of Inauguration Day, March 4, Johnson began to consider his final thrust against the hated Grant. On the cold, rainy morning of Grant's inauguration, Johnson's Cabinet assembled at the White House. They expected to travel together to the Capitol for the ceremony. Johnson sat at his desk, reviewing and signing legislation recently passed by Congress. Attorney General Evarts, anxious to move on to the Capitol, kept his overcoat on. Secretary of State Seward smoked a cigar. Johnson kept working. Grant arrived downstairs in his carriage, but Johnson did not stir. Grant's carriage left. At a few minutes past noon, Johnson shook hands with each Cabinet member and joined his family in his own carriage. He was the last president, and the only one not named Adams, to boycott the inauguration of his successor.

The ex-president took his lacerated feelings back home to Greeneville, Tennessee, but he had no thought of a quiet retirement. His ambition, now yoked to a powerful craving for vindication, drove him straight back into politics. When Senator Joseph Fowler announced he would not seek reelection, Johnson immediately began to angle for the post. The contest would not be easy. The ex-president had done something to anger every part of the Tennessee electorate. Democrats remembered that he stood with the Union while his state seceded, then ran on a ticket with Lincoln. Republicans resented his lax Reconstruction policies. Then there was the stigma of escaping removal from office by a single vote. Just as Johnson began his push for the Senate seat, his son Robert committed suicide. The ex-president did not relent.

In October 1869, the Tennessee legislature met to choose the state's next senator. Johnson stood first after the initial ballot. Edmund Cooper, now a member of the State Senate, led Johnson's forces. After more ballots, the ex-president crept to within two votes of the majority needed for victory. Cooper told Johnson he had the two votes, but they would cost $1,000 apiece. Johnson supposedly refused to approve the payment. Johnson's rivals then combined to support none other than Cooper's brother, Henry, who won the seat. It was Johnson's first electoral loss since 1837. He never forgave either of the Coopers.

In view of Cooper's central role in the bribery schemes during the impeachment trial, his resort to bribery in the Tennessee Senate contest seems unremarkable. The twist in the story is Johnson's supposed repudiation of Cooper's bribery. Was the Senate seat not worth the price? Had he grown weary of purchasing votes and making shady deals?

Johnson's return to Greeneville was not a happy one. Once resettled, he described himself as "so solitary as though I were in the wilds of Africa." He wrote in December 1871, "I long to be set free from this place forever." He ran for Congress in 1872, losing again. In 1875, he tried again for a Senate seat. This time, at the age of sixty-seven, he won.

Johnson managed only one major speech in his return to the Senate. On March 20, 1875, he took the floor to accuse Grant of imposing military despotism in Arkansas and Louisiana. Johnson also accused Grant of seeking a third term in office, predicting that if there were a third term, "farewell to the liberties of the country." Johnson quoted from his much-loved Addison's *Cato*, imploring Grant to discharge his military legions from the South and restore the Constitution in that region. The new senator expressed both disdain for the new constitutional amendments and undiminished fealty to the cause of states' rights. During a long congressional recess, Johnson suffered a stroke at his daughter's farm in Elizabethton, Tennessee. A second stroke carried him away two days later, on July 30, 1875. Three of his surviving children were with him.

Five thousand thronged the funeral in Greeneville, though his widow could not attend. Former Senator Fowler, whose vote helped save Johnson's term in office, delivered a eulogy. Johnson's body was wrapped in an American flag with thirty-seven stars. His head rested on his well-worn copy of the Constitution.

The Grant presidency, though it lasted for eight years, was inglorious. The former general seemed smaller in civilian office, sometimes inattentive. In sharp contrast to Johnson, Grant delegated much responsibility. A secretary who worked for both men found that Grant could dispatch work in one day that would take Johnson many days.

Grant's administration was rocked by scandals that reached his war secretary and his chief of staff. Grant retained modest qualities that are admirable in a human being but did not serve him well as the nation's leader. When urged that a St. Louis butcher was not qualified for an appointment, the president explained that when times had been hard for the Grant family, that man sold him meat on credit and loaned him money. "I intend to appoint this German butcher," Grant finished, "if it bursts the Republican party."

Under Grant, the federal government made efforts to protect the freedmen. The Justice Department effectively suppressed the Ku Klux Klan, securing criminal convictions of some 600 Klansmen. Though few went to prison, the campaign succeeded. For a time, antiblack violence flickered out in the South. Congress adopted more civil rights legislation in the early 1870s. The Fifteenth Amendment, ratified in 1870, guaranteed the right to vote to all Americans, though it was incompletely honored for the next nine decades.

By the time Grant left office in early 1877, Southern violence against blacks had revived. The tangled politics of Reconstruction snarled the presidential election of 1876. Democrat Samuel Tilden won a narrow victory in the popular vote, and had an 18-vote margin in the electoral college before votes arrived from the last three states—Florida, Louisiana, and South Carolina. Each of those states, however, returned two competing vote totals with opposite outcomes, each certified by a different, apparently official body. Many political agents (including Cincinnati lawyer Charles Woolley) spread cash around the three state capitols to acquire the results they wanted. When the election dispute landed in Congress, and then before a special commission, Republicans lined up Southern Democratic support for their candidate, Rutherford Hayes, by promising to withdraw federal troops from the South. That was the end of Reconstruction and the beginning of the Solid South. For the next four generations, few blacks in the South voted, most whites voted Democratic, and the principal success strategy for blacks was to leave. Andrew Johnson's vision for his region was realized.

26

---·◆·---

THE RORSCHACH BLOT

Surely God is on our side, for we have done what we could to
ruin ourselves, and yet we have failed to do it.

EDWIN STANTON

ANDREW JOHNSON'S IMPEACHMENT, like the entire Reconstruction era,
is one of the Rorschach blots of American history. Scavenging
through this political and legal train wreck, historians and writers have
drawn very different lessons, vividly illustrating the transitory nature of
historical judgments.

Beginning in the early years of the twentieth century, Andrew Johnson was celebrated as a healer of the sectional divisions of the war, while
the impeachers were depicted as hate-filled gorgons who wished only to
oppress noble Southern whites. Many writers insisted that Johnson
saved the nation from congressional Radicals who lusted to destroy the
presidency and Southern culture. Books by two future presidents, Woodrow Wilson and John F. Kennedy, presented both contentions. Wilson
portrayed Reconstruction as "the veritable overthrow of civilization in
the South," which placed the "white South" under the heel of the "black
South." Kennedy endorsed the view that Edmund Ross's vote was "the
most heroic act in American history." A chief justice of the Supreme
Court, William Rehnquist, proclaimed that the importance of the case

315

"can hardly be overstated" because Johnson's acquittal preserved "our tripartite federal system of government."

Popular culture followed this line. No early film was more powerful than D. W. Griffith's silent epic *The Birth of a Nation*, released in 1915, which glorified the Ku Klux Klan for staving off the horrors of black rule in the South. The abolitionist villain of the film, who endorses election fraud to empower blacks, was blatantly modeled on Thaddeus Stevens. Twenty-five years later, Hollywood reprised the theme in *Tennessee Johnson*. Strong-jawed Van Heflin portrayed Johnson contending against nasty old Thad Stevens, played this time by Lionel Barrymore (the actor who epitomized aging evil as Mr. Potter in *It's a Wonderful Life*).

By mid-century, the emergence of the civil rights movement began to change perspectives on Reconstruction. Johnson's solicitude for white Southerners seemed less admirable. His abandonment of the freedmen seemed misbegotten. His stubborn belief in the states' rights values of the pre–Civil War Constitution began to look like a bullheaded failure to notice how the war had revolutionized the nation. Johnson's defense lawyer, Benjamin Curtis, captured many of these elements in a short description: "He is a man of few ideas, but they are right and true, and he could suffer death sooner than yield up or violate one of them. He is honest, right-minded, and narrow-minded; he has no tact, and even lacks discretion and forecast. But he is as firm as a rock."

The impeachment trial of 1868 seethes with contradictions that have fostered equally contradictory views. As one congressman wrote later, Johnson "was impeached for one series of misdemeanors, and tried for another series." For many impeachers, Johnson had to be removed because he so effectively confounded congressional Reconstruction. Wielding his veto pen, his patronage powers, his ability to pardon ex-rebels, and his attorney general's willingness to misconstrue legislation, the president fought tenaciously against Congress's attempt, as he saw it, to Africanize the South. Johnson was uninterested in negotiation or compromise; his goal was obstruction. Even that was not enough to get him impeached. The first two impeachment attempts failed because they were overtly political, without any superficial gloss that Johnson had violated a criminal law. Despite a three-fourths Republican majority, the House of Representatives would not impeach the president unless it could accuse him of something that felt like a crime.

Stupidly, Johnson remedied that shortcoming when he sent Lorenzo Thomas to replace Stanton as war secretary. By flagrantly violating the Tenure of Office Act, he handed Stevens and the Radicals exactly the weapon they longed for. The president had incontestably committed a crime, or at least a high misdemeanor. Within days, the House adopted its impeachment resolution.

From that high-water mark, the impeachment effort bogged down in the legal arcana of the Tenure of Office Act and of impeachment itself. The schizophrenic nature of impeachment—a political process for removing a leader through judicial-like processes—vexed the effort, from the drafting of the impeachment articles, to the presentation of evidence, to the closing arguments. Ultimately, Stevens's unswerving view that impeachment was a political process was vindicated in part: the best chance to remove Johnson was under Article XI, which largely charged him with being an unfortunate president, not under those articles accusing him solely of violating a statute.

In the final days before the Senate vote, the political character of impeachment, which the House had rejected when it refused to adopt impeachment articles only months earlier, became undeniable. Johnson advocates and opponents lobbied fiercely. Political deals were struck, notably the personal assurances Johnson gave to Senator Grimes and the appointment of General Schofield as war secretary. Another battle—one fueled by greed, patronage promises, and cold cash—raged in murky corners where Butler and his spy network struggled against Edmund Cooper, the corrupt Kansans, and the Astor House group. One last political reality helped determine the outcome of the trial: the prospect of Ben Wade as president. "Andrew Johnson is innocent," one newspaper wrote after the acquittal, "because Benjamin Wade is guilty of being his successor."

Some of the Republicans who supported impeachment, including Ulysses Grant, later expressed remorse over the episode. After all, the republic made it through the last nine months of Johnson's presidency without any terrifying crises. The overheated rhetoric about the Great Criminal seemed hard to justify after Johnson had shrunk back to human scale, or less. The passion for impeachment began to seem unreal, a fever of the moment that would have cured itself. Johnson's defense— that conviction would damage the constitutional structure by weakening the presidency—seemed more powerful.

The regrets of hindsight, though, blinked at the exigencies of that moment in 1868 when the legacy of the Civil War seemed to hang in the balance. "An overwhelming majority of the loyal Union men North and South," recalled Carl Schurz, "saw in President Johnson a traitor bent upon turning over the National Government to the rebels again, and ardently wished to see him utterly stripped of power." When Johnson refused to negotiate over legislation with the vetoproof Republican majorities in Congress, his influence shriveled. When he used his executive powers to frustrate congressional policy, Congress adopted the Tenure of Office Act and the requirement that only General Grant could issue orders to the military. By systematically eliminating or restricting executive powers, those laws posed a far greater threat to the constitutional structure than impeachment did. Indeed, by February 1868, impeachment was the remaining tool for expressing Congress's titanic frustration with Johnson. At a time when many feared that blood would run in the streets, impeachment was an essential safety valve, providing—as Ben Franklin, eighty years before, had hoped it would—an alternative to political violence. The legalistic process of impeachment slowed events down, allowing cooler reflection and the consideration of consequences.

Much of the still-accepted wisdom about the Johnson impeachment is wrong. Johnson is sometimes portrayed as the true successor to Abraham Lincoln, reaching out the hand of fellowship to vanquished Southerners. After all, this argument goes, his initial plan for Southern state governments in 1865 had been developed for Lincoln before the assassination. Lincoln's closest adviser, Secretary of State Seward, performed the same role for Johnson and steadfastly insisted that the Tennessean acted as Lincoln would have. Embracing this theory, John Kennedy agreed that Johnson was "determined to carry out Abraham Lincoln's policies of reconciliation with the defeated South."

This theory, however, unrealistically assumes that Lincoln was incapable of changing his course to respond to events. Lincoln was far too good a politician to alienate Congress, as Johnson did. Lincoln was far too strong a leader to accept meekly the black codes and gruesome violence of the restored Southern states, as Johnson did. And Lincoln was far too compassionate a man to ignore the suffering and oppression of the freedmen and Southern Republicans, as Johnson did. That Seward embraced Johnson as Lincoln's successor reveals more about the secretary of state than it does about Johnson's stewardship of Lincoln's legacy. Seward shared with Johnson a lack of concern either for Negro rights or white Southern terrorism. At the end of his long career, having survived a brutal assassination attempt and the deaths of his wife and daughter, Seward desired peace and union far more than he cared about justice. But Johnson, to whom he pledged his all, could bring neither peace nor union.

After the war, the entire nation—North and South—had to unlearn the habits of rage and hate. Lincoln understood that and had begun to bend every energy to that goal. Johnson, in contrast, fed the fires of rage and hate. It was simply his rigid, combative nature. Far from being Lincoln's political heir, Johnson squandered Lincoln's legacy. At a most delicate moment in our history, when greatness of spirit was needed, the man from Tennessee could not be more than the forceful, intelligent, and intransigent politician he had always been. The times demanded more. Johnson's rise from abject poverty to the White House is an inspiring story, but his presidency was so calamitous that it can only be seen as a tragedy.

Many Republicans joined to resist Johnson's benighted policies after the war, but their undeniable leader was Thaddeus Stevens. A complex, sometimes ruthless man, Stevens sought to expand freedom and equality with sound strategic instincts and a single-minded focus that intimidated his contemporaries and those who have come after. His legacy includes the Fourteenth Amendment, which transformed the nation long after his death. The Reconstruction legislation championed by Stevens worked imperfectly, to be sure, but it honorably aimed to provide physical security and basic rights to the freedmen so they could become full participants in American society. Had he been granted six more months of health, Stevens likely would have won a Senate conviction and driven Johnson from the White House. It is long past time to reclaim Thaddeus Stevens as a great American figure.

Conversely, the myth should be abandoned that there was much of heroism in the acquittal votes of Edmund Ross and John Henderson. The national pantheon should be closed to those who trade votes for cash and patronage favors. As for the denials of misconduct offered by Ross and Henderson after the trial, Henderson's own observation as a prosecutor is irresistible: anyone capable of committing the crime is capable of denying it.

The notion has been widespread that the votes of the seven defectors "saved" either the presidency or the Constitution, or both. For John Kennedy, Ross's vote "may well have preserved for ourselves and posterity constitutional government in the United States." He quotes with approval the self-justifying claims of Senator Ross himself, who insisted twenty-five years after the trial that "the independence of the executive office as a coordinate branch of the government was on trial." The presidency, according to Ross and Kennedy, was at risk of being "ever after subordinated to the legislative will." This, too, is wrong.

Johnson's acquittal did not revive a weak and passive presidency. Indeed, exactly the opposite happened. Johnson's presidency was stronger than the office would be again until the 1890s. Lincoln exercised unprecedented powers during the Civil War. He called on the states to provide hundreds of thousands of soldiers and proclaimed a blockade of the South. His Emancipation Proclamation freed the slaves in the seceded states. He suspended the writ of habeas corpus in states that did not secede and hired an army of bureaucrats to collect the taxes needed to support a great military. No longer at war, Andrew Johnson's administration still collected the income tax and maintained an occupying army in ten Southern states. Johnson used every shred of executive power to battle Congress toe-to-toe for three years, pressing his own vision of reviving Southern state governments and Southern society with minimal federal intrusion. Indeed, he fought Congress so well that he brought on his own impeachment. For the next two decades, executive initiative would recede as Congress asserted itself as the dominant power in the national government.

The related claim has been made that Johnson's acquittal avoided a devastating precedent that would have sapped the power of future presidents, leaving them dangling at the end of strings manipulated by a malign Congress. In this vein, one historian has denounced the impeachment as "the most insidious assault on constitutional government in the nation's history," which threatened to alter the constitutional scheme forever. Again, the dramatic assertion is wrong.

What if Johnson had been convicted and removed from office? Would Ben Wade, in ten months as president, have changed the course of American history? That seems unlikely in the extreme. Would Ulysses Grant still have been elected president? Most likely, yes, though some Republicans feared a popular backlash against their party if they succeeded in deposing President Johnson. Would future Congresses have hastened to impeach and remove future presidents with wild abandon? That is difficult to imagine.

In most presidencies, impeachment has been irrelevant. After all, it requires a two-thirds vote of the Senate to convict a president. Most later presidents either enjoyed sufficient support in Congress, or managed not to enrage huge numbers of congressmen and senators, so impeachment never became part of the national conversation. More than all of his predecessors and successors as chief executive, Andrew Johnson was uniquely well suited to become a target for impeachment: the opposing party enjoyed a three-fourths majority in both houses of Congress, he disagreed with that majority on an explosive political issue (Reconstruction), and he aggressively pursued a policy of confrontation and obstruction over that issue, repeatedly vetoing congressional legislation. The wonder is not that he was impeached, but that Congress took so long to do it and then failed to convict him.

Moreover, Johnson's acquittal did not mark the death of impeachment as a constitutional tool. The House impeached several federal judges between Johnson's acquittal and 1935; some resigned and the Senate convicted two of them after trial. Richard Nixon resigned in 1974 rather than face near-certain impeachment and removal. The Johnson verdict did not prevent House Republicans from throwing the moralistic temper tantrum that led to the 1999 impeachment of Bill Clinton for actions totally unrelated to his official duties (though Clinton was acquitted by the Senate). Impeachment is an institutional safety valve, like the emergency lever in a train, to be used only in times of great exigency. Following the Johnson case, the safety valve continued to be available and continued to be used, rarely.

Based on the Johnson, Nixon, and Clinton cases, certain conditions seem to be necessary, if not sufficient, for presidential impeachment to be possible: Congress must be controlled by the opposing party, and the impeachers must be able to point to a legal violation by the president that can be portrayed as a crime. One further lesson from the Johnson and Clinton examples is that a president who has acted most unwisely can still avoid removal from office as long as he retains the support of his own party.

That presidential impeachment has been rare can hardly be attributed to Johnson's acquittal. It arose once, briefly, before the Johnson case; it has been an infrequent concern since. The triumphant generalizations offered by many historians and commentators about the Johnson impeachment have been so ill founded because the case unfolded in unique circumstances. Never again would the nation face a prolonged political struggle over how to reunite with a breakaway region that had started a civil war; never again would the party opposing the president enjoy such lopsided majorities in Congress; never again would assassination elevate to the White House someone who truly belonged to the other political party. The remarkable achievement was that impeachment produced a peaceful resolution of the angry contest, not that it saved the presidency from being subjugated to Congress.

When it came to restoring the constitutional balance of the government, Johnson's acquittal was far less important than Congress's repeal of much of the Tenure of Office Act, which began shortly after Johnson left the White House. In response to President Grant's demands, Congress promptly gave him control over firing Cabinet officers, and additional authority over the removal of lower officials. That controversial statute had, indeed, frozen some of the gears of government by stripping the president of the power to choose those who would implement his policies.

Almost sixty years later, the Supreme Court ruled on whether Senate approval could be required before specific executive officials could be fired—the constitutional issue that Johnson claimed he hoped to bring to the Supreme Court by replacing Edwin Stanton. In *Myers v. United States*, the Court held that the president could fire a postmaster without Senate approval. The Court's opinion was written by the only former president to serve on the Supreme Court. Chief Justice William Howard Taft decried congressional encroachment on executive powers and denied that Congress could reserve for itself the power to approve the firing of Postmaster Myers. Dissenting opinions by liberal Louis D. Brandeis and archconservative James McReynolds shredded Taft's historical arguments. As the dissenters saw it, Congress created executive offices under the Constitution, and established their salaries and duties.

Why could Congress also not prescribe specific terms for those offices, or require Senate concurrence in the removal of the people holding them? The dissenters were not fazed by Taft's insistence that it was unwise for the Senate to play a role in executive removals; wise or foolish, they insisted, the Constitution allowed it. Less than ten years later, the dissenters were partly vindicated after President Franklin Roosevelt dismissed the chairman of the Federal Trade Commission. The Supreme Court ruled that since Congress had created a five-year term for the position, the president could not fire the chairman before the end of his term.

Fourteen decades after Johnson's trial, several features of that constitutional confrontation still resonate. Stevens, Butler, and the other Republicans gave life to the impeachment clause as a response to a national crisis. They showed that it could be used to challenge a president directly. In our era of an increasingly imperial presidency, it is a powerful example: the direct representatives of the people possess the ultimate tool for curbing executive excess. It is an unwieldy tool, but an essential one. By coming so close to a conviction, the impeachers established that there are limits on presidential discretion, that the nation need not wait until the end of a four-year term to jettison a president. They also deserve credit for accepting their defeat peacefully, without any call to arms, respecting the constitutional process.

The positive results of the unsuccessful impeachment should not be overlooked. The accusers—and their supporters—had the cathartic experience of haling Johnson before the Senate, displaying his failings to the nation and the judgment of history. The experience chastened the most powerful person in the nation, who had committed many blunders, whether or not they warranted his removal from office. Unless he had been battered by that constitutional two-by-four, Johnson might well have left the clownish Lorenzo Thomas as interim secretary of war and could have embarked on other spiteful and ill-considered actions. Moreover, though hysterical rhetoric filled the air, the impeachment process itself was legalistic and peaceable, a constitutional outlet for violent political passions.

After three serious attempts to impeach a president, though, we are no closer than Thad Stevens and Benjamin Curtis were to knowing exactly what conduct justifies presidential removal. Indeed, in many ways the phrase "high crimes and misdemeanors" has proved to be its own Rorschach blot, sufficiently imprecise to permit intelligent arguments that it requires a true judicial "crime," or alternatively that it imposes no such requirement. But in the twenty-first century, when presidential powers have grown so vast and intrusive, it is an essential principle that *something* does.

In addition, though Johnson's acquittal was mortifying to Stevens and his fellow impeachers, it stigmatized Johnson forever as the man who escaped removal by the skin of his teeth. That the key acquittal votes were won by political bargaining and patronage payoffs, or by bribes, marks him even more.

Also, though the immediate cause of the impeachment effort was the firing of Stanton, underlying it was the firm conviction held by many Republicans that Johnson was undermining the nation's commitment to protect the freedmen and aid their emergence from slavery. That commitment would linger for only a few more years, then lie dormant for many decades. Yet it bears remembering that there were congressmen and senators in 1868 who almost drove a president from office in part because he would do nothing to stop the mistreatment of the former slaves.

Americans, perhaps all people, expect historical crises to be met by heroes—Washingtons, Franklins, Lincolns, and Roosevelts. A nation learns a great deal more about itself and its system of government when a crisis has to be met by people of lesser talents. In the impeachment crisis of 1868, none of the country's leaders was great, a few were good, all were angry, and far too many were despicable. Still, we survived.

ACKNOWLEDGMENTS

I SHOULD FIRST ACKNOWLEDGE three writers who traveled these serpentine historical trails before I set off and who shed important light on the story I have tried to tell. Coming upon Michael Les Benedict's *The Impeachment and Trial of Andrew Johnson* was a liberating moment. In this and other writings, Professor Benedict persuasively concludes that the Johnson impeachment effort was not the historical atrocity of popular myth. Equivalent liberation came from Mark W. Summers's *The Era of Good Stealings*, in which a serious scholar (arguably *the* serious scholar of American public corruption in the nineteenth century) takes seriously the possibility that bribery influenced the Senate impeachment vote. Finally, I must recognize Hans Trefousse, author of a half-dozen distinguished books about this historical period. On any subject central to this story—Andrew Johnson, Thaddeus Stevens, Ben Butler, Ben Wade, the impeachment trial itself—Professor Trefousse has published an important treatment. He has been courteous and generous in discussing this project with me. It is a gratifying coincidence that he and I are both graduates of George W. Curtis High School on Staten Island, where I took AP English from his late wife, Rachelle Trefousse. I learned much from both of them.

I have benefited from a great deal of help from archivists and reference librarians all around the country. These include most of the staff at the Library of Congress, of whom Thomas Mann is the most conspicuous and most consistently remarkable. Judy Atkins at the National Archives found records of the House impeachment managers that I have not seen cited by any other researchers. Teresa Coble of the Kansas State Historical Society, William A. Jones of the library at California State Univer-

Acknowledgments

sity, Chico, and Mark Patrick of the Detroit Public Library were generous and responsive in my efforts to track down the more obscure rascals of this story. Through Jodi Boyle, I received an early look at the Riggs Bank records at George Washington University. Great on-site support was available at the Huntington Library and Bancroft Library in California, the Wheaton College Library, the New York Public Library, and the New York Historical Society. Donald Ritchie of the Senate Historical Office graciously made available the resources of his office. I am also grateful for assistance from the Tennessee State Library and Archives, the Wisconsin Historical Society, the Massachusetts Historical Society, and Yale University Library. Bob McAvoy, whom I encountered through the genealogical wonders of the Internet, provided welcome leads on the elusive General Alonzo Adams.

Many friends provided insightful critiques of this book while it was in progress, beginning with James McGrath Morris, whose thoughts I sometimes resisted but usually came to embrace. Among those who have reminded me to tell the story clearly are Don Carr, Catherine Flanagan, Solveig Eggerz, Wayland Stallard, Katherine Lorr, Phil Harvey, Susan Clark, Joye Shepherd, Frank Joseph, Leslie Rollins, Robert Gibson, Linda Morefield, Paul Vamvas, Ken Ackerman, and Andrew Dayton. I am grateful to all of them. I also benefitted from Doris Kearns Goodwin's gracious counsel in trying to understand the course charted during the Johnson Administration by William Henry Seward.

This is my second book with Alice Mayhew, which is a stroke of unwarranted fortune for me. Her steady focus on what makes a good book, and her skill in putting those elements together, have been great gifts. The entire Simon & Schuster team—Roger Labrie, Karen Thompson, Dana Sloan, Katie Grinch, Gypsy da Silva, Fred Weimer—is unfailingly professional and talented. My agent, Philippa Brophy, has provided sound advice and guidance. My thanks to all.

My greatest debt, always, is to Nancy, my wife, who has learned to live with the guy pounding on the keyboard in the attic. She read the manuscript, with great discernment, more times than anyone should have to.

APPENDIX 1

THE IMPEACHMENT PROVISIONS IN THE CONSTITUTION

ARTICLE I:

Section 2: The House of Representatives . . . shall have the sole Power of Impeachment.

Section 3: The Senate shall have the sole Power to try all Impeachments. When sitting for that Purpose, they shall be on Oath or Affirmation. When the President of the United States is tried, the Chief Justice shall preside: And no Person shall be convicted without the Concurrence of two thirds of the Members present.

Judgment in Cases of Impeachment shall not extend further than to removal from Office, and disqualification to hold and enjoy any Office of honor, Trust or Profit under the United States: but the Party convicted shall nevertheless be liable and subject to Indictment, Trial, Judgment and Punishment, according to Law.

ARTICLE II:

Section 2: The President shall . . . have Power to Grant Reprieves and Pardons for Offenses against the United States, except in Cases of Impeachment.

• • •

Section 4: The President, Vice President and all civil Officers of the United States, shall be removed from Office on Impeachment for, and Conviction of, Treason, Bribery, or other high Crimes and Misdemeanors.

ARTICLE III:

Section 2: The Trial of all Crimes, except in Cases of Impeachment, shall be by Jury.

APPENDIX 2

THE TENURE OF OFFICE ACT

CHAPTER 154, STATUTES AT LARGE, 39TH CONGRESS, 2D SESSION, MARCH 2, 1867

Section 1. That every person holding any civil office to which he has been appointed by and with the advice and consent of the Senate, and every person who shall hereafter be appointed to any such office, and shall become duly qualified to act therein, is, and shall be entitled to hold such office until a successor shall have been in like manner appointed and duly qualified, except as herein otherwise provided: *Provided*, That the Secretaries of State, of the Treasury, of War, of the Navy, and of the Interior, the Postmaster-General, and the Attorney-General, shall hold their offices respectively for and during the term of the President by whom they may have been appointed and for one month thereafter, subject to removal by and with the advice and consent of the Senate.

Section 2. And be it further enacted, That when any officer appointed as aforesaid, excepting Judges of the United States courts, shall, during a recess of the Senate, be shown, by evidence satisfactory to the President, to be guilty of misconduct in office, or crime, or for any reason shall become incapable or legally disqualified to perform its duties, in such case, and in no other, the President may suspend such officer and designate some suitable person to perform temporarily the duties of such office until the next meeting of the Senate, and until the case shall be acted upon by the Senate, . . . and in such case it shall be the duty of the President, within twenty days after the first day of such next meeting of the Senate, to report to the Senate such suspension, with the evidence and reasons for his action in the case, and the name of the person so designated to perform the duties of such office. And if the Senate shall concur in such suspension and advise and consent to the removal of such officer, they shall so certify to the President, who may thereupon remove such officer. . . . But if the Senate shall refuse to concur in such suspension, such officer so suspended shall forthwith resume the functions of his office. . . .

* * *

Section 9 . . . [E]very person who shall violate any of the provisions of this section shall be deemed guilty of a high misdemeanor, and, upon trial and conviction thereof, shall be punished therefore by a fine not exceeding ten thousand dollars, or by imprisonment not exceeding ten years, or both said punishments, in the discretion of the court.

APPENDIX 3

IMPEACHMENT ARTICLES

ARTICLE I:

That said Andrew Johnson, President of the United States, on the 21st day of February, in the year of our Lord, 1868, at Washington, in the District of Columbia, unmindful of the high duties of his office, of his oath of office, and of the requirement of the Constitution that he should take care that the laws be faithfully executed, did unlawfully and in violation of the Constitution and laws of the United States issue and order in writing for the removal of Edwin M. Stanton from the office of Secretary for the Department of War, said Edwin M. Stanton having been theretofore duly appointed and commissioned, by and with the advice and consent of the Senate of the United States, as such Secretary, and said Andrew Johnson, President of the United States, on the 12th day of August, in the year of our Lord 1867, and during the recess of said Senate, having suspended by his order Edwin M. Stanton from said office, and within twenty days after the first day of the next meeting of said Senate, that is to say, on the 12th day of December, in the year last aforesaid, having reported to said Senate such suspension, with the evidence and reasons for his action in the case and the name of the person designated to perform the duties of such office temporarily until the next meeting of the Senate, and said Senate thereafterward, on the 13th day of January, in the year of our Lord 1868, having duly considered the evidence and reasons reported by said Andrew Johnson for said suspension, and did refuse to concur in said suspension, whereby and by force of the provisions of an act entitled "An act regulating the tenure of certain civil offices," passed March 2, 1867, said Edwin M. Stanton did forthwith resume the functions of his office, whereof the said Andrew Johnson had then and there due notice, and said Edwin Stanton, by reason of the premises, on said 21st day of February, being lawfully entitled to hold said office of Secretary for the Department of War, which said order for the removal of said Edwin M. Stanton is, in substance, as follows, that is to say:

Executive Mansion,
Washington, D.C., *February* 21, 1868
 SIR: By virtue of the power and authority vested in me, as President by the Constitution and laws of the United States, you are hereby removed from the office of Secretary for the Department of War, and your functions as such will terminate upon receipt of their communication. You will transfer to Brevet Major-General L. Thomas, Adjutant-General of the Army, who has this day been authorized and empowered to act as Secretary of War ad interim, all books, papers and other public property now in your custody and charge.
 Respectfully yours, ANDREW JOHNSON.
 Hon. E. M. Stanton, Secretary of War

Which order was unlawfully issued, and with intent then and there to violate the act entitled "An act regulating the tenure of certain civil offices," passed March 2, 1867; and, with the further intent contrary to the provisions of said act, and in violation thereof, and contrary to the provisions of the Constitution of the United States, and without the advice and consent of the Senate of the United States, the said Senate then and there being in session, to remove said Edwin M. Stanton from the office of Secretary for the Department of War, the said Edwin M. Stanton being then and there Secretary for the Department of War, and being then and there in the due and lawful execution of the duties of said office, whereby said Andrew Johnson, President of the United States, did then and there commit, and was guilty of a high misdemeanor in office.

ARTICLE II:

That on the 21st day of February, in the year of our Lord 1868, at Washington, in the District of Columbia, said Andrew Johnson, President of the United States, unmindful of the high duties of his office, of his oath of office, and in violation of the Constitution of the United States, and contrary to the provisions of an act entitled "An act regulating the tenure of certain civil offices," passed March 2, 1867, without the advice and consent of the Senate of the United States, said Senate then and there being in session, and without authority of law, did, with intent to violate the Constitution of the United States and the act aforesaid, issue and deliver to one Lorenzo Thomas a letter of authority, in substance as follows, that is to say:

Executive Mansion,
Washington, D.C., *February* 21, 1868
 SIR: The Hon. Edwin M. Stanton having been this day removed from office as Secretary for the Department of War, you are hereby

authorized and empowered to act as Secretary of War *ad interim*, and will immediately enter upon the discharge of the duties pertaining to that office.

Mr. Stanton has been instructed to transfer to you all the records, books, papers and other public property now in his custody and charge.

Respectfully yours, ANDREW JOHNSON

To Brevet Major-General Lorenzo Thomas, *Adjutant General United States Army, Washington, D.C.*

Then and there being no vacancy in said office of Secretary for the Department of War: whereby said Andrew Johnson, President of the United States, did then and there commit, and was guilty of a high misdemeanor in office.

ARTICLE III:

That said Andrew Johnson, President of the United States, on the 21st day of February, in the year of our Lord 1868, at Washington, in the District of Columbia, did commit, and was guilty of a high misdemeanor in office, in this, that, without authority of law, while the Senate of the United States was then and there in session, he did appoint one Lorenzo Thomas to be Secretary for the Department of War, *ad interim*, without the advice and consent of the Senate, and with intent to violate the Constitution of the United States, no vacancy having happened in said office of Secretary for the Department of War during the recess of the Senate, and no vacancy existing in said office at the time, and which said appointment, so made by Andrew Johnson, of said Lorenzo Thomas is in substance as follows, that is to say:

Executive Mansion,

Washington, D.C., *February* 21, 1868

SIR: The Hon. Edwin M. Stanton having been this day removed from office as Secretary for the Department of War, you are hereby authorized and empowered to act as Secretary of War *ad interim*, and will immediately enter upon the discharge of the duties pertaining to that office.

Mr. Stanton has been instructed to transfer to you all the records, books, papers and other public property now in his custody and charge.

Respectfully yours, ANDREW JOHNSON

To Brevet Major-General Lorenzo Thomas, *Adjutant General United States Army, Washington, D.C.*

ARTICLE IV:

That said Andrew Johnson, President of the United States, unmindful of the high duties of his office, and of his oath of office, in violation of the Constitution and laws of the United States, on the 21st day of February, in the year of our Lord 1868, at Washington, in the District of Columbia, did unlawfully conspire with one Lorenzo Thomas, and with other persons to the House of Representatives unknown, with intent by intimidation and threats unlawfully to hinder and prevent Edwin M. Stanton, then and there, the Secretary for the Department of War, duly appointed under the laws of the United States, from holding said office of Secretary for the Department of War, contrary to and in violation of the Constitution of the United States, and of the provisions of an act entitled "An act to define and punish certain conspiracies," approved July 31, 1861, whereby said Andrew Johnson, President of the United States, did then and there commit and was guilty of a high crime in office.

ARTICLE V:

That said Andrew Johnson, President of the United States, unmindful of the high duties of his office and of his oath of office, on the 21st of February, in the year of our Lord 1868, and on divers other days and times in said year before the 2d day of March, A.D. 1868, at Washington, in the District of Columbia, did unlawfully conspire with one Lorenzo Thomas, and with other persons to the House of Representatives unknown, to prevent and hinder the execution of an act entitled "An act regulating the tenure of certain civil office[s]," passed March 2, 1867, and in pursuance of said conspiracy, did unlawfully attempt to prevent Edwin M. Stanton, then and there being Secretary for the Department of War, duly appointed and commissioned under the laws of the United States, from holding said office, whereby the said Andrew Johnson, President of the United States, did then and there commit and was guilty of a high misdemeanor in office.

ARTICLE VI:

That said Andrew Johnson, President of the United States, unmindful of the high duties of his office and of his oath of office, on the 21st day of February, in the year of our Lord 1868, at Washington, in the District of Columbia, did unlawfully conspire with one Lorenzo Thomas, by force to seize, take, and possess the property of the United States in the Department of War, and then and there in the custody and charge of Edwin M. Stanton, Secretary for said Department, contrary to the provisions of an act entitled "An act to define and punish certain conspiracies," approved July 31, 1861, and with intent to violate and disregard an act entitled "An act regulating the tenure of certain civil offices," passed March 2, 1867, whereby said Andrew Johnson, President of the United States, did then and there commit a high crime in office.

ARTICLE VII:

That said Andrew Johnson, President of the United States, unmindful of the high duties of his office, and of his oath of office, on the 21st day of February, in the year of our Lord 1868, at Washington, in the District of Columbia, did unlawfully conspire with one Lorenzo Thomas with intent unlawfully to seize, take, and possess the property of the United States in the Department of War, in the custody and charge of Edwin M. Stanton, Secretary of said Department, with intent to violate and disregard the act entitled "An act regulating the tenure of certain civil offices," passed March 2, 1867, whereby said Andrew Johnson, President of the United States, did then and there commit a high misdemeanor in office.

ARTICLE VIII:

That said Andrew Johnson, President of the United States, unmindful of the high duties of his office and of his oath of office, with intent unlawfully to control the disbursements of the moneys appropriated for the military service and for the Department of War, on the 21st day of February, in the year of our Lord 1868, at Washington, in the District of Columbia, did unlawfully and contrary to the provisions of an act entitled "An act regulating the tenure of certain civil offices," passed March 2, 1867, and in violation of the Constitution of the United States, and without the advice and consent of the Senate of the United States, and while the Senate was then and there in session, there being no vacancy in the office of Secretary for the Department of War, with intent to violate and disregard the act aforesaid, then and there issue and deliver to one Lorenzo Thomas a letter of authority in writing, in substance as follows, that is to say:

> Execution Mansion,
> Washington, D.C., *February* 21, 1868
> SIR: The Hon. Edwin M. Stanton having been this day removed from office as Secretary for the Department of War, you are hereby authorized and empowered to act as Secretary of War *ad interim*, and will immediately enter upon the discharge of the duties pertaining to that office.
> Mr. Stanton has been instructed to transfer to you all the records,

books, papers and other public property now in his custody and charge.

Respectfully yours, ANDREW JOHNSON

To Brevet Major-General Lorenzo Thomas, *Adjutant General United States Army, Washington, D.C.*

Whereby said Andrew Johnson, President of the United States, did then and there commit and was guilty of a high misdemeanor in office.

ARTICLE IX:

That said Andrew Johnson, President of the United States, on the 22nd day of February, in the year of our Lord 1868, at Washington, in the District of Columbia, in disregard of the Constitution and the laws of the United States, duly enacted, as Commander-in-Chief of the Army of the United States, did bring before himself, then and there William H. Emory, a Major-General by brevet in the Army of the United States, actually in command of the department of Washington, and the military forces thereof, and did then and there, as such Commander-in-Chief, declare to, and instruct said Emory, that part of a law of the United States, passed March 2, 1867, entitled "An act for making appropriations for the support of the army for the year ending June 30, 1868, and for other purposes," especially the second section thereof, which provides, among other things, that "all orders and instructions relating to military operations issued by the President or Secretary of War, shall be issued through the General of the Army, and, in case of his inability, through the next in rank," was unconstitutional, and in contravention of the commission of said Emory, and which said provision of law had been theretofore duly and legally promulgated by general order for the government and direction of the Army of the United States, as the said Andrew Johnson then and there well knew, with intent thereby to induce said Emory, in his official capacity as Commander of the department of Washington, to violate the provisions of said act, and to take and receive, act upon and obey such orders as he, the said Andrew Johnson, might make and give, and which should not be issued through the General of the Army of the United States, according to the provisions of said act, and with the further intent thereby to enable him, the said Andrew Johnson, to prevent the execution of an act entitled "An act regulating the tenure of certain civil offices," passed March 2, 1867, and to unlawfully prevent Edwin M. Stanton, then being Secretary for the Department of War, from holding said office and discharging the duties thereof, whereby said Andrew Johnson, President of the United States, did then and there commit, and was guilty of a high misdemeanor in office.

ARTICLE X:

That said Andrew Johnson, President of the United States, unmindful of the high duties of his office and the dignity and proprieties thereof, and of the harmony and courtesies which ought to exist and be maintained between the executive and legislative branches of the Government of the United States, designing and intending to set aside the rightful authorities and powers of Congress, did attempt to bring into disgrace, ridicule, hatred, contempt and reproach the Congress of the United States, and the several branches thereof, to impair and destroy the regard and respect of all the good people of the United States for the Congress and legislative power thereof, (which all officers of the government ought inviolably to preserve and maintain,) and to excite the odium and resentment of all good people of the United States against Congress and the laws by it duly and constitutionally enacted; and in pursuance of his said design and intent, openly and publicly and before divers assemblages of citizens of the United States, convened in divers parts thereof, to meet and receive said Andrew Johnson as the Chief Magistrate of the United States, did, on the 18th day of August, in the year of our Lord 1866, and on divers other days and times, as well before as afterward, make and declare, with a loud voice certain intemperate, inflammatory, and scandalous harangues, and therein utter loud threats and bitter menaces, as well against Congress as the laws of the United States duly enacted thereby, amid the cries, jeers and laughter of the multitudes then assembled and in hearing, which are set forth in the several specifications hereinafter written, in substance and effect, that is to say:

Specification First. In this, that at Washington, in the District of Columbia, in the Executive Mansion, to a committee of citizens who called upon the President of the United States, speaking of and concerning the Congress of the United States, heretofore, to wit: On the 18th day of August, in the year of our Lord, 1866, in a loud voice, declare in substance and effect, among other things, that is to say:

"So far as the Executive Department of the government is concerned, the effort has been made to restore the Union, to heal the breach, to pour oil into the wounds which were consequent upon the struggle, and, to speak in a common phrase, to prepare, as the learned and wise physician would, a plaster healing in character and co-extensive with the wound. We thought and we think that we had partially succeeded, but as the work progressed, as reconstruction seemed to be taking place, and the country was becoming reunited, we found a disturbing and marring element opposing us. In alluding to that element, I shall go no further than your Convention, and the distinguished gentleman who has delivered the report of the proceedings. I shall make no reference that I do not believe the time and the occasion justify.

"We have witnessed in one department of the government every endeavor to prevent the restoration of peace, harmony and union. We have seen hanging upon the verge of the government, as it were, a body called or which assumes to be the Congress of the United States, while in fact it is a Congress of only a part of the States. We have seen this Congress pretend to be for the Union, when its every step and act tended to perpetuate disunion and make a disruption of the States inevitable.

"We have seen Congress gradually encroach, step by step, upon constitutional rights, and violate day after day, and month after month, fundamental principles of the government. We have seen a Congress that seemed to forget that there was a limit to the sphere and scope of legislation. We have seen a Congress in a minority assume to exercise power which, if allowed to be consummated, would result in despotism or monarchy itself."

Specification Second. In this, that at Cleveland, in the State of Ohio, heretofore to wit: On the third day of September, in the year of our Lord 1866, before a public assemblage of citizens and others, said Andrew Johnson, President of the United States, speaking of and concerning the Congress of the United States, did, in a loud voice, declare in substance and effect, among other things, that is to say:

"I will tell you what I did do? I called upon your Congress that is trying to break up the Government."

*   *   *

"In conclusion, beside that, Congress had taken much pains to poison their constituents against him. But what has Congress done? Have they done anything to restore the union of the States? No: On the contrary, they had done everything to prevent it: and because he stood now where he did when the rebellion commenced, he had been denounced as a traitor. Who had run greater risks or made greater sacrifices than himself? But Congress, factious and domineering, had undertaken to poison the minds of the American people."

Specification Third. In this case, that at St. Louis, in the State of Missouri, heretofore to wit: On the 8th day of September, in the year of our Lord 1866, before a public assemblage of citizens and others, said Andrew Johnson, President of the United States, speaking of acts concerning the Congress of the United States, did, in a loud voice, declare in substance and effect, among other things, that is to say:

"Go on. Perhaps if you had a word or two on the subject of New Orleans you might understand more about it than you do, and if you will go back and ascertain the cause of the riot at New Orleans, perhaps you will not be so prompt in calling out "New Orleans." If you will take up the riot of New Orleans and trace it back to its source and its immediate cause, you will find out who was responsible for the blood that was shed there. If you will take up the riot at New Orleans and trace it back to the Radical Congress, you will find that the riot at New Orleans was substantially planned. If you will take up the proceedings in their caucuses you will understand that they knew that a convention was to be called which was extinct by its powers having expired; that it was said that the intention was that a new government was to be organized, and on the organization of that government the intention was to enfranchise one portion of the population, called the colored population, who had been emancipated, and at the same time disfranchise white men. When you design to talk about New Orleans you ought to understand what you are talking about. When you read the speeches that were made, and take up the facts on the Friday and Saturday before that convention sat, you will find that speeches were made incendiary in their character, exciting that portion of the population, the black population, to arm themselves and prepare for the shedding of blood. You will also find that convention did assemble in violation of law, and the intention of that convention was to supersede the organized authorities in the State of Louisiana, which had been organized by the government of the United States, and every man engaged in that rebellion, in the convention, with the intention of superseding and upturning the civil government which had been recognized by the Government of the United States, I say that he was a traitor to the Constitution of the United States, and hence you find that another rebellion was commenced, having its origin in the Radical Congress."

* * *

"So much for the New Orleans riot. And there was the cause and the origin of the blood that was shed, and every drop of blood that was shed is upon their skirts and they are responsible for it. I could test this thing a little closer, but will not do it here to-night. But when you talk about the causes and consequences that resulted from proceedings of that kind, perhaps, as I have been introduced here and you have provoked questions of this kind, though it does not provoke me, I will tell you a few wholesome things that have been done by this Radical Congress in connection with New Orleans and the extension of the elective franchise.

"I know that I have been traduced and abused. I know it has come in advance of me here, as elsewhere, that I have attempted to exercise an arbitrary power in resisting laws that were intended to be forced upon the government; that I had exercised that power; that I had abandoned the party that elected me, and that I was a traitor, because I exercised the veto power in attempting, and did arrest for a time, that which was called a "Freedmen's Bureau" bill. Yes, that I was a traitor. And I have been traduced; I have been slandered; I have been maligned; I have been called Judas Iscariot, and all that. Now, my countrymen, here to-night, it is very easy to indulge in epithets; it is easy to call a man a Judas, and cry out traitor, but when he is called upon to give arguments and facts he is very often found wanting. Judas Iscariot? Judas! There was a Judas, and he was one of the twelve Apostles. O, yes, the twelve Apostles had a Christ, and he never could have had a Judas unless he had twelve Apostles. If I have played the Judas who has been my Christ that I have played the Judas with? Was it Thad. Stevens? Was it Wendell Phillips? Was it Charles Sumner? They are the men that stop and compare themselves with the Savior, and everybody that differs with them in opinion, and tries to stay and arrest their diabolical and nefarious policy is to be denounced as a Judas."

* * *

"Well, let me say to you, if you will stand by me in this action, if you will stand by me in trying to give the people a fair chance—soldiers and citizens—to participate in these offices, God be willing, I will kick them out. I will kick them out just as fast as I can.

"Let me say to you, in concluding, that what I have said is what I intended to say; I was not provoked into this, and care not for their menaces, the taunts and the jeers. I care not for threats, I do not intend to be bullied by enemies, nor overawed by my friends. But, God willing, with your help, I will veto their measures whenever any of them come to me."

Which said utterances, declarations, threats and harangues, highly censurable in any, are peculiarly indecent and unbecoming in the Chief Magistrate of the United States, by means whereof the said Andrew Johnson has brought the high office of the President of the United States into contempt, ridicule and disgrace, to the great scandal of all good citizens, whereby said Andrew Johnson, President of the United States, did commit, and was then and there guilty of a high misdemeanor in office.

ARTICLE XI:

That the said Andrew Johnson, President of the United States, unmindful of the high duties of his office and of his oath of office, and in disregard of the Constitution and laws of the United States, did, heretofore, to wit: On the 18th day of August, 1866, at the city of Washington, and in the District of Columbia, by public speech, declare and affirm in substance, that the Thirty-Ninth Congress of the United States was not a Congress of the United States authorized by the Constitution to exercise legislative power under the same; but, on the contrary, was a Congress of only part of the States, thereby denying and intending to deny, that the legislation of said Congress was valid or obligatory upon him, the said Andrew Johnson, except in so far as he saw fit to approve the same, and also thereby denying the power of the said Thirty-Ninth Congress to propose amendments to the Constitution of the United States. And in pursuance of said declaration, the said Andrew Johnson, President of the United States, afterwards, to wit: On the 21st day of February, 1868, at the city of Washington, D.C., did, unlawfully and in disregard of the requirements of the Constitution that he should take care that the laws be faithfully executed, attempt to prevent the execution of an act entitled "An act regulating the tenure of certain civil offices," passed March 2, 1867, by unlawfully devising and contriving and attempting to devise and contrive means by which he should prevent Edwin M. Stanton from forthwith resuming the functions of the office of Secretary for the Department of War, notwithstanding the refusal of the Senate to concur in the suspension therefore made by the said Andrew Johnson of said Edwin M. Stanton from said office of Secretary for the Department of War; and also by further unlawfully devising and contriving, and attempting to devise and contrive, means then and there to prevent the execution of an act entitled "An act making appropriations for the support of the army for the fiscal year ending June 30, 1868, and for other purposes," approved March 2, 1867. And also to prevent the execution of an act entitled "An act to provide for the more efficient government of the rebel States," passed March 2, 1867. Whereby the said Andrew Johnson, President of the United States, did then, to wit: on the 21st day of February, 1868, at the city of Washington, commit and was guilty of a high misdemeanor in office.

APPENDIX 4

THE SENATE VOTES

YEAS (VOTING TO CONVICT)—35:

Henry Anthony (R-Rhode Island), Simon Cameron (R-Pennsylvania), Alexander Cattell (R-New Jersey), Zachariah Chandler (R-Michigan), Cornelius Cole (R-California), Roscoe Conkling (R-New York), John Conness (R-California), Henry Corbett (R-Oregon), Aaron Cragin (R-New Hampshire), Charles Drake (R-Missouri), George Edmunds (R-Vermont), Orris Ferry (R-Connecticut), Frederick Frelinghuysen (R-New Jersey), James Harlan (R-Iowa), Jacob Howard (R-Michigan), Timothy Howe (R-Wisconsin), Edwin Morgan (R-New York), Justin Morrill (R-Vermont), Lot Morrill (R-Maine), Oliver Morton (R-Indiana), James Nye (R-Nevada), James Patterson (R-New Hampshire), Samuel Pomeroy (R-Kansas), Alexander Ramsey (R-Minnesota), John Sherman (R-Ohio), William Sprague (R-Rhode Island), William Stewart (R-Nevada), Charles Sumner (R-Massachusetts), John Thayer (R-Nebraska), Thomas Tipton (R-Nebraska), Benjamin Wade (R-Ohio), Waitman Willey (R-West Virginia), George Williams (R-Oregon), Henry Wilson (R-Massachusetts), Richard Yates (R-Illinois).

NAYS (VOTING TO ACQUIT)—19:

James Bayard (D-Delaware), Charles Buckalew (D-Pennsylvania), Garrett Davis (D-Kentucky), James Dixon (R-Connecticut), James Doolittle (R-Wisconsin), William Fessenden (R-Maine), Joseph Fowler (R-Tennessee), James Grimes (R-Iowa), John Henderson (R-Missouri), Thomas Hendricks (D-Indiana), Reverdy Johnson (D-Maryland), Thomas McCreery (D-Kentucky), Daniel Norton (R-Minnesota), David Patterson (D-Tennessee), Edmund Ross (R-Kansas), Willard Saulsbury (D-Delaware), Lyman Trumbull (R-Illinois), Peter Van Winkle (R-West Virginia), George Vickers (D-Maryland).

NOTES

Citations in the notes to published collections of original papers are as follows:

Grant Papers: John Y. Simon, ed., *The Papers of Ulysses S. Grant*, Carbondale: University of Southern Illinois Press (1967–2005).

Johnson Papers: LeRoy P. Graf and Ralph W. Haskins, eds., *The Papers of Andrew Johnson*, Knoxville: University of Tennessee Press (1967–2000).

Stevens Papers: Beverly Wilson Palmer and Holly Byers Ochoa, eds., *The Selected Papers of Thaddeus Stevens*, Pittsburgh: University of Pittsburgh Press (1998).

The following manuscript collections are found in the Library of Congress in Washington, D.C.:

Nathaniel Banks
Benjamin F. Butler
Ream-Hoxie
Thomas Ewing Family
Andrew Johnson
Logan Family
Manton Marble
Edward McPherson
Whitelaw Reid

Edmund G. Ross
William Henry Seward
John Sherman
Thaddeus Stevens
Benjamin Wade
Elihu Washburne
Thurlow Weed
James Russell Young

Other original manuscript collections and their locations:

Alonzo Adams Papers, Bancroft Library, Berkeley, California
Samuel L. M. Barlow Papers, Huntington Library, San Marino, California
John Armor Bingham Papers, Morgan Library, New York, New York
Cooper Family Papers, Tennessee State Library and Archives, Nashville, Tennessee
James F. Joy Collection, Detroit Public Library, Detroit, Michigan
Samuel Pomeroy Papers, Yale University, New Haven, Connecticut

Notes

The invaluable diary of Colonel William Moore was kept in his personal short-hand, which is difficult to translate. Because different parts of the diary have been translated at different times, the diary is cited in three different forms:

- "Moore Diary/AHR" refers to extracts that were translated by Colonel Moore himself and published as "Notes of Colonel W. G. Moore, Private Secretary to President Johnson, 1866–1868," *American Historical Review*, 19, 98 (1913).
- "Moore Diary/AJ" refers to those entries from July 8, 1866, through March 20, 1868, that were kept by Moore in a "small diary," and are available in the Johnson Papers in the Library of Congress, on Reel 50.
- "Moore Diary/Large Diary" refers to a second volume of shorthand notes with entries from March 21, 1868, through January 24, 1871, also available on microfilm Reel 50 in the Johnson Papers in the Library of Congress.

Finally, I have shortened the names of the following sources, as indicated:

House Committee on the Judiciary, "Impeachment of President Andrew Johnson: Various Papers," National Archives File 40B-A1: Archives, *Impeachment: Various House Papers*.

HR 40B-A1—"House Committee on the Judiciary, Impeachment of President Andrew Johnson, 40th Cong., "Various Papers," Committee's Journal of Managers ("Managers' Journal"): Archives, *Managers' Journal*.

Raising of Money to Be Used in Impeachment, House Report No. 75, 40th Cong., 2d sess. (July 3, 1868): *Impeachment Money*.

Impeachment Managers' Investigation, H.R. Rep. No. 44, 40th Cong., 2d sess. (May 25, 1868): *Impeachment Investigation*.

The impeachment trial record, in *Congressional Globe*, Supplement, 40th Cong., 2d sess. (1868): *Globe* Supp.

PREFACE

PAGE

1 [T]*his was no ordinary political crisis:* Adam Badeau, *Grant in Peace*, Hartford, CT: S. S. Scranton & Co. (1887), p. 86.

1. BAD BEGINNINGS

PAGE

5 *This Johnson:* Michael Burlingame, ed., Walter B. Stevens, *A Reporter's Lincoln*, Omaha: University of Nebraska Press (1998), p. 156.

5 *Or it might have been:* Benjamin C. Truman, "Anecdotes of Andrew Johnson," *Century* 85:438 (1913).

7 *On August 23:* Doris Kearns Goodwin, *Team of Rivals*, New York: Simon & Schuster (2005), p. 648. Lincoln could not afford to underestimate the Democrats. Traditionally identified with the South, the Democrats had won twelve out of sixteen presidential elections since 1800. In contrast, Lincoln's Republican Party, only eight years old, was an amalgamation of Whigs, Know-Nothings, and antislavery Democrats. Also, there was no presumption in 1864 that a president was entitled to a second term. Not since Andrew Jackson in 1832 had a president won reelection.

7 *"I am unwilling":* Cong. *Globe*, 36th Cong., 2d sess., p. 117 (December 18, 1860), pp. 1354–56 (March 2, 1861).

8 *Lincoln's seven-man Cabinet: New York Times*, March 6, 1865.

8 *Hamlin, an antislavery man:* As early as March of 1864, the press reported that Johnson might be the Republican pick for vice president. *New York Times*, March 24, 1864. Four years before, he had been Tennessee's "favorite son" candidate for the Democratic presidential nomination. In the 1860 Democratic Convention, his home state delegation voted for him on thirty-five ballots. Johnson then angled for the Democratic nod for vice president. Hans Trefousse, *Andrew Johnson, A Biography*, New York: W. W. Norton & Co. (1989), pp. 123–24. Now he might have an opportunity to run for the office on the opposing ticket.

Some 600 delegates arrived in Baltimore for the Republican convention on June 7, 1864. Reflecting the strategy of reaching out to Democratic voters, the gathering was called the "National Union Convention," and the party called itself the "National Union Party." Three candidates led the field for vice president: Johnson, the incumbent Hamlin, and Daniel Dickinson of New York, a former U.S. senator and a War Democrat. After unanimously choosing Lincoln for president, the convention turned to the second spot. Johnson led in the first balloting with 200 votes to Hamlin's 150 and Dickinson's 108. On the second roll call, Johnson won all but a handful of votes. *Proceedings of the First Three Republican National Conventions, 1856, 1860, and 1864, . . . As Reported by Horace Greeley*, Minneapolis: Charles W. Johnson (1893), pp. 188–89, 198–99, 236–39. Johnson's opponents suffered fatal defections from delegations that should have supported them. Dickinson commanded only half the votes of his own New York delegation. Those New Yorkers allied with Secretary of State William Seward supported Hamlin at first, then switched to Johnson. Seward, Lincoln's closest adviser, may have been implementing his boss's preferences. In so doing, Seward also protected his own job. Under the unwritten political rules of the 1860s, one state could not have two high officials in an administration. If Dickinson became vice president, Seward would have to leave office. Hamlin also came to grief in his home region, New England, when the Massachusetts delegation did not support him. P. J. Staudenraus, ed., Noah Brooks, *Mr. Lincoln's Washington*, Washington, DC: T. Yosellof (1967), p. 326 (June 7, 1864); James G. Blaine, *Twenty Years of Congress: From Lincoln to Garfield*, Norwich, CT: Henry Bill Publishing Co. (1886), vol. 2, pp. 64–69; *Diary of Gideon Welles*, Boston: Houghton Mifflin Co. (1911), vol. 2, p. 66; Glyndon Van Deusen, *William Henry Seward*, New York: Oxford University Press (1967), p. 433. Charles E. Hamlin, *The Life and Times of Hannibal Hamlin*, Cambridge, MA: Riverside Press (1899), pp. 464–76, 506; James F. Glonek, "Lincoln, Johnson, and the Baltimore Ticket," *Abraham Lincoln Quarterly* 6:270–71 (March 1951); Don E. Fehrenbacher, "The Making of a Myth: Lincoln and the Vice-Presidential Nomination in 1864," *Civil War History* 41:273 (1995).

Did Lincoln drive Johnson's selection? Before the convention, Lincoln said several times that he was neutral as to the choice of his running mate, hardly a vote of confidence for Hamlin. Lincoln's official neutrality probably was a smokescreen. The president likely sought to nudge the party toward Johnson while still appearing to be above the fray. One Republican congressman wrote, "It was understood that the President favored Johnson, though certain I am that he made no open declaration of his wishes." Albert G. Riddle, *Recollections of War Times: Reminiscences of Men and Events in Washington, 1860–1865*, New York: G. P. Putnam's Sons (1895), p. 282.

8 *"[K]nowing that Johnson":* Hamlin, p. 497.

10 *A Supreme Court justice:* Noah Brooks, *Washington in Lincoln's Time*, Herbert Mitgang, ed., New York: Rinehart & Co. (1958), pp. 211–12. Senator John Sherman of Ohio remembered Johnson's address similarly, though with different details. John Sherman, *John Sherman's Recollections of Forty Years in the House, Senate, and Cabinet: An Autobiography*, Chicago: Werner Co. (1895), p. 351:

> He was plainly intoxicated and delivered a stump speech unworthy of the occasion. . . . He went on in a maudlin and rambling way for twenty minutes or more, until finally he was suppressed by the suggestion of the secretary that the time for the inauguration had arrived, and he must close.

10 *Brandishing it before the crowd:* Brooks, p. 213.

10 *As the tall president:* Staudenraus, ed., p. 425.

11 *A visitor to Johnson's office:* J. B. Brownlow, quoted in David Bowen,

Andrew Johnson and the Negro, Knoxville: University of Tennessee Press (1989), p. 174 n. 35; Charles A. Dana, *Recollections of the Civil War*, Lincoln: University of Nebraska Press (1996), p. 106. Numerous other observations confirm these accounts. Harriott S. Turner, "Recollections of Andrew Johnson," *Harpers Monthly* 120:173 (1910); Oliver P. Temple, *Notable Men of Tennessee*, New York: Cosmopolitan Press (1912), p. 366; Garrett Epps, *Democracy Reborn, the Fourteenth Amendment and the Fight for Equal Rights in Post–Civil War America*, New York: Henry Holt & Co. (2006), p. 26; Chauncey M. Depew, *My Memories of Eighty Years*, New York: Charles Scribner's Sons (1922), p. 48.

11 *"I have known Andy Johnson":* Hugh McCulloch, *Men and Measures of Half a Century*, New York: Charles Scribner's Sons (1889), p. 373.

11 *"The Vice President Elect":* Letter of Senator Zachariah Chandler to his wife, quoted in Howard Means, *The Avenger Takes His Place: Andrew Johnson and the 45 Days that Changed the Nation*, New York: Harcourt (2006), p. 92.

11 *A future member: John Sherman's Recollections*, p. 351; Hamlin, p. 498; Welles Diary, vol. 2, p. 252; Staudenraus, ed., pp. 422–23 (March 12, 1865); *The Diary of Orville Hickman Browning*, Springfield: Illinois State Historical Society (1933), vol. 2, p. 9.

11 *All eyes: Times* (London), March 20, 1865.

12 *From that day on: Chicago Tribune*, March 13, 1865; Carl Schurz, *The Reminiscences of Carl Schurz*, New York: McClure Co. (1908), vol. 3, p. 227.

2. PRESIDENT JOHNSON

PAGE

14 *I am for a white man's government:* John W. Gorham to Johnson, June 3, 1865, in *Johnson Papers* 8:173 (quoting prior statement by Johnson).

14 *Notable among them:* Trefousse, *Andrew Johnson*, p. 208.

14 *Johnson was fastidious:* Truman, p. 435.

14 *After meeting the president:* Quoted in Trefousse, *Andrew Johnson*, p. 346; ibid., pp. 20–24.

15 *After long seconds of silence: Life, Speeches, and Services of Andrew Johnson* (T. B. Peterson, 1865), pp. 112–13.

15 *One of the president's few recreations:* W. H. Crook, *Memories of the White House*, Boston: Little, Brown & Co. (1911) (Henry Rood, ed.), pp. 45, 57, 61.

15 *During the White House years:* Frank Cowan, *Andrew Johnson, President of the United States: Reminiscences of his Private Life and Character*, Greenesburgh, PA: Oliver Publishing House (1894), p. 7.

15 *A White House worker:* Nancy Beck Young, "Eliza (McCardle) Johnson,"

in Lewis L. Gould, ed., *American First Ladies: Their Lives and Their Legacy*, New York: Garland Publishing (1996), p. 196.

15 *Their older surviving son:* Trefousse, *Andrew Johnson*, p. 168; Bowen, p. 82.

15 *Johnson's bodyguard:* Johnson to Mary Johnson, December 7, 1856, in *Johnson Papers* 1:592–93; Cowan, pp. 7, 11, 14; Moore Diary/AJ, p. 27 (February 24, 1867); Blaine, vol. 1, p. 325; McCulloch, p. 404; Margarita Spalding Gerry, "Andrew Johnson in the White House, Being the Reminiscences of William H. Crook," *Century* 126: 877 (1908).

16 *He once claimed to like circuses:* Cowan, p. 6 and passim; Turner, p. 170; George Fort Milton, *The Age of Hate: Andrew Johnson and the Radicals*, New York: Coward-McCann (1930), p. 121.

16 *Those who met with Johnson: Cong. Globe*, 28th Cong., 1st sess., app. 96 (January 31, 1844), in *Johnson Papers* 1:140; Bowen, p. 2; George W. Julian, *Political Recollections, 1840 to 1872*, New York: Jansen, McClurg & Co. (1884), p. 243.

16 *"Of all the dangers":* Benjamin B. French to Johnson, February 8, 1866, in *Johnson Papers* 10:57; *Cong. Globe*, 40th Cong., 2d sess., app. 2–3 (December 3, 1867).

17 *When Wade suggested:* Trefousse, *Andrew Johnson*, pp. 197–98; "Interview with Pennsylvania Delegation," May 3, 1865, in *Johnson Papers* 8:22; Mary Land, "Ben Wade," in Kenneth Wheeler, ed., *For the Union: Ohio Leaders in the Civil War*, Columbus: Ohio State University Press (1998), p. 217; *Memoirs of W. W. Holden*, Durham (NC): Seeman Printery (1911), pp. 55–56.

17 *Ultimately, the president abandoned:* Testimony before House Judiciary Committee, July 18, 1867, in *Grant Papers* 17:212–16.

17 *With Secretary of State Seward:* James L. Swanson, *Manhunt*, New York: HarperCollins (2006), pp. 202–3; Henry Dawes, "Recollections of Stanton Under Johnson," *Atlantic Monthly* 74:497 (October 1894).

18 *"The prim conservatives":* "Reconstruction," September 6, 1865, in *Stevens Papers* 2:23.

18 *He thought the nation:* Charles O. Lerche, Jr., "Congressional Interpretation of the Guarantee of a Republican Form of Government During Reconstruction," *Journal of Southern History* 15:192 (1949); quoted in James M. Scovel, "Thaddeus Stevens," *Lippincott's Monthly*, April 1898, p. 546.

18 *The States had brought:* "Interview with *The Times* (London) Correspondent," January 10, 1867, in *Johnson Papers* 11:596.

19 *He might nudge:* Johnson to William L. Sharkey, August 15, 1868, in *Johnson Papers* 8:599–600; "Interview with George L. Stearns," October 3, 1865, in *Johnson Papers* 9:180; Johnson to Sharkey, August 21, 1865, in *Johnson Papers* 8:635; Circular to Provisional Governors, August 22, 1865,

ibid., p. 639; Johnson to Sharkey, November 17, 1865, in *Johnson Papers* 8:400.

19 *An aide remarked:* "Interview with John A. Logan," May 31, 1865, in *Johnson Papers* 8:153–54; "Interview with South Carolina Delegation," June 24, 1865, in *Johnson Papers* 8:282–83; Cowan, p. 14.

20 *"According to the constitution":* Seward to Gasparin, July 10, 1865, in Seward Papers. In 1867, Johnson described Seward as "an Old Roman." A Johnson aide declared that the president had "a most sincere and friendly feeling" for his secretary of state. The aide marveled at Seward's "equanimity under all circumstances." Moore Diary/AJ, May 7, 1867.

20 *His proclamation granted amnesty: New York Times,* June 26, 1865; Michael Perman, *Reunion Without Compromise: The South and Reconstruction, 1865–1868,* London: Cambridge University Press (1973), pp. 4–12, 70–71.

20 *Only six weeks:* George Baber, "Johnson, Grant, Seward, Sumner," *North American Review* 145:72 (1887); Trefousse, *Andrew Johnson,* pp. 216–17.

20 *Stevens's father:* Ralph Korngold, *Thaddeus Stevens, A Being Darkly Wise and Rudely Great,* New York: Harcourt Brace & Co. (1955), p. 6; Fawn M. Brodie, *Thaddeus Stevens, Scourge of the South,* New York: W. W. Norton & Co. (1959), pp. 23–24.

20 *A neighbor recalled: New York Times,* August 14, 1868, quoting *Philadelphia Press.*

20 *Though he ultimately:* Brodie, p. 25.

20 *A congressional colleague: Cong. Globe,* 40th Cong., 3d sess., p. 139 (December 17, 1868) (Ignatius Donnelly).

21 *He never answered:* Alexander Harris, *A Biographical History of Lancaster County,* Baltimore: Genealogical Publishing Co. (1974; originally 1872), p. 575; interview with David Foulk, Lancaster Historical Society, June 29, 2007; Scovel, p. 460; Trefousse, *Thaddeus Stevens: Nineteenth Century Egalitarian,* Chapel Hill, NC: University of North Carolina Press (1997), pp. 69–70. In his final year, Stevens was accused of living in "open adultery" with Mrs. Smith. Brodie, p. 89. This attack elicited from him a textbook nondenial. After recounting his longtime practice of hiring housekeepers, he wrote, "I believe I can say that no child was ever raised or, so far as I know, begotten under my roof." Stevens to W. B. Melius, September 14, 1867, in *Stevens Papers* 2:328. That was, as he knew, not the question.

With no further statement from Stevens, the evidence is suggestive, but not definitive. One friend referred to their "unwritten romance," praising Mrs. Smith's "unselfish and tender devotion" to Stevens. Scovel, p. 550. When a minister friend faced accusations that he approved of Stevens "living out of wedlock with the woman who kept his house," the minister confessed he should have been "more guarded." J. Blanchard to E. McPherson, January 28, 1869, in McPherson Papers. One biographer, Fawn Brodie, concluded that Stevens and Mrs. Smith must have been sexual intimates. She emphasized that Stevens paid for a fine portrait of Lydia Smith, something he would not do for "a colored woman who was merely his respected housekeeper." Brodie, p. 88. In his will, Stevens left Mrs. Smith his furniture, as well as her choice of a yearly payment of $500 for life or a lump sum of $5,000. Trefousse, *Thaddeus Stevens*, p. 244.

21 *One enchanted observer:* George S. Boutwell, *Reminiscences of Sixty Years in Public Affairs*, New York: Greenwood Press (1968), vol. 2, p. 10; Schurz, *Reminiscences*, vol. 3, p. 217; Staudenraus, p. 104.

22 *He reminded Lincoln:* Schurz, *Reminiscences*, vol. 3, p. 214; Brodie, p. 95; Scovel, p. 549; Korngold, p. 112. The appointee with larcenous tendencies was Secretary of War Simon Cameron.

22 *One observer thought:* Schurz, *Reminiscences*, vol. 3, p. 214. A congressional colleague emphasized how Stevens limped on "his short, club-footed leg." Riddle, *Recollections of War Times*, p. 31.

22 *Ever gallant:* Trefousse, *Thaddeus Stevens*, pp. 7–8.

22 *Otherwise, many would "think":* Stevens to Johnson, May 16, 1865, in *Stevens Papers* 2:5.

22 *"Among all the leading":* Stevens to Johnson, July 6, 1865, in ibid., 2:7.

23 *Johnson's designee:* Benjamin Perry, *Reminiscences of Public Men, with Speeches and Addresses*, Philadelphia: J. D. Avil & Co., (1883), pp. 248–49; Dan T. Carter, *When the War Was Over: The Failure of Self-Reconstruction in the South, 1865–67*, Baton Rouge: Louisiana State University Press (1985), p. 31.

24 *The presence of such men:* Report of the Joint Committee on Reconstruction, 39th Cong., 1st sess., p. x (1866); Epps, p. 56; Carter, pp. 228–29; Milton, p. 256; Blaine, vol. 2, p. 113.

24 *Yet the president:* Johnson to James Johnson, November 26, 1865, in *Johnson Papers* 9:432; Johnson to James B. Steedman, November 24, 1865, ibid., 9:434.

24 *Equally incendiary:* Blaine, vol. 2, p. 94.

24 *One Republican called them:* Kenneth M. Stampp, *The Era of Reconstruction, 1865–1877*, New York: Alfred A. Knopf (1965), p. 80 (quoting Schurz).

24 *Though specific terms:* Blaine, vol. 2, p. 94.

24 *Vagrancy laws:* One traveler observed a chain gang of Negroes working on the streets of Selma, Alabama. They seemed no different from slaves. The prisoners had committed

> a list of misdemeanors, one of the gravest of which was "using abusive language towards a white man." Some had transgressed certain municipal regulations, of which, coming in from the country, they were

very likely ignorant. One had sold farm produce within the town limits, contrary to an ordinance which prohibits market men from selling so much as an egg before they have reached the market and the bell has rung. For this offense he had been fined twenty dollars, which being unable to pay, he had been put upon the chain. Others had been guilty of disorderly conduct, vagrancy, and petty theft, which it was of course necessary to punish. But it was a singular fact that no white men were ever sentenced to the chain gang—being, I suppose, all virtuous.

John T. Trowbridge, *The Desolate South, 1865–1866*, Gordon Carroll, ed., New York: Duell, Sloan & Pearce (1956), pp. 225–26. As one Southern scholar has concluded, the black codes were "unequivocally discriminatory and designed to keep blacks in a subordinate economic and social relationship to whites." Carter, p. 218.

24 *In a Mississippi hotel:* John Richard Dennett, *The South As It Is*, Henry M. Christman, ed., New York: Viking Press (1965; originally 1866), p. 351.

24 *According to one traveler:* Whitelaw Reid, *After the War: A Southern Tour, May 1, 1865, to May 1, 1866*, New York: Moore, Wilstach & Baldwin (1866), p. 237; ibid., 219; Leon Plossom to Butler, December 5, 1866, in Butler Papers, Box 41.

25 *Northerners began to fret: Chicago Tribune*, December 15, 1865; Stampp, p. 85; Carter, pp. 227–28.

25 *"[i]f Andy Johnson were a snake":* Turner, p. 170.

25 *By 1866, Johnson had granted:* Reid, pp. 304–6. This theme is discussed in a variety of sources. Stampp, p. 71; Temple, p. 419; Bowen, p. 43; Eric Foner, *Reconstruction: America's Unfinished Revolution, 1863–1877*, New York: Harper & Row (1988), pp. 191–92; Jonathan Truman Dorris, "Pardon and Amnesty During the Civil War and Reconstruction," Abstract of Ph.D. thesis, University of Illinois, 1926, pp. 9–12.

3. LAND OF REVOLUTION

PAGE

27 *Nothing renders society:* Frederick Bancroft, ed., *Speeches, Correspondence and Political Papers of Carl Schurz*, New York: G. P. Putnam's Sons (1913), vol. I, p. 354.

28 *A city of ruins:* Trowbridge, pp. 39, 314; Dennett, pp. 8, 230, 237; Andrews, p. 1.

28 *"People on Main Street":* Report to Johnson by William Elder, Treasury Department, May 23, 1868, in Johnson Papers, Reel 14; Charles M. Blackford, *Letters from Lee's Army*, Susan L. Blackford, ed., New York: Charles Scribner's Sons (1947), p. 295. Other travelers described similar scenes in 1865 and 1866. Dennett, p. 45; Trowbridge, p. 153.

28 *Political rights for the former slaves:* Andrews, p. 87.

29 *As one visitor observed:* Carter, p. 202, quoting *Philadelphia Inquirer*, August 9, 1865.

29 *"You know how a bird":* Schurz, *Reminiscences*, vol. 3, p. 174; Dennett, pp. 95, 364; Trowbridge, p. 38.

29 *As one Northern correspondent:* Dennett, pp. 39, 79, 124; James M. Smallwood, *Time of Hope, Time of Despair: Black Texans During Reconstruction*, Port Washington, NY: Kennikat Press (1981), p. 29. Trowbridge, p. 56; Reid, pp. 44, 173; Foner, p. 199; Andrews, pp. 127, 178, 188, 322, 370–71; Hans Trefousse, ed., *Background for Radical Reconstruction*, New York: Little Brown & Co. (1970), pp. 11 and 52 (testimony of Orlando Brown, Freedmen's Bureau official in Richmond: "By vagrant laws, and by availing themselves of the ignorance of the Negroes in the making of contracts, by getting them in debt, and otherwise, they would place them, I think, in a worse condition than they were when slaves.") This pattern is discussed in Stampp, pp. 199–201.

30 *A Virginian acknowledged:* Reid, p. 218; Dennett, pp. 42, 109.

30 *Indeed, many government records:* Reid, pp. 33–34, 221; Dennett, pp. 48, 102, 290, 294–301; Trowbridge, pp. 47–48, 78.

30 *Problems quickly emerged:* Dennett, pp. 76, 155, 163, 169, 191, 193; Andrews, pp. 157, 177; William McFeely, *Yankee Stepfather*, New York: W. W. Norton & Co. (1994), pp. 215–16. Trowbridge, pp. 314, 316; Trefousse, *Background*, p. 8 (testimony of Richard Hill, former slave).

30 *"If we let a nigger":* General Bennett in Pineville, SC, to Carl Schurz, July 25, 1865, in Johnson Papers, Reel 16; Dennett, p. 116.

30 *A New York correspondent wrote:* Reid, pp. 325, 386–87; Dennett, p. 74.

31 *When a black mistakenly:* Dennett, pp. 110, 182–83; Trefousse, *Background*, pp. 143–45 (testimony of Dexter H. Clapp, Freedmen's Bureau agent) and p. 10 (testimony of Rev. William Thornton); Andrews, p. 100.

31 *I saw in various hospitals:* Schurz, *Reminiscences*, vol. 3, p. 175. For a collection of similar descriptions of the random violence of the time, see W. E. B. DuBois, *Black Reconstruction in America*, New York: Free Press (1992), pp. 671–77.

31 *In South Carolina:* William W. Boyce to Francis P. Blair, Sr., October 7, 1865, Johnson Papers, Reel 18.

32 *As many as a hundred:* Smallwood, pp. 131–32, 145.

32 *A stableman in South Carolina:* Andrews, pp. 219–20.

32 *He knew of no occasion:* Dennett, pp. 182–83, 221; Trefousse, *Background*, pp. 21–22 (testimony of T. J. Markey) and 145 (Clapp testimony); Testimony before the Select Committee on the Murder of Union Soldiers in South Carolina, 39th Cong., 2d sess., in National Archives, File HR 39A—F28.2, p. 104 (January 28, 1867) (testimony of General Thomas Wood).

Markey, the former Texas state official, told Congress that "the prevailing sentiment is so adverse to the Negro that acts of monstrous crime against him are winked at." Trefousse, *Background*, p. 21.

32 *Much of the violence:* Grant to Johnson, February 17, 1866, in *Grant Papers* 16:69–70.

33 *[The] freedman did not remove:* S. Rep. No. 41, Part 1, 42d Cong., 2d sess., p. 19; Smallwood, p. 32; Claude Elliott, "The Freedmen's Bureau in Texas," *Southwestern Historical Quarterly* 56:6 (July 1952). See Trefousse, *Background*, p. 150 (H. S. Hall).

33 *During the 1868 election:* Smallwood, p. 33; *Hearings on 1868 Elections*, 40th Cong., 3rd sess., House Misc. Docs. No. 52–53; *The Nation* 7:42 (July 16, 1868); Brodie, p. 328.

33 *Men, who are honorable:* Col. Samuel Thomas [head of the Freedmen's Bureau in Mississippi] to O. O. Howard, September 6, 1865, Letters Received, Ser. 15, Washington Headquarters, RG 105 NA [FSSP A-9206], quoted in Foner, p. 150.

33 *In September 1865:* James E. Sefton, *The United States Army and Reconstruction, 1865–1877*, Baton Rouge: Louisiana State University Press (1967), pp. 27, 50–51.

34 *Freedom for the slaves:* Reid, p. 213; Myrta Avary, *Dixie After the War*, Boston: Houghton Mifflin Co. (1937; originally 1906), pp. 158, 182.

34 *The commander replied:* Johnson to General George Thomas, September 4, 1865, Official Records of the Secretary of War, RG 107, 2:1865-77, quoted in Bowen, p. 154; George Thomas to Johnson, September 7, 1865, in *Johnson Papers* 8:41.

34 *A third general:* M. C. Post, ed., *Life and Memoirs of Comte Regis de Trobriand*, New York: E. P. Dutton & Co. (1910), pp. 347–48 (Gen. George C. Meade to Col. P. Regis de Trobriand, August 28, 1867); William Conant Church, *Ulysses S. Grant and the Period of National Preservation and Reconstruction*, New York: G. P. Putnam's Sons (1897), p. 349; Trefousse, *Background*, p. 70 (Gen. Rufus Saxton).

35 *State militias and "home guards":* Chase to Johnson, May 17, 1865, in Johnson Papers, Reel 14; Brownlow to Johnson (telegram), May 19, 1865, ibid.; Sefton, pp. 57–66, 80; *Committee on the Murder of Union Soldiers in South Carolina*, passim; Andrews, pp. 220–21; Stephen Budiansky, *The Bloody Shirt*, New York: Viking (2008), pp. 26–27; McFeely, pp. 135, 294; Church, p. 350; Smallwood, pp. 144–45; Trowbridge, p. 197; Dennett, p. 247.

35 *"We ought not":* Memoirs of Gen. W. T. Sherman, New York: Charles L. Webster & Co. (1891), vol. 2, p. 424.

35 *At its peak:* McFeely, pp. 157, 289.

35 *To patrol the Rio Grande:* Smallwood, p. 39.

4. THE OPPOSITION GATHERS

PAGE

36 *Contemning all applause:* J. D. Binckley, "The Leader of the House," *Galaxy* 1:500 (July 1866).

36 *In late November:* Korngold, p. 293; Trefousse, *Thaddeus Stevens*, p. 175.

37 *Sumner costumed himself:* Blaine, vol. 2, p. 317; Brooks, *Washington in Lincoln's Time*, pp. 32–33.

37 *Though Sumner's credentials:* Welles Diary, vol. 1, p. 502.

37 *A Radical colleague:* Boutwell, *Sixty Years in Public Affairs*, vol. 2, p. 47.

37 *When an old friend:* David Donald, *The Politics of Reconstruction, 1863–1867*, Cambridge, MA: Harvard University Press (1965, 1984), p. 25. The old acquaintance was Julia Ward Howe, who wrote the stirring words to "The Battle Hymn of the Republic." Her brother, Sam Ward, played a role in the impeachment trial, covered in chaps. 15 through 24.

37 *Told that Sumner:* Alexander K. McClure, *Recollections of Half a Century*, Salem, MA: Salem Press Co. (1902), p. 96.

38 *One Northerner exulted:* Mary Land, "Bluff Ben Wade's New England Background," *New England Quarterly* 27:507 (1954); *Cong. Globe*, 34th Cong., 1st sess., 1304–6; John B. Ellis, *The Sights and Secrets of the National Capital: A Work Descriptive of Washington City in All Its Various Phases*, New York: United States Publishing Co. (1869), p. 124; H. L. Trefousse, *Benjamin Franklin Wade: Radical Republican from Ohio*, New York: Twayne Publishers Inc. (1963), p. 103; Land, "Ben Wade," p. 160; Brooks, *Washington in Lincoln's Time*, p. 34.

38 *Facing "the onflowing torrent":* Riddle, p. 244.

39 *According to future President:* Ellis, p. 124; Blaine, vol. 1, p. 320; Julian, *Political Recollections*, pp. 356–57; Garfield to James Harrison Rhodes, May 7, 1868, in Theodore Clarke Smith, *Life and Letters of James Abram Garfield*, New Haven: Yale University Press (1925), vol. 1, p. 425.

39 *In 1864, Wade's frustration:* Land, "Ben Wade," p. 163; Emily Edson Briggs, *The Olivia Letters*, New York: Neale Publishing Co. (1906), p. 66; William Frank Zornow, " 'Bluff Ben' Wade in Lawrence, Kansas: The Issue of Class Conflict," *Ohio Historical Quarterly* 65:46 (1956); Foner, p. 335; ibid., p. 61. The reconstruction program in the Wade-Davis bill of 1864 was actually fairly mild; Thad Stevens abstained from voting on it because he thought it was too weak. Trefousse, *Thaddeus Stevens*, p. 149.

39 *"That's all that hell wants":* Chicago Tribune, March 4, 1864; Schurz, *Reminiscences*, vol. 3, pp. 217–18; Brooks, *Men of Lincoln's Time*, p. 35.

39 *Sumner fired back:* Maunsell Field, *Memories of Many Men and of Some Women*, London: Sampson Low, Marston, Low & Searle (1874), p. 306; Schurz, *Reminiscences*, vol. 3, p. 218; Michael Les Benedict, *A Compromise of Principle, Congressional Republicans and Reconstruction, 1863–*

1869, New York: W. W. Norton & Co. (1974), p. 39; Francis Fessenden, *Life and Public Services of William Pitt Fessenden*, Boston: Houghton, Mifflin & Co. (1907), vol. 2, p. 148; *Boston Advertiser*, August 30, 1867. Some accounts blame the enmity between Sumner and Fessenden for the nomination of Andrew Johnson for vice president in 1864. The accusation is circuitous, but not impossible. Sumner is supposed to have persuaded the Massachusetts delegation to abandon the renomination of Vice President Hannibal Hamlin of Maine, so that Hamlin would then oust Fessenden from the Senate. Hamlin, pp. 464–67. This was one of several explanations offered for Johnson's nomination in 1864, an action that seemed so horrible to Republicans in retrospect that they searched for guilty parties to blame.

39 *With his "cold, dry, severe manner"*: Brooks, *Men of Lincoln's Time*, p. 34.

40 *"Say what they will"*: Benedict, *Compromise of Principle*, p. 56, (Sen. Zach Chandler of Michigan, attacking Fessenden as "the Conservative Senator from Maine"); Fessenden, vol. 2, p. 12; Benedict, *Compromise of Principle*, p. 132. Stevens complained to the press about Fessenden's gentle feelings toward the President. McPherson Papers, Box 12 (Article from *Meriden* [CT] *Recorder*, September 18, 1867).

40 *With long fair hair*: Donald, p. 46; Staudenraus, ed., p. 109; Reid, p. 431.

40 *Bingham also*: Erving E. Beauregard, *Bingham of the Hills: Politician and Diplomat Extraordinary*, New York: Peter Lang (1989), pp. 68, 83–84. As detailed by Beauregard, Bingham had a complex relationship with the Lincoln assassination. On his deathbed, the Ohio congressman claimed he experienced a vision, as Lincoln was being shot, of the tragic event. Ibid., p. 88. Also while on his deathbed, Bingham supposedly told his doctor that Mrs. Mary Suratt–one of the executed conspirators–had revealed to him and Secretary of War Stanton certain information "so shocking that its publication would threaten the Republic." Bingham and Stanton agreed it should not be disclosed, and Stanton on his own deathbed made Bingham swear to preserve the confidence. Bingham took the secret to his grave with him, saying, "The truth must remain sealed."

40 *His lasting legacy*: Welles Diary, vol. 3, p. 274; Benjamin B. Kendrick, *The Journal of the Joint Committee of Fifteen on Reconstruction*, New York, (1914), p. 183; Richard L. Aynes, "The Continuing Importance of Congressman John A. Bingham and the Fourteenth Amendment," *Akron Law Review* 36:590 (2003).

40 *One observer thought*: Brooks, *Washington in Lincoln's Time*, pp. 108–9; Donald, pp. 68, 75; Benedict, *Compromise*, p. 36; Blaine, vol. 1, p. 328; Donald C. Swift, "John A. Bingham and Reconstruction: The Dilemma of a Moderate," *Ohio History* (1968) 77:86–87.

41 *"I always liked him for it"*: Undated memorandum to McPherson, McPher-

son Papers, Box 60; John Law to McPherson, January 23, 1869, ibid., Box 12; William D. Reed to McPherson, January 13, 1869, and E. G. Spaulding to McPherson, January 23, 1869, ibid., Box 60; "Interview with Benjamin Eggleston," December 22, 1866, in *Johnson Papers* 11:558.

41 *Plain homes:* Riddle, *Recollections of War Times*, pp. 7–9.

41 *For four years:* Ellis, pp. 50, 494. Ellis pithily summarized his view of the behavioral changes wrought by the war: "Honesty, both private and official, was thrown aside, and rascality took its place. Female virtue was at a discount."

41 *Government buildings:* Ellis, p. 55; George Alfred Townsend, *Washington, Outside and Inside*, Hartford, CT: James Betts & Co. (1873), p. 124.

41 *Due to the limited hygienic resources:* Ellis, p. 111.

42 *"Members of Congress":* Donald, *The Politics of Reconstruction*, p. 54.

42 *Near the Capitol: New York Sun*, October 25, 1896 (recollections of Gen. Daniel Sickles).

42 *There is no record: Meriden* (CT) *Recorder*, September 18, 1867, in McPherson Papers, Box 12; Riddle, *Recollections of War Times*, p. 9. Korngold, p. 292, quoting *New York Tribune*; Scovel, p. 549; Harris, p. 580; Korngold, p. 66; Ellis, pp. 406–7. The game of faro was described as follows: "In front of the dealer is a table with a green cloth, upon which a number of cards are laid. . . . A pack of cards . . . is then placed in a patent silver case, and the dealer shuffles them out one by one upon the 'lay out.' A player deposits his stake upon a card, the Jack of diamonds, for instance. If the dealer . . . throws the corresponding Jack from the pack [on the lay out], the player wins from the bank; but if a different card falls upon it he loses his stake." In a "first-class house, the shuffling is done fairly by the dealer." Betting was done with "counters," bought from the proprietor and cashed out promptly, because "the law forbids gambling for money, and if, in case of a descent by the police, no money is visible, it is hard to make a case against the proprietor and his friends." Ellis, pp. 402–3.

43 *The Republican leaders unanimously:* Shelby Cullom, *Fifty Years of Public Service*, Chicago: A. C. McClurg & Co. (1911), p. 147; Brodie, p. 240; Charles R. Williams, ed., *Diary and Letters of Rutherford Birchard Hayes*, Columbus: Ohio State Historical Society (1922–26), vol. 3, p. 33.

43 *"I cannot yield": Cong. Globe*, 39th Cong., 1st sess., p. 4 (December 4, 1865).

43 *To ensure that the Southern representatives:* Foner, p. 239; *Chicago Tribune*, December 12, 1865.

44 *Without debate: Cong. Globe*, 39th Cong., 1st sess., p. 6 (December 4, 1865), p. 30 (December 12, 1865).

45 *If Stevens had heard:* Welles, vol. 2, pp. 387, 438; Blaine, vol. 2, p. 112.

5. A GOVERNMENT DIVIDED AGAINST ITSELF

46 *The war between the President:* Georges Clemenceau, *American Reconstruction: 1865–1870*, Fernand Baldensperger, ed., New York: Lincoln McVeagh/Dial Press (1928), pp. 102–3 (September 10, 1867). Clemenceau, who would become the French premier during World War I, completed his medical studies in 1865 but was not ready to settle down. His father underwrote a lengthy stay in the United States, during which Clemenceau practiced some medicine and gloried in roughhouse American politics. He began contributing letters about American politics to *Le Temps* in Paris, and ultimately was paid for his dispatches. He also acquired an American wife.

47 *The hearings assembled:* Kendrick, pp. 39, 41; Report of the Joint Committee of Reconstruction, passim; Eric L. McKitrick, *Andrew Johnson and Reconstruction*, Chicago: University of Chicago Press (1960), pp. 330–31 and n. 3. One scholar concluded that the Joint Committee hearings "dramatized conclusions already held rather than uncovered the whole truth." Joseph B. James, "Southern Reaction to the Proposal of the Fourteenth Amendment," *Journal of Southern History* 22:480 (November 1956).

47 *With four million:* Blaine, vol. 2, p. 189; *Cong. Globe*, 39th Cong., 1st sess., pp. 356–57 (January 22, 1866) (Roscoe Conkling).

48 *But blacks were in a majority:* Ibid., p. 351; Leslie H. Fishel, Jr., "Northern Prejudice and Negro Suffrage, 1865–1870," *Journal of Negro History* 39:8 (January 1954); *Cong. Globe*, 39th Cong., 1st sess., p. 683 (February 6, 1866). The population estimates are based on 1860 census figures.

48 *Harkening to the 200,000 blacks: Cong. Globe*, 39th Cong., 1st sess., pp. 674–87 (February 6, 1866).

48 *With the proposed amendment:* Ibid., p. 380 (January 23, 1866) (Rep. Brooks); Foner, pp. 252–53; *Washington Daily National Intelligencer*, January 29, 1866; "Interview with James Dixon," January 28, 1866, in *Johnson Papers* 9:647–48.

49 *It specifically conferred: Cong. Globe*, 39th Cong., 1st sess., p. 1760 (April 4, 1866) (Sen. Trumbull); McKitrick, p. 278; Edward McPherson, *The Political History of the United States of America During the Period of Reconstruction*, New York: Da Capo Press (1972; originally 1871), pp. 72–74, 78.

50 *Thad Stevens and his allies:* Welles Diary, vol. 2, p. 432.

50 *The president's concern:* McPherson, pp. 69–71; *Chicago Tribune*, February 9, 1866. Johnson met a delegation of Negro leaders in early February but offered no support for their petition for protection for the former slaves. McPherson, p. 54. Johnson confided to his secretary after the meeting, "I know that d—d [Frederick] Douglass," adding, "he's just like any

nigger, & he would sooner cut a white man's throat than not." Reported by Philip Ripley in letter to Manton Marble, February 8, 1868, Manton Marble Papers.

50 *Yet Johnson ignored:* John H. Cox and LaWanda Cox, "Andrew Johnson and His Ghost Writers: An Analysis of the Freedmen's Bureau and Civil Rights Veto Messages," *Mississippi Valley Historical Review* 48:470–71 (December 1961); McPherson, pp. 71–72. In a masterful analysis of drafts of two Johnson veto messages, the Coxes demonstrated that Johnson carefully managed those documents, though others drafted large portions of them. The challenge to Congress's authority in the veto of the Freedmen's Bureau bill, however, appears in no drafts, so the Coxes conclude that Johnson himself inserted it.

50 *Johnson's veto:* McKitrick, pp. 290–91.

51 *One pronounced him:* McGregor [IA] *News,* reprinted in *Chicago Tribune,* February 27, 1866; *Chicago Tribune,* February 21, 1866; *Pittsburgh Commercial* editorial reprinted in *Chicago Tribune,* February 27, 1866; *Richmond Whig, Vicksburg Herald,* reprinted in *Chicago Tribune,* February 27, 1866.

51 *Nevertheless, the Senate failed: Cong. Globe,* 39th Cong., 1st sess., p. 943 (February 20, 1866, Sen. Trumbull). With the battle lines hardening between the president and Congress, Stevens secured House approval of a resolution declaring flatly that no Southern legislator would enter Congress "until Congress shall have declared such state entitled to such representation." Kendrick, pp. 233–34; *Cong. Globe,* 39th Cong., 1st sess., p. 950 (February 20, 1866).

52 *Stirred by his looming martyrdom: Washington Daily National Intelligencer,* February 23, 1866. Struck by the peculiarly self-righteous tone of this oration, one scholar counted each use by Johnson of a personal pronoun—I, me, myself, my, Andrew Johnson, and even the occasional third-person "he." The scholar found that Johnson referred to himself 210 times, or approximately three times a minute, or about twice as often as Lincoln had referred to himself in his final speech. McKitrick, p. 293 n. 46.

53 *A Johnson ally:* Blaine, vol. 2, p. 182; Welles Diary, vol. 2, p. 439; James H. Geiger to John Sherman, February 24, 1866, John Sherman Papers; McCulloch, p. 381; Browning Diary, vol. 2, p. 93 n. 1 (letter of Sen. Doolittle of Wisconsin, October 7, 1866).

53 *The Maine senator wrote:* Fessenden to Elizabeth F. Warriner (February 25, 1866), in Fessenden Papers, Bowdoin College, quoted in McKitrick, p. 297 n. 51.

53 *His real dismay:* McPherson, pp. 74–78.

53 *Over a glass of claret: Cong. Globe,* 39th Cong., 1st sess., pp. 1755–61 (April 4, 1866), p. 1809 (April 6, 1866) (Senate), p. 1861 (April 9, 1866) (House); Moore Diary/AJ, p. 15 (undated entry).

54 *To ensure that Johnson:* Foner, p. 251; LaWanda Cox and John H. Cox, *Politics, Principle, and Prejudice 1865–1866*, New York: Atheneum (1976), pp. 202–3; Cox and Cox, "Andrew Johnson and His Ghost Writers," p. 478.

54 *"A year ago they were willing":* Foner, p. 262; McFeeley, pp. 275–81, quoting *Memphis Avalanche*, May 6, 1866; *New York Times*, May 24, 1866.

55 *A day later, Sheridan's feelings:* James G. Hollandsworth, Jr., *An Absolute Massacre: The New Orleans Race Riot of July 30, 1866*, Baton Rouge: Louisiana State University Press (2001), pp. 139–41, 144.

55 *A few Johnson loyalists:* Welles Diary, vol. 2, p. 569.

55 *Yet the same report:* Schurz, *Reminiscences*, vol. 3, pp. 239–40; George S. Boutwell, "The Usurpation," *Atlantic Monthly* 18:509 (October 1866); *New York Times*, May 19, 1868.

55 *After Charles Sumner's insistence:* Foner, pp. 252–53; *Cong. Globe*, 39th Cong., 1st sess., p. 1289 (March 9, 1866).

55 *Seated in Stevens's parlor:* James M. Scovel, "Thad Stevens," undated article, in Stevens Papers, Box 8.

56 *Owen had less luck:* Robert Dale Owen, "Political Results from the Varioloid," *Atlantic Monthly* 35:662–64 (June 1875).

56 *During the first half of April:* Kendrick, pp. 82, 89, 97.

56 *When the revised version:* Owen, pp. 665–66; *New York Independent*, May 31, 1866 (quoting Sen. Jacob Howard of Michigan); Welles Diary, vol. 2, pp. 495–98.

56 *Focusing on practical matters: New York Herald*, May 2, 1866.

57 *That provision would survive:* By 1875, Robert Dale Owen was critical of the failure to enforce this provision: "[W]hile various States have abridged suffrage by imposing qualifications [such as literacy tests and poll taxes], no attempt has been made, or is likely to be made, to ascertain how many adult males are thereby excluded, or to deduct, *proportionately*, from the basis of representation in these States." Owen, p. 667.

57 *When he closed: Cong. Globe*, 39th Cong., 1st sess., pp. 3042–3149 (May 5 through June 13, 1866); Owen, p. 665; "A Woman in Washington," *The Independent*, June 14, 1866.

57 *Do you inquire why: Cong. Globe*, 39th Cong., 1st sess., p. 3148 (June 13, 1866).

58 *Meeting with one Cabinet member:* Senate Ex. Doc. No. 57, 39th Cong., 1st sess. (June 22, 1866); "Message re Amending the Constitution," June 22, 1866, in *Johnson Papers* 10:615; Browning Diary, vol. 2, p. 80; Temple, p. 343 (Tennessee); testimony of T. C. Wetherly, April 2, 1868, in Archives, *Impeachment: Various House Papers* (South Carolina); Trefousse, *Andrew Johnson*, p. 275 (Alabama); James, p. 497 (Johnson's opposition to the Fourteenth Amendment was "decisive" in persuading Southern states to reject it). Most Southern state officials opposed the Fourteenth Amend-

ment, and no Southern states ratified it until their governments were re-constituted after the Reconstruction Acts of 1867 took effect. Perman, *Reunion Without Compromise*, pp. 249–53.

58 *Thereafter, the two congressmen:* Cullom, p. 153.

6. POLITICAL WAR

PAGE

59 *We have got to fight:* Mark M. Krug, *Lyman Trumbull, Conservative Radical*, New York: A. S. Barnes (1965), p. 244.

59 *The president, according to his own treasury secretary:* McCulloch, pp. 404–5.

59 *In mid-June:* Carter, p. 237; Welles Diary, vol. 2, pp. 528–31.

60 *In the year since the assassination:* Moore Diary/AJ (May 2, 1866).

60 *One contemporary called:* Brooks, *Men in Lincoln's Time*, pp. 35–36; Blaine, vol. 2, pp. 65, 108; Goodwin, pp. 11–13, 506–7; Field, p. 262; Donn Piatt, *Memories of the Men Who Saved the Union*, New York: Belford, Clarke & Co. (1887), p. 135; Van Deusen, pp. 428–30; John M. Taylor, *William Henry Seward: Lincoln's Right Hand*, New York: HarperCollins (1991), pp. 245–46, 250; Frederic Bancroft, *The Life of William H. Seward*, Gloucester, MA: Peter Smith (1967), vol. 2, pp. 462–63; *Washington Daily National Intelligencer*, June 22, 1865. Navy Secretary Gideon Welles held a grudging admiration for Seward's political skills, claiming that the secretary of state "made constant mistakes, but recovered with a facility that was wonderful and almost always without injury to himself." Welles Diary, vol. 1, p. 139.

60 *One Republican thought:* Blaine, vol. 2, p. 67.

60 *Some attributed:* Staudenraus, ed., p. 326 (June 7, 1864); Blaine, vol. 2, pp. 64–69; Hamlin, p. 506; Van Deusen, p. 433. Dickinson also was a "War Democrat." Had the New York delegation supported Dickinson aggressively, he might well have won the nomination, but some New York strength was siphoned off to Johnson. Hamlin, pp. 464–76; Glonek, p. 291.

61 *He strongly approved:* Seward to Johnson, February 23, 1866, in *Johnson Papers* 10: 164; *Milwaukee Daily Sentinel*, March 31, 1866 (reprinting column from *Cincinnati Gazette*).

61 *In a public letter:* Goodwin, pp. 300–304, 467–68; *Washington National Daily Intelligencer*, March 8, 1866 and July 16, 1866; *Milwaukee Daily Sentinel*, February 24, 1866; *Yankton (SD) Union and Dakotan*, September 15, 1866 (reprinting Seward speech).

61 *According to his new secretary of the interior:* Welles Diary, vol. 2, pp. 551–52 (July 11, 1866); Trefousse, *Andrew Johnson*, p. 257; William Dennison to Johnson, July 11, 1866, in *Johnson Papers* 10: 668–69; James

Harlan to Johnson, July 27, 1866, in *Johnson Papers* 10:741; Browning Diary, vol. 2, p. 79.

61 *In the seven months:* Sauerevein of Baltimore to McPherson (August 1, 1865), in McPherson Papers, Box 49R ("The contest for Federal appointments here is over, . . . Mr. Johnson has not forgotten his democracy."); Krug, *Trumbull*, p. 244 (In April, Johnson's purge of federal officials in Illinois harmed Trumbull's political organization); *Cong. Globe*, 39th Cong., 1st sess., p. 2308 (Sen. Henderson) (May 1, 1866) ("I have nothing to ask from the present Executive in the way of patronage; and I can safely express the opinion here that if I had the President would not grant it"); McKitrick, pp. 387–89. Michael Les Benedict, *The Impeachment and Trial of Andrew Johnson*, New York: W. W. Norton & Co. (1973), p. 48.

61 *Those highly coveted jobs:* Blaine, vol. 2, p. 125; Harry J. Carman and Reinhard H. Luthin, *Lincoln and the Patronage*, Gloucester, MA: Peter Smith (1964), p. 60.

62 *Johnson's use of patronage:* Benedict, *Impeachment*, p. 47; Foner, p. 266.

62 *In Ohio, Senator John Sherman:* Quoted in Herbert S. Schell, "Hugh McCulloch and the Treasury Department, 1865–1869," *Mississippi Valley Historical Review* 17:417 (December 1930); John Sherman to William Sherman, October 26, 1866, in Rachel Sherman Thorndike, ed., *The Sherman Letters: Correspondence Between General and Senator Sherman from 1837 to 1891*, New York: Charles Scribner's Books (1894), p. 278.

62 *For six months:* Welles Diary, vol. 2, p. 498; Browning Diary, vol. 2, p. 63 (February 23, 1866) (discussion with the President of need to replace Stanton); Benjamin P. Thomas and Harold M. Hyman, *Stanton: The Life and Times of Lincoln's Secretary of War*, Westport, CT: Greenwood Press (1962), pp. 491–92.

62 *The war secretary seemed:* Ulysses S. Grant, *The Personal Reminiscences of Ulysses S. Grant*, New York: Konecky & Konecky (originally 1885), p. 656; McClure, p. 156.

63 *When stress laid him low:* Goodwin, pp. 176–78, 449; Welles Diary, vol. 1, p. 70 (July 13, 1862); Thomas & Hyman, p. 501. Goodwin's portrayal of Stanton is sensitive and compelling.

63 *Referring to Abraham Lincoln:* Walter Gaston Shotwell, *Driftwood*, London: Longmans, Green & Co. (1927), p. 69; Ward Lamon, *Recollections of Abraham Lincoln*, Chicago: A. C. McClurg & Co. (1895), p. 231.

64 *"Folks come up here":* Welles Diary, vol. 1, p. 355 (July 2, 1863); Stephen B. Oates, *Abraham Lincoln: The Man Behind the Myths*, New York: Harper & Row (1984), p. 173; Riddle, *Recollections of War Times*, p. 318.

64 *According to one contemporary:* Piatt, p. 63.

64 *Tensions arose quickly:* Stanton to Johnson, March 3, 1865, in *Johnson Papers* 7:498–99; George Baber, "Johnson, Grant, Seward, Sumner," *North American Review* 145:72 (1887); Trefousse, *Andrew Johnson*, pp. 216–17.

64 *In truth, Johnson referred:* Welles Diary, vol. 2, p. 424 (February 2, 1866); Moore Diary/AJ, p. 32 (March 1867).

65 *According to Grant's aide:* Badeau, p. 84; Harold M. Hyman, "Stanton and Grant: A Reconsideration of the Army's Role in the Events Leading to Impeachment," *American Historical Review* 66:91–92 (October 1960).

65 *By summertime:* Thomas and Hyman, p. 483; Welles Diary, vol. 3, pp. 133–34 (July 15, 1866).

65 *Stanton attended Cabinet meetings:* Moore Diary/AJ, p. 2 (July 14, 1866); Welles Diary, vol. 3, p. 25 (January 19, 1867); Richard Taylor, *Destruction and Reconstruction*, New York: Arno Press (1973) (originally 1879), pp. 252–53; McCulloch, p. 391.

66 *The Secretary's personal integrity:* Boutwell, vol. 2, pp. 91–93.

66 *Pledging to remain at his post:* Dawes, p. 305.

67 *The president blamed:* Foner, p. 264; Martin E. Mantell, *Johnson, Grant, and the Politics of Reconstruction*, New York: Columbia University Press (1973), p. 20.

67 *He accused a minority:* McPherson, p. 127.

68 *One supporter:* Harriett Weed, ed., *Autobiography of Thurlow Weed*, Boston: Houghton, Mifflin & Co. (1884), pp. 630–31; Trefousse, *Andrew Johnson*, p. 263; "Speech in New York," August 29, 1866, in *Johnson Papers* 11:164. Most of Johnson's speeches included a description of his rise through public offices. "Remarks to Citizens of Montana," February 7, 1866, in *Johnson Papers* 10:51.

68 *If I have played the Judas:* McPherson, pp. 134–40.

69 *For many, Johnson's speeches:* Rutherford B. Hayes to Guy M. Bryan, October 1, 1866, in *Hayes Diary*, vol. 3, p. 33; Cullom, p. 153 (during the Swing Around the Circle, when the president's speeches were "intemperate and extreme," "many people thought [Johnson] was intoxicated most of the time"). The humorist David Locke, writing as Petroleum V. Nasby, lampooned Johnson in an exaggerated country dialect that Lincoln (a Nasby enthusiast) had loved to read aloud to visitors:

> [Johnson] was sacrificing hisself for them—who hed made greater sacrifices? He hed bin Alderman uv his native town, and Vice-President; he wuz too modest to make a speech; but ef he was Joodas Iskariot, who wuz the Saviour? He hed swung around the circle, and hadn't found none so far.

David Ross Locke, *The Struggles of Petroleum V. Nasby*, Boston: Beacon Press (1963), p. 219.

69 *A Johnson ally:* Grant to Julia Grant, September 9, 1866, in *Grant Papers* 16:308; Foner, p. 265.

69 *Republicans sat:* http://www.senate.gov/pagelayout/history/one_item_and _teasers/partydiv.htm; http://www.clerk.house.gov/art_history/house_his tory/index.html.

69 *Wary of both Virginians:* Senator John Sherman to General William T. Sherman, July 8, 1866, in Thorndike, ed., *The Sherman Letters,* p. 276; *New York Times,* July 16, 1866; Hyman, p. 93.

70 *Another Republican senator:* Margaret Shortreed, "The Antislavery Radicals: From Crusade to Revolution," *Past and Present* (November 1959), p. 83; John Thayer, "A Night with Stanton in the War Office," *McClure's* 8:439 (March 1, 1897).

70 *One report had him: Baltimore American,* October 11, 1866. This report was promptly repudiated, but received wide distribution. *Baltimore American,* October 12, 1866.

70 *Grant's reported response:* George S. Boutwell, "Johnson's Plot and Motives," *North American Review* 141:574 (December 1885); Ulysses S. Grant III, *Ulysses S. Grant: Warrior and Statesman,* New York: William Morrow (1969), pp. 279, 297; Grant Testimony, Judiciary Committee, in *Grant Papers* 17:226. Another version of this Johnson-Grant exchange appears in a recollection by a boyhood chum of Grant's. Daniel Ammen, "Recollections and Letters of Grant," *North American Review* 141:367 (October 1885). Though these recountings of the episode vary from each other, the basic exchange plainly occurred, and it alarmed General Grant and many others.

70 *An Ohio congressman formed:* Thomas and Hyman, p. 493; Grant to General Cyrus B. Comstock, September 24, 1866, in *Grant Papers* 16:314; A. G. Riddle, *The Life of Benjamin Wade,* Cleveland: William W. Williams (1887), p. 272n. Grant later reported to Johnson that his investigator found "no cause for apprehension . . . at least for the present." Grant to Johnson, October 12, 1866, in *Johnson Papers* 11:344–45.

70 *As a precaution:* Grant to Sheridan, October 12, 1866, in *Grant Papers* 16:330–31; Smith, pp. 427–28.

71 *A North Carolina newspaper: Chicago Tribune,* October 23, 1866; Mary R. Dearing, *Veterans in Politics: The Story of the G.A.R.,* Baton Rouge: Louisiana State University Press (1952), pp. 105–7; Browning Diary, vol. 2, p. 94; *Chicago Tribune,* September 20, 1866, quoting *New Bern [NC] Progress.*

71 *"If insurrection does come":* Clemenceau, p. 121; *Baltimore American and Commercial Advertiser,* October 10, 1866; Moore Diary/AHR, p. 103; Browning Diary, vol. 2, pp. 102, 105; Welles Diary, vol. 2, pp. 620–21 (November 17, 1866); Grant to Johnson, October 24, 1866, in *Grant Papers* 16:350.

71 *Then he walked out:* Grant to Johnson, October 21, 1866, in *Johnson Papers* 11:375; Welles Diary, vol. 2, p. 621; Grant to Stanton, October 27, 1866, in *Grant Papers* 16:357; Boutwell, "Johnson's Plot," p. 575.

71 *To his wife:* William Sherman to John Sherman, October 31, 1866, in Thorndike, *Sherman Letters,* p. 280; Smith, p. 427; Sherman to Ellen Ewing Sherman, October 26, 1866, in *Grant Papers* 16:339–40n.

72 *Another congressman countered: The Independent*, March 29, 1866 (Wendell Phillips); *Chicago Tribune*, April 10, 1866; *Cong. Globe*, 39th Cong., 1st sess., p. 2849; Stevens to Robert C. Schenck, August 31, 1866, in *Stevens Papers* 2:191; Schenck to Stevens, September 23, 1866, ibid. 2:195.

72 *"Did we fight down the rebellion"*: Hamlin, pp. 510–11. Increasing interest in impeachment can be tracked in the correspondence of leading Radicals through 1866. W. Jones to Butler, May 18, 1866, Butler Papers, Box 40; H. Willis to Thaddeus Stevens, October 23, 1866, Stevens Papers, Box 4.

72 *Before a Brooklyn crowd: Chicago Tribune*, October 18, 1866 (reporting on Butler speech in Chicago), and November 28, 1866; Trefousse, *Butler*, p. 189; *Littell's Living Age* (November 17, 1866). At the same time as Butler's speech, Wendell Philips induced a "vast audience" in Philadelphia to begin "stomping" for Johnson's impeachment. R. D. Mussey to Butler, November 25, 1866, Butler Papers, Box 41. Another urgent proponent of impeachment in the fall of 1866 was Rep. James Ashley of Ohio. Robert F. Horowitz, *The Great Impeacher: A Political Biography of James M. Ashley*, New York: Brooklyn College Press (1979), p. 127.

73 *To another Radical: Washington Daily National Intelligencer*, November 24, 1866; Trefousse, *Thaddeus Stevens*, p. 203.

73 *His annual statement:* McPherson, pp. 143–47.

7. FALSE START ON IMPEACHMENT

74 *I do impeach: Cong. Globe*, 39th Cong., 2d sess., p. 320.

74 *"[T]he great war"*: Clemenceau, pp. 74–75 (January 5, 1867).

75 *Called "a calculating fanatic"*: William Lawrence to Butler, December 3, 1866, Butler Papers, Box 41; Horowitz, pp. 128–29; Welles Diary, vol. 3, p. 12.

75 *They poured in: New York Times*, January 7, 1867; National Archives, File HR 39A-H14.7-"Records of the Committee on the Judiciary" (containing petitions); E. B. Ward to Butler, January 27, 1867, in Butler Papers, Box 42 (reporting circulation of 30,000 petitions demanding Johnson's impeachment and removal from office).

75 *Nebraska but not Colorado: Cong. Globe*, 39th Cong., 2d sess., p. 344 (January 8, 1867); Trefousse, *Andrew Johnson*, pp. 273–74.

75 *"I approve your taking"*: Boutwell, *Reminiscences*, vol. 2, pp. 107–8; Moore Diary/AHR, p. 106 (March 4, 1867).

75 *For some time: Cong. Globe*, 39th Cong., 2d sess., p. 5 (December 3, 1866); *Chicago Tribune*, December 6, 1866.

76 *Stevens and his allies: Cong. Globe*, 39th Cong., 2d sess., pp. 547–48 (January 18, 1867), 943 (February 1, 1867).

76 *Even though the law:* Welles Diary, vol. 3, pp. 50, 54.

77 *Impeachment dates back:* Raoul Berger, "Impeachment for 'High Crimes and Misdemeanors,'" in *Impeachment: Selected Materials*, House Comm. on the Judiciary, 93d Cong., 1st sess. (October 1973), p. 621.

78 *Otherwise, as Ben Franklin:* Max Farrand, ed., *The Records of the Federal Convention of 1787*, New Haven: Yale University Press (1911), vol. 2, p. 65 (July 20, 1787).

78 *The Constitution devotes:* Article 1, Section 2, states, "The House of Representatives . . . shall have the sole power of impeachment." Article 1, Section 3 provides: "The Senate shall have the sole power to try all impeachments. When sitting for that purpose, they shall be on oath or affirmation. When the President of the United States is tried, the Chief Justice shall preside: And no person shall be convicted without the concurrence of two thirds of the members present." It also states that "Judgment in cases of impeachment shall not extend further than to removal from office, and disqualification to hold and enjoy any office of honor, trust or profit under the United States: but the party convicted shall nevertheless be liable and subject to indictment, trial, judgment and punishment, according to law."

Under Article 2, Section 2, "the President . . . shall have power to grant reprieves and pardons for offenses against the United States, except in cases of impeachment." Section 4 of Article 2 states that "the President, Vice President and all civil officers of the United States, shall be removed from office on impeachment for, and conviction of, treason, bribery, or other high crimes and misdemeanors."

79 *James Madison criticized:* Farrand, vol. 2, p. 550 (September 8, 1787).

79 *Others have argued:* Clinton Rossiter, ed., *The Federalist Papers*, New York: Mentor (1999), No. 77, p. 432; ibid., No. 79, p. 442.

79 *With little debate: Cong. Globe*, 27th Cong., 3d sess., pp. 144–46 (January 10, 1843); Robert J. Morgan, *A Whig Embattled, The Presidency Under John Tyler*, Hamden, CT: Archon Books (1974), pp. 53–54.

80 *After a five-week trial:* David Kyvig, *The Age of Impeachment: American Constitutional Culture Since 1960*, Lawrence: University Press of Kansas (2008), p. 25.

81 *"The President has usurped": New York Times*, January 19, 1867.

81 *Some Republican newspapers: New York Times*, January 11, 1867 (reprinting editorials from many newspapers).

81 *"There is nothing judicial or fair":* Welles Diary, vol. 3, p. 20 (January 14, 1867); John Nugent to S. L. M. Barlow, January 10, 1867, in Barlow Papers, Box 64.

81 *The House committee began:* Nugent to S. L. M. Barlow, January 10, 1867, in Barlow Papers, Box 64; E. B. Ward to Ben Butler, January 27, 1867, in Butler Papers, Box 42; Horowitz, p. 130.

81 *Supposedly, Mrs. Cobb:* "Impeachment Investigation," H. Rep. No. 7,

40th Cong., 1st sess., pp. 2–13 (testimony taken before the House Judiciary Committee, 1867).

82 *It also inquired:* Ibid., pp. 28–29, 45, 60–66.

82 *The government did not know:* Ibid., pp. 159–75, 183–86.

82 *When the Thirty-Ninth Congress expired: Cong. Globe,* 39th Cong., 2d sess., pp. 1754–55 (March 2, 1867).

83 *Ashley darkly told the House: New York Times,* March 7, 1867; *Cong. Globe,* 40th Cong., 1st sess., pp. 18–19.

83 *"I have had a son killed":* Welles Diary, vol. 3, p. 90 (May 4, 1867); Moore Diary/AJ, p. 33 (March 1867).

84 *The reaction in the South:* Perman, *Reunion Without Compromise,* pp. 270–71, 286–87.

84 *He reclaimed land:* "Interview with *Cincinnati Commercial* Correspondent," July 2, 1867, in *Johnson Papers* 12:368; Benedict, *Impeachment,* pp. 44, 90; McFeely, pp. 112–18, 128, 130, 294.

84 *The Republican congressmen:* Thomas and Hyman, pp. 542–44; Welles Diary, vol. 3, p. 105 (June 11, 1867); ibid., pp. 110–11 (June 20, 1867); *Washington Daily National Intelligencer,* May 28, 1867; U.S. Department of Justice, *Opinions of the Attorneys General* 12:141 (May 24, 1867); ibid., 12:182 (June 12, 1867); Michael Les Benedict, "From Our Archives: A New Look At the Impeachment of Andrew Johnson," *Political Science Quarterly,* 113:493 (1998).

84 *"The whole force":* Brooks D. Simpson, *Let Us Have Peace: Ulysses S. Grant and the Politics of War and Reconstruction, 1861–1868,* Chapel Hill: University of North Carolina Press (1991); Blaine, vol. 2, p. 294; Badeau, p. 65.

85 *He called for a time:* Welles Diary, vol. 3, p. 107 (June 14, 1867); *Cong. Globe,* 40th Cong., 1st sess., pp. 565–67 (July 10, 1867), 592–93 (July 11, 1867), 725, 730–32, 741–47 (July 19, 1867); Blaine, vol. 3, p. 294; "Veto of the Third Military Reconstruction Act," July 19, 1867, in *Johnson Papers* 12:416, 423.

85 *He called the investigation: Cong. Globe,* 40th Cong., 1st sess., p. 450 (March 29, 1867). In early March, Senator John Sherman of Ohio called the impeachment effort "a complete failure." John Sherman to William Sherman, March 7, 1867, in *Sherman Letters,* p. 289.

85 *Stevens predicted: New York Herald,* July 8, 1867.

85 *Smythe's employees kicked back:* Carman and Luthin, pp. 59–60.

86 *Smythe gained the plum position:* Cox and Cox, *Politics, Principle, and Prejudice,* p. 127.

86 *In mid-March, the committee chairman: Cong. Globe,* 40th Cong., 1st sess., pp. 120–23 (March 15, 1867).

86 *Smythe customarily received:* Mark Wahlgren Summers, *The Era of Good Stealings,* New York: Oxford University Press (1993), p. 91.

86 *He succeeded in riding out the storm:* Samuel Barlow to Ward, March 29, 1867, Barlow Papers, Box 64; House Report No. 30, 39th Cong., 2d sess.; *Cong. Globe*, 40th Cong., 1st sess., p. 394 (March 27, 1867); *Boston Daily Advertiser*, March 19, 1867; *Daily Cleveland Herald*, March 23, 1867; James B. Steedman to Johnson, March 22, 1867, in *Johnson Papers* 12:174.

8. THE DANGEROUS SPHINX

PAGE

87 *The President don't comprehend:* Sherman to Ellen Sherman, October 7, 1867, in Mark DeWolfe Howe, ed., *The Home Letters of General Sherman*, New York: Charles Scribner's Sons (1909), p. 361.

87 *"Grant quarrels with no one":* Tyler Dennett, ed., *Lincoln and the Civil War in the Diaries and Letters of John Hay*, New York, DaCapo Press (2000), p. 176.

88 *"I am disgusted":* Simpson, p. 149, quoting Sylvanus Cadwallader, "Four Years With Grant," unpublished manuscript in Illinois Historical Society library, pp. 186–87, 151.

88 *Abraham Lincoln described him:* George Meade, *Life and Letters of George Gordon Meade*, New York: Charles Scribner's Sons (1913), vol. 2, p. 191 (Meade to Mrs. Meade, April 24, 1864); William O. Stoddard, Jr., *William O. Stoddard: Lincoln's Third Secretary*, New York: Exposition Press (1955), p. 307.

88 *Ben Wade of Ohio:* Shelby Foote, *The Civil War: A Narrative*, New York: Random House (2006) (reissued), vol. 3, p. 12; *New York Times*, November 8, 1867.

88 *One of his officers:* Dana, *Recollections of the Civil War*, p. 61; James McPherson, *The Battle Cry of Freedom*, New York: Oxford University Press (1988), p. 721.

89 *Grant accepted all three changes:* Smith, *Grant*, p. 26; *Personal Memoirs of U. S. Grant*, New York: Charles L. Webster & Co. (1885), vol. 1, pp. 34–35; Smith, *Grant*, pp. 24–25.

89 *At final exercises:* James B. Fry, "An Acquaintance with Grant," *North American Review* 141:540 (1885).

90 *"For years afterward":* New York Times, July 24, 1885.

90 *An officer who served under Taylor:* Meade, vol. 2, p. 191 (April 24, 1864).

90 *"I do not know that I felt":* Grant to John Lowe, June 26, 1846, in *Grant Papers* 1:97.

90 *Within six years:* Grant's recent biographer, Jean Smith, provides a persuasive account both of his resignation from the army and his problems with alcohol. Smith, *Grant*, pp. 83–89.

90 *In a brief exchange:* Church, *Grant,* at 57.

91 *Another wrote home:* Horace Porter, *Campaigning with Grant,* New York: Century (1897), p. 16; T. Harry Williams, *McClellan, Sherman, and Grant,* New Brunswick: Rutgers University Press (1962), pp. 82–83 (quoting Charles Francis Adams, Jr.).

91 *General Grant is a great general:* Badeau, pp. 373–74; L. P. Brockett, *Our Great Captains: Grant, Sherman, Thomas, Sheridan, Farragut,* New York: Charles P. Richardson (1866), p. 175.

91 *"I am becoming impressed":* Welles Diary, vol. 3, pp. 15 (January 10, 1867), 177 (August 22, 1867), 244 (December 24, 1867).

92 *Grant, who was moved:* Testimony of Ulysses S. Grant before House Impeachment Committee, July 18, 1867, in *Grant Papers* 17:216–18; Badeau, pp. 35–36; Grant to Johnson, December 18, 1865, in *Grant Papers* 15:434–37. Just after the Southern surrender, Grant wrote his wife from North Carolina that "the suffering that must exist in the South the next year, even with the war ending now, will be beyond conception. People who talk of further retaliation and punishment, except of the political leaders, either do not conceive of the suffering endured already or they are heartless and unfeeling and wish to stay at home out of danger while the punishment is being inflicted." Grant to Julia Grant, April 25, 1865, in Badeau, p. 31.

92 *"early in the rebellion":* Grant to Elihu Washburne, August 30, 1863, in *Grant Papers* 9:217–18.

92 *Grant directed his commanders:* Grant to Thomas et al., December 26, 1865, in *Grant Papers* 16:69–70.

93 *Noting that Stanton:* Smith, p. 433, quoting Comstock Papers, Library of Congress; John Y. Simon, ed., *Personal Memoirs of Julia Dent Grant,* Carbondale: Southern Illinois University Press (1975), p. 165.

93 *Grant's senior aide:* Grant to Oliver O. Howard, January 18, 1867, in Badeau, p. 59; Welles Diary, vol. 3, pp. 42–43 (February 15, 1867); Smith, *Grant,* pp. 432–33; Grant to Elihu Washburne, March 4, 1867, in *Grant Papers* 17:76–77; Grant to Philip Sheridan, June 24, 1867, ibid., 17:196; Thomas and Hyman, p. 546; Badeau, p. 71.

94 *Wherever Grant went:* Badeau, pp. 62, 69; *Chicago Tribune,* August 8, 1867.

94 *When Johnson offered:* Moore Diary/AHR, pp. 107–8 (August 1, 1867).

94 *Sheridan, in short:* Sefton, p. 140; Badeau, p. 102; "Interview with *Cincinnati Commercial* Correspondent," July 2, 1867, in *Johnson Papers* 12:369–70; Welles to Johnson, August 4, 1867, in *Johnson Papers* 12:454.

95 *Indeed, those feelings:* Badeau, pp. 62, 95.

95 *Dismissal of Stanton and Sheridan:* Grant to Johnson, August 1, 1867, in *Grant Papers* 17:250–52.

95 *"Public considerations":* Moore Diary/AHR, p. 107; Welles Diary, vol. 3,

pp. 149–56 (August 2, 3, 1867); Stanton to Johnson, August 5, 1867, in *Johnson Papers* 12:461; Badeau, p. 90.

96 *"The turning point":* Moore Diary/AHR, p. 109.

96 *Removing Sheridan:* Grant to Johnson, August 17, 1867, in *Johnson Papers* 12:489–90.

96 *In a bitter letter:* Grant to Johnson, August 26, 1867, in *Grant Papers* 17:303.

96 *Grant asked to be excused:* Moore Diary/AHR, pp. 112–13 (August 28, 1867); Johnson to Grant, August 28, 1867, in *Johnson Papers* 12:519; "Statement from Andrew Johnson," October 12, 1867, ibid., 13:166–67.

97 *Now he pardoned:* "Second Amnesty Proclamation," September 7, 1867, in *Johnson Papers* 13:40; Order of August 26, 1867, ibid., 12:514; Johnson to Grant, August 26, 1867, ibid., 12:512–13.

97 *Similar demands came:* William A. Russ, Jr., "Was There Danger of a Second Civil War During Reconstruction?" *Mississippi Valley Historical Review* 25:39, 41 (June 1938), quoting *Missouri Democrat*, August 30, 1867; Schurz to Mrs. Schurz, August 31, 1867, in *Intimate Letters of Carl Schurz*, Joseph Schafer, ed., Madison: State Historical Society of Wisconsin (1928), p. 392; Brodie, p. 331, quoting Francis Lieber to Theodore W. Dwight, August 27, 1867, Lieber Papers, Huntington Library; Trefousse, *Andrew Johnson*, p. 300, quoting Fessenden to McCulloch, September 2, 1867, in McCulloch Papers, Library of Congress, Box 3; *Chicago Tribune*, August 21, 1867; *The Nation*, August 29, 1867; H. Taylor to Butler, August 28, 1867, and W. G. Upham to Butler, September 16, 1867, in Butler Papers, Box 43. Even the *New York Times*, ordinarily not anti-Johnson, began to denounce the president. *New York Times*, September 11, 1867.

97 *"I have always had an abiding confidence":* New York Times, November 14, 1867.

97 *The Democratic candidate:* Fishel, pp. 8, 18, 19–20, quoting *Boston Evening Transcript*, November 8, 1866; Foner, p. 313. The Frenchman Clemenceau observed that "any Democrat who did not manage to hint in his speech that the negro is a degenerate gorilla would be considered lacking in enthusiasm. The idea of giving political power to a lot of wild men, incapable of civilization, whose intelligence is no higher than that of animals! That is the theme of all the Democratic speeches." Clemenceau, p. 131 (November 1, 1867).

97 *Ben Wade, firmly committed:* New York Times, November 8, 1867.

98 *"I take the occasion":* New York Herald, November 7, 1867.

98 *Sherman spurned:* William Sherman to John Sherman, October 11, 1867, in Thorndike, *Sherman Letters*, p. 297.

98 *In a triumphal procession:* Clemenceau, p. 122 (October 4, 1867).

9. IMPEACHMENT, ROUND TWO

PAGE

100 *"They swept through the air":* Washington Daily National Intelligencer, November 18, 1867, reprinting *Boston Post* article of November 15, 1867; "Impeachment Investigation," H. Rep. No. 7, 40th Cong., 1st sess. (1867), pp. 1166–94; *New York World*, November 15, 1867.

101 *I have always believed:* Ellis, p. 169; Horowitz, pp. 133–40; *Impeachment Investigation*, pp. 1198–99.

102 *Churchill gave his reasons: New York Times*, December 6, 1867.

102 *The Associated Press: New York Times*, November 23, 1867; *Daily Cleveland Herald*, November 29, 1867; *New York Times*, November 30, 1867, reprinting November 29, 1867, article in the *Philadelphia Bulletin*.

102 *When he left Lancaster:* Stevens to Simon Stevens, August 3, 1867, in Stevens Papers, Box 4; Henry Carpenter to Stevens, November 17, 1867, in Stevens Papers, Box 4. Dr. Carpenter's remedies included:
- Taking three times a day the "tonic mixture in the vial," which could be omitted "if the stomach should become disturbed with weakness of appetite," in favor of "the vegetable tonic, infused with half a pint of boiling water, poured off after standing a few hours and a tablespoonful taken every 4 hours until better," when the tonic mixture could be resumed.
- If other ill effects should arise, "as indicated by the gray or ash coloured stools, a blue pill may be taken at bedtime and repeated next morning or evening as may be necessary."
- "If the effusion into the pericardium—or the dropsical affection of the heart, should increase—as you will know by the usual oppression, as experienced before, take one of the 'diuretic pills' at bedtime, and repeated every 6 to 8 hours if necessary, until relieved."
- "Take as much nourishing food as your stomach will comfortably receive and digest—with as much of the punch wine, brandy, whisky or beer, as may be necessary and agreeable."

103 *He could flash into coherence: New York World*, November 15, 1867 ("looks very feeble"); *Chicago Tribune*, November 23, 1867 ("more haggard and bloodless in the face"); *New York Herald*, November 20, 1867; *Washington Daily National Intelligencer*, November 18, 1867.

103 *When colleagues offered: New York Herald*, November 19 and 21, 1867; *New York Times*, November 22, 1867.

103 *"Why, I'll take that man's record":* Ben Perley Poore, *Perley's Reminiscences of Sixty Years in the National Metropolis*, Philadelphia: Hubbard Brothers (1886), vol. 2, p. 229.

103 *When the report: New York World*, November 26, 1867.

103 *In dealing with the former rebels:* House Rep. No. 7, 40th Cong., 1st sess., p. 2.

104 *One stated, for example:* The quoted language, included in the majority report, came from a popular constitutional treatise by George Ticknor Curtis—*History of the Origin, Formation, and Adoption of the Constitution of the United States*, New York: Harper & Row (1865), vol. 2, p. 261. Ironically, the author of the treatise was the brother of former Supreme Court Justice Benjamin Curtis, who would serve as one of Johnson's defense counsel in the impeachment trial. With unofficial help from brother George, Benjamin Curtis would argue the opposite position during the trial.

105 *Rather than contrive: The Nation* framed the problem: "Mr. Johnson is mischievous in this—that small, feeble, and insignificant though he be, the precautions which it is necessary to take against him are likely to become precedents, and to lead to serious changes in the character of the government." August 22, 1867, p. 150; Benedict, *Compromise*, pp. 292–93.

105 *Wilson, called by one newspaper: New York Times*, March 16, 1868.

106 *By rough force:* For example, Wilson pointed to the constitutional provision stating that an official, after removal by impeachment, may be prosecuted in a criminal court. That shows, Wilson proclaimed, that impeachment must be for a crime. Yet the Constitution does not *require* criminal prosecution of the removed official. Nor does it state that *only* a criminal offense may be the basis for impeachment. Rather, it preserves the possibility of a later criminal prosecution if the conduct at issue justifies it. Wilson also trumpeted the constitutional provision that "the trial of all crimes, except in cases of impeachment, shall be by jury." By placing impeachment and "crimes" in adjacent clauses, this statement proved to Wilson that impeachment can only be for a crime. But the constitutional language states only that criminal cases must be decided by juries *except* when an impeachment trial happens to include allegations of a crime. The provision does not exclude impeachment for noncriminal conduct. Finally, Wilson stressed the provision that the president's power to pardon "offences against the Constitution" does not apply "in cases of impeachment." Because Wilson thought "offences" could mean only crimes, he argued that this provision also limited impeachment to criminal offenses. But if the definition of impeachment offenses ("high crimes and misdemeanors") includes conduct *other* than crimes, then such conduct constitutes an "offence against the Constitution" that the president cannot pardon.

107 *One Republican congressman: Harper's Weekly*, December 14, 1867; *Chicago Tribune*, November 27, 1867. The *New York Times* gathered similar views expressed by newspapers in Providence; Albany; Springfield, Mas-

sachusetts; and Buffalo. *New York Times*, November 29, 1867; *New York Times*, December 3, 1867; Blaine, vol. 2, p. 343.

108 *Though Stevens continued to endorse: New York Herald*, November 26 and November 19, 1867; *Charleston Courier*, December 5, 1867; *Harper's Weekly*, October 19, 1867; Welles Diary, vol. 3, pp. 234 (October 19, 1867), 237–38 (November 30, 1867); "Memorandum to the Cabinet," November 30, 1867, in *Johnson Papers* 13:269–71; Farrand, vol. 2, pp. 612–13 (September 14, 1868). Senator Reverdy Johnson, a Maryland Democrat who argued and won the *Dred Scott* case in 1857, offered a constitutional attack on the notion that the president could be suspended from office pending an impeachment trial. *New York Times*, November 26, 1867. Congress never voted on the legislation. *Chicago Tribune*, February 10, 1868.

108 *In apocalyptic tones: Cong. Globe*, 40th Cong., 2d sess., p. 1 (December 3, 1867). Johnson's annual message was leaked to the press before Congress received it, which annoyed many congressmen. *New York World*, December 4, 1867. The source of the leak is not clear, though one Johnson aide sometimes sold exclusive stories to newspapers—Donald A. Ritchie, *The Press Gallery: Congress and the Washington Correspondents*, Cambridge, MA: Harvard University Press (1991), pp. 80–81—while Johnson met regularly with favored reporters to trade information.

108 *Although civil war should be avoided:* Remarkably, Johnson's annual message stated that "enormous frauds have been perpetrated on the Treasury, and colossal fortunes have been made at the public expense." *Cong. Globe*, 40th Cong., 2d sess., p. 4 (December 3, 1867), p. 4. That sort of confession rarely comes from an incumbent who has been managing the bureaucracy for almost three years. The president blamed the "enormous frauds" on the Tenure of Office Act, which required Senate action concurring in the dismissal of many officials. Though the statute surely had been an obstacle to dismissals of executive officials for the preceding eight months, the widespread fraud predated the law and thrived both with and without it.

108 *The telling consideration:* Some Republicans thought Johnson's message could provoke civil war. Moorfield Storey to his father, December 4, 1867, in M. A. DeWolfe Howe, *Portrait of an Independent: Moorfield Storey*, Boston: Houghton Mifflin Co. (1932), p. 47.

109 *He could be long-winded:* Julian, p. 312; *New York Times*, December 6, 1867; *New York Herald*, December 7, 1867; Blaine, vol. 2, p. 361; Brodie, p. 340.

109 *Over the next six months:* Boutwell, "The Usurpation," p. 508; Clemenceau, p. 175 (April 24, 1868); Ellis, p. 169. The only full biography of Boutwell is Thomas H. Brown, *George Sewall Boutwell: Human Rights Advocate*, Groton, MA: Groton Historical Society (1989). Navy Secretary

Welles wrote in his diary that Boutwell "is a fanatic, a little insincere, violent, and yet has much of the demagogic cunning." Welles Diary, vol. 3, p. 235 (October 23, 1867).

109 *After paying tribute:* Cong. Globe, 40th Cong., 2d sess., app., p. 54 (December 5, 1867).

110 *In a disingenuous opening:* Cong. Globe, 40th Cong., 2d sess., app., p. 63 (December 6, 1867).

111 *With Wilson and John Bingham:* New York World, December 9, 1867; New York Times, December 9, 1867; New York Herald, December 8, 1867; Chicago Tribune, December 21, 1867; Cong. Globe, 40th Cong., 2d sess., p. 66 (December 7, 1867).

111 *As remembered by:* Sherman, Recollections, p. 414.

112 *Two days before Boutwell began:* A political operative allied with Johnson, Cornelius Wendell, reported strong pro-Grant feelings in New England. He wrote from western Massachusetts: "Six weeks spent here and hereabouts satisfy me that Radical managers in this section will be forced to go Grant. The public voice is unanimous for him. Of hundreds whom I have listened to, not one dissentient have I heard." Wendell to Thurlow Weed, August 2, 1867, Seward Papers. New York Herald, November 12, 1867. Chicago Tribune, January 28, 1868; New York Herald, December 4, 1867; New York World, December 5, 1867. The New York Times hailed the "spontaneous uprisings for Gen. Grant, which are without precedent in our political history. They did not originate with politicians, and cannot be controlled by schemers." New York Times, December 4, 1867.

112 *That reasoning provoked:* One of the principal political sports of the day was speculating about what Grant's political views really were. New York Herald, November 12, 1867. Jacob William Schuckers, The Life and Public Services of Salmon P. Chase (1874), p. 548; Trefousse, Andrew Johnson, p. 303.

112 *If that argument could not be sustained:* That Boutwell had the better of the legal argument was reinforced a few days after the vote, when a Democratic congressman from Pennsylvania and former chief justice of that state's supreme court rose to speak. Having been persuaded by fellow Democrats to hold his tongue before the vote on the impeachment resolution, George Woodward seized the moment to outline his complete agreement with Boutwell's definition of an impeachable offense. Cong. Globe, 40th Cong., 2d sess., pp. 177–79 (December 13, 1867); Chicago Tribune, December 14, 1867.

112 *As a Republican remembered:* Anti-Slavery Standard, December 9, 1867, reprinted in New York Times, December 13, 1867; Blaine, vol. 2, p. 347. With one eye fixed on posterity, Stevens continued sitting for the teenage sculptress from Kansas, Vinnie Ream. Because he could no longer manage

stairs, he asked her to come to his home. Stevens to Vinnie Ream, December 10, 1867, Stevens Papers.

113 *No one ever accounted: Impeachment Money*, pp. 2–3.

10. IMPEACHMENT, ROUND THREE

PAGE

114 *I regard [the president]:* John Sherman to W. T. Sherman, March 1, 1868, *John Sherman's Recollections of Forty Years in the House, Senate, and Cabinet: An Autobiography*, Chicago: Werner Co. (1895), p. 424.

114 *The Freedmen's Bureau: Chicago Tribune*, January 4, 1868.

114 *In New York, financial titans:* Stephen Ambrose, *Nothing Like It In The World: The Men Who Built The Transcontinental Railroad, 1863–1869*, New York: Simon & Schuster (2000), pp. 261–306; *New York Times*, March 31 and April 16, 1868; Maury Klein, *The Life and Legend of Jay Gould*, Baltimore: Johns Hopkins University Press (1986), pp. 77–87.

115 *Soon Congress would have to appropriate:* Trefousse, *Andrew Johnson*, p. 288.

115 *New York newspapers: New York World*, November 21, 1867; *Boston Daily Advertiser*, December 10, 1867.

115 *To speed his manager's recovery: Washington Daily National Intelligencer*, January 11, 1867; *Washington Star*, January 10, 1867.

115 *The army arrested:* Richard G. Lowe, "Virginia's Reconstruction Convention," *Virginia Magazine of History and Biography* 80:341, 342 (1972); *New York Herald*, November 13, 1867. A delegate to the South Carolina Convention reported being "grossly insulted at the dinner table for being a member of a Yankee and Negro convention." C. Hopkins to T. Stevens, January 3, 1868, in Stevens Papers. The voting statistics for the elections of each Southern state convention are reproduced in an appendix in Perman, *Reunion Without Compromise*.

115 *State constitutional conventions: New York World*, November 16 and 20, 1867; Joseph B. James, *The Ratification of the Fourteenth Amendment*, Macon, GA: Mercer University Press (1984), pp. 234–35, 269; James E. Bond, *No Easy Walk to Freedom: Reconstruction and the Ratification of the Fourteenth Amendment*, Westport, CT: Praeger Publishers (1997), pp. 90, 108, 131; Bond, pp. 242–43.

116 *The state conventions:* Foner, pp. 316–33; Peggy Lamson, *The Glorious Failure: Black Congressman Robert Brown Elliott and the Reconstruction of South Carolina*, New York: W. W. Norton & Co. (1973), pp. 47–67; Jack B. Scroggs, "Carpetbagger Constitutional Reform in the Southern Atlantic States, 1867–68," *Journal of Southern History* 27:475 (1962).

116 *The injury did not limit:* Cowan, p. 8; Trefousse, *Andrew Johnson*, pp. 229, 285; *Hearings of Select Committee on Alleged Private Meetings of Mem-*

bers of the House with a View to a Corrupt Bargain with the President, National Archives, HR39A-F28.1; Testimony of William Warden, February 21, 1867, pp. 46–48; Testimony of Jerome Stillson, February 8, 1868, pp. 2–5, in Archives, *Impeachment: Various House Papers;* Glenna R. Schroeder-Lein and Richard Zuczek, *Andrew Johnson: A Biographical Companion*, Santa Barbara, CA: ABC Clio (2001), pp. 138–39.

117 *It is a misnomer:* Pope to Grant, December 30, 1867, *Grant Papers* 18:95–96; Peter Cozzens, *General John Pope: A Life for the Nation*, Urbana: University of Illinois Press (2000), pp. 294–95.

117 *"The rebels are rejoicing":* Foster Blodgett to Benjamin Butler, December 30, 1867, in Butler Papers, Box 44. For Pope's Reconstruction experiences, see Cozzens, pp. 276–95.

117 *In both Houses:* Welles Diary, vol. 3, p. 242 (December 19, 1867); Smith, *Grant*, pp. 444–45; Clemenceau, p. 139 (January 3, 1868).

118 *He concluded with the incontestable:* Johnson's report was printed in the *Senate Executive Journal*, vol. 16, pp. 95–105 (December 12, 1868). His assertion about Lincoln's approach to reconstruction is accurate, but quite incomplete. Johnson implies that the black codes and racial violence in the South would not have caused Lincoln to revise his policy—as, indeed, they had not caused Johnson to reevaluate his. It also assumes that Lincoln would have alienated congressional Republicans in the same fashion that Johnson had. On the New Orleans episode, Stanton acknowledged that he did not send to Johnson a message from the Louisiana army commander outlining his plans and asking for additional instructions. In arbitrary Stanton fashion, he did not respond to that commander because he could not think of any other action that should be taken. Stanton's biographers criticize him for this lapse, though it was consistent with the war secretary's practice of acting without consultation with superiors or colleagues. Thomas and Hyman, p. 496.

118 *On January 10, a Senate committee: Chicago Tribune*, December 15, 1867, January 11, 1868.

118 *Or, if Grant returned:* Johnson to Grant, January 31, 1868, in *Johnson Papers* 13:508–9; Simpson, p. 203.

119 *After discussing the law's penalties:* Grant to Johnson, February 3, 1868, in *Johnson Papers* 13:523; Welles Diary, vol. 3, pp. 259–60 (January 14, 1868); *Memoirs of Gen. W. T. Sherman*, p. 421.

120 *The full dimensions:* Grant to Johnson, January 28, 1868, *Johnson Papers* 13:502; Johnson to Grant, January 31, 1868, ibid., 13:508; Badeau, p. 111. Johnson's version of the conversation was described in congressional testimony by a favored reporter, Jerome Stillson of the *New York World*, who had been called in to receive and republish the president's side of the story. Archives, *Impeachment: Various Papers*, February 8, 1868.

120 *Grant and Johnson saw each other:* Grant to Johnson, January 28, 1868, in

Johnson Papers 13:502; Badeau, p. 111; *Memoirs of Gen. W. T. Sherman*, pp. 421–22. Johnson's interior secretary, Orville Browning, had proposed Governor Cox as war secretary several months before. Welles Diary, vol. 3, pp. 231–32 (October 8, 1867).

120 *Many Republican senators supported Stanton:* Senate Executive Journal, vol. 18, pp. 129–30 (January 13, 1868); *New York Herald,* January 14, 1868; Clemenceau, p. 140 (January 18, 1868).

120 *There, Grant sent a letter:* Ellis, p. 319; Badeau, pp. 111–12; Grant to Johnson, January 14, 1868, in *Johnson Papers* 13:468.

121 *Stanton spent the afternoon:* Simpson, pp. 228–29; Thomas and Hyman, p. 570; *Baltimore Sun,* January 15, 1868. Edward Townsend, *Anecdotes of the Civil War,* New York: D. Appleton & Co. (1884), p. 124; Sherman to Grant, January 27, 1868, *Grant Papers* 17:106n; *New York Herald,* January 15, 1868; *Cincinnati Gazette,* January 15, 1868.

121 *Navy Secretary Welles thought:* Browning Diary, vol. 2, pp. 173–75; Welles Diary, vol. 3, p. 261 (January 14, 1868).

121 *When other Cabinet members sided:* Gerry, p. 865; Badeau, p. 113.

121 *Stanton, master of the positive:* Grant to Sherman, January 29, 1868, in *Memoirs of Gen. W. T. Sherman,* p. 424; Simpson, pp. 231–32.

121 *Johnson preferred to leave:* Moore Diary/AHR, p. 117 (January 26, 1868).

122 *As for the Cabinet meeting: New York Herald,* January 15, 1868; *Chicago Tribune,* January 15, 1868; Archives, *Impeachment: Various House Papers* (testimony of Jerome Stillson, reporter for the *New York World*) (February 8, 1868), pp. 2–5. Another correspondent with access to Johnson reported that the president "has told me things that were not always in accordance with truth." Ibid., March 5, 1868 (testimony of W. Scott Smith), pp. 9–10; *Washington Daily National Intelligencer,* January 30, 1868; Badeau, p. 112; McPherson, p. 283; *Johnson Papers* 13:500.

122 *Another encouraged Johnson:* Ewing to Johnson, January 29, 1868, in *Johnson Papers* 13:502; Robert W. Latham to Johnson, January 29, 1868, ibid., 13:503.

122 *Unimpressed by the massed moral power:* Grant to Johnson, February 3, 1868, in *Johnson Papers* 13:524.

122 *Even some who disliked Johnson:* Clemenceau, p. 144 (January 24, 1868). Statements supporting Johnson from the Cabinet secretaries were read to the House of Representatives on February 11. The statement by Secretary of State Seward elicited laughter because of its evasiveness, while that of Navy Secretary Welles drew laughs because of its bellicosity. *Chicago Tribune,* February 12, 1868.

123 *In a question of veracity: New York Tribune,* January 17, 1868. Similar views were expressed by the *Boston Daily Advertiser* on January 17, 1868, and the *Chicago Tribune* on February 11 and 18, 1868. The *New York Times*'s correspondent wrote on February 15, 1868, that if the dispute

between Grant and Johnson were decided "as the Dutch Justice decided his cases, by counting up the number of witnesses on each side, and then deciding in favor of the party who had the greatest number, then unquestionably the President has the best of the case. But if it be decided according to the credibility of the witnesses, and the reasonable probabilities of what did occur, . . . then unquestionably General Grant stands fully vindicated."

123 *Within days, Stevens: Chicago Tribune*, February 5, 7, and 8, 1868; *New York Times*, February 5, 1868; Brodie, p. 333, citing *Philadelphia Ledger*, February 10, 1868; *New York Times*, February 6, 1868.

123 *He persuaded the House: Cong. Globe*, 40th Cong., 2d sess., p. 1087 (February 11, 1868).

123 *Now the Pennsylvanian:* The Judiciary Committee had taken testimony from the Washington correspondent of the *New York World*, a pro-Johnson paper, about how the president leaked information during the nasty exchanges with Grant. Archives, *Impeachment: Various House Papers*, Testimony of Jerome Stillson (February 8 and 11, 1868).

124 *After brandishing correspondence: New York Times*, February 15, 1868, reprinting from *Cincinnati Commercial*, February 10, 1868 (interview with "Mac," Joseph B. McCullagh).

124 *As summed up by old Thomas Ewing:* Welles Diary, vol. 3, p. 269 (February 5, 1868); Johnson to Grant, February 10, 1868, in *Johnson Papers* 13:547. The letters from Secretary of the Interior Browning, Treasury Secretary McCulloch, Postmaster General Randall, and Secretary of State Seward are in *Johnson Papers* 13:526–31, 532–34. Ewing to Ellen Ewing Sherman, February 15, 1868, in Ewing Family Papers. Ewing implored the president to take no action against Stanton. "It is better to let Stanton alone," he argued. "Public opinion is against him and his backers and by an imprudent act you may turn it in his favor." Ewing to Johnson, January 29, 1868, in *Johnson Papers* 13:502–3.

124 *As for "the question of veracity":* Undated memorandum, Stevens Papers, Box 6; *New York World*, February 14, 1868; *New York Herald*, February 14, 1868.

125 *His motion won: Cincinnati Gazette*, February 13, 1868; *Philadelphia Press*, February 13, 1868; Jerome Stillson to Samuel Barlow, February 12, 1868, in Barlow Papers, Box 68.

125 *Once more, he pronounced: Cincinnati Gazette*, February 14, 1868; *New York Herald*, February 14, 1868. Stevens also made more philosophical statements to the press about the loss, promising to revive impeachment when events warranted. *Philadelphia Press*, February 14, 1868; *New York Times*, February 14, 1868.

125 *His failure was so plain: Chicago Republican*, February 19, 1868. As Stevens pressed his impeachment initiative, the House of Representatives

was taking initial steps to consider impeachment of Supreme Court Justice Steven Field. At issue was a dinner-table conversation during which the judge was supposed to have stated that he opposed Negro suffrage and thought the government should follow a more "conservative" course. This was alleged to show prejudgment of the legal issues surrounding the Reconstruction Acts, which would be reviewed by the Supreme Court later that year. *Chicago Tribune*, February 5, 1868. The inquiry into Field's impeachment was dropped. *Cincinnati Gazette*, February 8, 1868; *Chicago Republican*, February 8, 1868; *New York Times*, February 5, 1868.

125 *Stevens's Reconstruction Committee:* Clemenceau, p. 138 (January 3, 1868); *Chicago Tribune*, January 12 and 24, 1868; *New York Herald*, January 19, 1868. *Cong. Globe*, 40th Cong., 2d sess., pp. 476–89, 664; (January 13, 1868); *New York Herald*, February 13 and 19, 1868.

125 *A reporter who visited:* Stillson to Barlow, February 12, 1868, in Barlow Papers, Box 68.

126 *To many Americans:* The *Boston Daily Advertiser* wrote on February 6, 1868, that Johnson's dispute with Grant was a "petty attempt to raise an issue of personal veracity on a collateral incident." Presidents, the newspaper continued, "have usually found more important and creditable business to occupy their time and thoughts." The *Chicago Tribune* wrote on that day that a "more miserable exhibition of official turpitude and littleness is not to be found in the history of the United States."

11. SHOWDOWN ON SEVENTEENTH STREET

PAGE

127 *The President called upon:* Clemenceau, p. 151 (February 28, 1868).

127 *His terms were so magnanimous:* Simpson, p. 96; Charles Bracelen Flood, *Grant and Sherman: The Friendship That Won The Civil War*, New York: Farrar, Straus & Giroux (2005), pp. 337–46.

128 *One Cabinet member:* Michael Fellman, "Lincoln and Sherman," in Gabor S. Borritt, ed., *Lincoln's Generals*, New York: Oxford University Press (1994), pp. 141, 142 (citing Sherman to John Sherman, April 26, 1863, in Sherman Papers); Lloyd Lewis, *Sherman: Fighting Prophet*, New York: Harcourt, Brace & Co. (1932), p. 303; Sherman to Salmon P. Chase, January 11, 1865, in Brooks D. Simpson and Jean V. Bertin, eds., *Sherman's Civil War: Selected Correspondence of William T. Sherman, 1860–1865*, Chapel Hill: University of North Carolina Press (1999), p. 795; Sefton, p. 23, quoting *Army and Navy Journal*, 4:514 (March 30, 1867), as reprinted from the *Worcester (MA) Spy*; W. Sherman to J. Sherman, February 23, 1866, in Thorndike, *Sherman Letters*, p. 263; Welles Diary, vol. 3, p. 163 (October 9, 1867). Sherman's racist views—which he mostly recanted at the end of his life—are discussed at length by Michael Fellman

in *Citizen Sherman: A Life of William Tecumseh Sherman*, New York: Random House (1995).

129 *Johnson's attorney general:* Ewing to Johnson, March 15, 1866, in *Johnson Papers* 10:257.

129 *"Washington is as corrupt as Hell":* Sherman to Ellen Ewing Sherman, May 8, 1865, in Howe, The *Home Letters of General Sherman*, p. 352.

129 *Stanton would be gone:* Moore Diary/AHR, February 19, 1868, p. 120 and January 26, 1868, p. 116.

129 *I have been with General Grant:* Sherman to Johnson, January 31, 1868, *Memoirs of Gen. W. T. Sherman*, p. 427.

130 *Johnson finally issued:* Welles Diary, vol. 3, p. 60 (March 6, 1867); Moore Diary/AHR, February 6, 7, and 8, 1868, p. 117; Johnson to Grant, February 12, 1868, in *Memoirs of Gen. W. T. Sherman*, p. 426.

130 *When Johnson received:* Sherman to Grant, February 14, 1868; Sherman to John Sherman, February 14, 1868; Sherman to Johnson, February 14, 1868, in *John Sherman's Recollections*, pp. 418–19; Johnson to Sherman, February 19, 1868, in *Memoirs of Gen. W. T. Sherman*, p. 433.

131 *To buoy his troops' flagging spirits:* Willard Sterne Randall, *George Washington: A Life*, New York: Henry Holt & Co. (1997), pp. 42–43.

131 *Johnson, Colonel Moore concluded:* Moore Diary/AJ, February 16, 1868, p. 87. Another Johnson aide also reported the president's fondness for *Cato*. Upon discovering that the aide knew the play, the president spoke more often with him. Cowan, p. 12. Though political leadership and literary taste are not necessarily related, Johnson's enthusiasm for the wooden *Cato* contrasts with Lincoln's devotion to Shakespeare's complex tragedies *Hamlet, Macbeth,* and *King Lear*. Lincoln's favorite speech from Shakespeare is delivered by Claudius, the uncle of Hamlet, as he despairs over how he murdered his brother. Johnson had no such taste for moral ambiguities.

131 *Navy Secretary Welles wondered: New York Times*, February 4, 1868, reprinting report from *New York Evening Post*, February 3, 1868; Welles Diary, vol. 3, p. 291 (February 24, 1868).

132 *Anticipating that both Potts:* Moore Diary/AJ, February 17, 1868, pp. 87–89.

132 *[Johnson] said he was determined:* Moore Diary/AJ, February 19, 1868, p. 93.

132 *One contemporary recalled Stanton:* Piatt, p. 58. Newsman Noah Brooks reported encountering Thomas in 1863 "with all his glory and epaulets on." Staudenraus, ed., p. 62.

132 *Stanton never flushed:* Michael T. Meier, "Lorenzo Thomas and the Recruitment of Blacks in the Mississippi Valley, 1863–1865," in John David Smith, *Black Soldiers in Blue*, Chapel Hill: University of North Carolina Press (2003); Fellman, "Lincoln and Sherman," pp. 141–42; Ezra Warner,

Generals in Blue, Baton Rouge: Louisiana State University Press (1994), p. 503; Handon B. Hargrove, *Black Union Soldiers in the Civil War*, Jefferson, NC: McFarland & Co. (1988), p. 89.

133 *On February 13, the president: Globe* Supp., pp. 136, 142 (April 10, 1868) (testimony of Lorenzo Thomas); Welles Diary, vol. 3, p. 279 (February 13, 1868); Johnson to Grant, February 13, 1868, in Archives, *Impeachment: Various House Papers; New York Herald*, February 15, 1868; Townsend, *Anecdotes of the Civil War*, p. 125. At the beginning of the Civil War, desperate for a command, Ulysses Grant wrote to Thomas for help, invoking their shared service in Mexico in the 1840s. Grant to Thomas, May 24, 1861, in Grant, *Memoirs*, vol. 1, pp. 239–40. Thomas never responded to Grant's plea. The delicacy of the adjutant general's position, and the ease with which he could make enemies, was illustrated by his experience with General William Sherman in 1861, when Sherman's erratic behavior led to his temporary removal from command. Sherman's wife—the sister-in-law of a senator, the daughter of Washington power Thomas Ewing—wrote to Lincoln accusing Thomas of being part of a "conspiracy" against her husband. Ellen Ewing Sherman to Lincoln, December 19, 1861, Sherman Papers, cited in Fellman, p. 136; Flood, p. 76. Neither episode would have endeared Thomas to General Grant.

134 *With conscious dignity:* Moore Diary/AJ, February 20, 1868, p. 93; ibid., February 21, 1868, p. 94; *Globe* Supp., p. 137 (April 10, 1868) (Thomas testimony). Johnson also ordered Moore to prepare papers promoting George H. Thomas to full general.

134 *The situation drove Navy Secretary Welles:* Welles Diary, vol. 3, p. 289 (February 22, 1868); Smith, *Grant*, p. 453; The *Chicago Tribune* wrote, "Upon comparing notes . . . it appears that everyone was taken by surprise by the President's action, not only the Republicans, but the Conservatives and Democrats, who are supposed to be in constant communication with Mr. Johnson."

134 *The general-in-chief added:* Thomas and Hyman, p. 585; *Globe* Supp., p. 137 (April 10, 1868) (testimony of Lorenzo Thomas).

135 *"Very well," the president said:* Townsend, p. 125; *Globe* Supp., p. 143 (April 10, 1868) (testimony of Lorenzo Thomas).

135 *The news struck "like a thunderbolt":* New York Times, February 22, 1868; *New York Herald*, February 22, 1868.

135 *Others sent messages:* Thomas and Hyman, p. 585; *New York Times*, February 22, 1868; *Baltimore Sun*, February 22, 1868.

135 *Radicals Ben Butler, George Boutwell: New York Herald*, February 22, 1868; *Cong. Globe*, 40th Cong., 2d sess., pp. 1329–30 (February 21, 1868); *Baltimore Sun*, February 22, 1868.

136 *"If you don't kill the beast":* Clemenceau, pp. 153–54; *New York Herald*, February 22, 1868.

136 *Political Washington: New York Times,* February 22, 1868; *Chicago Tribune,* February 23, 1868; *Baltimore Sun,* February 22, 1868. Senator Fessenden of Maine thought that the Senate's resolution on February 21 forced the House to impeach the president, making the Senate "responsible both as accuser and judge." Fessenden, p. 204 (letter of May 3, 1868).

136 *By 3 A.M.: New York Herald,* February 23, 1868; *Chicago Tribune,* February 23, 1868; *Philadelphia Press,* February 24, 1868.

136 *As one newspaper phrased it:* Archives, *Impeachment: Various House Papers* (testimony of John F. Coyle, April 11, 1868); *Globe* Supp., p. 53 (testimony of J. W. Jones, keeper of the stationery of the Senate); ibid., p. 71 (April 1, 1868) (testimony of Walter Burleigh, delegate from the Dakota territories); ibid., p. 75 (April 1, 1868) (testimony of Samuel Wilkeson); *Philadelphia Press,* February 25, 1868.

137 *It was a false alarm:* John M. Thayer, "A Night with Stanton in the War Office," *McClure's* 8:441–42 (March 1, 1897); *New York Herald,* February 24, 1868.

137 *"Either I am very stupid":* Fessenden, pp. 154–55.

12. THE DAM BURSTS

PAGE

138 *There was a widespread feeling:* Schurz, *Reminiscences,* vol. 3, p. 252.

138 *Two local merchants: Chicago Tribune,* February 23, 1868; *Globe* Supp., p. 140 (April 10, 1868) (testimony of Lorenzo Thomas). Thomas's bail was provided by George B. Hall, a coachmaker in Washington, and Elias A. Eliason, a tanner in Georgetown. *New York Times,* February 23, 1868; *Philadelphia Press,* February 24, 1868.

138 *After reporting to the attorney general:* Moore Diary/AJ, February 22, 1868, pp. 95–96; *Globe* Supp., p. 140 (testimony of Lorenzo Thomas).

139 *Thomas: I shall act as Secretary of War:* Townsend, pp. 126–27. Rep. Burt Van Horn from Niagara County, New York, was the scribe for the encounter. Also present in Stanton's office were Gen. Charles Van Wyck and Rep. Freeman Clarke of New York, Rep. G. M. Dodge of Iowa, Rep. J. K. Moorhead and Rep. W. D. Kelley of Pennsylvania, Rep. Columbus Delano of Ohio, Rep. Thomas Perry of Michigan, and Secretary Stanton's son, who served as his assistant.

140 *Pouring drinks: Globe* Supp., pp. 140–41.

140 *In the coming days:* Ibid., p. 141; *New York Herald,* February 23, 1868; Archives, *Impeachment: Various House Papers,* testimony of Lorenzo Thomas, pp. 10–11 (February 26, 1868).

140 *The spectacle smacked:* The *New York Herald* observed on February 25

that the removal of "an obnoxious Cabinet Minister . . . has never been questioned [before], much less characterized as a 'high crime and misdemeanor.' "

140 *Arriving in the midst: New York Herald*, February 22 and 23, 1868; *New York Times*, February 22, 1868; *New York Tribune*, March 2, 1868; *Chicago Tribune*, February 28, 1868. The *Baltimore Sun* reported on February 22 that "habitués of the Capitol say that for years there has not been such excitement as that of to-day," a remarkable judgment for a city that had endured four years of civil war that included several frights over possible assault by nearby Confederate armies.

141 *A number of congressmen: Chicago Tribune*, February 25, 1868; *New York Times*, February 25, 1868; *New York Herald*, February 24, 1868; *Baltimore Sun*, February 26, 1868; Russ, p. 39; *New York Times*, February 28, 1868.

141 *The* New York Herald *reported: New York Herald*, February 24, 1868.

141 *I hope you will quietly: New York Herald*, February 24 and 25, 1868; Logan Family Papers, February 22, 1868. Many years later, while a judge in California, former Gen. N. P. Chipman confirmed that after receiving Logan's note, he "organized the members of the Grand Army Posts and held them in readiness to rally at a signal in defense of Secretary Stanton or the Congress." N. P. Chipman to Mary Logan, June 5, 1907, Logan Family Papers.

141 *That evening, a reporter:* Mary Logan, *Reminiscences of the Civil War and Reconstruction*, Carbondale: Southern Illinois University Press (1970), p. 154; *Illinois Daily State Journal*, February 22, 1868; James Pickett Jones, *John A. Logan, Stalwart Republican from Illinois*, Carbondale: Southern Illinois University Press (1982), pp. 21–22; Townsend, p. 129; *New York Herald*, February 22 and 24, 1868; *The Independent*, February 27, 1868.

142 *During the evening the President: New York Herald*, February 26, 1868.

142 *Early in the crisis:* Thayer, pp. 438, 441; *New York Herald*, February 24, 1868; *Baltimore Sun*, February 22, 1868.

142 *Soon the newspapers: New York Times*, February 26, 1868; *New York Herald*, February 25, 1868.

143 *During an hour's recess: Cong. Globe*, 40th Cong., 2d sess., p. 1336 (February 22, 1868). This narrative draws on the contemporaneous reports, published on February 23, 1868, in the *New York Times*, the *New York Herald*, and the *Chicago Tribune*.

143 *He settled back: Philadelphia Press*, February 24, 1868; *New York Times*, February 23, 1868; *Chicago Tribune*, February 23, 1868; *Washington Daily National Intelligencer*, February 24, 1868. Ten days later, another newspaper proclaimed that the impeachment effort, for Stevens, was "the fountain of youth" that allowed him to "muster and bluster about the House with the vigor and energy of fifty." *Cincinnati Commercial*, March 5, 1868.

143 *He struck a threatening note: Philadelphia Press*, February 24, 1868. Navy Secretary Welles thought that Democratic leaders "secretly desire the conviction and deposition of the President." Welles Diary, vol. 3, p. 319, (March 23, 1868). *Cong. Globe*, 40th Cong., 2d sess., pp. 1336–37 (February 22, 1868).

144 *Third, that the Tenure of Office Act: Cong. Globe*, 40th Cong., 2d sess., pp. 1338–39 (February 22, 1868) (Rep. Brooks).

144 *A Tennessean won the prize: Globe* Supp., p. 1342 (Rep. Bingham) (February 22, 1868); p. 1348 (Rep. Kelley) (February 22, 1868); p. 1391 (Rep. Clarke) (February 24, 1868). *Globe* App., p. 189 (Rep. Newcomb) (February 22, 1868); *Globe* App., p. 160 (Rep. Plants); *Cong. Globe*, 40th Cong., 2d sess., p. 1396 (Rep. Shanks); ibid. (Rep. Stokes).

144 *The Republicans were "blind with rage": Globe* App., p. 249 (Rep. Demas Barnes); *Cong. Globe*, 40th Cong., 2d sess., p. 1397 (Rep. Eldridge), p. 1353 (Rep. Phelps), p. 1349 (Rep. Beck) (February 22, 1868); *Globe* App., p. 164 (Rep. Kerr) (February 24, 1868), p. 195 (Rep. Golladay).

144 *Would troops march:* Welles Diary, vol. 3, p. 289 (February 22, 1868).

145 *Assuring Johnson:* Archives, *Impeachment: Various House Papers*, testimony of Gen. William Emory (February 26, 1868); *Cong. Globe*, 40th Cong., 2d sess., Supp., pp. 79–80; *New York Times*, February 24, 1868.

145 *Senator Ben Wade of Ohio: Chicago Tribune*, February 23, 1868; *Philadelphia Press*, February 24, 1868; *New York Herald*, February 23 & 24, 1868.

145 *Johnson insisted that his course:* Cowan, p. 11; *New York Herald*, February 22, 1868; *Chicago Tribune*, February 23, 1868; *Philadelphia Press*, February 24, 1868; Moore Diary, February 22, 1868, p. 98.

145 *The Senate never did take up:* Moore Diary, February 22, 1868, p. 98; *Philadelphia Press*, February 24, 1868; *Washington Daily National Intelligencer*, February 24, 1868; Ward to Barlow, February 27, 1868, in Barlow Papers, Box 68. The *Chicago Tribune* reported on March 8 that the Senate Military Committee resolved not to act on the Ewing appointment until the impeachment proceedings were completed. Silvia Tsoldos, "The Political Career of Thomas Ewing, Sr.," Ph.D. thesis, University of Delaware (1977), p. 298.

146 *One newspaper gushed:* Lately Thomas, *Sam Ward, "King of the Lobby,"* Boston: Houghton Mifflin Co. (1965), p. 342; *Chicago Inter-Ocean*, February 20, 1875. A correspondent described Ward as "pudgy as a neatly cooked dumpling." *San Francisco Daily Evening Bulletin*, January 28, 1875; *Chicago Tribune*, May 29, 1868.

146 *One newspaper acknowledged: New York Times*, October 11, 1868.

147 *Though this was surely good advice: New York Times*, May 20, 1884; *New York Tribune*, May 20, 1884; *New York World*, May 20, 1884; Maude Howe Elliott, *Uncle Sam Ward and His Circle*, New York: The Macmillan Co.

(1938), p. 489. Johnson quickly leaned toward retaining as his lawyers both Attorney General Henry Stanberry of Ohio and Jeremiah Black of Pennsylvania. *New York Times*, February 25, 1868. Black had served as attorney general in the last Democratic administration, that of James Buchanan, while Stanberry had been a Whig (precursor to the Republican Party). Stanberry also was a former law partner of Thomas Ewing, Sr., who served in the Cabinets of two Whig administrations and was one of Johnson's few trusted advisers.

147 *Cherokee Chief John Ross:* Craig Miner and William E. Unrau, *The End of Indian Kansas*, Lawrence: University of Kansas Press (2d ed., 1990), pp. 64–65; Annie Louise Abel, *The American Indian and the End of the Confederacy, 1863–1866*, Lincoln: University of Nebraska Press (1993; originally 1925), pp. 70–71, 82–97, 280; John Ross to Johnson, June 28, 1866, in *Johnson Papers* 10:634.

147 *To prove his dedication:* Miner and Unrau, pp. 64–65; Report of Kansas Legislature Joint Committee to Investigate Senatorial Elections, February 24, 1872, excerpted in Daniel W. Wilder, *Annals of Kansas*, Topeka: Geo. W. Martin, Kansas Publishing House (1872), pp. 572–74; *Report of the Joint Committee of Investigation, Appointed by the Kansas Legislature of 1872*, Topeka, KS: S. S. Prouty, Public Printer (1872), pp. 195, 162, 243, 253 (testimony that Perry Fuller paid as much as $40,000 to secure the election of Edmund G. Ross to the Senate); H. B. Denman to Thomas Ewing, Jr., January 12, 1868, Thomas Ewing Family Papers, Box 74; *Chicago Tribune*, September 1, 1868; *Rea v. Missouri*, 84 U.S. 532 (1873); Fuller to Johnson, December 30, 1867, in *Johnson Papers* 13:382–83; Daniel Voorhees to Johnson, January 24, 1868, ibid., pp. 494–95; Fuller to Johnson, January 25, 1868, ibid., pp. 495–96.

148 *Adjutant General Thomas:* *New York Times*, February 24, 1868; Moore Diary/AJ, February 23, 1868, p. 99; Archives, *Impeachment: Various House Papers*, testimony of Lorenzo Thomas (February 26, 1868), p. 13.

148 *From ten in the morning:* *New York Herald*, February 25, 1868; *New York Times*, February 25, 1868.

149 *They were choosing: Cong. Globe*, 40th Cong., 2d sess., p. 1400 (February 24, 1868).

149 *When the tally was announced: New York Herald*, February 25, 1868.

149 *Stevens, Boutwell, and Bingham: Cong. Globe*, 40th Cong., 2d sess., p. 1402 (February 24, 1868).

149 *Not for several more days:* Thomas and Hyman, pp. 595–96, citing the sergeant's reminiscences in the *New York Commercial Advertiser* of March 24, 1903.

150 *"Make your calculations":* Ward to Barlow, February 25, 1868, in Barlow Papers, Box 68.

13. THE WATERLOO STRUGGLE

PAGE

151 *If he was impeached:* Fessenden, vol. 2, p. 184 (March 31, 1868, letter to his cousin).

151 *The president, he intoned:* J. W. Binckley, "The Leader of the House," *Galaxy* 1:496 (July 1866); *The Independent,* February 27, 1868; *Cong. Globe,* 40th Cong., 2d sess., p. 1399 (February 24, 1868).

152 *The falling snow: Chicago Tribune,* February 26, 1868; Briggs, p. 44; Ellis, pp. 92–93.

153 *Wade appointed a committee: New York Times,* February 26, 1868; *Cong. Globe,* 40th Cong., 2d sess., pp. 1405–6 (February 25, 1868).

153 *Then Stevens lay down: Chicago Tribune,* February 26, 1868; *Cong. Globe,* 40th Cong., 2d sess., p. 1421 (February 25, 1868); *Boston Advertiser,* February 26, 1868.

153 *The committee members braved: Chicago Tribune,* February 25, 1868.

153 *Asked if he still despised: Baltimore Sun,* February 26, 1868; *New York Times,* February 26, 1868; *New York Times,* February 26, 1868.

154 *[T]here was not a moment:* Francis A. Richardson, "Recollections of a Washington Newspaper Correspondent," *Records of the Columbia Historical Society,* Washington, D.C., 1903, pp. 24, 37.

154 *The facts, though:* Archives, *Impeachment: Various House Papers.* Transcripts of testimony by General Emory and his second, Colonel George Wallace, appeared in the *New York Herald* on March 1, and the *New York Times* on March 2, 1868; *New York Times,* February 25, 1868.

154 *Looking thin and haggard:* Beauregard, p. 126, quoting diary of Rep. George Julian, March 1, 1868, Indiana State Library, Indianapolis (March 1, 1868); Julian, p. 314. George Boutwell remembered that Stevens's "health was much impaired, but his intellectual faculties were free from any cloud." Boutwell, *Reminiscences,* vol. 2, p. 120.

154 *Reviving those claims: New York Times,* February 28, 1868, and February 27, 1868.

155 *No one thought: New York Times,* February 26 and 27, 1868.

155 *When Thomas called for his mail: New York Times,* February 27, 1868; Townsend, p. 130; Thomas and Hyman, pp. 597–98.

155 *As the Radical* Philadelphia Press: *Philadelphia Press,* March 2, 1868; *New York Times,* February 28, 1868; Gerry, p. 863.

156 *The case was destined: New York Times,* February 28 and 29, 1868.

156 *As* The Nation *observed: The Nation* 6:166 (February 27, 1868).

157 *Having many overlapping: Cong. Globe,* 40th Cong., 2d sess., pp. 1542–44 (February 29, 1868).

157 *That Emory's testimony:* During the debate, one New York Democrat

found that the impeachment article based on General Emory's testimony "is considered by all candid minds as amounting to nothing and the charges utterly frivolous." Jerome Mushkat, "The Impeachment of Andrew Johnson: A Contemporary View," *New York History* 48:278 (1967) (Rep. Pruyn's diary, February 29, 1868).

158 *Boutwell betrayed no embarrassment:* Storey to his father, March 3, 1868, in Howe, *Portrait of an Independent,* p. 77.

158 *A Democrat denounced: Cong. Globe,* 40th Cong., 2d sess., p. 1554 (Rep. Burr) (February 29, 1868); pp. 1554–55 (Rep. Morgan) (February 29, 1868); p. 1563 (Rep. Loughridge) (February 29, 1868); p. 1549 (Rep. Lawrence); pp. 1557–58 (Rep. Mullins); pp. 1553–54 (Rep. Stevens of New Hampshire); p. 1545 (Rep. Bromwell); p. 1544 (Rep. Burr) (February 29, 1868); p. 1563 (Rep. Kerr).

159 *The House then approved: Cong. Globe,* 40th Cong., 2d sess., pp. 1612–18 (March 2, 1868); *Chicago Tribune,* March 3, 1868. The seventh draft impeachment article was dropped. *New York Times,* March 2, 1868.

159 *On a second ballot: Chicago Tribune,* March 2, 1868; *New York Times,* February 29, 1868.

160 *With his head set: New York Times,* March 2, 1868; *Chicago Tribune,* March 2, 1868; Hans L. Trefousse, *Ben Butler: The South Called Him BEAST!,* New York: Twayne Publishers (1957), p. 18; George R. Agassiz, ed., Theodore Lyman, *Meade's Headquarters, 1864–1865,* Boston: Atlantic Monthly Press (1922), p. 192.

160 *One war-derived nickname:* Louis Taylor Merrill, "General Benjamin Butler in the Presidential Campaign of 1864," *Mississippi Valley Historical Review* 33:537 (March 1947); Trefousse, *Ben Butler,* pp. 111, 121, 154.

161 *Many, however, doubt:* Benjamin F. Butler, *Butler's Book,* Boston: A. M. Thayer & Co. (1892), pp. 633–35; Butler, "Vice Presidential Politics in '64," *North American Review* 151:331–35 (October 1885); Alexander McClure, *Abraham Lincoln and Men of War Times,* Philadelphia: Times Publishing Co. (1892), p. 118; Merrill (see the previous note). The doubters include Murray M. Horowitz, "Benjamin F. Butler: Seventeenth President," *Lincoln Herald* 77:191 (1975), and Don E. Fehrenbacher, "The Making of a Myth: Lincoln and the Vice-Presidential Nomination in 1864," *Civil War History* 41:273 (1992).

161 *One Republican was not surprised:* Blaine, vol. 2, p. 289.

161 *Thought by many:* Benedict, *Compromise,* p. 35. Stevens took a distinctly astringent view of the cross-eyed congressman from Massachusetts, calling him "a false alarm, at once superficial, weak and impracticable. Indeed, a 'humbug.'" *New York Herald,* July 11, 1867; Brodie, p. 397 n. 43.

161 *Butler replied: Cong. Globe,* 40th Cong., 1st sess., pp. 262–63 (March 21, 1867).

161 *Drawing on the rich store:* Ibid., p. 364 (March 26, 1867).

161 *"I'll be damned":* New York Herald, March 3, 1868.

161 *Because Bingham led:* Cong. Globe, 40th Cong., 2d sess., pp. 1619–20 (March 2, 1868); Boutwell, *Reminiscences*, p. 120; Benedict, *Impeachment*, pp. 113–14; *Butler's Book*, p. 927.

162 *The full House was restrained:* New York Times, March 4, 1868; Cong. Globe, 40th Cong., 2d sess., pp. 1639–42 (March 3, 1868); New York Times, March 4, 1868.

162 *Even if there is no two-thirds majority:* Cong. Globe, 40th Cong., 2d sess., p. 1642 (March 3, 1868); Washington Daily National Intelligencer, March 4, 1868; Trefousse, *Impeachment*, p. 138; Archives, *Managers' Journal*. This pattern can be seen in the two impeachment articles voted against President Clinton in 1999, both of which mingled unrelated allegations of wrongdoing. The impeachment trial of Judge Halsted Ritter in 1936 vividly illustrates this dubious practice. Judge Ritter, who sat in the Southern District of Florida, faced six specific impeachment articles and a seventh catchall article that gathered together the allegations in the first six. The Senate acquitted him on the first six articles but convicted him on the last. Elizabeth B. Bazan, "Impeachment: An Overview of Constitutional Provisions, Procedure, and Practice," Congressional Research Service, February 27, 1998, p. 25.

163 *Bingham read through:* New York Herald, March 5, 1868; Philadelphia Press, March 5, 1868; Chicago Tribune, March 5, 1868; Cong. Globe, 40th Cong., 2d sess., pp. 1647–49 (March 4, 1868); Zion's Herald, March 12, 1868.

164 *Johnson's short remarks:* Browning Diary, vol. 2, p. 183 (February 28, 1868); Blaine, vol. 2, p. 362; New York Herald, February 27, 1868.

164 *The president also consulted:* New York Times, February 25, 1868.

164 *Three Republican senators:* James Dixon of Connecticut, James Doolittle of Wisconsin, and Daniel Norton of Minnesota. Benedict, *Impeachment*, p. 127.

164 *"I will do nothing of the kind":* Moore Diary/AJ, February 29, 1868, p. 123.

165 *"Nothing is being done":* New York Times, March 7, 1868; Petersburg (VA) Index, March 30, 1868.

165 *In Philadelphia and Cincinnati:* New York Herald, February 26, 1868; New York Times, February 25 and 26, 1868; Washington Daily National Intelligencer, March 3, 1868.

165 *The nation's financial market:* The Nation, 6:161 (February 27, 1868). Senator Sherman of Ohio found it "strange" that the impeachment proceedings "have so little effect on prices and business. The struggle has been so long that the effect has been discounted." Thorndike, *Sherman Letters*, p. 315.

165 *There was room:* Philadelphia Press, March 2, 1868.

165 *Through the week when the House:* New York Times, February 29, 1868; *Philadelphia Press*, March 2, 1868; *Chicago Tribune*, March 2, 1868.

166 *Wherever society met:* Mary Logan, *Reminiscences*, pp. 156–59.

166 *The war secretary, ever the pedant:* Thomas and Hyman, p. 575.

166 *A sure sign of reduced tensions:* Philadelphia Press, March 4, 1868.

166 *Each sent his orders:* Townsend, p. 131; Archives, *Impeachment: Various House Papers*, testimony of Col. William Moore, pp. 35–36, 43, 45 (March 12, 1868).

166 *As for the reports:* Thomas and Hyman, p. 599.

166 *Yet the specter:* Chicago Tribune, March 2, 1868; *New York Times*, February 25, 26, 28, and 29, 1868; *New York Herald*, February 25, 1868; Henry J. Harker to Wade, March 5, 1868, in Wade Papers, Reel 7; S. Barnett to C. A. Trowbridge, March 14, 1868, in Wade Papers, Reel 7 (proposing candidate for secretary of the treasury); Briggs, p. 50; *New York Herald*, February 26, 1868; Welles Diary, vol. 3, p. 293 (February 25, 1868).

14. SEND IN THE LAWYERS

167 *We are all nervous:* Medill to John Logan, March 18, 1868, Logan Family Papers, Box 2.

167 *John Bingham led:* McClure, *Lincoln and Men of War-Times*, p. 270; *Ex Parte Milligan*, 71 U.S. 2 (1866); Beauregard, *Bingham of the Hills*, p. 126.

168 *He missed meetings:* Butler's Book, p. 927. According to the committee's journal, Stevens missed five sessions in March alone. Archives, *Managers' Journal*. Stevens was reported to be "perilously ill" on March 10 by the *New York Tribune*, and again by the *Philadelphia Press* on March 17, 1868.

168 *Even with Stanton:* Archives, *Impeachment: Various House Papers* (transcripts of testimony); *Chicago Tribune*, March 12, 1868; *New York Times*, March 13, 1868; Stanton to Butler, March 11, 1868; Stanton to Butler, March 17, 1868; Butler to Bingham, March 21, 1868, in Butler Papers, Box 44.

169 *Distracted from their studies:* New York Times, March 23, 1868, reprinting letter to *Cincinnati Commercial*, March 16, 1868.

170 *Butler issued:* Philadelphia Press, March 11 and 13, 1868; *New York Times*, March 13, 1868; *New York Times*, March 26, 1868, reprinting letter from the *Salem (MA) Gazette*, March 16, 1868.

170 *hell's blackest imp:* Briggs, p. 35; John Forney, *Anecdotes of Public Men*, New York: Harper & Brothers (1881) (reprinted, Da Capo Press, 1970),

p. 82; Murray M. Horowitz, "Benjamin F. Butler: Seventeenth President," *Lincoln Herald* 77:193 (winter 1975), quoting David Macrae, "The Americans at Home," (Edinburgh, 1870), at 370n.

171 *Perhaps as important:* Welles Diary, vol. 1, p. 365 (August 22, 1865); George F. Hoar, *Autobiography of Seventy Years*, New York: Charles Scribner's Sons (1903), p. 329; Blaine, vol. 2, p. 289.

171 *His colleagues fell for it: Butler's Book*, pp. 927–28.

171 *When the defense: Globe* Supp., pp. 8–9 (March 13, 1868).

171 *It was a blunder:* A perceptive dissection of Butler's trial strategy appears in a pamphlet, George P. Brockway, *Political Deals That Saved Andrew Johnson*, New York: Coalition of Publishers for Employment (1977).

173 *He resigned that post:* Moore Diary/AHR, p. 123 (March 10 and 11, 1868); Stanberry to Johnson, March 11, 1868, in *Johnson Papers* 13:647.

173 *The last lawyer: Washington Daily National Intelligencer*, March 4, 1868 (Curtis at White House); *New York Times*, March 7, 1868 (Groesbeck at White House); Browning Diary, vol. 2, p. 185 (March 7, 1868). Some Republicans hoped that Evarts would refuse to act as Johnson's counsel, but were disappointed. *Chicago Tribune*, March 8, 1868; *The Independent*, May 14, 1868; Chester Leonard Barrows, *William M. Evarts, Lawyer, Diplomat, Statesman*, Chapel Hill: University of North Carolina Press (1941), p. 141.

174 *One Cabinet member called: Washington Daily National Intelligencer*, March 12, 1868, reprinting interview in *New York World* on March 11, 1868; Welles Diary, vol. 3, p. 311 (March 12, 1868).

175 *Stanton was not protected:* Stuart Streichler, *Justice Curtis in the Civil War Era*, Charlottesville: University of Virginia Press (2005), p. 172; George Ticknor Curtis, *A Memoir of Benjamin Robbins Curtis, LL.D.*, Boston: Little, Brown & Co. (1879), vol. 1, pp. 409–10; *Globe* Supp., pp. 12–18 (March 23, 1868).

175 *Stanberry had no idea:* Moore Diary/AHR, p. 124 (March 16, 1868).

175 *In Cabinet meetings:* Moore Diary/AHR, p. 123 (March 14, 1868); p. 125 (March 17, 1868); p. 127 (March 19, 20, 21, and 22, 1868); p. 128 (March 25, 1868); *New York Times*, March 18, 1868; Welles Diary, vol. 3, pp. 313 (March 14, 1868), 315 (March 17, 1868).

175 *Johnson bade Black farewell:* Cowan, p. 11; Moore Diary/AHR, March 21, 1868; p. 128 (March 24, 1868). Black's withdrawal was explained in the press as well. *New York Herald*, March 25, 1868. A few years later, Black defended Secretary of War William Belknap against impeachment charges based on bribes from an Indian trader. Belknap resigned after the House of Representatives approved an impeachment resolution, but the Senate conducted a trial anyway, falling short of the two-thirds majority required for conviction. Several senators voted to acquit because they thought the

Senate had no jurisdiction to try a former official. *Perley's Reminiscences*, vol. 2, p. 313; "Impeachment: Selected Materials," House Judiciary Committee, 93d Cong., 1st sess. (October 1973), p. 717.

175 *Their task may have been:* Moore Diary/AHR, p. 127 (March 22, 1868).

176 *The blacks in the rotunda: New York Times*, March 11, 13, and 24, 1868; *New York Herald*, March 5, 1868; *Washington Daily National Intelligencer*, March 15, 1868 ("Every body remarks the unusual absence of the African"); *Philadelphia Press*, March 14, 1868 ("no colored people were present, and it is understood that no applications for tickets were made by them").

177 *The debate blew itself out: Cong. Globe*, 40th Cong., 2d sess., pp. 1671–81, 1701 (March 5, 1868); *New York Times*, March 6 and 7, 1868; *New York Herald*, March 6, 1868.

177 *The reaction was amplified: New York Herald*, March 5, 1868; Senate Misc. Doc. No. 43, 40th Cong., 2d sess. (Letter from the Hon. S. P. Chase, Chief Justice, March 4, 1868).

178 *Chase's "theology is unsound":* Goodwin, pp. 17–18, 34–43; Piatt, pp. 96, 97; Dennett, p. 53.

179 *Chase hedged his bets:* Goodwin, p. 634; Julian, *Political Recollections*, p. 236; Robert B. Warden, *An Account of the Private Life and the Public Services of Salmon Portland Chase*, Cincinnati: Wilstach, Baldwin & Co. (1874), pp. 669–70; Warden, p. 681 (Chase to J. E. Snodgrass, March 16, 1868); Perman, *Reunion Without Compromise*, p. 255; John Hanxhurst to Elihu Washburne, March 23, 1868, in Washburne Papers, vol. 58; Warden, pp. 669–70 (in an August 5, 1867, letter to Horace Greeley, Chase reported discussing with President Johnson the constitutionality of the Reconstruction Acts, an issue that certainly would come before the Supreme Court), p. 681 (March 18, 1868 letter to J. Snodgrass); *Cincinnati Commercial*, March 22, 1868; Frederick Bancroft, "Some Radicals as Statesmen: Chase, Sumner, Adams, and Stevens," *Atlantic Monthly* 86:279 (August 1900).

179 *He has an unhappy way:* Carl Schurz to Mrs. Schurz, April 12, 1868, in *Intimate Letters*, p. 433. A Radical newspaper described Chase as "mad with Presidential fever and . . . meanly jealous of Wade, and, perhaps, cherishing the forlorn hope of a Democratic nomination." *Anti-Slavery Standard*, March 9, 1868.

179 *Republican senators:* Thomas W. Egan to Johnson, October 7, 1867, in *Johnson Papers* 13:141. There was a further awkwardness to having Chase preside over the pretrial proceedings in March. At the beginning of the month, the Supreme Court heard four days of argument in *Ex Parte McCardle*, a case that might define Reconstruction. In the fall of 1867, the Army arrested William McCardle, editor of the *Vicksburg Times*, for editorials denouncing army commanders as "infamous, cowardly, and aban-

doned villains" who should be jailed. Pursuing a writ of habeas corpus—the device Lorenzo Thomas had wanted to use to challenge the Tenure of Office Act—McCardle argued that the Reconstruction laws violated his rights by subjecting him to army power. Johnson actively helped McCardle. One of the president's lawyers, Jeremiah Black, represented the editor, and Attorney General Stanberry refused to defend the government in the case. Congress authorized the secretary of war to retain a lawyer to defend the statute. Stanton hired Senator Lyman Trumbull of Illinois. After twelve hours of argument before the Court, Republicans feared a ruling that would derail Reconstruction. Charles Fairman, *Reconstruction and Reunion, Part One*, New York: Macmillan Publishing Co. (1971), pp. 437–40; *Chicago Tribune*, March 3, 1868; *Washington Daily National Intelligencer*, March 26, 1868.

Trumbull contrived a legislative evasion. With Congress about to approve a law on Supreme Court jurisdiction over tax cases, Trumbull inserted legislative language eliminating the Court's power to hear habeas corpus appeals. House Manager Wilson, chair of the Judiciary Committee, slipped the bill through the House in mid-March without describing it. Asked a week later why he had not explained it, Wilson replied that he would "never trouble the House with any unnecessary remarks." *Cong. Globe*, 40th Cong., 2d sess., p. 2060 (March 21, 1868); *New York Times*, March 16, 1868; Fairman, p. 464. The *New York Times* reported on March 23 that House Democrats complained "good-humoredly that they had been caught napping."

The president was not caught napping. He vetoed the bill, but Congress overrode his veto. The Court, having not yet decided McCardle's case, scheduled reargument on the question whether Congress had the power to eliminate habeas corpus appeals. *Cong. Globe*, 40th Cong., 2d sess., pp. 2128 (March 26, 1868), 2170 (March 27, 1868). The Court ultimately upheld Congress on that question. *Ex Parte McCardle*, 74 U.S. 506 (1869).

179 *And Thaddeus Stevens:* Moore Diary/AHR, March 14, 1868, p. 122; *Philadelphia Press*, March 17, 1868.

179 *"People who never could":* New York Herald, March 14 and 29, 1868.

180 *Baron Gerolt: Washington Daily National Intelligencer*, March 15, 1868.

180 *During a recess: New York Herald*, March 14, 1868; *Philadelphia Press*, March 14 and 24, 1868; *New York Times*, March 24, 1868.

180 *They set the trial's opening day: Globe* Supp., p. 8 (March 13, 1868), p. 25 (March 23, 1868), p. 29 (March 24, 1868).

15. INFLUENCE AND EDMUND COOPER

181 *I told him:* Testimony of James Legate before House Impeachment Committee, May 22, 1868, p. 11, in Butler Papers, Box 175.

182 *Newspapers across the country: Anti-Slavery Standard,* March 2, 1868, March 9, 1868; *New York Times,* April 6, 1868, reprinting report in *Baltimore Sun,* April 3, 1868; *Charleston (SC) Courier,* April 9, 1868, reprinting report from *New York World,* April 1, 1868; Benedict, *Compromise,* p. 299; Storey to his father, March 17 and April 19, 1868, in Howe, *Portrait of an Independent,* pp. 78, 97–98; *New York Herald,* April 11, 1868; Edmond L. Goold to Barlow, March 21, 1868, Barlow Papers, Box 66; *The Independent,* April 9, 1868; Colfax to Young, April 9, 1868, Young Papers.

182 *Once impeachment proceedings began:* Schuyler Colfax to John Russell Young, April 16, 1868, Young Papers; Benedict, *Compromise,* p. 299. Fowler, a teacher, strongly supported Andrew Johnson's pro-Union stance in late 1860. While Johnson was military governor of Tennessee, Fowler was his comptroller. He also was a floor leader for Johnson at the 1864 Republican Convention. Clifton H. Hall, *Andrew Johnson, Military Governor of Tennessee,* Princeton, NJ: Princeton University Press (1916), p. 42; Walter T. Durham, "How Say You, Senator Fowler?" *Tennessee Historical Quarterly* 42:43–45 (1983).

182 *He came from:* William G. Brownlow to Johnson, June 8, 1865, in *Johnson Papers* 8:200; "A Distinguished Tennessean, Hon. Edmund Cooper," www .usgennet.org/usa/ga/county/macon/newspapers/CV/cv1911pg_14.htm; Archibald Yell Smith Memories, in "Tullahoma Time Table," published by the Tullahoma Historical Preservation Society, October 1989, http:// drbobyoung.net/Dad%20Website/unpublished/page3.htm.

183 *Despite a period of detention: Hinds County Gazette,* November 10, 1869; James Patton, *Unionism and Reconstruction in Tennessee,* Gloucester, MA: Peter Smith (1966; originally 1934), p. 34; Edmund Cooper to D. B. Cooper, October 20, 1862, and December 10, 1862, in Cooper Family Papers, Box 8.

183 *Cooper artfully called:* Francis C. LeBlond to Johnson, February 8, 1867, in *Johnson Papers* 12:16; *Cong. Globe,* 39th Cong., 2d sess., pp. 713–14 (January 24, 1867); *Daily Cleveland Herald,* January 29, 1867; Constance J. Cooper, "Tennessee Returns to Congress," *Tennessee Historical Quarterly* 37:53–54.

183 *After imploring Johnson:* Cooper to Johnson, April 5, 1867, in *Johnson Papers* 12:205–6; Cooper to Johnson, June 27, 1867, ibid., pp. 357–58.

183 *"The more boldly":* Cooper to Johnson, August 30, 1867, ibid., p. 526.

183 *I would forego:* Cooper to Johnson, September 12, 1867, ibid., 13:63.

183 *"The President needs":* Welles Diary, vol. 3, p. 221 (October 4, 1867); *The War of the Rebellion*, Series II, Vol. IV, Washington, DC: Government Printing Office (1899); *New York Times*, August 15, 1865; Joshua W. Caldwell, ed., *Studies in Constitutional History of Tennessee*, Cincinnati: Robert Clarke Co. (1907), pp. 278–79; Cooper to Johnson, November 1, 1863, in James B. Jones, Jr., ed., *Tennessee Civil War Sourcebook*, www.tennessee.civilwarsourcebook.com (January 6, 2006); Archives, *Impeachment: Various House Papers*, testimony of C. E. Creecy, March 19, 1868.

184 *Cooper lauded:* Johnson to E. Cooper, April 6, 1866, and E. Cooper to D. B. Cooper, October 28, 1867, in Cooper Family Papers, Box 8.

184 *Periodically questioning McCulloch's loyalty:* Moore Diary/AHR, p. 125 (March 18, 1868); Moore Diary/Large Diary, p. 64 (July 23, 1868); William W. Warden to Johnson, July 1, 1868, in *Johnson Papers* 14:296.

184 *Cooper's "interim" posting: Globe* Supp., p. 87 (April 2, 1868); Robert W. Latham to Johnson, January 10, 1868, in *Johnson Papers* 13:463–64; Trefousse, *Andrew Johnson*, pp. 324, 344.

184 *When his leave was about to expire: Impeachment Money*, pp. 4, 7; Temple, *Notable Men of Tennessee*, pp. 198–202.

186 *Gaylord, again acting for Senator Pomeroy:* Legate's account of the bribery efforts in the spring of 1868 is preserved in a transcript of his testimony taken in late May, and in portions disclosed in a report by the impeachment committee afterward. Testimony of James Legate, before House Impeachment Committee, May 22, 1868, in Butler Papers, Box 175, pp. 1–19; *Impeachment Money*, passim. David G. Taylor, "Thomas Ewing, Jr., and the Origins of the Kansas Pacific Railway Company," *Kansas Historical Quarterly* 42:162, 164–65 and app.

186 *They were willing to pay: Impeachment Money*, p. 5; *New York Times*, August 21, 1865; Temple, p. 343; *Chicago Tribune*, January 11, 1868.

187 *He became a regular visitor:* A. J. Bleecker to Butler, attaching letter from Pomeroy to Bleecker, June 21, 1868, in Butler Papers, Box 45; *Impeachment Money*, pp. 5–6, 7–8.

187 *Gaylord declined the payment: Impeachment Money*, p. 7; *New York World*, July 29, 1868, in Thomas Ewing Family Papers; *Ross's Paper* (Coffeyville, KS), January 19, 1872.

187 *Cooper claimed: Impeachment Money*, p. 8; *Washington Daily National Intelligencer*, May 22, 1868; undated news report, Thomas Ewing Family Papers.

189 *He replied that he preferred:* Moore Diary/Large Diary, March 27, 1868, p. 6. Colonel Moore decorously declined to name Legate's representative, even in his diary, indicating him only by a blank line—"————"—and referring to him as someone who had lived in Kansas for some time. Fuller had made his fortune in Kansas swindles, while Thomas Ewing, Jr., served

as a general of the army in Kansas and was a justice of the Kansas Supreme Court before moving to Washington City to join his father's law practice.

189 *Pomeroy, a Radical:* Moore Diary/AHR, March 17, 1868, p. 125; Martha B. Caldwell, "Pomeroy's 'Ross Letter': Genuine or Forgery?," *Kansas Historical Quarterly* 13:463 (1945); Taylor, p. 155 (appendix details the grant to Pomeroy of $113,000 of stock in the Leavenworth, Pawnee & Western Railroad).

189 *After a "very friendly" talk:* Moore Diary/AHR, March 18, 1868, p. 126.

190 *In a six-year period:* Mark Summers, *The Plundering Generation,* New York: Oxford University Press (1987), pp. 45–46, 253–55; H. Rep. 249, 36th Cong., 1st sess., 120–28, 178, 185–86.

190 *In but one example:* "Covode Report," H. Rep. No. 648, 36th Cong., 1st sess. (1860); Edwin Erle Speaks, ed., *The Lincoln-Douglas Debates of 1858,* Springfield: Illinois State Historical Library (1908), p. 180.

190 *That sponsor later recanted:* Arthur M. Schlesinger, Jr. and Roger Bruns, eds., *Congress Investigates: A Documented History, 1792–1974,* New York: Chelsea House Publishers (1975), vol. 2, pp. 1092–1103; *Chicago Press,* April 25, 1860; House Report No. 648, 36th Cong., 1st sess. (1860); Emerson David Fite, *The Presidential Campaign of 1860,* New York: Macmillan Co. (1911), p. 135; John G. Nicolay and John Hay, eds., *Abraham Lincoln, Complete Works,* New York: Century Co. (1907), vol. 1, p. 329; Francis P. Blair, Sr. to Johnson, February 4, 1867, in *Johnson Papers* 12:6. Johnson appointed Wendell to office at the request of the publisher of the *Washington Daily National Intelligencer,* a loyal Johnson supporter, who seems to have been relying on Wendell to give him enough government printing work to stay afloat. John F. Coyle to Johnson, July 31, 1866, in *Johnson Papers* 13:765.

191 *Much was raised: Cincinnati Gazette,* December 20 and 25, 1869.

191 *Some came from employees: Impeachment Money,* p. 13; *Cincinnati Gazette,* December 20 and 25, 1869; Ben Perley Poore, *Perley's Reminiscences,* Boston: Hubbard Brothers, Publishers (1886), vol. 2, p. 313.

191 *Moore warned:* Smythe to Johnson, February 21, 1868, in *Johnson Papers* 13:576–77; Moore Diary/Large Diary, March 29, 1868, p. 13. Smythe directed yet another murky overture to Colonel Moore, this one from S. Taylor Suit, a Wall Street operator who had opened a bank in Virginia. *New York Times,* October 2, 1888. Smythe's letter to Moore explained that Suit "had the ear of certain senators and could accomplish some things others could not." Suit was closeted with Moore at the White House on March 29. Moore Diary/Large Diary, March 29, 1868, p. 15.

191 *"Here in the South":* Quoted in Hans L. Trefousse, "The Acquittal of Andrew Johnson and the Decline of the Radicals," *Civil War History,* 14:155–56 (1968). A Mississippian wrote to Butler: "Impeachment is not only

peace—it is Reconstruction. These people [Southern whites] are supercilious and servile in the presence of power, but cruel and inhuman when they have the advantage." J. Tarbell to Butler, March 15, 1868, in Butler Papers, Box 44.

192 *No other manager:* The *Philadelphia Press* on March 23, 1868, described the group photograph as "imperial"; Vinnie Ream to Nathaniel Banks, March 23, 1868, in Nathaniel Banks Papers; *Butler's Book*, p. 928; *New York Herald*, March 30, 1868.

192 *For Johnson, the parallel:* Moore Diary/AHR, March 29, 1868, p. 130; Moore Diary/Large Diary, March 28, 1868, p. 10. Johnson's self-education left him with an intimate knowledge of specific works. He sometimes recited long passages from poems, such as Gray's *Elegy*, and from famous orations. Moore Diary/AJ, January 10, 1867, p. 27.

192 *Navy Secretary Welles judged:* Welles Diary, vol. 3, p. 324 (March 27, 1868); Barlow to R. Taylor, March 20, 1868, in Barlow Papers, Box 64.

16. BEN BUTLER'S HORSE CASE

PAGE

193 *Waiting to give: Butler's Book*, p. 929.

193 *Cowed by the significance:* G. A. Townsend, *Washington, Outside and Inside*, p. 371; *Zion's Herald*, April 16, 1868; Riddle, *Life of Wade*, p. 283; *Washington Daily National Intelligencer*, March 31, 1868; *Cincinnati Commercial*, March 31, 1868.

194 *Johnson should remain: Butler's Book*, p. 929; *Washington Daily National Intelligencer*, March 31, 1868; Briggs, p. 60; Samuel Sullivan Cox, *Union—Disunion—Reunion: Three Decades of Federal Legislation, 1855 to 1885* (1886), pp. 586–87; Moore Diary/AHR, March 30, 1868, p. 130; *Cincinnati Commercial*, March 31, 1868.

195 *The manager admitted:* Briggs, p. 60; Schurz to Mrs. Schurz, April 4, 1868, in Schurz, *Intimate Letters*, p. 432; *Charleston (SC) Courier*, April 4, 1868; *Globe* Supp., p. 32 (March 30, 1868).

195 *The senators, he continued: Globe* Supp., pp. 29–30 (March 30, 1868).

195 *"[T]hat peril": The Federalist*, No. 77; *Globe* Supp., pp. 34–36 (March 30, 1868).

196 *On the Senate's verdict: Globe* Supp., pp. 40–41 (March 30, 1868). The *New York Times* complained in its editorial the next day about Butler's "unnecessary violence of language" and "appeals that might be very effective in a stump speech."

196 *When Butler announced: Milwaukee Daily Sentinel*, April 6, 1868; *Philadelphia Press*, April 1, 1868; *New York Herald*, April 4 and 5, 1868; *New York Times*, April 5, 1868; *Globe* Supp., 40th Cong., 2d sess., p. 120 (April 4, 1868); *Washington Daily National Intelligencer*, April 6, 1868; *New York*

Times, April 6, 1868, reprinting report from *Baltimore Sun*, April 4, 1868.

196 *President Johnson's unfortunate addresses:* A correspondent wrote on the opening day of the trial: "the excitement that would have been occasioned by each fresh development has been, to a certain extent, anticipated, and the great trial no longer arouses that exciting interest that manifested itself when impeachment became a fixed fact, and for a fortnight thereafter." *New York Herald*, April 1, 1868.

197 *Another Republican congressman: Globe* Supp., pp. 56–57 (March 31, 1868) (testimony of Rep. Burt Van Horn; Rep. James Moorhead).

197 *"We have had a Johnson": Globe* Supp., pp. 59–61 (March 31, 1868).

198 *Adjournment at 6:30 P.M.: Globe* Supp., pp. 62–63 (March 31, 1868); *New York Times*, April 1, 1868.

198 *The motion lost: Globe* Supp., p. 63 (March 31, 1868); Archives, *Managers' Journal*, pp. 32–33 (April 1, 1868).

198 *Butler had used: Globe* Supp., p. 71 (April 1, 1868).

199 *Having been advised: Cincinnati Commercial*, April 2, 1868; *New York Times*, April 2 and 4, 1868; *Petersburg (VA) Index*, April 3, 1868. The correspondents scored the lawyers as though they were prizefighters, and agreed that Evarts v. Butler was a worthy matchup. *New York Times*, April 2, 1868.

200 *It became a catchphrase: Globe* Supp., p. 76 (April 1, 1868); *Chicago Tribune*, April 2, 1868. The *New York Herald* on April 3 applauded Karsner's "rustic humor [which] diverted the dullness of the court yesterday."

200 *As one Radical wrote in dismay: New York Times*, April 3, 1868; Storey to his father, May 17, 1868, in Howe, *Portrait of an Independent*, p. 112.

200 *The Senate agreed: Globe* Supp., pp. 86–89 (April 2, 1868).

201 *With this modest flourish: Chicago Tribune*, April 6, 1868; *New York Times*, April 5, 1868.

201 *Stanberry, maintaining the defense position: Philadelphia Press*, April 6, 1868; *New York Herald*, April 7, 1868; *Cincinnati Commercial*, April 5, 1868.

201 *Thad Stevens, who "uses stimulants": Washington Daily National Intelligencer*, April 1, 1868; *New York Times*, April 5, 1868; *New York Herald*, April 3, 1868; *Chicago Tribune*, April 11, 1868.

202 *One rummaged through:* Archives, *Managers' Journal*, pp. 31–38; testimony of T. C. Westerly, April 2, 1868; testimony of H. H. Van Dyck, April 4, 1868, in Archives, *Impeachment: Various House Papers*. Butler to Hugh McCulloch, April 6, 1868, Butler Papers. In fact, many government clerks were engaged in exactly the process described in Butler's letter, to assist the president's defense. They were examining all presidential appointments and firings since 1789 to find examples that might support Johnson's legal arguments. *Cincinnati Commercial*, April 8, 1868; Hoar, p. 343.

202 *Evarts matched Butler's whimsical mood:* Morefield Storey to Susan Storey, April 6, 1868, in Howe, *Portrait of an Independent*, p. 91.

203 *Moore despaired:* Moore Diary/AJ, April 4, 1868, p. 17; Moore Diary/ Large Diary, April 8, 1868, p. 4. Johnson's hostility toward blacks relaxed in individual cases. In mid-March, he attended the funeral of the black former steward at the White House, William Slade. *Philadelphia Press*, March 19, 1868.

203 *He seemed to take comfort:* Moore Diary/Large Diary, April 9, 1868, p. 5; Cowan, pp. 12–13.

204 *"If I used any rough expressions":* Cincinnati Commercial, April 6, 1868.

204 *Then he blamed the reporter:* Moore Diary/Large Diary, April 7, 1868, p. 3.

204 *He finally concluded:* Moore Diary/AHR, pp. 131–32, April 4 and 7, 1868. General Sherman confirmed to Colonel Moore that Grant never made the statements attributed to him, which had been printed to try to draw him into making a public statement on the impeachment. Moore Diary/Large Diary, April 7, 1868, p. 2; *New York Times*, April 4, 1868.

204 *Speaker of the House Schuyler Colfax: North American and United States Gazette*, April 24, 1868.

205 *This time, Johnson:* Diary, April 5, 1868, in Gustavus Fox Papers, New York Historical Society; Welles Diary, vol. 3, pp. 338–39.

17. DEFENDING THE PRESIDENT

PAGE

206 *The president either:* Clemenceau, p. 175 (April 10, 1868).

206 *He cautioned his audience: New York Tribune*, April 10, 1868; *Chicago Tribune*, April 10 and 11, 1868; *Globe* Supp., p. 123 (April 9, 1868).

207 *After Curtis's speech: New York Times*, April 10, 1868; *Chicago Tribune*, April 10, 1868; *New York Herald*, April 11, 1868; *Butler's Book*, p. 930 (emphasis in original).

208 *Accordingly, the Tenure of Office Act: Globe* Supp., pp. 122–25 (April 9, 1868).

208 *If Lincoln's term:* "The Evidence Against the President," *Harper's Weekly*, April 18, 1868, p. 242.

209 *Holding the president: Globe* Supp., p. 129 (April 9, 1868).

209 *The Boston lawyer: Globe* Supp., p. 135 (April 10, 1868).

209 *Though many other factors:* Streichler, p. 173; Browning Diary, vol. 2, p. 192 (April 10, 1868).

210 *Managers Butler and Bingham: New York Herald*, April 11, 1868; *Globe* Supp., p. 140 (April 10, 1868); *New York Times*, April 11, 1868.

210 *When Thomas left the stand: Globe* Supp., pp. 146 (April 10, 1868), 150

(April 11, 1868); *Cincinnati Commercial*, April 12, 1868; *Philadelphia Press*, April 11, 1868; *Washington Daily National Intelligencer*, April 11, 1868; Briggs, p. 63.

211 *The House managers erupted:* New York Herald, April 14, 1868; *Cincinnati Commercial*, April 12, 1868; *Globe* Supp., pp. 150–51 (April 11, 1868).

211 *Stanberry brought Sherman back:* Globe Supp., pp. 151–60 (April 11, 1868), 164–66 (April 13, 1868).

211 *The defense contrived:* New York Herald, April 13, 1868.

211 *Wisely, the managers:* Globe Supp., p. 170 (April 13, 1868).

212 *These arbitrary changes:* Globe Supp., pp. 171–73 (April 11, 1868); *New York Herald*, April 14, 1868; *New York Times*, April 14, 1868; Storey to Miss Helen Appleton, April 20, 1868, in Howe, *Portrait of an Independent*, p. 98. The *New York Herald* said the Senate allowed the question to be put to Sherman out of "pity for the President's counsel." *New York Herald*, April 14, 1868.

212 *Stanberry would not be able:* New York Times, April 15, 1868; Browning to Seward, April 14, 1868, in Seward Papers, LOC.

212 *After a lifetime:* Welles Diary, vol. 3, p. 330 (April 13, 1868); Cox, pp. 591–92; Moore Diary/Large Diary, April 12, 1868, April 13, 1868, pp. 8–10.

212 *The next day:* Moore Diary/Large Diary, April 15, 1868, p. 11.

213 *Department heads reported:* Washington Daily National Intelligencer, April 16, 1868; *New York Herald*, April 16, 1868; *Cincinnati Commercial*, April 15, 1868.

213 *Johnson complained that a military display:* Cincinnati Commercial, April 17, 1868; *Washington Daily National Intelligencer*, April 18, 1868; Moore Diary/Large Diary, April 16, 1868, pp. 11–12.

213 *A message on a window shutter:* Allen W. Trelease, *White Terror: The Ku Klux Klan Conspiracy and Southern Reconstruction*, Baton Rouge: Louisiana State University Press (1971), pp. 27–116; *New York Herald*, April 9, 1868; *New York Times*, April 7 and 8, 1868; Ku Klux Klan to Stevens, April 4, 1868, Stevens Papers, Box 4; undated paper, Butler Papers, Box 45.

214 *He brought General Sherman:* Archives, *Managers' Journal*, April 10–14, pp. 41–45.

214 *The Senate ducked:* New York Herald, April 9, 10, and 11, 1868; *Globe* Supp., p. 251 (April 22, 1868).

214 *Stanton continued to provide:* Moore Diary/Large Diary, April 7, 1868, p. 2; Thomas and Hyman, p. 601; Stanton to Butler, March 11, 1868; Stanton to Butler, March 17, 1868; Butler to Bingham, March 21, 1868, in Butler Papers, Box 44; Stanton to Butler, April 1, 1868, and Stanton to Butler, April 11, 1868, in Butler Papers, Box 45.

215 *He was proving:* Globe Supp., pp. 181–94 (April 15, 1868).

215 *Defense lawyer Evarts calmly disparaged: Globe* Supp., pp. 208–9 (April 16, 1868); *Cincinnati Commercial*, April 18, 1868.

215 *He considered telling: New York Herald*, April 18, 1868; *Cincinnati Commercial*, April 18, 1868; Moore Diary/Large Diary, April 19, 1868, p. 15.

216 *They also were expected:* Browning Diary, vol. 2, pp. 189–90 (March 31, 1868).

216 *That argument over the president's intent: New York Times*, April 19 and 20, 1868.

216 *With a tart New England outlook: Cincinnati Commercial*, April 18, 1868.

217 *In his sober and ingratiating manner: New York Times*, April 19, 1868.

217 *Though other Cabinet members: Globe* Supp., pp. 225–34 (April 17, 1868); *Cincinnati Commercial*, April 19, 1868.

217 *By muzzling some: New York Herald*, April 22, 1868; *Chicago Tribune*, April 19, 1868; Blaine, vol. 2, p. 365.

217 *They talked too much: New York Times*, April 19, 1868; Brockway, p. 4.

218 *"[T]he evidence sheds": Globe* Supp., pp. 239–47 (April 22, 1868); *The Nation* 6:324 (April 23, 1868).

218 *For Frenchmen: Washington Daily National Intelligencer*, May 11, 1868, reprinting from the *London Times* of April 23, 1868; *New Orleans Commercial Bulletin*, April 14, 1868, reprinting from *Constitutiennel*.

18. COUNTING TO SEVEN

PAGE

219 *[I]t is certain that no man:* Lady Trevelyan, ed., *The Works of Lord Macaulay*, New York: Longmans, Green & Co. (1897), pp. 634–35.

219 *It was all conjecture:* Moore Diary/Large Diary, April 19, 1868, p. 14.

220 *The* Petersburg Index *in Virginia: Chicago Tribune*, April 11 and 17, 1868; *New York Herald*, April 16, 1868; *Springfield Republican*, April 20, 1868, reprinted in *New York Herald*, April 21, 1868; *New York Independent*, April 23, 1868; *Petersburg (VA) Index*, April 22, 1868. "There are 12 Democrats and conservatives certain and seven out of the Republican ranks wanting," wrote old Thomas Ewing to his son in Europe. "These we think we can count, but it is not at all certain." Thomas Ewing to Hugh Ewing, April 3, 1868, in Thomas Ewing Family Papers.

220 *Barlow remained skeptical:* William Shaffer to Barlow, April 4, 1868, and Jerome Stillson to Barlow, April 19, 1868, Barlow Papers, Box 68; Barlow to Stillson, April 21, 1868, Barlow Papers, Box 64.

220 *Grimes insisted:* Curtis to George Ticknor, April 10, 1868, in Curtis, vol. 1, pp. 416–17; *John Sherman's Recollections*, vol. I, p. 427; William Salter, *Life of James W. Grimes*, New York: D. Appleton & Co. (1876), p. 336 (Grimes to H. W. Starr, March 6, 1868). The *New York Herald* correspondent agreed that the Democratic senators and the Radical Republicans

knew how they would vote before the trial was held, but insisted on March 25 that "the greater number" of senators would "judge of Andrew Johnson's acts as charged in the articles of impeachment in a spirit of fairness."

220 *The senator told a companion: New York Herald*, April 11, 1868.

221 *Colfax named four more Republicans:* Colfax to Barlow, April 16, 1868, in Young Papers.

221 *Colfax, like several newspapers: Chicago Tribune*, April 17, 1868; *The Independent*, April 23, 1868 (letter dated April 17, 1868).

221 *A half-million dollars: Milwaukee Sentinel*, April 16, 1868 (letter of April 11, 1868).

222 *Bent collectors:* Thurlow Weed to Seward, January 28, 1868, in Seward Papers; Jeremiah Jenks, "The Development of the Whiskey Trust," *Political Science Quarterly* 4:296, 298–99 (1889); *New York Times*, October 4, 1867, December 31, 1867, May 20, 1868, May 30, 1868, June 30, 1868, October 23, 1868; Hearings before the House Committee on Ways & Means, 40th Cong., 2d sess., January 6, 7, 13, 15, 23, and March 12, 1868, 40 HWAY .T1 through .T6 (handwritten records of testimony in the Law Library, Library of Congress).

222 *Colonel Moore at the White House: Washington Daily National Intelligencer*, April 25, 1868, reprinted from *New York Times; New York Herald*, April 22, 1868; *Philadelphia Press*, April 18, 1868; Moore Diary/Large Diary, April 21, 1868, p. 16.

222 *Wade's disposition:* Though Wade did not preserve much of his correspondence, throughout the impeachment season another Radical congressman, Elihu Washburne of Illinois, was besieged with requests for appointments in the new Wade administration. Edwin Johns to Washburne, March 23, 1868; John Shank to Washburne, March 24, 1868; L. H. Whitney to Washburne, March 31; S. S. Patterson to Washburne, April 8, 1868; James Rowen to Washburne, April 30, 1868, in Washburne Papers, vols. 58 and 59; Garfield to Rhodes, May 7, 1868, in Smith, *Life and Letters of James Abram Garfield*, vol. 1, p. 425.

223 *"The set of men": Milwaukee Daily Sentinel*, April 6, 1868; *Chicago Tribune*, April 25, 1868; Sumner to Lieber, May 1868, in Edward L. Pierce, *The Life and Public Services of Charles Sumner*, Boston: Roberts Brothers (1893), vol. 4, p. 351; *Washington Daily National Intelligencer*, April 24, 1868; *Washington Herald*, April 22, 1868; Colfax to Young, April 28, 1868, in Young Papers.

223 *For Republicans who preferred: Chicago Tribune*, April 25, 1868; *New York Herald*, April 25, 1868; *New York Herald*, May 4, 1868.

223 *"I prefer tar and feathers":* J. R. Briggs, Jr., to Young, April 17, 1868, in Young Papers; Fessenden, p. 185 (letter to cousin, dated April 12, 1868).

224 *Two more years of misrule:* Salter, p. 323 (Grimes to Mrs. Grimes, March 12, 1867).

224 *In early April:* Fox Diary (April 5, 1868). Some who were skeptical of impeachment nevertheless feared Johnson's reaction to an acquittal. *The Nation*, April 30, 1868, p. 344.

224 *Republicans might vote:* Colfax to Young, April 9, 1868, in Young Papers.

225 *The president, he assured them:* Cox, pp. 592–94.

225 *Johnson could be acquitted: Cincinnati Commercial*, April 16, 1868.

225 *The president did not care:* Sefton, p. 102; Donald B. Connelly, *John M. Schofield and the Politics of Generalship*, Chapel Hill: University of North Carolina Press (2006), p. 207.

226 *When Evarts objected:* John McAllister Schofield, *Forty-Six Years in the Army*, New York: Century Co. (1897), pp. 413–18 (memorandum prepared by Schofield in May 1868, reflecting conversations with Evarts).

227 *This time, Evarts nodded yes: Chicago Tribune*, April 25, 1868.

227 *The press reported:* Moore Diary/Large Diary, April 23 and 24, 1868, pp. 18–19; *Cincinnati Commercial*, April 26, 1868; *Chicago Tribune*, April 27, 1868.

227 *In reply, Schofield:* Grant to Schofield, April 12, 1868, in *Grant Papers* 18:235; John M. Schofield, "Controversies in the War Department," *Century* 54:581 (1897).

227 *Because Grant's commission:* Moore Diary/Large Diary, April 26, 1868, p. 21.

228 *The news must have:* Moore Diary/Large Diary, April 21 and 24, 1868, pp. 17, 18.

228 *Though he deplored:* Cullom, *Fifty Years of Public Service*, p. 154; *New York Herald*, April 19, 1868; Mark M. Krug, *Lyman Trumbull, Conservative Radical*, New York: A. S. Barnes & Co. (1965), pp. 266–67.

228 *Uncertainty also surrounded:* J. R. Briggs, Jr., to Young, April 17, 1868, in Young Papers; R. W. Bayless, "Peter G. Van Winkle and Waitman T. Willey in the Impeachment Trial of Andrew Johnson," *West Virginia History* 12:79 (1952).

19. AN AVALANCHE OF TALK

PAGE

229 *[W]e have been wading:* Garfield to Rhodes, April 28, 1868, in Smith, *Life and Letters of James Abram Garfield*, vol. 1, p. 424.

230 *Nevertheless, the number: Globe* Supp., pp. 251–68 (April 22, 1868).

230 *The ladies turned:* Briggs, p. 69; *New York Herald*, April 23, 1868.

231 *If this earth: Globe* Supp., pp. 274, 284–85 (April 22 and 23, 1868); *New York Herald*, April 24, 1868.

232 *Of the managers: Globe* Supp., pp. 306–7 (April 23, 1868); Bowen, p. 98; Temple, pp. 167–80; Briggs, p. 72; *Chicago Tribune*, April 24, 1868; *New York Herald*, April 24, 1868; *New York Times*, April 25, 1868; *Phila-*

delphia Press, April 24 and 25, 1868; *Chicago Tribune*, April 24 and 30, 1868.

232 *In truth, the letter: Globe* Supp., pp. 295–96 (April 24, 1868).

232 *One listener claimed: New York Herald*, April 26 and 27, 1868; *New York Times*, April 26, 1868; Cox, p. 589; Welles Diary, vol. 3, p. 193 (April 25, 1868); *Chicago Tribune*, April 30, 1868.

233 *Ah, he was too eager: Globe* Supp., p. 319 (April 25, 1868).

234 *His gaunt face: Washington Daily National Intelligencer*, April 27, 1868; *Cincinnati Commercial*, April 29, 1868.

234 *Stevens accepted: New York Times*, April 28, 1868; *Philadelphia Press*, April 28, 1868.

234 *If the president was unwilling: Globe* Supp., pp. 322–33 (April 27, 1868).

234 *Following the sepulchral: Globe* Supp., pp. 324–35 (April 27 and 28, 1868); *New York Times*, April 30, 1868; *New York Herald*, April 28 and 29, 1868; *Washington Daily National Intelligencer*, April 29, 1868 (Williams, "having nothing to say, could not get through it in a single day").

234 *During a recess: New York Times*, April 29, 1868; Howe, *Portrait of an Independent*, p. 116; *Chicago Tribune*, April 30, 1868.

234 *Nelson scornfully answered: Globe* Supp., p. 337 (April 28, 1868). Nelson's words were: "So far as any question that [Butler] desires to make of a personal character with me is concerned, this is not the place to make it. Let him make it elsewhere if he desires to do it." The *New York Herald* on April 29 described Nelson as "hinting at pistols," while the *Philadelphia Press* on that day dismissed Nelson's "characteristic plantation braggadocio."

234 *After their squall erupted: Philadelphia Press*, May 1, 1868.

235 *A slim figure:* Barrows, p. 153.

235 *As one observer noted: New York Herald*, April 30, 1868.

235 *Joined by Boutwell: Globe* Supp., p. 348 (April 29, 1868); *New York Times*, April 29, 1868.

236 *Evarts's marathon performance: Globe* Supp., pp. 357–59 (April 30, 1868); *New York Herald*, May 1, 1868; *Philadelphia Press*, April 30, 1868.

236 *Stanberry made little contribution: Philadelphia Press*, April 4, 1868; *Globe* Supp., pp. 378–79 (May 2, 1868).

236 *Some onlookers: Philadelphia Press*, May 6, 1868; Bingham to Lucy and Emma Bingham, February 26 and April 11, 1868, John Armor Bingham Papers, Morgan Library.

237 *"Yesterday the supremacy": Globe* Supp., p. 379 (May 4, 1868).

238 *He ranged far beyond: Cincinnati Gazette*, May 8, 1868.

238 *Chase directed that: Globe* Supp., p. 406; *Philadelphia Press*, May 7, 1868; *New York Herald*, May 7, 1868; *New York Times*, May 7, 1868; *New York World*, May 7, 1868.

238 *"God knows I have tried":* Chicago Tribune, May 9, 1868; Briggs, p. 81.

239 *"We are not as strong":* Colfax to Young, April 16 and 28, 1868, Young Papers.

20. THE DARK MEN

240 *We should go through:* Butler to Young, May 12, 1868, Young Papers.

240 *With the outcome uncertain:* Archives, *Managers' Journal*, p. 62 (May 5, 1868).

241 *The hulking Weed: Perley's Reminiscences*, vol. 1, p. 59; *Impeachment Managers' Investigation*, pp. 3–5; *Impeachment Money*, pp. 24–25.

241 *Now Weed had assembled:* Welles Diary, vol. 3, p. 345 (May 5, 1868). Postmaster General Randall attempted to deny he was in New York on May 5, but his denial was authoritatively contradicted. The secretary of the interior noted Randall's absence from the May 5 Cabinet meeting, Browning Diary, vol. 2, p. 195 (May 5, 1868), while an aide to Randall telegraphed the Astor House that he and Randall would arrive there on the evening of May 4, which was confirmed by the hotel's guest register. *Impeachment Money*, pp. 24–25.

241 *Adams won election:* Theodore H. Hittell, *History of California*, vol. 4, San Francisco: N. J. Stone & Co. (1898), p. 67.

241 *In early 1851:* Roger D. Hunt and Jack R. Brown, *Brevet Brigadier Generals in Blue*, Lake Monticello, VA: Olde Soldier Books (1998), p. 4; Hubert Bancroft, *History of California*, San Francisco: The History Co. (1888), vol. 6, p. 647 n. 11; *Oroville Weekly Mercury*, December 31, 1875. The records from the State Senate inquiry into Adams's tax-collecting suggest he also backdated mining licenses in return for payments directly to him and a local sheriff. Alonzo Adams Papers, Bancroft Library, University of California at Berkeley; *New York Times*, July 22, 1856.

242 *By war's end:* James H. Stevenson, *A History of the First Volunteer Cavalry of the War Known as the First New York (Lincoln) Cavalry*, Harrisburg, PA: Patriot Publishing Co. (1879), pp. 7, 24–26, 74–75, 117–18, 312, 352, 355–58; William H. Beach, *The First New York (Lincoln) Cavalry from April 18, 1861 to July 7, 1865*, New York: Lincoln Cavalry Association (1902), pp. 461–62.

242 *Adams boasted:* S. F. Norton to Benjamin Butler, May 26, 1868, in Butler Papers, Box 45.

242 *Smythe, who himself:* Smythe to "My Dear Colonel" (Col. Moore in the White House), April 17, 1868, in Butler Papers, Box 45 (pressing for appointment as minister to Austria).

242 *Although Weed later said: Impeachment Money*, p. 26.

243 *As pay for supporting:* Welles Diary, vol. 1, p. 155 (September 22, 1865); Summers, *The Plundering Generation*, pp. 112, 229, 268; Goodwin, pp. 70–71, 80–81.

243 *He had long followed:* Glyndon G. Van Deusen, "Thurlow Weed: A Character Study," *American Historical Review* 48:427–31 (1944).

243 *As chief federal revenue collector:* HWAY.T5, Hearings Before the House Ways and Means Committee, January 23, 1868 (testimony of Mr. Bailey); HWAY.T6, Hearings Before the House Ways and Means Committee, March 12, 1868 (testimony of Col. Burr Porter).

243 *He also served:* New York Times, January 3, 1867; *Impeachment Managers' Investigation*, pp. 3–7; James R. Doolittle to Johnson, December 3, 1868, in *Johnson Papers* 15:267.

243 *For the impeachment trial:* Van Deusen, p. 480; *Chicago Tribune*, May 29, 1868; *New York Times*, April 19, 1869, November 3, 1870; *Johnson Papers* 15:501 n. 1.

243 *To support his taste: Impeachment Money*, p. 3.

244 *Through long careers:* E.g., Samuel Ward to Thurlow Weed, July 20, 1865; Erastus Webster to Weed, June 30, 1864; Cornelius Wendell to Weed, October 15, 1865; Wendell to Weed, August 2, 1867, all in Thurlow Weed Papers, Box 1; *Chicago Tribune*, May 29, 1868 (Ward and Webster are "fast friend[s]").

245 *Webster joined Woolley: Impeachment Money*, p. 25.

245 *Hastings was needed: Impeachment Managers' Investigation*, pp. 4, 6.

245 *"My business is adjusted": Impeachment Managers' Investigation*, p. 9.

245 *"He will do it": Impeachment Managers' Investigation*, pp. 6–7.

246 *At the same moment: Impeachment Money*, pp. 24, 27. The Wall Street operator was S. Taylor Suit, who opened a bank in Virginia after the war, and for whom the city of Suitland, Maryland, is named.

246 *Still, possession of the letter:* Moore Diary/Large Diary, pp. 28–29, 36 (May 2, 1868, May 9, 1868). Among the many perplexing features of the Pomeroy-Legate letter of April 1867 is that it fell into the possession of Cornelius Wendell, the former superintendent of public printing who advised Johnson's supporters on corrupt ways to secure an acquittal. Postmaster General Randall testified that Wendell showed him the Pomeroy-Legate letter but refused to allow Randall to keep the original. *Impeachment Money*, p. 11. How Wendell acquired the latter is not known.

247 *Smythe's account:* Moore Diary/Large Diary, p. 26 (April 30, 1868).

247 *Because the letters:* Moore Diary/Large Diary, p. 28 (May 1, 1868).

247 *Gaylord still offered:* Fuller letter to *New York World*, July 29, 1868, in Thomas Ewing Family Papers, Box 251; *Impeachment Money*, p. 8.

247 *Indeed, after his initial flirtation: Kansas Patriot* (Burlington, KS), June 20, 1868 (letter of Henry C. Whitney to S. S. Prouty); Eugene Berwanger,

"Ross and the Impeachment: A New Look at a Critical Vote," *Kansas History* 1:239–40 (1978).

248 *Shortly thereafter: New York World*, May 25, 1868; *Washington National Daily Intelligencer*, May 22, 1868; Moore Diary/Large Diary, January 8, 1870, p. 82; Legate Testimony, May 22, 1868, before Impeachment Investigation Committee, pp. 35, 38, Butler Papers, Box 175.

248 *After a day of anxiety: Impeachment Managers' Investigation*, pp. 4, 7; *Impeachment Money*, pp. 26, 34.

248 *The president's lawyers:* Barlow to Ward, May 9, 1868, in Barlow Papers, Box 64. This was confirmed by testimony before the Impeachment Committee. *Impeachment Money*, p. 13.

249 *At the trial's end: Impeachment Money*, p. 13; Richard Schell to Seward, March 16 and April 2, 1868, Seward Papers. Stanberry acted as paymaster for the defense lawyers, as reflected in his deposit records with Riggs & Co., a bank, which are currently housed at George Washington University. PNC-Riggs National Bank Records, Ledger 185, Riggs & Co. (1866–68). Stanberry's ledger sheet reflecting the payments to the other lawyers is preserved in Evarts's papers at the Library of Congress.

249 *"Raising money for the President's counsel": Impeachment Money*, pp. 14, 46.

249 *He may have wondered: Cincinnati Daily Gazette*, December 20, 1869; George Wilkes to Butler, May 23, 1868, in Butler Papers, Box 45.

21. SCRAMBLING FOR VOTES

PAGE

250 *There is much the same feeling:* Garfield to Rhodes, April 28, 1868, in Smith, *Life and Letters of James Abram Garfield*, vol. 1, p. 425.

250 *The impeachers met: New York Herald*, May 10, 1868. After seeing Ben Butler with New York Republican Senator Roscoe Conkling together in late April, Navy Secretary Welles called it an "ominous and discreditable conjunction." Welles Diary, vol. 3, p. 336 (April 22, 1868).

250 *More Republican officials: New York Herald*, April 19, 1868.

250 *According to some: New York Herald*, May 5, 1868.

251 *He asked Stevens:* Greeley to Stevens, April 20, 1868, in Stevens Papers, Box 4.

251 *Senator Fessenden of Maine:* Fessenden, p. 205 (May 3, 1868).

251 *If he went the other way:* Morrill to Fessenden, May 10, 1868, in Fessenden, p. 206.

251 *Anti-Johnson forces: New York Herald*, May 9, 1868.

251 *He visited the Indiana Avenue home:* Badeau, p. 136.

251 *Henderson later recalled:* John S. Henderson, "Emancipation and Impeachment," *Century* (December 1912), p. 207; Simpson, p. 244.

252 *Senators who feared: New York Herald*, May 10, 1868; Moore Diary/Large Diary, p. 32 (May 6, 1868); *Chicago Tribune*, May 12, 1868; Ellis, p. 158.

252 *Plans went forward: Philadelphia Press*, May 9, 1868.

252 *"The gathering of evil birds":* Horace White to Elihu Washburne, May 1, 1868, in Washburne Papers, vol. 59; *Washington Daily National Intelligencer*, May 9, 1868; *New York Times*, May 11, 1868.

252 *Two Union generals: Leavenworth (KS) Daily Times*, May 10, 1868; *New York Times*, May 11, 1868.

253 *If Johnson had to leave: New York Times*, May 12, 1868, reprinting interview from the *Boston Post*, dated May 10, 1868. Warden's overlapping employments—some might call them conflicting—were well known at the time. Ritchie, pp. 80–81; Summers, *The Press Gang*, p. 102.

253 *Though he liked: New York World*, May 15, 1868.

253 *The atmosphere mingled: New York Herald*, May 12, 1868.

253 *Ever partisan: New York Times*, May 14, 1868.

254 *Charles Woolley, the Whiskey Ring lawyer:* Woolley to Benjamin Robinson, May 11, 1868, in *Impeachment Money*, p. 47.

254 *Predictions about:* Democratic lawyer Samuel Barlow, following the drama from New York, rode this roller-coaster of emotions. On May 6, he wrote Sam Ward, "I am afraid you are over sanguine as to the President's acquittal as I find the friends of the impeachers are as sanguine as ever. Don't bet too heavily on the result unless you have better means of knowledge." The next day, he wrote to Jerome Stillson, correspondent for the *New York World:* "I still fear your wishes are the foundation for the opinion that there will be no conviction, as I find today that the impeachers' friends here are as earnest as ever in their assertions as to the result. Day before yesterday they were scared—but they are again confident." One day later, Barlow confided to Ward, he met a Radical Republican who was brimming with optimism and "offered large bets" on the verdict, "which I did not take." Barlow Papers, Box 64.

254 *By May 11:* Moore Diary/Large Diary, p. 35 (May 9, 1868).

255 *But Sherman also said: New York Times*, May 12, 1868; Roger D. Bridges, "John Sherman and the Impeachment of Andrew Johnson," *Ohio History* 82:178 (1973).

255 *Maddeningly, time expired: Chicago Tribune*, May 12, 1868; *New York Herald*, May 12, 1868; *Philadelphia Press*, May 12, 1868.

255 *Another described the experience:* Julian, p. 316; *Baltimore Sun*, May 12, 1868.

255 *Bingham talked with friends:* Storey to Susan Storey, May 14, 1868, in Howe, *Portrait of an Independent*, p. 105; *New York Herald*, May 12, 1868.

255 *Even doubtfuls who opposed: New York Times*, May 12, 1868.

256 *On May 7, the managers:* Archives, *Managers' Journal*, p. 64 (May 7, 1868); *Philadelphia Press*, May 8, 1868.

256 *The separate allegations: Globe* Supp., p. 409 (May 11, 1868).

256 *For the big day: Impeachment Managers' Investigation*, p. 9; *Impeachment Money*, p. 27.

257 *Smelling presidential victory: New York Herald*, May 12, 1868.

257 *Those seeking to remove him: Baltimore Sun*, May 11, 1868; *New York Times*, May 12, 1868.

257 *Some slept not at all: New York Herald*, May 13, 1868.

257 *At 5 A.M.:* William King to Washburne, May 12, 1868, in Washburne Papers, vol. 59; *New York Times*, May 13, 1868.

258 *Henderson's vote: New York Herald*, May 13, 1868; *New York Times*, May 13, 1868; *Impeachment Money*, pp. 15–16.

258 *Not able to spare: Globe* Supp., pp. 409–10 (May 11 and 12, 1868).

258 *Deflated, the murmuring spectators: New York World*, May 13, 1868.

259 *The impeachment clauses:* Farrand 2:65 (July 20, 1787).

259 *Within weeks those states: Chicago Tribune*, May 13, 1868.

259 *Western Union: Petersburg* (VA) *Index*, May 12, 1868 (reprinting from the *Baltimore Sun*); *New York Herald*, May 12, 1868.

22. DESPERATE DAYS

PAGE

260 *Have been the rounds: Impeachment Money*, p. 28.

260 *Before Saturday: New York Times*, May 12, 13, and 14, 1868; *Philadelphia Press*, May 13, 1868.

260 *A "perfect avalanche": Baltimore Sun*, May 13, 1868.

261 *The* Philadelphia Press *applauded: Philadelphia Press*, May 14, 1868.

261 *A pro-Johnson newspaper:* Ibid.; W. G. Brownlow to Butler, June 29, 1868, Butler Papers; *Impeachment Money*, p. 29; Durham, pp. 48, 55; *New York Herald*, May 14, 1868. Ben Butler claimed that Fowler had been hot for impeachment as early as 1866. *Cincinnati Gazette*, June 22, 1866.

261 *The impeachers gave up: New York Times*, May 15, 1868; *New York Herald*, May 15, 1868.

261 *Before the final ballot: Wheeling Intelligencer*, March 16, 1868; Philip Sturm, "Senator Peter G. Van Winkle and the Andrew Johnson Impeachment Trial: A Comprehensive View," *West Virginia History* 58:39 (1999–2000); R. W. Bayless, "Peter G. Van Winkle and Waitman T. Willey in the Impeachment Trial of Andrew Johnson," *West Virginia History* 13:83 (1952); *Philadelphia Press*, May 13, 1868; *New York Times*, May 14, 1868 (Van Winkle may vote "guilty" on Article XI); *New York Times*, May 15, 1868 (for acquittal on all articles); *Cleveland Daily Herald*, June 5, 1868 (Chase persuaded Van Winkle to vote for acquittal).

262 *Henderson often voted:* Chicago Tribune, January 21, 1862; *Washington Daily National Intelligencer*, April 21, 1866; *Milwaukee Daily Sentinel*, November 1, 1865; *Milwaukee Daily Sentinel*, November 1, 1867; *Newark (OH) Advocate*, September 27, 1867; *Savannah (GA) Daily News and Herald*, June 22, 1867.

262 *"The vote of Henderson":* Welles Diary, vol. 3, p. 349, May 8, 1868; Arthur Mattingly, *Senator John Brooks Henderson, U.S. Senator from Missouri*, Ph.D. dissertation, Kansas State University (1971), p. 136. One account has Mary Foote visiting Washington as a young woman "to see a real senator, and what capital parties were like." Evidently, John Henderson looked like a real senator, as she set her sights on the Missouri senator early in her visit. *Washington Post*, December 30, 2000, p. 12.

262 *In May 1868:* Legate Testimony of May 22, 1868, before the Impeachment Investigation Committee, p. 43 in Butler Papers; Craig to James F. Joy (March 17, 1867), and Craig to Joy (April 10, 1868), Joy Collection; Paul Wallace Gates, *Fifty Million Acres: Conflicts Over Kansas Land Policy 1854–1890*, University of Oklahoma Press (1997), pp. 156–65; Miner and Unrau, pp. 117–19; Lula Lemon Brown, *Cherokee Neutral Lands Controversy*, M.A. thesis, Kansas State Teachers College (1930), pp. 6–10.

263 *"The Henderson matter":* Impeachment Money, pp. 16–17.

263 *He promised to "throw myself . . .":* New York Times, May 14, 1868; Cox, p. 594; Warden, p. 696; *Washington Daily National Intelligencer*, May 16, 1868.

263 *Possibly someone pointed out:* Moore Diary/Large Diary, pp. 83–84 (January 6, 1870); *New York World*, May 19, 1868; Moore Diary/Large Diary, p. 44 (June 8, 1868); *New York Times*, May 15, 1868; *New York Herald*, May 14, 1868; *New York Tribune*, May 15, 1868.

264 *When the war came:* Edward Bumgardner, *The Life of Edmund G. Ross, the Man Whose Vote Saved a President*, Kansas City, MO: Fielding-Turner Press (1949), pp. 15–51; Earl C. Kubicek, "Pioneer, Soldier, and Statesman: The Story of Edmund Gibson Ross," *Lincoln Herald* (Fall 1982), pp. 147–48.

264 *Ross was not charged:* G. Raymond Gaeddert, *The Birth of Kansas*, Philadelphia: Porcupine Press (1974), pp. 176–77.

264 *Ten days later:* Leverett Wilson Spring, *Kansas: The prelude to the war for the Union*, Boston: Houghton Mifflin & Co. (1885), pp. 300–303; Kendall E. Bailes, *Rider on the Wind: Jim Lane and Kansas*, Shawnee Mission, KS: Wagon Wheel Press (1962), p. 205; *Lincoln and the Civil War in the Diaries and Letters of John Hay*, New York: Da Capo Press (1988), p. 289.

264 *For $42,000 in bribes:* Mark A. Plummer, "Governor Crawford's Appointment of Edmund G. Ross to the United States Senate," *Kansas Historical Quarterly* 28:145 (1962). The 1873 investigation of this bribery is outlined

in Daniel W. Wilder, *The Annals of Kansas*, Topeka, KS: George W. Martin, Kansas Publishing House (1875), pp. 570–74.

265 *Ben Wade also sponsored:* Ross to Wyman Spooner, January 15, 1868, Ross to Ream, February 24, 1868, and Wade to Fairchild, February 11, 1868, in Hoxie-Ream Papers; Vinnie Ream to Stevens, April 3 and July 21, 1868, and Simon Stevens to Ream, March 19, 1868, all in Stevens Papers, Box 4; Edward S. Cooper, *Vinnie Ream: An American Sculptor*, Chicago: Academy Chicago Publishers (2004), p. 59. "She just talked pretty, girlish talk to some of these impotent iron-clad old politicians—Congressmen, of course," wrote Samuel Clemens as Mark Twain, "and got out her mud and made busts of some of the others; and she kept on in this fashion until she over-mastered them all with her charming little ways." *Chicago Republican*, February 19, 1868.

265 *To complete the circle:* Cooper, pp. 17–42. A former Democratic congressman from Indiana, Daniel Voorhees, had urged Johnson to appoint Robert Ream as a consul to a city in southern Europe so he could accompany his daughter Vinnie to Rome, where she wished to complete her commission for a sculpture of Lincoln. The president did not make the appointment. Voorhees to Johnson, May 13, 1867, in *Johnson Papers* 12:266.

265 *Others pegged him:* E.g., *Globe* Supp., p. 231 (April 18, 1868) (Ross votes to admit testimony of Cabinet members); *Baltimore Sun*, May 12, 1868, and *New York Herald*, May 13, 1868 (Ross doubtful); *New York Times*, May 11, 12, and 14, 1868 (Ross for conviction on four articles); Mark A. Plummer, "Profile in Courage? Edmund G. Ross and the Impeachment Trial," *Midwest Quarterly* 27:30, 35 (1985) (Kansas newspapers recording Ross as voting to convict).

266 *"I never allow":* C. C. Warner to Butler, April 15, 1868, in Butler Papers, Box 45 (Butler's cover note is written in the margins of the letter).

267 *if the President:* Browning Diary, vol. 2, p. 195 (May 4, 1868).

267 *A deal between Wade and Pomeroy:* Plummer, "Profile in Courage?" pp. 33–34; Berwanger, pp. 236, 239; *Kansas Weekly Patriot* (Burlington, KS), June 20, 1868. Accounts at the time were not clear on whether Pomeroy expected to be trusted with Kansas patronage under a Wade presidency or would have even larger influence.

267 *Ross confirmed: Impeachment Money*, p. 31.

268 *Ross's position seemed: Cincinnati Gazette*, May 18, 1868; *Daily Cleveland Herald*, May 19, 1868 (the newspaper correspondent was the respected Henry Van Ness Boynton; the senator was Alexander Cattell, a New Jersey Republican); *Impeachment Money*, p. 30 (testimony of Mr. Green).

268 *Without being specific: Impeachment Money*, p. 32; *New York Tribune*, May 16, 1868.

268 *Supposedly offered $20,000: Philadelphia Press*, May 18, 1868; *Bangor*

Daily Whig and Courier, May 27, 1868, reprinting report of *Rochester Express*; Bumgardner, p. 78.

268 *Kansas repudiates you:* Text of telegrams copied in memorandum, Ross Papers; Plummer, "Profile in Courage?" p. 36. Though he came from Rochester, New York, Anthony had a frontier swagger. One report has him tracking down Ross in the early 1870s and beating the former senator with his cane. Kubicek, p. 151. Anthony later survived a dramatic shooting at the Leavenworth Opera House, *New York Times*, September 18, 1875. His son, Daniel Anthony, Jr., succeeded him as editor of the newspaper and represented Kansas in Congress for twenty-two years.

269 *He left the Pomeroys:* Bumgardner, p. 79; *Impeachment Money*, p. 32.

269 *At midnight: Impeachment Money*, p. 30; Ross to Major Hoxie, November 2, 1896, in Hoxie-Ream Papers, Box 3.

269 *Out in the early morning hours:* In Kansas, it was said during the Johnson Administration that "a good fee, and Thomas Ewing, Jr., on one's side, is all that is necessary to secure almost anything in the line of Indian contracts or government lands from the Department of the Interior." Gates, *Fifty Million Acres*, p. 158.

269 *Ross then assured Sickles:* Stanton was Sickles's defense lawyer in an 1859 murder trial. Sickles had shot and killed Philip Barton Key, son of Francis Scott Key, because of an affair between Key and Sickles's wife. Stanton argued that Sickles, stunned by his wife's betrayal, was temporarily insane, and won his client's acquittal. Nat Brandt, *The Congressman Who Got Away with Murder*, Syracuse, NY: Syracuse University Press (1991), pp. 113–89; Thomas Kenneally, *American Scoundrel: The Life of the Notorious Civil War General Dan Sickles*, New York: Nan A. Talese/Doubleday (2002), pp. 122–200.

270 *When young Vinnie: Baltimore Gazette*, May 29, 1868; *Washington Daily National Intelligencer*, May 30, 1868; *Cong. Globe*, 40th Cong., 2d sess. (May 29, 1868), pp. 2674–75 (Rep. Morgan; Rep. Julian).

270 *Miss Ream differed: New York Sun*, October 25, 1896; Vinnie Ream Hoxie to General O. O. Howard, November 14, 1896, in Hoxie-Ream Papers.

270 *This time, with Thad Stevens: Impeachment Money*, pp. 30, 32.

271 *Shook came to Washington: Impeachment Managers' Investigation*, p. 10; *Impeachment Money*, pp. 21–22.

271 *He then reported:* Handwritten table of telegrams, Butler Papers, Box 45.

271 *On May 15, the day before the vote:* Barlow to Ward, May 12 and 15, 1868, in Barlow Papers, Box 64.

271 *They did not need it: Impeachment Managers' Investigation*, pp. 10–11, 20, 27, 28. In any event, Craig, the railroad man from Missouri, viewed Pomeroy as "a Blow-gun and blatherskite." Craig to Joy, April 10, 1868, in Joy Collection.

271 *In his dinner invitation: Impeachment Money*, p. 20. Ward explained that

he signed his note to Evarts as "Horace" because he had given Evarts a volume of Horace that Ward had received from the British novelist William Makepeace Thackeray. Henry A. Beers, *The Connecticut Wits and Other Essays*, New Haven, CT: Yale University Press (1920), p. 112.

271 *Woolley and Sheridan Shook:* Thomas, pp. 345, 427–29; *Galveston Daily News*, May 28, 1875; *Impeachment Money*, p. 19.

272 *Most of the rumored commitments:* Mark Wahlgren Summers, *The Era of Good Stealings*, New York: Oxford University Press (1993), p. 41.

272 *Paradoxically, the future president: New York Herald*, May 14, 1868, reprinting article from *Chicago Republican*.

272 *Better yet: Philadelphia Press*, May 11, 12, and 14, 1868; *New York World*, May 16, 1868; *Washington Daily National Intelligencer*, May 15, 1868. John D. Candel to Butler, May 12, 1868, in Butler Papers, Box 43: "If the present Senate will not convict Andrew Johnson, can not the taking of the vote be adjourned till such time as the new senators are admitted from the southern states and then his conviction will be sure?"

273 *In debate on the day: New York Times*, May 15, 1868; *Washington Daily National Intelligencer*, May 16, 1868, reprinting editorial from *Philadelphia Press*, May 15, 1868; *Cong. Globe*, 40th Cong., 2d sess., p. 2465 (May 15, 1868); Brodie, pp. 352–53; *Washington Daily National Intelligencer*, May 15, 1868; *New York World*, May 16, 1868; *Philadelphia Press*, March 10 and 26, 1868; *New York Herald*, May 8, 1868.

273 *Pomeroy assured them: New York Herald*, May 16, 1868; *New York Times*, May 16, 1868; Badeau, p. 136.

273 *In one sermon: New York Herald*, May 16, 1868.

274 *A warning went out: Cincinnati Gazette*, May 14, 1868.

274 *More shocking: New York Times*, May 14, 1868; *Baltimore Sun*, May 14, 1868; Gustavus Fox Diary, May 15, 1868.

23. FREE AGAIN

PAGE

275 *"Glory enough": Impeachment Money*, p. 28.

275 *The Republicans resolved: Chicago Tribune*, May 18, 1868; *Philadelphia Press*, May 18, 1868; *Cincinnati Gazette*, May 18, 1868.

276 *Ignoring reporters: New York World*, May 17, 1868; Howe, *Portrait of An Independent*, p. 108.

276 *The quiet: New York Tribune*, May 18, 1868.

276 *Though it was a warm day: New York World*, May 17, 1868.

276 *"All turns on Ross' vote": Baltimore Gazette*, May 17, 1868; *Chicago Tribune*, May 18, 1868; *New York Herald*, May 17, 1868; *Washington Daily National Intelligencer*, May 18, 1868; Henderson, "Emancipation and Impeachment," p. 207; *Cincinnati Gazette*, May 18, 1868.

276 *He said, clearly: New York Tribune*, May 18, 1868.

277 *Colleagues around him:* Julian, p. 316.

277 *Aware that every eye:* Edmund Ross, "Historic Moments: The Impeachment Trial," *Scribner's* 11:524 (1892); "A Woman's Letters from Washington," *The Independent*, May 28, 1868; *New York World*, May 17, 1868; *New York Tribune*, May 18, 1868.

277 *John Logan spat:* Blaine, vol. 2, p. 317; *Baltimore Gazette*, May 18, 1868; Mushkat, p. 283; Henderson, p. 208.

278 *"Black with rage":* W. H. Crook, *Through Five Administrations*, New York: Harper & Brothers (1910) (edited by Margarita Spalding Gerry), p. 133.

278 *Johnson and his men:* Ibid., p. 134; *New York World*, May 17, 1868.

278 *"Men's consciences":* **New York Times**, May 18, 1868; *Washington Daily National Intelligencer*, May 18, 1868. Mrs. Johnson received the news of the acquittal separately, from the White House steward. "I knew he'd be acquitted," she said in response. "I knew it." Crook, *Memories of the White House*, p. 67.

278 *After congratulating:* Samuel J. Barrows and Isabel C. Barrows, "Personal Reminiscences of William H. Seward," *Atlantic Monthly* 63:379, 389 (1889); Van Deusen, p. 480.

278 *"There goes the rascal":* Bumgardner, p. 86; *Cincinnati Gazette*, May 18, 1868.

279 *They were still drunk: Impeachment Managers' Investigation*, p. 11; *Impeachment Money*, p. 41.

279 *The president also attended:* Unsigned Memorandum, May 16–18, 1868, in Butler Papers; *Cincinnati Gazette*, May 18, 1868; *New York World*, May 17, 1868.

279 *Less than three hours: Cong. Globe*, 40th Cong., 2d sess., pp. 2503–5 (May 16, 1868); Archives, *Impeachment: Various House Papers* (resolution drafted by John Bingham).

279 *He denied knowledge:* Archives, *Managers' Journal*, pp. 71–72. *Philadelphia Press*, May 18, 1868.

279 *"How does it happen":* Butler to James Russell Young, May 16, 1868, in Young Papers. Republican assumptions that bribery occurred are described in correspondence from Morefield Storey, aide to Massachusetts Senator Charles Sumner, and in newspapers. Storey to his father, May 17, 1868, in Howe, *Portrait of an Independent*, pp. 112–14; *Daily Cleveland Herald*, May 18, 1868.

279 *Richmond received:* **New York Times**, May 17, 1868; *Washington Daily National Intelligencer*, May 18, 1868; *Daily News and Herald* (Savannah, GA), May 18, 1868.

280 *Those supporting impeachment:* Henderson, "Emancipation and Impeachment," p. 208; *Cincinnati Gazette*, May 19, 1868 (the defectors "have been deeply mortified and greatly disappointed at the universal cry of shame,

where they had expected, at least toleration, if not applause"); *Arkansas Daily Gazette*, June 4, 1868; Bayless, p. 86; *The Independent*, May 21, 1868.

280 *1. Bad articles: Chicago Tribune*, May 17, 1868.

280 *Despairing of bringing Ross: Impeachment Managers' Investigation*; Blaine, vol. 2, p. 375; Archives, *Managers' Journal*, p. 73 (May 23, 1868); *Cincinnati Gazette*, May 23, 1868; *Chicago Tribune*, May 23 and 26, 1868; Trefousse, *Benjamin Butler*, p. 204.

281 *The Senate never voted: Globe* Supp., pp. 413–15 (May 26, 1868).

281 *The officer delivered:* E. P. Townsend, pp. 132–33; Thomas and Hyman, pp. 608–9.

281 *Much of his booty:* Richardson, pp. 24, 38; Ritchie, p. 87.

281 *Grimes called the incumbent: Globe* Supp., pp. 419–20, 424.

281 *Henderson's explanation: Globe* Supp., pp. 457, 520.

282 *Finally, the senator denied:* Ibid., pp. 432–33. A brief flurry of attention surrounded a report in the *New York Tribune* that Chief Justice Chase persuaded Van Winkle to vote for acquittal. As the story evolved, Van Winkle supposedly was influenced only by Chase's description to the Senate of the impeachment charge in Article XI, but there was no private conversation between the two men on the subject. *Daily Cleveland Herald*, June 5, 1868; *Washington Daily National Intelligencer*, May 25, 1868. Chase was certainly capable of discussing his views of the impeachment articles with individual senators, and acknowledged that he did so in a letter to the *Tribune's* editor (Horace Greeley) on May 19, 1868. Warden, p. 696.

282 *Calling them "parasitic insects": Globe* Supp., p. 472.

282 *Decrying the impeachment effort: Daily Cleveland Herald*, June 16, 1868.

282 *He denied that his vote:* Ross to Mrs. Ross, May 22, 1868, in Bumgardner, p. 89; *Cong. Globe*, 40th Cong., 2d sess., p. 2599 (May 27, 1868) (Sen. Ross); *Cincinnati Gazette*, May 28, 1868.

282 *An ally of the Astor House group: Impeachment Money*, p. 12.

283 *The listing of Nye:* Trefousse, *Impeachment of the President*, p. 169; *Chicago Tribune*, May 18, 1868; Benjamin C. Truman, "Anecdotes of Andrew Johnson," *Century* 85:435–40 (1913); Henderson, "Emancipation and Impeachment," p. 207; Horace White, *The Life of Lyman Trumbull*, Boston: Houghton Mifflin Co. (1913), p. 321; *Impeachment Money*, p. 22. Senator Nye, who voted to convict, was originally from New York, where he was an ally of Seward and Thurlow Weed. Michael Green, "Diehard or Swing Man: Senator James W. Nye and Andrew Johnson's Impeachment and Trial," *Nevada Historical Society Quarterly* 29:176 (1986); *Cincinnati Commercial*, March 9, 1868. Nye was described as leaning toward the president by one observer. Edmund Goold to Samuel Barlow, March 26, 1868, Barlow Papers, Box 66. Nye is listed as a vote for sale in an undated news-

paper article about postal agent James Legate of Kansas, in Box 74 of the Thomas Ewing Family Papers. *Chicago Tribune*, May 29, 1868.

283 *Johnson also had expected:* Moore Diary/Large Diary, p. 39 (May 17, 1868).

24. SEARCHING FOR SCANDAL

PAGE

284 *People here [in Washington]:* Barlow Papers, Box 68.

285 *What about the businessman:* John Bisk to Butler, May 21, 1868; Morris Alberger to Butler, June 1, 1868; Sidney Bates to Butler, May 25, 1868; S. F. Norton to Butler, May 26, 1868; G. Weitzel to Butler, May 28, 1868; R. Bartiteu to Butler, May 19, 1868; "Justice" to Butler, May 20, 1868; Thomas Church to Butler, May 19, 1868; James Pine to Butler, May 21, 1868; L. B. Halsey to Butler, all in Butler Papers, Box 45.

285 *Like many sporting men:* Alexander Saxton, "George Wilkes: The Transformation of a Radical Ideology," *American Quarterly* 33:437 (1981); *New York World*, May 7, 13, and 19, 1868; *New York Tribune*, May 15, 1868.

285 *Charley Morgan, Wilkes pointed out:* Wilkes to Butler, May 21 and 23, 1868, in Butler Papers, Box 45. For a lurid description of Morrissey's colorful life, there is William E. Harding, *John Morrissey: His Life, Battles, and Wrangles*, New York: Police Gazette (1881).

286 *Butler never proved: New York Times*, June 1, 1868. M. Alberger to Butler, June 1, 1868, in Butler Papers, Box 45; Ward to Barlow, June 19, 1868, in Barlow Papers, Box 68. According to Ward, Butler "took me aside and begged me to believe that he had no hand in Charley's arrest—on the contrary, he had resisted attempts of parties to have him subpoenaed and brought before the Committee to mortify me."

286 *Missouri's Henderson appeared: Chicago Tribune*, May 29, 1868; Archives, *Managers' Journal*, p. 75; *Washington Daily National Intelligencer*, May 21, 1868; *St. Louis Morning Republican*, May 22, 1868. Henderson's resentment of Butler's methods led him to propose that the Senate investigate Butler's investigation. *Cincinnati Gazette*, May 23, 1868; *New York World*, May 21, 1868. Such a Senate committee was approved, but it took no significant actions. *Cong. Globe*, 40th Cong., 3d sess., p. 1865 (March 3, 1869); Ellis Paxson Oberholtzer, *A History of the United States Since the Civil War*, New York: Macmillan Co. (1928), pp. 146–47.

286 *Butler, acutely aware: Impeachment Managers' Investigation*, p. 5; *Boston Post*, undated, in Young Papers; Matthew Carey, Jr., *The Democratic Speaker's Handbook*, Cincinnati: Miami Printing & Publishing Co. (1868), p. 59.

287 *Unfortunately for Woolley:* Archives, *Managers' Journal*, pp. 73–75; *Chi-*

cago Tribune, May 21, 1868; *Chicago Tribune*, May 20, 1868; *Impeachment Money*, p. 39; *Cong. Globe*, 40th Cong., 2d sess., p. 2947 (June 8, 1868).

287 *Woolley accompanied that message:* D. H. Bliss to Butler, May 21, 1868, in Butler Papers, Box 45; affidavit of Charles Woolley, May 21, 1868, in Butler Papers, Box 45; *Washington Daily National Intelligencer*, May 22, 1868.

287 *That report admitted: Impeachment Managers' Investigation*, p. 12; *Cincinnati Gazette*, May 24, 1868.

287 *The House found him: Cong. Globe*, 40th Cong., 2d sess., pp. 2585–90 (May 26, 1868).

289 *She was forced: Washington Daily National Intelligencer*, May 27 and 28, 1868; *New York Times*, May 30, 1868; *Bangor Daily Whig & Courier*, May 29, 1868.

289 *Another Seward intimate:* Ransom Van Valkenburg served as a mid-level courier for Seward, and was involved in the secretary of state's negotiation with Denmark to acquire the Virgin Islands. *Impeachment Money*, p. 40; Seward to Butler, October 26, 1864, in *Private and Official Correspondence of General Benjamin F. Butler During the Period of Civil War*, Norwood, MA: Plimpton Press (1917), p. 286.

289 *After the committee first questioned:* The *New York Times* of January 22, 1893, reported that in 1868 the ride from Jersey City to Washington took eight hours and fifty-two minutes, an average speed of 25 miles per hour.

289 *In one of the most convincing passages: Impeachment Money*, pp. 41–44.

289 *Stymied by this "mass of corruption":* Archives, *Managers' Journal*, pp. 81, 91–94 (June 8–11, 1868); *Cong. Globe*, 40th Cong., 2d sess., pp. 2937–47 (June 8, 1868). *Impeachment Money*, pp. 42, 44; *Fort Wayne Daily Gazette*, June 13, 1868; *Daily Cleveland Herald*, June 17, 1868. Woolley was told that his release was purchased by a deal between Butler and the president on the appointment of a new head of the revenue service. Woolley to Johnson, June 11, 1868, in *Johnson Papers* 14:101–2. Johnson, however, never made the rumored appointment, preferring Perry Fuller for the position. The correspondent for the *New York Tribune* eviscerated Woolley's claim that the $20,000 had been intended to support lobbying efforts on tax legislation. That would mean, the *Tribune* writer pointed out, that the money was to be used in a *different* corrupt effort, one to influence legislation that had died two weeks before May 17, the date on which Van Valkenburg supposedly took custody of the money from the inebriated Woolley and Shook. *New York Tribune*, June 10, 1868.

290 *John Bingham and the governor:* W. G. Brownlow to Butler, June 29, 1868, in Butler Papers; *Cincinnati Gazette*, June 22, 1868; *Impeachment Money*, pp. 28–29. Butler claimed that Fowler demanded the impeachment of President Johnson as early as 1866. *Cincinnati Gazette*, June 22, 1868; Erving E. Beauregard, "The Chief Prosecutor of Andrew Johnson," *Mid-*

west Quarterly 31:419 (1990), citing James R. Therry, "The Life of General Robert Cumming Schenck," Ph.D. dissertation, Georgetown University (1968); *Cincinnati Gazette*, June 12, 1868.

290 *The Indian trader's purpose:* Legate Testimony of May 22, 1868, before Impeachment Investigation Committee, p. 3, in Butler Papers, Box 175; *Impeachment Money*, pp. 8–9.

290 *Because Butler never found out:* Ward to Barlow, June 19, 1868, in Barlow Papers, Box 68; Letter of Samuel Ward, *New York World*, May 26, 1868; *The Nation*, May 28, 1868, p. 422.

290 *Whatever Butler missed:* Ward to Butler, June 14, 1868, in Butler Papers, Box 45; Ward letter, undated, in Papers of Samuel Ward, New York Public Library, Box 1.

291 *He meticulously traced: Impeachment Money*, p. 45.

291 *Yet Butler took no action:* Archives, *Managers' Journal*, p. 86 (June 2, 1868), p. 93 (June 10, 1868), p. 101 (June 19, 1868), p. 106 (June 25, 1868), p. 108 (June 27, 1868); A. W. Adams to Butler, June 19, 1869, in Butler Papers, Box 45; *Impeachment Money*, p. 24. Possibly the least explained recollection of the trial came from President Johnson's bodyguard, who claimed he carried "many messages" between the president and Butler during the later stages of the trial. What could the president and his chief prosecutor have been communicating to each other? Did the president's lawyers know about the communications? No one has provided a well-founded explanation. Gerry, p. 870.

291 *Postal agent Legate:* Moore Diary/Large Diary, p. 82 (January 8, 1870).

291 *In the final committee report: Impeachment Money*, p. 33.

292 *In a letter to his father:* Thomas Ewing, Jr. to Thomas Ewing, Sr., June 3, 1868, in Papers of Thomas Ewing Family, Box 74.

292 *Ross's denunciation: Cong. Globe*, 40th Cong., 2d sess., app., pp. 4463–65 (July 26, 1868); 4507–8, 4509–17 (July 27, 1868).

292 *As Henderson himself:* David A. Logan, "Historical Uses of a Special Prosecutor: The Administrations of Presidents Grant, Coolidge, and Truman," Congressional Research Service (November 23, 1973), p. 11. The most dramatic response to the committee investigation and report came from Thurlow Weed, who suffered on June 26 what was described as "partial sunstroke." Weed left for Europe on the steamship *Cimbria* four days after the report issued. Thurlow Weed Barnes, *Life of Thurlow Weed*, Boston: Houghton, Mifflin & Co. (1884), p. 460; *New York Times*, July 8, 1868.

292 *Though a firm Republican:* Mark Wahlgren Summers, *The Press Gang*, University of North Carolina Press (1994), p. 85; Ritchie, *Press Gallery*, pp. 74, 113; Richardson, p. 27.

293 *Boynton was disgusted:* In the 1860s, Congress did not have regular procedures for preserving the records of its committees. The committee's

journal of its activities survives in the National Archives, along with the transcripts of testimony of a few minor witnesses. Butler retained copies of some correspondence in his personal records, along with a couple of additional transcripts. Fragments of other testimony, and references to many telegrams and other correspondence, appear in the two reports prepared by the committee. Some witnesses claimed that the excerpts of testimony in the reports omitted important information.

293 *Having expected to prove: Cincinnati Gazette*, December 20, 1868; Boynton to Whitelaw Reid, October 23, 1869, Whitelaw Reid Papers. The biographer James Parton wrote in *Atlantic Monthly* in August 1869 that Johnson's acquittal was "wholly the lobby's doing." He claimed that senators' votes were purchased for $25,000 or $50,000 per vote, or by the intentional loss of large sums in card games. He concurred with Boynton that much of the money raised for bribery purposes was siphoned off by middlemen, and that patronage appointments and "commodities of another description" purchased some votes. He also claimed that Butler and the impeachers could have purchased a conviction for $110,000. Because Parton offered no particulars to support his statements, they are difficult to evaluate. James Parton, "The 'Strikers' of the Washington Lobby," *Atlantic Monthly*, August 1869, pp. 229–30.

293 *Wendell added: Cincinnati Gazette*, December 25, 1868; *New York Herald*, January 8, 1870.

293 *Without directly asking:* Wendell to Johnson, March 3, 1868, in *Johnson Papers* 15:500–501.

294 *Sixty thousand dollars:* Moore Diary/Large Diary, p. 83 (January 6, 1870).

295 *House Speaker Colfax:* Summers, *The Era of Good Stealings*, pp. 231–37.

295 *Seward, who had accepted:* After the trial, Clemenceau described Seward as "Mr. Johnson's mentor," adding that "[t]he influence, or at least the maneuvers, of the Secretary of State played a considerable part in the President's acquittal." Clemenceau, p. 189 (May 29, 1868).

295 *The president's men: Cincinnati Gazette*, December 20, 1869.

296 *"As matters stand now": New York Tribune*, May 24, 1868.

296 *"I have been saved by so many men":* Moore Diary/Large Diary, p. 39 (May 18, 1868).

297 *Three days later:* Ross to Johnson, June 23, 1868, in *Johnson Papers* 14:258.

297 *When the Senate Finance Committee: Cincinnati Gazette*, June 25, 1868; *Chicago Tribune*, June 25, 1868; *Boston Daily Advertiser*, June 25, 1868; *Chicago Tribune*, June 28, 1868. The *Newport (RI) Journal* asked on June 27, 1868, whether there was a connection between Fuller's appointment and the vote of Edmund Ross on impeachment.

297 *"The man who can give":* Fuller to Johnson, August 23, 1868, in *Johnson Papers* 14:530 and n. 2; *Chicago Tribune*, September 1, 1868.

297 *Fuller's overhaul: Washington Daily National Intelligencer*, September 30, 1868; McCulloch to Johnson, October 20, 1868, in *Johnson Papers* 15:159.

298 *The criminal charges: New York Herald*, September 22, 1869; *Chicago Tribune*, May 1, 1869; *New York Times*, September 16, 1869; *Lowell Daily Citizen & News*, February 7, 1868; *Chicago Tribune*, December 10, 1870; Abel, p. 85 n. 177; *New York Times*, January 29, 1875.

298 *The appointment was "vital": Chicago Tribune*, September 1, 1868; Ross to Johnson, June 6, 1868, in *Johnson Papers* 14:177–78.

298 *The Kansas senator:* Ross to Johnson, June 13, July 1, 10, 1868, in *Johnson Papers* 14:215–16, 295, 346; Charles A. Jellison, "The Ross Impeachment Vote: A Need for Reappraisal," *Southwestern Social Science Quarterly* 41:151, 154 (1960); Gerry, p. 872.

298 *Van Winkle of West Virginia:* Bayless, p. 88; Brockway, p. 15; Van Winkle to Johnson, June 19, 1868, and Fowler to Johnson, July 18, 1868, Johnson Papers, Reel 33; Grimes to Johnson, January 28, 1869, Johnson Papers, Reel 36. The president also granted an appointment desired by Fessenden of Maine. Smythe to Johnson, June 22, 1868, in *Johnson Papers* 14:251.

298 *Cornelius Wendell, the corruption consultant: New York Times*, October 22, 1868.

299 *The Senate promptly confirmed: Cincinnati Gazette*, May 26, June 1, 1868; *Washington Daily National Intelligencer*, June 26, 1868; *Janesville (WI) Gazette*, June 29, 1868; Ann S. Stephens to Johnson, June 2, 1868, in *Johnson Papers* 14:157.

299 *It was, Welles noted tersely:* Welles Diary, vol. 3, p. 391 (May 25, 1868); *New York Tribune*, July 4, 1868. About the nomination of Perry Fuller as commissioner of internal revenue, Welles harrumphed that it was "an improper selection."

299 *One historian estimated: Chicago Tribune*, September 3, 1868; Albert S. Bolles, *The Financial History of the United States, from 1861 to 1885*, 2d ed., New York: D. Appleton & Co. (1894), p. 495.

299 *Despite Johnson's dogged efforts: New York Tribune*, February 13, 1868; *Boston Daily Advertiser*, January 30, 1868; *North American Review* (April 1869), p. 625. Noting the Fuller, Smythe, and Foote appointments, the *Janesville (WI) Gazette* observed dryly on June 28, 1868, "The president is going through the list. He has not yet reached Woolley."

25. THE CARAVAN MOVES ON

PAGE

301 *Mrs. Johnson came downstairs:* Gerry, p. 873.

301 *Noble Hurdle: New York Times*, January 2, 1869; *Bangor Daily Whig and Courier*, January 2, 1869; Ellis, pp. 242–43.

301 *Did this fraternal feeling:* Butler spent the rest of New Year's Day calling at the homes of Johnson's Cabinet secretaries, most of whom could not stand the sight of him. Plainly, the Massachusetts congressman had embarked on a major fence-mending effort. Welles Diary, vol. 3, p. 497 (January 2, 1869).

301 *With a laugh:* Moore Diary/Large Diary, pp. 41–42 (May 27, 29, and 30, 1868); E. P. Townsend, pp. 135–36.

302 *Congress enacted both bills: Chicago Tribune,* June 22, 1868. Johnson vetoed other legislation as well. "Veto of Restrictions on Electoral Votes," July 20, 1868, in *Johnson Papers* 14:388; "Veto of Freedmen's Bureau Bill," July 25, 1868, in ibid., 14:429.

302 *Using terror tactics:* Report of Senate Select Committee on "The Causes of the Removal of the Negroes from the Southern States to the Northern States," S. Rep. No. 693, 46th Cong., 2d sess., Part I, p. xviii (1880); Trefousse, *Andrew Johnson,* pp. 340–41, 349–50; Johnson to Grant, March 14, 1868, in *Johnson Papers* 13:650. The Senate Select Committee report in 1880 included a remarkable study compiled by a freed slave and former Union soldier from Louisiana, Henry Adams, who was shocked by the antiblack violence when he returned to the South in 1868. Adams recruited a group of some 500 freedmen who attempted to document atrocities committed by whites and to report on conditions for the freed people throughout the South. Their goal was to identify areas where black people might live in safety. Adams's listing of the victims of white slaughter includes gruesome entries like: "Alex. Nelson (colored) tongue cut out, skinned and beat, and then killed by Old Dority and other white men, on John Orley's place, in 1868." Most are more prosaic: "Frank Jeffrew (colored), killed by white men on Seward Angrel's place, 1868." Senate Select Comm. Report, Part II, p. 196.

302 *The Ku Klux Klan claimed credit:* Memorandum for election of 41st Congress, Butler Papers, Box 43; Trelease, p. 117; Connelly, p. 211; Smallwood, p. 62; Michael W. Fitzgerald, *Splendid Failure: Postwar Reconstruction in the American South,* Chicago: Ivan R. Dee (2007), p. 91; *New York Times,* August 6, 1868; Trelease, p. 116.

302 *Others were compelled:* Benjamin Leas to Butler (July 4, 1868); J. C. Lucas to Butler (July 1, 1868); J. Tarbell to Butler (July 3, 1868), all in Butler Papers, Box 45; see Hans L. Trefousse, "The Acquittal of Andrew Johnson and the Decline of the Radicals," *Civil War History* 14:158–59 (1968).

302 *Twenty-five freedmen: New York Times,* May 11, 1868; Smallwood, pp. 142–45.

303 *If the man in the White House: Report of the Secretary of War,* Part I, House Ex. Doc. No. 1, 40th Cong., 3d Sess. (1868), pp. xix–xxxii.

303 *On the twenty-second ballot:* Cooper to Johnson, July 3, 1868, in *Johnson Papers* 14:306–7; Smythe to Johnson, July 6, 1868, in ibid., 14:328; Cooper

to Johnson, July 7, 1868, in ibid., 14:328–29; Moore Diary/Large Diary, pp. 57–58, 60 (July 3, 7, 8, and 9, 1868); Johnson to Cooper, July 8, 1868, in *Johnson Papers* 14:332; Trefousse, *Andrew Johnson*, p. 339.

304 *The new state governments:* Joseph B. James, *Ratification of the Fourteenth Amendment*, Macon, GA: Mercer University Press (1984), pp. 280–98.

304 *The president's annual message:* Edward McPherson, p. 385 (Annual Message of the President, December 7, 1868).

305 *The House took no action: Cong. Globe*, 40th Cong., 2d sess., pp. 3786–91, 3792–93 (July 7, 1868); *Cincinnati Gazette*, July 8, 1868.

305 *He was not concerned: New York Times*, August 8, 1868; *San Francisco Daily Evening Bulletin*, August 31, 1868, reprinted from the *New York Tribune*; J. Hickman to McPherson, January 14, 1869, in McPherson Papers, Box 12.

306 *In Stevens's final moments: New York Times*, August 14, 1868; *New Hampshire Statesman*, August 21, 1868; *Newark (OH) Advocate*, August 14, 1868.

306 *Before his death: Lowell (MA) Daily Citizen*, August 15 and 18, 1868; *Washington Daily National Intelligencer*, August 14, 1868; *New York Times*, August 13, 1868; *New York Times*, August 13 and 18, 1868.

306 *He won easily:* Brodie, p. 366.

307 *Johnson nominated Evarts:* Welles Diary, vol. 3, pp. 375, 390 (June 3 and 14, 1868).

307 *Stanberry returned to private law practice:* Charles Lane, *The Day Freedom Died: The Colfax Massacre, the Supreme Court, and the Betrayal of Reconstruction*, New York: Henry Holt & Co. (2008), pp. 116–17.

307 *Four days later:* Dawes, p. 504.

307 *Grant appointed him:* Land, p. 222.

308 *"Not a single one of them":* John F. Kennedy, *Profiles in Courage*, New York: Harper & Row (1955), p. 165.

308 *Poor health forced:* Grimes to Henry W. Starr, March 18, 1869, in Salter, p. 367. A denunciation of Grimes in the newspaper in Burlington, Iowa, offers a flavor of the passions of the time: "Republicans of Iowa mourn over the studied perfidiousness of the reptile [Grimes] they have warmed into life and to whose fangs they have added the poison of power to destroy them." George A. Boeck, "Senator Grimes and the Iowa Press, 1867–1868," *Mid-America* 48:157 (1966), quoting the *Burlington Daily Hawk-Eye*, May 23, 1868.

308 *Only a few months earlier:* Fessenden, p. 326.

308 *He retired from the Senate:* Bayless, pp. 86–87; Sturm, p. 39.

308 *Indeed, their careers:* Richard J. Roske, "The Seven Martyrs?" *American Historical Review* 64:324 (1959).

308 *On a memorable evening: New York Times*, September 26, 1872, September 21, 1875, May 18, 1906, and April 2, 1911; *Sedalia Daily Democrat*,

September 7, 1872 and September 25, 1872. Roske, p. 328; Poore, pp. 313–14; *Washington Post*, December 20, 2000.

309 *He later ran for governor:* Krug, p. 269; Roske, p. 329.

309 *In 1872, he campaigned:* New York Times, February 7, 1870; *Newark (OH) Advocate*, June 12, 1868, reprinted from the *Cincinnati Commercial*; Walter T. Dunham, "How Say You, Senator Fowler?" *Tennessee Historical Quarterly*, 62:55–56 (1983).

309 *In his final years:* Charleston Courier, April 17, 1869, reprinted from *New York Herald*; Plummer, "Profile in Courage?" pp. 42–45; Kubicek, p. 151; "Hon. Edmund G. Ross, Governor of New Mexico," *Frank Leslie's Illustrated Newspaper*, June 13, 1885; Edmund G. Ross, "Historic Moments: The Impeachment Trial," *Scribner's* 11:519 (April 1892); Edmund G. Ross, *History of the Impeachment of Andrew Johnson*, Santa Fe: New Mexican Printing Co. (1896); undated letter from Ross in New Mexico to Major Hoxie, in Hoxie-Ream Papers.

310 *He ran for president:* Albert R. Kitzhaber, "*Götterdämmerung* in Topeka: The Downfall of Senator Pomeroy," *Kansas Historical Quarterly* 18:243 (1950).

310 *Eight years after that:* Harper's New Monthly Magazine, April 1872, p. 790; *Chicago Daily*, January 19, 1873; *Chicago Tribune*, January 11 and 13, 1885; *San Francisco Bulletin*, January 12, 1885; *New York Times*, March 4, 1893; *Chicago Tribune*, March 22, 1893; *Rocky Mountain News*, March 22, 1893; *Chicago Daily*, July 23, 1894.

310 *After winning dismissal:* New York Herald, September 16 and 17, 1869; *New York Times*, April 28, 1899; *Milwaukee Sentinel*, July 11, 1886.

310 *Smythe again escaped:* New York Herald, November 26, 1869.

310 *Woolley, who was then president:* Chicago Tribune, March 1, 1871, and February 11, 1876, October 13, 14, and 21, 1878; *New York Times*, May 3, 1878 and February 8, 1879.

311 *In his remaining years:* Evarts to Ward, December 8, 1880, in Samuel Ward Papers, Box 1; *New York World*, May 20, 1884.

311 *Confined for weeks:* Philadelphia North American, November 19, 1889 and January 4, 1890. The *Raleigh News and Observer* described Gaylord as "for years a heavy manipulator of railroad securities." January 4, 1890.

311 *One hundred sixty-two blacks:* "Louisiana Contested Elections," Testimony taken by House Subcommittee of Elections in Louisiana, House Misc. Doc. No. 154, 41st Cong., 2d sess., pp. 127–28 (testimony of C. W. Keeting); Oberholtzer, p. 366; Tracy Campbell, *Deliver the Vote: A History of Election Fraud, an American Political Tradition, 1742–2004*, New York: Carroll & Graf (2005), pp. 60–61.

312 *Grant struck back:* Smith, *Grant*, pp. 463–64; Welles Diary, vol. 3, pp. 497–98 (January 2, 1869).

312 *He was the last president:* Welles Diary, vol. 3, p. 542 (March 4, 1869); Smith, *Grant*, p. 466; Gerry, p. 874.

312 *He never forgave:* This anecdote comes from a remembrance written in 1926 by E. C. Reeves, who was Johnson's private secretary in Greeneville, Tennessee, from 1869 to 1875. Unhappily, Reeves, who was a strong partisan of the former president, waited some forty-five years before reporting this incident, a delay that could call into question his memory of the event. Nevertheless, he was employed by Johnson at the time of the incident and likely had the broad outlines of the event correct. Reeves denounced Edmund Cooper's "treachery" in supporting his own brother after Johnson fell short in the contest. Reeves's memorandum appears as an appendix in Lloyd Paul Stryker, *Andrew Johnson*, New York: Macmillan Co. (1929), pp. 825–37. Stryker's book admires Johnson greatly. *New York Times*, October 20, 22, and 23, 1869; Dewitt, p. 619; Temple, p. 439.

313 *He wrote in December 1871:* Trefousse, *Andrew Johnson*, pp. 360–61 (quoting letters from Johnson to his daughter).

313 *The new senator: Cong. Record*, 44th Cong., Special sess., pp. 121–27 (March 20, 1875).

313 *His head rested:* Trefousse, *Andrew Johnson*, pp. 352–77; Baber, p. 70.

313 *A secretary:* Cowan, p. 8.

314 *"I intend to appoint":* Smith, *Grant*, p. 555.

314 *For a time:* Ibid., p. 547.

26. THE RORSCHACH BLOT

315 *Surely God is on our side:* Dawes, p. 503.

315 *A chief justice:* William H. Rehnquist, *Grand Inquests: The Historic Impeachments of Justice Samuel Chase and President Andrew Johnson*, New York: William Morrow & Co. (1992), p. 278; Woodrow Wilson, *History of the American People*, New York: Harper & Brothers, vol. 9 (1918), pp. 49–50, 54–55. The chapter-length treatment of Johnson and Ross in the Kennedy book is particularly incomplete. For example, Kennedy portrays the appointment of Ross to the Senate in 1866 as part of a Radical conspiracy to impeach the president. There is no evidence to support such a claim. Ross was appointed by the Kansas governor in August 1866, when impeachment was just beginning to be mentioned by Radical newspapers and some Republicans. Kennedy describes the Tenure of Office Act as a "cry for more patronage," when it was actually an attempt to tie Johnson's hands in firing officials. Kennedy also describes Johnson as eager for a court test of the Tenure of Office Act, an assertion contradicted by Johnson's repeated compliance with the statute and then his violation of it. Johnson never tried to bring a court challenge to it. When Kennedy refers to "[a]ttempted bribery and other forms of pressure" surrounding the Senate vote, he means that the so-called Radical fanatics were engaged in such

actions. Yet most of the attempts at bribery were made by the president's men. Kennedy also makes simple factual errors. He claims that twelve Senate Democrats supported Johnson; there were only nine Democrats in the Senate. He asserts that Republicans sought the admission of Colorado and Nebraska in order to secure the votes of senators from those states on impeachment. The fight over admitting those two states came in early 1867, when impeachment was not a serious goal of the Republican Party. When Kennedy quotes Butler's statement that there was a "bushel of money" available for Ross, he places the remark at the wrong point in the trial, putting it before the first impeachment vote on May 16. The statement was made after that date, after the vote. John F. Kennedy, *Profiles in Courage*, New York: Harper & Row (1955), pp. 146–71. A recent work on Reconstruction in Mississippi, Nicholas Lemann's *Redemption*, identifies comparable errors and omissions in Kennedy's chapter celebrating Mississippi Senator Lucius Lamar.

316 *"He is a man of few ideas":* Curtis to Ticknor, April 10, 1868, in Curtis, p. 417.

316 *As one congressman wrote later:* Blaine, vol. 2, p. 376.

317 *"Andrew Johnson is innocent":* New York Tribune, May 19, 1868, quoting *Detroit Post*. The *Cincinnati Gazette* wrote that "Ninety out of every hundred politicians will admit that had Fessenden been presiding officer of the Senate, the President would have been convicted." *Cincinnati Gazette*, June 1, 1868. Senator George Edmunds of Vermont made the same point in a magazine article forty-five years later. "Ex-Senator Edmunds on Reconstruction and Impeachment," *Century* 85:863–64 (April 1913), p. 864.

317 *Some of the Republicans:* Blaine, vol. 2, p. 376; Julian, pp. 318–19; Badeau, p. 137; Henderson, p. 209 (Senator Charles Sumner).

318 *"An overwhelming majority":* Schurz, *Reminiscences*, vol. 3, p. 282.

318 *Embracing this theory:* Kennedy, p. 146.

320 *The presidency, according to Ross and Kennedy:* Kennedy, pp. 128–29, quoting Edmund G. Ross, *History of the Impeachment of Andrew Johnson*, Whitefish, MT: Kessinger Publishing (2006; originally 1892), p. 206.

320 *For the next two decades:* Robert V. Remini, *The House: The History of the House of Representatives*, New York: Smithsonian Books/HarperCollins (2006), p. 206.

320 *In this vein:* Irving Brant, *Impeachment: Trials and Errors*, New York: Alfred A. Knopf (1972), p. 4.

321 *Richard Nixon resigned:* Kyvig, pp. 29–33.

322 *In response to President Grant's demands:* Smith, p. 479.

323 *The dissenters were not fazed:* 272 U.S. 52 (1926). Few judges have ever shrugged their shoulders as eloquently as Justice Oliver Wendell Holmes, Jr., who joined Brandeis and McReynolds in dissent, writing: "I have no

more trouble in believing that Congress has power to prescribe a term of
life for [a federal office] free from any interference than I have in accepting the undoubted power of Congress to decree its end. I have equally
little trouble in accepting its power to prolong the tenure of an incumbent
until Congress or the Senate shall have assented to his removal. The duty
of the President to see that the laws be executed is a duty that does not go
beyond the laws or require him to achieve more than Congress sees fit to
leave within his power."

323 *The Supreme Court ruled: Humphrey's Executor (Rathbun) v. United
States*, 295 U.S. 602 (1935).

323 *Indeed, in many ways:* Kyvig, pp. 392–94.

INDEX

Note: Page numbers in *italics* refer to illustrations.

ABOUT THE AUTHOR

———•◦•———

DAVID O. STEWART is the author of *The Summer of 1787*, a *Washington Post* bestseller and winner of the Washington Writing Prize for Best Book of 2007. He was principal defense counsel in a 1989 Senate impeachment trial of a Mississippi judge. He has practiced law in Washington, D.C., for more than a quarter-century. He has argued appeals all the way to the U.S. Supreme Court and was law clerk to Justice Lewis Powell of that Court. He lives in Garrett Park, Maryland.